HISTORICAL REPRESENTATION

Cultural Memory
in
the
Present

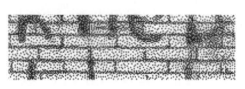

Mieke Bal and Hent de Vries, Editors

HISTORICAL REPRESENTATION

F. R. Ankersmit

STANFORD UNIVERSITY PRESS

STANFORD, CALIFORNIA

2001

Stanford University Press
Stanford, California

© 2001 by the Board of Trustees of the
Leland Stanford Junior University

Printed in the United States of America
on acid-free, archival-quality paper.

Library of Congress Cataloging-in-Publication Data

Ankersmit, F. R.
   Historical representation / F.R. Ankersmit
     p. cm. — (Cultural memory in the present)
   Includes bibliographical references and index.
   ISBN 0-8047-3979-X (alk. paper) — ISBN 0-8047-3980-3 (pbk. : alk. paper)
   1. Historiography. 2. Memory—Social aspects. 3. History—Philosophy.
4. Objectivity. 5. Realism. I. Title. II. Series.
D13 .A637   2002
907'.2—dc21   2001048427

Original Printing 2001
Last figure below indicates year of this printing:
10 09 08 07 06 05 04 03 02 01

Typeset by James P. Brommer in 11/13.5 Garamond

CONTENTS

	Acknowledgments	ix
	Introduction	1
PART I	HISTORICAL THEORY	
1	The Linguistic Turn: Literary Theory and Historical Theory	29
2	In Praise of Subjectivity	75
PART II	HISTORICAL CONSCIOUSNESS	
3	Gibbon and Ovid: History as Metamorphosis	107
4	The Dialectics of Narrativist Historism	123
5	The Postmodernist "Privatization" of the Past	149
6	Remembering the Holocaust: Mourning and Melancholia	176
PART III	THEORISTS	
7	Why Realism? Auerbach on the Representation of Reality	197
8	Danto on Representation, Identity, and Indiscernibles	218
9	Hayden White's Appeal to the Historians	249
10	Rüsen on History and Politics	262
	Epilogue	281
	Notes	289
	Index	317

ACKNOWLEDGMENTS

Chapter 3 was previously published as "History and/as Cultural Analysis: Gibbon and Ovid," in M. Bal and H. de Vries, eds., *The Practice of Cultural Analysis: Exposing Literary Interpretation* (Stanford, Calif., 1999), 151–71.

Chapter 4 is a revised version of "Historicism: An Attempt at Synthesis," *History and Theory* 34, no. 3 (1995): 143–62.

A German-language version of Chapter 5, "Die postmodern 'Privatisierung' der Vergangenheit," was published in H. Nagl-Docekal, *Der Sinn des Historischen: Geschichtsphilosophische Debatten* (Frankfurt am Main, 1996), 201–35.

Chapter 6 was previously published in P. Ahokas and M. Chard-Hutchinson, *Reclaiming Memory: American Representations of the Holocaust* (Turku, Fin., 1997), 62–87.

Chapter 7 was previously published in *Poetics Today* 20 (1999): 53–77.

Chapter 8 was previously published in *History and Theory* 37, no. 1 (1998): 44–71.

Chapter 9 was previously published in *History and Theory* 37, no. 4 (1998): 182–94.

Chapter 10 was previously published as "Representation: History and Politics," in H. W. Blanke, F. Jaeger, and T. Sandkühkler, eds., *Dimensionen der Historik: Wissenschafsgeschichte und Geschichtskultur heute* (Cologne, 1998), 27–41.

I would like to thank the editors of these journals and collections for having graciously permitted me to republish these essays in this book.

HISTORICAL REPRESENTATION

INTRODUCTION

"If we were to try a provisional definition: history is the form in which a culture becomes conscious of its past. All would go into this," Johan Huizinga wrote triumphantly in the margins of his lecture notes for a course on historical theory in the academic year 1928.[1] Wessel Krul correctly observes that this note does not offer a definition of history as "a critical science" or "a profession." Huizinga had something else in mind. His point was that, though individual historians sincerely wish to tell the truth about the past, each phase in the history of historical writing can nevertheless be seen as "the form in which a culture expresses its consciousness of its past."[2] That is to say, apart from what the historical writing produced in a period may say about the past, it can also be seen as the expression of how this period related to its past. And this is by no means an accidental or peripheral aspect of a culture. Just as psychoanalysis has taught us to get access to individual identity by taking into account the person's past, so it is with a culture or a civilization. We do not know who we are unless we have an adequate understanding of our past. From this perspective historians can be seen as the psychoanalysts *malgré eux* of the time in which they are living and writing. As the psychoanalyst may understand people's personalities on the basis of how they describe their past, so may we expect to be able to discern a culture's fears, expectations, desires, and repressed elements by taking into account how it gave form to its past.

CONTEMPORARY HISTORICAL WRITING AND THE PRESENT

Let us now apply this insight to our own time and see how the relevant features of contemporary culture and contemporary historical writing may mutually clarify each other. Some fifteen years ago Jürgen Habermas characterized our time with the label *die neue Unübersichtlichkeit*—"the new confusion"—and in spite of its lumbering and ungainly literalness this epithet has gained considerable popularity.[3] For, indeed, our time no longer has any recognizable intellectual, cultural, or political program in the way this had been the case with the Renaissance, the Enlightenment, or even in the 1960s and 1970s. This is not merely so because it always is difficult to precisely name the distinguishing characteristic of the present—the owl of Minerva flies out at the dusk, as we all know—but primarily because our time has opted, to put it paradoxically, to have as its program not having a program. We do not like well defined cultural points of view anymore and have all accepted more or less Derrida's point of view of not having a point of view.

So it is in contemporary historical writing. We live in an age without any new Braudels, Foucaults, Arièses, Fogels, Ginzburgs, or Hayden Whites, and even if some of them such as John Pocock or Simon Schama are still alive and still prodigiously active, their writings no longer have the impact and capacity to determine contemporary historical thought. The Golden Age of theory, when exciting and provocative theories were fired off in a breathtaking tempo and hotly discussed by everyone, has been succeeded by the Silver Age of modesty and of the solid practice of the craft of history. The writings of the great and famous authors no longer function as the reliable compass enabling us to see where we are and what really happens in contemporary historical writing. Not only are these great and famous authors a group threatened with extinction; even more so, we have lost our interest and our respect for the bold synthesis and for the daring new program that will present us with a wholly new and different picture of the past. We simply seem to have lost all confidence in points of view pretending to offer a synopsis of either the past itself or of how to best deal with it.

In contrast with this, the style of contemporary historical writing and thought comes closest to what Hans Kellner once described as that of the "Menippean satire." Following Northrop Frye, he defined this style as follows: "the Menippean satirist shows his exuberance in intellectual ways, by piling up an enormous mass of erudition about his theme or by overwhelming his targets with an avalanche of their own jargon."[4] In the Menippean satire the reader is buried under a huge mass of information while no real effort is made to bring some order in it that might enable the reader to get a firm grasp upon it. From this perspective, the *neue Unübersichtlichkeit* of contemporary historical writing should not be interpreted as a regrettable shortcoming, but instead as proof that it, too, has understood the signs of the time and has abandoned the naive hope to achieve a reliable mimesis of the past. And in order to give expression to the mentality of the *neue Unübersichtlichkeit*, contemporary historical writing has a fascination for the contingent in the past (as exemplified by "micro-storie") and for the historical sublime (as exemplified by the Holocaust)[5]—in other words, precisely for those aspects of the past that successfully resist the effort to force the complexities of the past into a neat synthesis.

A second characteristic of contemporary historical writing directly follows from this. It will be obvious that in terms of the Menippean satire the rise or decline of a civilization cannot be established: the Menippean satire drowns us with its facts and will frustrate each attempt to gain a point of view transcending these facts and from which a certain order can be discerned in them. The implication is that the Menippean satire will preferably consider the past as a Schopenhauerian *semper eadem sed aliter*: the time-transcendent forms enabling us to see progress or decline are *sui generis* ruled out by the Menippean satire. And it is precisely in this way that the Menippean satire in historical writing makes contemporary historical writing agree with the *neue Unübersichtlichkeit* so characteristic of the realities of the beginning of the third millennium. This may also explain the fact why much of what is really new in contemporary historical writing can be found in what has recently been written on the Middle Ages and of early modern Europe. Whereas until the sixties and the seventies the history of modernity was the obvious topic of the most important historical writing, interest recently shifted into the direction of the more static periods of the Western European past, hence toward those periods that have a congeniality of their own with the Menippean satire, and that are themselves characterized already by an intrinsic *Unübersichtlichkeit*. But this affinity of contemporary historical writing with these relatively static periods does not have its origins in an explicit rejection of the idea of progress, nor in an explicit embrace of the idea of decline, but rather in the conviction that the models of progress or decline poorly fit both our own world and that of the past.

The question arises what our contemporary preference for the Menippean satire as the model of our relationship to the past must mean for our historical consciousness. Is history still possible under the aegis of a *semper eadem sed aliter*? Does historical writing not necessarily have change as its subject matter, and does it therefore not presuppose the applicability of the categories such as those of progress and decline? What meaning can the past still have for us, and what use is the writing of history if the events of past and present are like the Brownian swarming of the molecules in a gas chamber? Who would wish to be informed about these records of purposelessness and futility? What lesson could there be in this, except the lesson that there is *no* lesson to be learned from it? It may seem that the past has only to tell us something if we approach it with a certain brutality; that is, with categories such as progress or decline. Only when seen in the light of these categories does the past obtain a *clair-obscur* in which its contours can articulate themselves. It is true that such categories may sometimes invite us to violate the past; nevertheless if we never risk this violation, the past will forever keep itself closed to us. Machiavelli famously compared the prince to a young man trying to win his beloved: and both in politics and in the affairs of love nothing is accomplished by patient abstention. Fortune is a woman, isn't she?[6] And then intervention is necessary, though all depends on doing the right thing at the right time; one inappropriate move at the wrong moment may spoil everything. So it is in history: the past will retain all its secrets for the historian approaching it with the fearful respect of the timid lover. The past will only yield itself to the historian who is not afraid of clasping it within his embrace—if it is prepared to do so at all.

THE IDEA OF PROGRESS IN THE ENLIGHTENMENT AND NOW

Perhaps no better illustration can be found of Huizinga's thesis of the correspondence of the self-interpretation of a culture and of its concept of the past than the Enlightenment. Even more so, each phase of the Enlightenment was reflected in its relationship to the past. For example, Pierre Bayle's *Dictionnaire historique et critique* of 1691 is characteristic of the early Enlightenment that was still uncertain of itself and attempted to express its superiority over the past in pedantry, smart little dodges, and in an ostentatious and provocative manifestation of not being impressed by the great authorities from the past.[7] *Ipse dixit* now had served its turn. But just as the adolescent may outgrow the dependency and uncertainty of youth with this, for older persons, somewhat tiring propensity to contradiction, so did Bayle's book testify to Europe's "recovery of nerve," as Gay called it, now that the terrors of the wars of religion had gradually receded into the background. The self-confidence of the Enlightenment fully announced itself in Voltaire's *Essai sur les moeurs* of 1756, in which Voltaire declared "le siècle de Louis XIV" to surpass the glories of Greek and Roman antiquity and the Renaissance.[8] But even Voltaire was still susceptible to the doubts of cultural despair, as may become clear from his description of human beings:

> des atomes tourmentés sur cet amas de boue,
> que la mort engloutit et dont le sort se joue.
>
> tormented atoms on this clod of mud,
> swallowed by death and with whom fate plays its games.

But in the course of the century the conviction that Reason had ushered in the era of the triumphs of Enlightened reason had grown so strong that the marquis of Condorcet, one of the high priests of Reason, did not doubt progress for a moment, even though he was condemned to the guillotine by progressivist reason in its earthly, revolutionary manifestation.

At the beginning of the present century the idea of progress seems to have lost all attraction that it had. Which is all the more remarkable since all that used to be considered as the true and reliable signs of progress—freedom, peace, education, science, technology—have all been realized to an extent that would have seemed wildly utopian a mere fifteen to twenty years ago. Illustrative is Francis Fukuyama's eulogy of liberal capitalism, which was phrased as "the end of history" rather than as the triumph of progress. The triumphs of science and of liberal democracy seem to have stalled history rather than be the promise of a new era of progress and liberation. It is as if the course of history no longer permits of extrapolation, so that the end of a certain phase of the historical process or an eternal and unchanging present (as in the case of Fukuyama) is all that is left of the pathos of historical progress.

It will rightly be pointed out that the catastrophes of the last century have made us wary of the notion of progress. But if we survey the intellectual *Durcharbeitung* ("working through") of these catastrophes over the past fifty years, the picture is more complicated than this easy comment suggests. For we should discern two stages in the process. In the first place there were numerous authors in the fifties and the sixties—such as Karl Popper, Jakob Talmon, Maurice Mandelbaum, or Friedrich von Hayek—who accused the totalitarian ideologies, responsible for a major part of the disasters of the twentieth century, of the use of a corrupted reason. For example, Popper made clear in *The Open Society and Its Enemies* and in his immensely influential *The Poverty of Historicism* that the apparent scientific analyses of history and society on which totalitarian ideologies were founded had, in fact, nothing to do with science and scientific reason in the proper sense of the word. But about the value of scientific reason Popper *cum suis* had no doubts at all. On the contrary, if the process of the testing of scientific knowledge were applied to society as well—think of his notion of "piecemeal social engineering" (or of Talmon's related notion of "trial and error")—this would tremendously contribute to the victory of freedom and liberalism over tyranny and despotism. And it follows that these authors were, in the end, still quite close to the Enlightened ideology of progress. Like their Enlightenment predecessors they still believed that our salvation and freedom lay in (scientific) reason. Only a thorough critique of reason was required in order to ruthlessly and totally eradicate all the misuses of reason. But reason in its purified form they believed to be our only reliable compass for the future.

This is different with a later group of theorists dealing with the disasters of the previous century. These theorists took a far bleaker view of Enlightened, scientific reason than we will find in the writings by Popper. This was the case already with Adorno and Horkheimer's *Dialektik der Aufklärung*, published a mere three years after the end of World War II; and several of Hannah Arendt's writings should certainly be placed in this tradition of thought as well. But this disillusioned view of Enlightened reason would find its clearest expression only in the work of postmodernist authors such François Lyotard, Zygmunt Bauman, or Berel Lang, theorists who argued that scientific reason *itself* had partly been responsible for the derailment of reason in the twentieth century. Minimally, scientific reason does not always offer sufficient warning and protection against the aberrations of the human mind such as those that had been responsible for the disasters of the last century. But, even worse, these authors also intimated that even pure reason, *die reine Vernunft*, may have a political agenda of its own that can well be at odds with the requirements of the free and humane society. For example, as Berel Lang wrote, Kantian pure reason on the one hand gave us an undoubtedly impressive model of what the just society should look like, but on the other hand also suggested a strong and rigorous program of marginalization of all that with which reason does not feel comfortable. And from this perspective there *is* a line running from the sublimity of Kantian reason and ethics to the fate of the Jews in the Holocaust—admittedly, the line is thin and uncertain, but nevertheless it is there. Pure reason indulges in politics and its politics is not always the politics of freedom. This has been, arguably, the most important contribution of postmodernism. Postmodernists refined the political critique of Enlightened reason as had been proposed by Popper and others. They made us aware of the fact that pure reason in its political manifestation is double faced, that its pure formalism inevitably entails a political content and that we, therefore, are in need of a higher court of appeal where Enlightened Reason is not the judge but may well be the defendant.

TRANSVERSAL REASON AND HISTORICAL REASON

Obviously, this should provoke our interest in the nature of this higher court of appeal. Does it exist? Or is such a court of appeal only an empty illusion that is merely elicited by our painful awareness of the political shortcomings of Enlightened reason? If we recall that the postmodernist critique of the politics of Enlightened reason mainly focuses on its propensity to exclusion, we may expect that, if this higher court of appeal exists, it should not only be open to all voices that wish to make themselves heard, but also adequately weigh what these voices are saying. When we bear this in mind we have every reason to be interested in Wolfgang Welsch's notion of so-called transversal reason. The notion is introduced by Welsch as follows:

Traditionally (since the end of the eighteenth century) the notion of understanding is used for referring to our use of concepts enabling the practice of isolated and specific domains of intellectual pursuit. In this sense we can still speak of ethical, aesthetic, religious, technical, etc., understanding. In contrast to this use of concepts tied to specific domains, reason is the kind of intellectual faculty transcending all these uses. So reason comes into the picture, where and when we are confronted with the restrictions and the limitations of understanding.[9]

When explicating how transversal reason may transcend the barriers between the different domains of intellectual activity and the domain-specific form of rationality obtaining there, Welsch reminds us, first, that these different rationalities tend to interact with each other. For example, an aesthetics embracing the *l'art pour l'art* formula will keep its doors firmly shut against ethical rationality, whereas an aesthetics of "art and life" will see there one of its main sources of inspiration. In this way, different aesthetics imply different definitions of the relationship between aesthetics and ethics and it follows to a certain extent that these local rationalities will influence one another. Considerations such as these (for they obviously can be expanded with observations on what happens in the marginal areas between other domains of intellectual activity) legitimate the notion of a "transversal reason" (i.e., of a reason that succeeds in creating, analyzing, and discussing the "transversal" interconnections between these domains). And without much further clarification Welsch circumscribes the nature and tasks of this transversal reason as follows:

> Reflecting on the structure and the relationship between different forms of understanding—hence on unity, plurality, coherence, transgression, implication, analogy etc.—is only possible as an achievement of transversal reason. Reason is a meta-rational faculty, primarily so because of its capacity to function "between and betwixt." Its proper domain is transition. Reason is precisely the faculty controlling transitions—and for revealing how identity and difference then relate to each other.[10]

Obviously, this is the kind of reason to which we should turn in order to avoid the dangers, ethical or political, that the postmodernist theorists mentioned just now feared from pure, scientific reason. For scientific reason's one-dimensionality, its congeniality with the one-track mind and its tendency to marginalize what falls outside its scope, were where its triumphs but also its demoniac potentialities originated. By its very nature we may expect transversal reason, as defined by Welsch, to be the court of appeal where the transgressions of scientific reason can be set down for trial. Thanks to its (alleged) capacity to transcend the barriers separating all the domains of human life and endeavor, transversal reason will have its ears open to all who are in danger of being victimized by scientific reason.

I expect that most readers will react ambivalently to Welsch's introduction of the notion of transversal reason. On the one hand they will enthusiastically agree with Welsch that we badly need such a thing as his transversal reason, as a protection against the dangers of one-dimensional scientific reason. It clearly seems to be the kind of reason we need in a democratic society that respects the rights and the freedom of all its members. Moreover, it will enable us to create *Übergänge*, or transitions, between the different disciplines and restore some order to our fragmented postmodernist world. This may render to us at least some of the comfortable surveyability of modernism without the accompanying dangers of surveyability—and it is already clear from the title of Welsch's book that he is eager to satisfy this desire of ours.

But we may also have our doubts. We will be ready to recognize that transversal reason undoubtedly is a crucial faculty of the human mind, of no less importance than those forms of rationality that were so eagerly and thoroughly investigated by thinkers since Descartes, Locke, or Kant, down to the philosophers of language and of science of our own time. But, we will ask, is it really likely that all these eminent philosophers have so completely overlooked what Welsch calls to our attention? Doubting this, we will ask ourselves whether Welsch's transversal reason does not have its antecedents in the work of other philosophers and whether, therefore, it might not be a variant of a faculty of the human mind that has been discussed already in the long and venerable history of philosophical reflection.

Welsch himself already takes a first step in this direction by relating transversal reason to the faculty of judgment that Kant discussed in his third *Critique*. This is a most helpful suggestion, for not only did Kant investigate in this *Critique* the nature of aesthetic judgment, he also considered the third *Critique* to be the keystone to all his critical writings. So aesthetic judgment was for Kant already the domain of a "transversal reason," integrating pure reason (the topic of the first *Critique*) and practical reason (the topic of the second *Critique*).

But there is an even more obvious and familiar candidate. For when Welsch assigns to transversal reason the task of discerning "unity," "difference," "cohesion," "transitions," and "identity and difference," and of dealing with "the genesis, renovation, and adaptation" of disciplines, he clearly is talking about the professional historian's field of activity. Most, if not all of what the historian does can be understood in terms of these categories. Nineteenth-century historians had already contended that the historian should discern a "cohesion" or a "unity" in the chaotic manifold of the data left to us by the past, that this will enable him to see "identity and difference" in the phenomena of the past and that this will lead, finally, to the discovery of "transitions" and, in the end, to an understanding of processes of "genesis, renovation, and adaptation." In sum, Welsch's transversal reason is not something new that was hitherto wholly unknown to us: for more than two hundred years it has been the historian's main intellectual instrument in his effort to make sense of the past.

Moreover, Welsch insists that we need transversal reason now that we no longer believe the grand narratives in terms of which one used to give meaning to the past: the postmodern world has disintegrated into an infinitely complex mosaic of *petits récits*, in Lyotard's terminology, giving an only local cohesion to subdomains of knowledge without any pretension of a larger scale coherence. The important implication is that transversal reason operates on the modest scale of the interaction of already existing *petits récits* and should not be seen as a transcendental structure antedating and organizing our knowledge of the world. Indeed, transversal reason functions a posteriori and does not offer a schematism existing a priori (which probably is the explanation of its ethical and political salutariness). There are no formal schemes structuring all experience and knowledge; insofar as form can be discerned at all it can never be dissociated from the content in which it has its origins. Transversal reason is a *material* and not a *formal* reason. Its nature cannot be defined a priori and will only manifest itself in its dealings with specific topics—just as an individual's character is not something that can be defined apart from his actions, but something that only *shows* itself in his actions and behavior. In logic and in some domains of epistemology we will find reason in its a priori form; transversal reason gives us reason in its less often perceived a posteriori manifestation. Nor is transversal reason a practical reason (in the non-Kantian sense) telling us how to apply an abstract rule to a complex social or legal reality. For even this practical reason still has an a priori certainty in that the rules of law are given to us independently of their application.

And all this has its exact counterpart in the historist conception of the nature of historical writing: historism developed, at least partly, in opposition to speculative philosophies of history, such as the Enlightenment's belief in progress or Hegel's speculations about the Absolute Mind. Instead of these a priori–deduced metanarratives, historism was content with the *petits récits* that the historist's transversal reason allowed him to construct a posteriori on the basis of archival data. In this way historism can be seen as an anticipation of postmodernism.[11]

THE RATIONALITY OF HISTORICAL WRITING

It follows that we had best look at historical writing if we wish to come to a better understanding of the nature of Welsch's transversal reason, of this kind of reason having the most peculiar capacity of uniting *and* respecting the heterogeneous. As will be shown in Chapter 1, historical writing gives us *representations* of the past.

There is an ontological, an epistemological, and a methodological aspect to the notion of (historical) representation that I will briefly expound here. The etymology of the word "representation" will give us access to its ontological properties: we may "re-present" something by presenting a substitute of this thing in its absence. The real thing is not, or is no longer available to us, and something else is given to us in order to replace it. In this sense it can be said that we have historical writing in order to compensate for the absence of the past itself. The same is true of the work of art: the statue of a God, of an emperor, the painting of a person, castle, or landscape, all function as substitutes for the absent God, emperor, and so on, and they are all made in such a way as to be most successful in functioning as such a substitute. Since the work of art belongs to the domain of aesthetics, the same is true for all representation—and thus also for historical representation. We can agree, therefore, with Welsch when he relates transversal reason—that is, the kind of reason operative in historical representation—to Kant's third *Critique*. And, as I have attempted to demonstrate elsewhere, this will also commit us to an aesthetization of democratic politics insofar as democracy is determined by the logic of political representation.[12] And in all these cases the crucial insight is that the represented and its representation have the same ontological status. For think of the paradigmatic example: the sitter for a portrait and the portrait itself have the same ontological status—both belong to the inventory of the world— and precisely this fact explains why representations can often be for us such satisfactory substitutes for what they represent.

Second, representation falls outside the scope of epistemology. Epistemology relates words to things, whereas representation relates things to things. In Chapter 1 this claim will be elaborated by opposing description to representation. The paradigmatic model of description is the true statement: the subject-term of the statement identifies and refers to a thing in reality whereas its predicate-term attributes a certain property to it. This distinction between subject- and predicate-term cannot be made in representations. If we look at a painting or a photograph we cannot distinguish between components that refer and those that attribute. And this is what we would expect, since representations and what they represent are ontologically equivalent. For since the distinction, obviously, makes no sense for the represented thing, this must be true of the thing representing it as well. It follows that the whole technical apparatus developed by epistemologists over the centuries (and by contemporary philosophy of science) cannot be of any use to us when we are dealing with representation—and with the question of what may make one representation better than another. The main shortcoming of (most) contemporary philosophy of history is that it takes description—instead of representation—as its model in its attempt to deal with the problem of historical writing.

If, then, epistemological notions such as reference, truth, and meaning will not enable us to understand historical writing and how it relates to what it is about, what alternative is left to us? This brings us to the methodological aspect of historical writing and to the issue of how transversal, historical reason is operative in historical debate, and hence, to the issue of the rationality of historical writing and of historical discussion.

In order to deal with these questions, two preliminary remarks have to be made. In the first place, we tend to believe that everything is either a thing or language, either part of the world or part of the language we use for speaking about the world. There is, however, a third category that combines the defining features of both.[13] This is the case with historical narratives, which on the one hand consist of language but on the other are representations and, therefore (as we saw a moment ago), things—just like chairs, trees, or human beings. Things are things insofar as they can be spoken about in language without being themselves part of the language that is used for speaking about them. You can speak about a chair but the chair will never be part of the statement you make about it. This is different with true descriptions. The meaning of a description will be part of the statement that you make about it because the statement that is made about it will be about the same thing as what the original statement was about. The statement (1) *"p* is false," where *p* stands for (2) "this person is male," is no less a statement about "this person" than (2) is. True descriptions are, so to speak, transparent from the perspective of the statements that are made about them and they are so because the reference of the subject-term is maintained in the transition from the statement itself to the statement that is made about it. Narrative language, language that is used for expressing a representation, is, on the other hand, opaque—as things are. Admittedly, there is a sliding scale between transparency and opacity, and much if not all will depend on whether language is being used extensionally or intensionally, but both extremes are formed by description on the one hand and representation on the other. Description is "pure" language, whereas historical representation combines the features of both things and language. Or, put differently, a historical representation is a thing that is made of language.

This brings me to my second remark. We know how to find out about the truth or falsity of descriptions. The subject-term identifies a certain object in the world, so we look at this object and then see whether it does in fact possess the property that the predicate-term attributes to it. Of course, things may be far more complex in practice, but this will always remain the gist of it. Obviously, this procedure will not work in the case of representations, since, as we have seen, representations do not refer to objects in reality. Representations are things, and things do not refer. Surely, this does not imply that there should be no relationship between a representation and what it represents. A portrait relates somehow to the sitter depicted in it and the same is true of a historical representation and a certain part of the past. We had perhaps best say that a historical representation "is about" a certain part of the past—and avoid reducing "aboutness" to reference. In Chapter 1 this notion of "aboutness" will be further investigated. But at this stage it will be sufficient to point out that "aboutness" is, above all, a relationship between things, and that therefore all the instruments developed by epistemology will be of no avail to us in order to clarify the nature of this relationship of "aboutness" or what reason we might have for preferring one representation to another. So where should we now turn for help?

The answer lies in the notion of metaphor. Think, for example, of the metaphor "the earth is a spaceship." The first thing to be noted about this utterance is that it is not a description. If we were to read it in this way, the utterance would be false. For the earth is not a spaceship. Yet, the utterance makes sense to us somehow and if we wish to see how it does so, we should avoid seeing the phrase "is a spaceship" as a predicate-term attributing some property to the earth. We should, instead, see the utterance for what it is: a link between two *things*, the earth on the one hand and a spaceship on the other. The "is" in the utterance invites us to see one *thing* (the earth) in terms of another *thing* (a spaceship). Obviously, this is what we are in need of when we have to compare two things, such as a represented and its representation, with each other. And in this way it makes sense to say that historical representation is metaphorical. It should be remembered, however, that metaphor is not operative here exclusively in the domain of the historical text or in that of the representation: the metaphor ties the past itself to its representation. Theorists (such as Hayden White) sometimes say that historical writing is metaphorical, but they then appear to restrict the activity of metaphor only to the text, to the level of the representation.[14] Actually, however, the scope of metaphor in historical writing comprises both the past itself and its representation.

Having established this, we have made an important step toward an understanding of the workings of transversal, historical reason and of the rationality of historical writing. For we should observe, next, that a rational discussion about the relative merits of different metaphors is possible. Compare, for example, the following three metaphors: (1) the earth is a spaceship; (2) the earth is a garden; and (3) the earth is a living room. Each of these three metaphors expresses in its own way that there are certain limits to what the global ecological system can tolerate. But whereas the second metaphor permits, or maybe even recommends, the use of pesticides, and whereas the third implicitly sanctions us to do anything we want as long as we do not hinder our neighbors, such conclusions are not likely to be derived from the first metaphor. The first metaphor, then, is the most successful of the three since it organizes into a logical interrelationship more aspects and desiderata with regard to the environment than is the case with the other two.

Two considerations follow from this. In the first place, we are relatively helpless if we have only one metaphor. Only if more metaphors are available can a comparison be made and only then can their relative shortcomings and merits be discussed. This may explain why we don't have in history just one more or less authoritative account, accepted by all historians, of a phenomenon such as the French Revolution, but, instead, a wild proliferation of histories of it. If there was just one such account and no others to compare it with, nothing could be said about its plausibility. The (im)plausibility of historical accounts only manifests itself in the presence of many such accounts. And we may observe here a striking illustration of the a posteriori character of transversal, historical reason that was mentioned above. In history there are no a priori criteria enabling us to establish to what extent one *individual* account of the past matches with the past or not. Such criteria develop simultaneously with the proliferation of the accounts that we have of some part of the past. Hence, the more accounts of the past we have, and the more complex the web is of their agreements and differences, the closer we may come to historical truth. But this is not because a Darwinian struggle between accounts of the past will then have been most effective in eliminating the wrong ones (as is the case in the sciences), but because the proliferation of accounts of the past will contribute to a perfection of the criteria we may apply to each of them in order to establish their plausibility. No theories or accounts of the past are eliminated in the process (and, indeed, each contains part of the truth), but the *criteria* are perfected for how to understand part of the past. Put differently, the historian, having properly weighed all rival accounts of a part of the past, does not actually know, in the end, which account is the right one, but rather which criteria will have to be satisfied in order to understand that part of the past. In this way the discipline of history aims at education, or *Bildung*, rather than at knowledge.

A second consideration concerns the often lamented indeterminacy of historical writing. In the first place, this indeterminacy is already to be expected because the relationship between the historical text and past reality should be phrased, as we have seen, in terms of "aboutness" rather than in those of reference. Think, for example, of the contrast between a statement on Louis XIV and a representation of him. The statement is precise in that it picks with absolute precision one individual out of all the human individuals who have peopled the past. A representation is more ambitious because it wishes to express something "about" Louis XIV, although no precision is possible in this expression since we often only become aware of what it is about thanks to the representation itself. It might be objected now, of course, that much the same is true of statements on Louis XIV. For example, we only know that he became king of France in 1643 thanks to statements saying this about him. However, when we move to the level of representation a complication arises because of the intertextual interaction that we observed a moment ago, one that is absent at the levels of the statement and description. For the merits (or shortcomings) of what a representation expresses on what it "is about" will be codetermined by other representations of a part of the past, a fact that introduces a double indeterminacy. In the first place it will not be easy to establish how (the presence of) these other representations will require us to look at *this* one. How should we weigh the merits of *this* account against those of all the others? And in the second place, even if we came here to the right conclusion, the problem would still remain that the set of accounts that we do have is only a sample of all the possible accounts that could be produced about a certain part of the past. And this implies that the a posteriori criteria that we have for assessing the merits of this representation will necessarily be imperfect. These criteria could only be perfect if we were in possession of *all* the possible representations of a part of the past. A really "true" representation of the past, a representation of the past matching the represented part of the past just as the true statement matches what it is about, is only possible after all possible representations of this part of the past have been realized. As long as this condition is not met, a greater or smaller indeterminacy in the relationship between a representation and what it is about will be inevitable.

It follows that determinacy and complete precision can never really be achieved in historical writing—a disappointing conclusion, for some of us. But one can instead take a more sanguine and above all more realistic view of this fact by interpreting the foregoing argument as a demonstration that indeterminacy and lack of precision are the indispensable prerequisites of historical writing. And once again, the contrast with the sciences here is striking. Precision and determinacy are a necessary requirement for all meaningful scientific debate, and progress in the sciences is, to a large extent, the ongoing process of achieving ever greater precision. But we have seen that (historical) representation puts a premium on a proliferation of representations, hence not on the refinement of one representation but on the production of an ever more variegated set of representations. Historical insight is not a matter of a continuous "narrowing down" of previous options, not of an approximation of the truth, but, on the contrary, is an "explosion" of possible points of view. It therefore aims at the unmasking of previous illusions of determinacy and precision by the production of new and alternative representations, rather than at achieving truth by a careful analysis of what was right and wrong in those previous representations. And from this

Introduction   17

perspective, the development of historical insight may indeed be regarded by the outsider as a process of creating ever more confusion, a continuous questioning of certainty and precision seemingly achieved already, rather than, as in the sciences, an ever greater approximation to the truth. But as the above discussion shows, the outsider would be mistaken, since he misapplies to history the paradigms of the sciences. Though historical writing and historical discussion may often seem to move into a direction that is radically opposed to what we are accustomed to in the sciences, this does not in the least imply that we should doubt the rationality of history and of historical debate.

Historical representations and the metaphors proposed in such representations can be rationally discussed, and we can well explain why some metaphors are better than others and why we may have good reasons to prefer a representation to some other. This can be demonstrated by considering a few examples, although a handicap in discussions of such examples is that they would require us to quote complete historical texts.[15] The reader may well suspect manipulation in the absence of such complete texts. But unfortunately the introduction of complete historical texts in a theoretical discussion is ruled out by practical considerations. In order to obviate this problem as thoroughly as possible, I shall discuss it here with a few very well known historical texts, so that readers can establish for themselves whether or not what I am saying about these texts is convincing.

GIBBON, BURCKHARDT, AND HUIZINGA

It is clear that Edward Gibbon's *The History of the Decline and Fall of the Roman Empire* (1776–88), Jakob Burckhardt's *Die Kultur der Renaissance in Italien* (The civilization of the Renaissance in Italy; 1860), and Johan Huizinga's *Herfsttij der middeleeuwen* (The autumn of the Middle Ages; 1919)[16] each supplies a (very strong) metaphor. The Roman empire cannot *really* fall, a culture cannot *really* be reborn, and a part of the Middle Ages cannot *really* be an autumn. Next, the scope of these metaphors is not restricted to their titles only; they also aptly summarize the contents of these books. In this sense, they are metaphors of the books themselves. But, more importantly, these metaphors are an integral part of the logic of the whole of each book. Consider Gibbon, for example, when he comments on the deposition of the last Roman Emperor in 476 A.D.:

The rise of a city, which swelled into an Empire, may deserve, as a singular prodigy, the reflection of a philosophic mind. But the decline of Rome was the natural and inevitable effect of immoderate greatness. Prosperity ripened the principle of decay, the causes of destruction multiplied with the extent of conquest; and as soon as time or accident had removed the artificial supports, the stupendous fabric yielded under the pressure of its own weight.

This "swelling" of the city of Rome, the "ripening" of the principle of decay, the "artificial supports" that kept Rome upright, the image of a building destroyed by its own weight—these are all naturalist and even mechanistic metaphors emanating directly from the title and expressing the logic of Gibbon's narrative.

The same is true of how Burckhardt's contrasts the mind of the Middle Ages with that of the Renaissance:

In the Middle Ages both sides of human consciousness—turned towards the world and turned towards the individual's inner self—were as covered by a common veil, and as if still dreaming or half awake. This veil was woven of belief, and of a childish diffidence and illusion. . . . In Italy this veil is blown away for the first time into the fresh air; an *objective* approach to politics and to all things of the world comes into being; and together with this *subjectivity* acquires the fullness of its potentialities: man becomes a spiritual human being.

The human individual (slumbering, waking up, growing up as a child into adulthood) is the source of inspiration of Burckhardt's metaphorics: just as the human individual discovers both the world and itself on its journey to full maturity, just as this will for each individual be a rediscovery of what others had already discovered before, so it has been with Renaissance culture. But most amazing, undoubtedly, is how Huizinga develops in the preface to the original Dutch version of his book the metaphorics of its title:

When writing this book it was as if my gaze directed into the depth of an evening sky—but a sky full of a bloody red, heavy, and fierce lead-gray, full of a false copper shine.[17]

Huizinga's metaphor of this evening sky so full of threat and of the announcement of an indefinite and uncanny evil lends to Huizinga's autumnal metaphor of the Middle Ages a deep and intense emotion; we shudder as we read it.

Next, metaphors organize knowledge. The metaphor "the earth is a spaceship" organizes all that we know about the earth in such a way as to invite a solicitude for the earth as an ecological system. This capacity of metaphor—as unique as it is remarkable—is fully exploited in historical writing. And this should not surprise us—for what are historical narratives other than organizations of knowledge, organizations into a coherent and meaningful whole of what we know about the past on the basis of archival data and other relics from the past? And so it is with the three specimens of historical writing discussed here. When Gibbon uses the metaphor of a structure destroyed by its own weight in order to describe the decline and fall of Rome, this metaphor enables him to place within a coherent whole, not only Rome's decay and "the triumph of barbarism and Christian religion," but paradoxically also all that had contributed to Rome's greatness. Next, Burckhardt's metaphor of the Renaissance as the discovery of the human individual has undoubtedly been one of the most powerful metaphors that have ever been proposed in all of the history of historical writing. This epochal discovery, giving to the Western world both the subjectivity of the self and an objective natural reality, was related by Burckhardt in a magisterial way to such diverging themes as the *virtù* of the *condottiere*, the awareness that political and social reality is man-made, the explosion of artistic talent in fifteenth-century Italy, amazing the world down to the present, the birth of the sciences or of the brutal, worldly humor of a Paolo Giovio or a Piero Aretino. Lastly, Huizinga's metaphor of the late Northern Middle Ages as an autumn was fulfilled in the image of an age "full of a false copper shine," of a wild and uncontrolled festering of forms in all domains of life, in that of religion, in those of sentiments of life, love, and death, and to which often a content was given bluntly contradicting its form. The late-medieval mind, with its for us unimaginable extremes and fierce contrasts between pious mortification and raw worldliness, between the stillness of a van Eyck on the one hand and the boisterous ostentation of public life on the other, acquired an impressive authenticity thanks to Huizinga's metaphorics. In this way the power of all of these three masterworks in the history of historical writing lies in their singular capacity to comprise a complex and multiform historical reality within strong metaphorical images lending unity to historical complexity.

Next, each of the three metaphors was for a long time more successful than any alternative in organizing manifold historical data. Gibbon wrote at a time when the fall of Rome was still often seen in terms of the four-empires theory dating back to the prophecies of Daniel. But even more important is that, although we will find Gibbon's thesis about the fall of Rome already in Montesquieu and the facts he used for proving his thesis in the works of the seventeenth- and eighteenth-century *érudits*, as Momigliano has rightly pointed out, it was Gibbon's unique genius that enabled him to combine the two.[18] Hence, insofar as it is the task of historical metaphorics to unite historical data within one powerful thesis, Gibbon can be said to have contributed more to the discovery of historical metaphor than any other historian. Burckhardt's metaphor of the Renaissance is of no less interest. His presentation of this metaphor was so extraordinarily successful that few people will now recall that the metaphor was originally proposed by Michelet in 1855 in his *Histoire de France*. But since Michelet saw the Renaissance only as an anticipation of the French Revolution, he was interested only in the anticlericalism and in the reborn paganism of the Renaissance. It was therefore only Burckhardt who succeeded in exploiting all the possibilities of the metaphor and who knew how to give it such a tremendous impact that up till now we would find it very difficult to imagine fifteenth- and sixteenth-century Italian culture apart from Burckhardt's metaphor. It is almost as if historical reality tends to adapt itself to Burckhardt's metaphor instead of the other way round. (Historical) representation is clearly stronger than reality itself here. And this automatically brings us to Huizinga. For the sheer force of Burckhardt's metaphor was a standing invitation to project it also on the late Northern Middle Ages—as was done, for example, by H. Fierens Gevaert in his *La Renaissance septentrionale et les premiers maîtres de Flandres* (1905). In his *Autumn of the Middle Ages*, however, Huizinga attacked this transposition of Burckhardt's metaphorics by presenting the culture of the late Northern Middle Ages as an endless and often hollow proliferation of medieval forms.

The chapters in this book are divided into three categories. The first two chapters deal with systematic issues in historical theory; Chapters 3 through 6 discuss topics of the history of historical writing and of historical consciousness; and Chapters 7 through 10, while including conclusions of a more general purport, are each devoted to the work of an individual theorist.

The first two chapters aim to elaborate the claim, sketched out above, of the rationality of history as a discipline. Contemporary historical theory has often been accused—especially in the case of theorists having an affinity with postmodernism or with Hayden White's views, because of their alleged eulogy of irrationality and arbitrariness—of doubting or rejecting the rationality of historical writing. And it cannot be denied that there is more than a kernel of truth in this accusation. Admittedly, contemporary historical theorists, especially in the wake of the work of White and of postmodernism, have rightly pointed out that no theory of history can be taken seriously that does not account for the role of language in historical writing. But this most welcome and necessary correction of the shortcomings of traditional historical theory has been radicalized by some into a kind of linguistic idealism, leaving no room at all for reference, truth, and rational debate. So the time has come to find the *juste milieu* between the linguistic innocence of traditional historical theory and the hyperbole of some postmodernist theorists—an attempt that is the gist of Chapter 1. My main claim in this chapter is that the so-called linguistic turn should be fully accepted in historical theory but that one should also be wary of introducing literary theory into historical theory. Since the philosophy of language never developed a theory of narrative or of the text, it is quite understandable that historical theorists resorted to literary theory. And it cannot be doubted that some of the insights developed by literary theorists proved to be most valuable for historical theory. White's tropological reading of nineteenth-century historians and Gossman's deconstructivist reading of Thierry and Michelet are convincing examples. The problem with literary theory however, is that it has a hidden agenda for a philosophy of language. And unfortunately, in literary theory's philosophy of language, reference and meaning are rarely more than a set of pathetic and ill-considered *obiter dicta*. This has no disastrous consequences for literary theory's aim to clarify literature, since truth and reference have no very prominent role to play there; but obviously this is not the case with historical writing, in which the weaknesses of literary theory as a philosophy of language may become a serious handicap, inviting historical theorists to cut through all the ties between historical narrative and what it is about.[19] Hence—and this is the conclusion of the first chapter—historical theory should indeed embrace the linguistic turn, but should do so only in the domain of the history of historical writing, not allowing it to infringe on the critical philosophy of history that investigates the nature of historical knowledge.

The second chapter deals with the question of what makes one representation of the past better than others. This argument develops in two stages: In the first place, in agreement with the implications of the linguistic turn, historical language is granted a certain autonomy with regard to the past itself. Historical narrative is not a passive linguistic mirror of past reality. But recognizing this autonomy of the historian's language emphatically does not imply that no criteria can be given for the plausibility of historical representations. The chapter investigates the nature of these criteria and shows that they must combine doing justice to actual historical fact with certain linguistic requirements. These latter requirements can be summarized in the claim that the best historical representation is the most original one, the least conventional one, *the one that is least likely to be true—and that yet cannot be refuted on the basis of existing historical evidence.* Intellectual courage is the condition of all success in historical writing—as it is in the sciences.

Chapters 3 to 6 deal with the coming into being of modern historical writing and with contemporary historical consciousness. The familiar claim that Ranke's historism is the birth of modern historical writing is accepted, supported by an analysis, or rather a rational reconstruction, of what happened in the transition from Enlightenment historical writing, as exemplified by its unparalleled master, Edward Gibbon, to historism. This transition is explained in terms of the notion of substance. Enlightenment historical writing conceived of historical change as the changes in or of an immutable substance (in the way that we could say that the routine of daily experience leaves our personality unchanged). Change there is, but fundamentally all remains the same. This conception of change is *metamorphosis*, as it was defined in Ovid's *Metamorphoses*. Historism involved substance also in processes of change. Though this gave us modern historical writing, this new, historist conception of change involved a number of difficult philosophical problems that, even now, have only been dealt with tangentially. The main problem is that if change involves substance, no answer can be given to the question of *what* changes. For all change presupposes an immutable subject of change. The historists were vaguely aware of the problem and answered it by postulating an Aristotelian subject of change, whose entelechy predetermined it to pass through exactly those same processes of change that are recorded in actual historical fact. Obviously, this miraculous identity of a predetermined entelechy and historical fact will not recommend itself to the philosopher—though the practice of historist historical writing was not hampered by this weird theoretical curiosity. The problem can be solved by situating the subject of change not in (historical) *reality* but in the *language* we use for speaking about the past.[20] Obviously, this solution to the philosophical problem of historical change is in agreement with the linguistic turn.

Chapter 3 uses the similarities between Ovid's and Gibbon's conceptions of change in order to clarify the Enlightenment's prehistorist notion of historical change. The main insight is that change is conceived by both Ovid and Gibbon as metamorphosis and that metamorphosis is, in principle, no less capable of accounting for change than the later historist model. However, since metamorphosis will present change always as merely peripheral—that is, as change in the accidental properties of an unchanging substance—it had an built-in brake on the historicization of the world that could only be taken away by historism insofar as historicism also historicized substance. Chapter 3 explains how historism liberated historical writing from the fetters of metamorphosis. Nevertheless, as is suggested at the end of Chapter 3, something was lost as well in the abandonment of change as Ovidian metamorphosis to the historist conception of change as substantial change. Apparently the history of historical writing should not be written in terms of the triumphs over the shortcomings of the past but rather in those of a balance of gains and losses.

However, at the end of Chapter 4 it is argued that historism is, or rather has been, subject to a dialectical logic of its own, a logic, peculiar to historism, that can be explained and accounted for on the basis of an analysis inspired by the linguistic turn. For if language provides the historist historian with his subject of change, this implies that there is no coherence lying in the *past itself* (as would be suggested by the realist account of historical writing), but that coherence at the level of language decide how we conceive of the past (as is suggested by the linguistic turn). At this stage we should realize that coherence at the level of language will be subject to its own dialectics. We need only recall here that in history textual coherence is achieved by metaphor: the unity pervading the text of a book on the Renaissance can be defined in terms of how its author has operationalized the metaphor of a culture that was "reborn." Now, metaphor takes some things to the foreground while relegating others to the background. For example, the metaphor of the Renaissance will accentuate what fifteenth-century Italian culture owed to antiquity but, at the same time, invite us to disregard scholarly continuity between the Middle Ages and early modern Europe. But precisely this will invite historians to investigate this continuity between the Middle Ages and a later period and to develop a metaphor for understanding this aspect of the past. And so on. In sum, the logic of historical debate will stimulate an endless proliferation of different metaphorical viewpoints from which we are invited to see the past.

Or to use a metaphor (for understanding historical metaphor): the initially smooth surface of our understanding of the past will, in the course of the evolution of historical debate, be littered by myriad little bumps all having some metaphorical proposal for how to see (part of) the past in its center. Some of the bumps will be higher and larger than others—these have proven to be relatively successful in the history of historical writing. The more successful ones will not only be higher than others, but also tend to produce new bumps on themselves—as a volcano may sometimes sprout many smaller volcanoes on its lower slopes. But the most successful ones will be those that are surrounded by a whole host of smaller and lower bumps in a relative isolation from other such systems of bumps. Here we may think of a Ranke, Hegel, or Marx, or of a Namier, Braudel, Foucault, or Pocock. Hence of those historians who have given us historical subdisciplines.

When we consider this dialectics of historical writing, it will be clear that it possesses an intrinsic tendency to fragmentation, to exchange this initially smooth surface for myriad archipelagoes of historical metaphors, with some isolated raisings in the empty space between them. In this way, large-scale coherence will be exchanged for extremes of coherence in small isolated areas and which consume all of the available "capital of coherence"—so that nothing of it will be left over for the system of these archipelagoes itself. Overall coherence will be exchanged for local coherence. Consequently, with the historism of the beginning of the nineteenth century a process of fragmentation of the past had begun—a process that would find its logical point of culmination in the history of mentalities and, more specifically, in the so-called micro-storie.[21] Some of the consequences this has had for contemporary historical writing and for contemporary historical consciousness are detailed in Chapters 5 and 6. As one might expect from the fragmentation of past reality, the fragments of the past will be claimed by those historians who, for either disciplinary reasons or for reasons lying outside history as a discipline, will feel a special affinity with a specific (kind of) fragment. The process can be described as a "privatization of the past"—the title of Chapter 5. The fact that "privatization" is one of the most cherished items in our contemporary political discourse has undoubtedly further contributed to its success in transforming contemporary historical writing. The profound interest for memory and for commemoration in contemporary historical writing testifies to this urge to "privatize" the past.[22] For memory is a private affair; my memories are necessarily and exclusively mine even if I would remember exactly the same thing as you. In Chapter 6 the memory of the Holocaust and the monuments assembled at Yad Vashem are discussed as examples of the contemporary interest for memory.

The final chapters deal with individual theorists, though many of the themes indicated above are addressed in them as well. Thus in Chapter 7 Erich Auerbach's conception of the realist representation of reality is discussed. Since all historical writing aims at a realist representation of past reality, Auerbach's magisterial work is of the highest relevance for the historical theorist as well. When discussing historism above it became clear that the notion of the subject of change is central to the historist's theoretical position. Needless to say, an entity's subject of change ordinarily is where we would locate its identity. Identity, then, is the main topic in the discussion in Chapter 8 of Arthur Danto's theories on art, history, and the history of art. As mentioned above in the discussion of Chapter 1, much of contemporary historical theory focuses on what implications the linguistic turn should have for historical writing and for historical theory. The best point of departure for dealing with this issue are the writings of Hayden White, whose works are analyzed therefore in Chapter 9. The *communis opinio* among White's enemies—that he is not interested in historical reality or in a truthful and responsible historical representation of the past—is demonstrated to be false. Lastly, Chapter 10 deals with the work of Jörn Rüsen, who presently is the most influential German historical theorist but whose work still is insufficiently known among Anglo-Saxon theorists. As one might expect of a German theorist, trying to come to grips with Germany's dismal past in the first half of the last century, the political dimension is more pronounced in his theoretical writings than will be the case with Anglo-Saxon theorists. Because my *Political Representation*, the companion volume to the present book, focuses on political thought, the discussion of Rüsen's work is the natural *trait d'union* between these two books.

PART I

HISTORICAL THEORY

1

THE LINGUISTIC TURN: LITERARY THEORY AND HISTORICAL THEORY

In 1973 Hayden White published his by now famous *Metahistory*, a book that is generally regarded as a turning point—as is most suitable for a theory on *tropology*—in the history of historical theory. And, surely, one need only be superficially aware of the evolution of historical theory since World War II in order to recognize that historical theory has become a fundamentally different discipline since the publication of White's magnum opus. Different questions are now being asked, different aspects of historical writing are now being investigated, and it would be no exaggeration to say that thanks to White the kind of historical writing that now is the object of theoretical studies is much different from the kind of history that a previous generation of historical theorists believed to be exemplary of historical writing.

Three decades later now, at the beginning of the new century, it is arguable that this is an appropriate moment in which to assess what has and has not been achieved. In order to do so, I will address mainly the question of the relationship between the so-called linguistic turn and the introduction of literary theory as an instrument for understanding historical writing. My conclusion will be (1) that there is an asymmetry between the claims of the linguistic turn and those of literary theory; (2) that confusion between these two sets of claims has been most unfortunate from the perspective of historical theory; and (3) that literary theory has a lot to teach to the historian of historical writing but has no bearing on the kind of problems that is traditionally investigated by the historical theorist.

THE LINGUISTIC TURN AND HISTORICAL THEORY

The revolution effected by White in contemporary historical theory has often been related to the so-called linguistic turn. And quite rightly so, since White's main thesis has been that our understanding of the past is determined not only by what the past has been like but also by the *language* used by the historian for speaking about it—or, as he liked to put it himself, that historical knowledge is as much "made" (by the historian's language) as it is "found" (in the archives). Nonetheless, when White makes this claim he sometimes has things in mind different from the philosophers who argue for the linguistic turn. For a satisfactory appraisal of what White's revolution has done to historical theory, it will be worthwhile to identify these differences and to consider their implications.

"I shall mean by 'linguistic philosophy' the view that philosophical problems are problems which may be solved (or dissolved) either by reforming language, or by understanding more about the language we presently use": thus Rorty in the introduction to his influential collection on the linguistic turn.[1] Philosophical problems arise when, as in Wittgenstein's famous formulation, "language goes on holiday" and begins to create a pseudo world in addition to the world that language has to deal with on its ordinary workdays. Initially this may seem to strengthen the empiricist's position: for does not the linguistic philosopher's program recommend that we dismiss all philosophical problems as illusory that are not reducible to either the construction of an ideal language (that cannot give rise to philosophical pseudo problems) or to empirical enquiry? And is this not in agreement with empiricist orthodoxy, as formulated already by David Hume,[2] that all true belief can be reduced to either empirical or analytical truth? Surely, this intuition is not wholly mistaken: one need only think of Ayer's *Language, Truth, and Logic* in order to realize that one can be both an empiricist and an advocate of the linguistic turn.

But the linguistic turn can be shown at a deeper level to have antiempiricist implications. Empiricists and the advocates of the linguistic turn will pleasantly travel together to the station of the necessity to distinguish between speaking and speaking about speaking. Both will argue that the failure to distinguish between these two levels gave rise to the many pseudo problems that occupied traditional philosophy. But after having reached that station, each will follow his or her own route. The empiricist will tend to identify the distinction of these two levels with the distinction between empirical or synthetic truth (the level of "speaking") and analytical truth (the level of "speaking about speaking"). But here the more radical advocates of the linguistic turn will express their doubts. They will point out that this identification sins against the empiricist's own claims since it cannot be reduced to either logical truth or empirical truth—so, even on empiricist assumptions, the identification should be stigmatized as a hitherto unproven "dogma of empiricism." Next, they will emphasize that the identification is profoundly at odds with what we know about how one proceeds in the sciences: for here speaking about speaking will often be part of the acquisition of empirical knowledge. This is the procedure that Quine called "semantic ascent." And in order to illustrate what he has in mind with this notion, he asks us to consider the following example: "Einstein's theory of relativity was accepted in consequence not just of reflections on time, light, headlong bodies, and the perturbations of Mercury [hence, the level of 'speaking'], but of reflections on the theory itself, as discourse, and its simplicity in comparison with alternative theories [hence, the level of 'speaking about speaking']."[3] Self-evidently, Quine was not advocating here a return to prelinguistic philosophy, since he proposes here a theory on what the "semantic ascent" from the first to the second level may contribute to empirical knowledge—and this presupposes the distinction between the two levels that had so often been ignored by prelinguistic philosophy.

In a classic essay of 1951, "Two Dogmas of Empiricism," Quine had already used the linguistic turn for a frontal attack on empiricism. The dogma in question he described as the "belief in some fundamental cleavage between truths which are *analytic*, or grounded in meanings independent of fact, and truths which are *synthetic* or grounded in fact."[4] The dogma in question is the empiricist claim that (1) all true belief can be retraced to two sources of truth (i.e., firstly, what we know by empirical experience and, secondly, what we can derive by analytical deduction from true premises); (2) that there are no other sources of truth; and (3) that empirical truth can always be distinguished from analytical truth. Quine objected that there are true statements that can fit either category, and that, therefore, the distinction between synthetic and analytic truth is not as watertight as empiricists like(d) to believe. For an illustration of Quine's intentions, we may think, for example, of Newton's law according to which force is the product of mass and acceleration. We might say that the statement is empirically true because it is in agreement with the observed behavior of physical objects. And then it is an empirical or synthetic truth (to be situated on the level of "speaking"). But we can also say that the law is a conceptual truth about the notions of force, mass, and acceleration. Then it is an analytical truth, since it is true because of the meaning of the concepts (to be situated on the level of "speaking about speaking"). Summarizing the implications of Quine's argument against the synthetic/analytic distinction, Rorty wrote:

> Quine's "Two Dogmas of Empiricism" challenged this distinction, and with it the standard notion (common to Kant, Husserl, and Russell) that philosophy stood to empirical science as the study of structure to the study of content. Given Quine's doubts (buttressed by similar doubts in Wittgenstein's *Philosophical Investigations*) about how to tell when we are responding to the compulsion of "language" rather than that of "experience", it became difficult to explain in what sense philosophy had a separate "formal" field of inquiry, and thus how it might have the desired apodictic character.[5]

Hence, the crucial implication is that we cannot always be sure whether our beliefs have their origins in the "compulsion of experience"—in what empirical reality demonstrates to be the case—or in the "compulsion of language," so in what we believe on the basis of a priori, analytical, or philosophical argument. This is also why one speaks of the linguistic turn: contrary to empiricist conviction, what we believe to be true can, at least sometimes, be interpreted as a statement about reality *and* as a statement about the meaning of language and of the words that we use in language. So, language can be a truth maker no less than reality.

Now, a similar antiempiricist argument can be defended for historical writing as well. Even more so, as we shall see in a moment, the significance of the linguistic turn is far greater for the humanities than for the sciences. Think of a study of the Renaissance or of the Enlightenment. Then, just as in the case of Newton's law, one can say two things of such a study: In the first place it could well be argued that a historical investigation of the relevant part of the past is the *empirical* basis for this specific view of the Renaissance or the Enlightenment. But it could be said equally well that this study presents us with a definition—or with the proposal of a definition—of the Renaissance or the Enlightenment. Other historians have written other books on the Renaissance or the Enlightenment and associated the Renaissance or the Enlightenment with a different set of aspects of the relevant part of the past—or, rather, with a different set of statements about the past—and this is why they came up with a different *definition* of the Renaissance or the Enlightenment. And if this is how they decide to *define* the Renaissance or the Enlightenment, then all that they have been saying about it must be (analytically) true, since what they have said about it can be derived analytically from the meaning they want to give to the terms "Renaissance" or "Enlightenment." What has been said about these historical texts is then a conceptual truth, just as Newton's law can be interpreted as a conceptual truth.

Much the same can be argued with regard to terms like "revolution," "social class," and probably even for such seemingly unambiguous and well-defined terms as "war" or "peace." Take "revolution," for example. In Crane Brinton's well-known *The Anatomy of Revolution*, he discusses four revolutions: "the English revolution of the 1640's, the American Revolution, the great French Revolution, and the recent—or present—revolution in Russia."[6] As the book's title already suggests, Brinton wanted to discern some features or patterns that are shared by all revolutions, and found these mainly in the fact that all revolutions seem to pass from the phase of an *ancien régime*, through the reign of the moderates, to the subsequent reign of the extremists and the ultimate phase of "Thermidor." In this way a comparative analysis of revolutions allowed Brinton to discover some empirical truths about revolutions.

However, the problem of the systematization of phenomena such as revolutions is that they seem to depend as much on what one actually finds in the past as in how one decides to define the word "revolution." This observation is exemplified already by Brinton's choices of revolutions to discuss, for, while he includes the American Revolution in his study, Marxist historians will argue that this was not a revolution at all since it lacked the aspect of class struggle that Marxists see as a *conditio sine qua non* for a historical conflict to count as a revolution. If Brinton had adopted a different *definition* of the word "revolution," he would probably have ended up with different *empirical* findings about revolutions. Next, what would Brinton do with a social conflict resembling his revolutions in all relevant respects except for the fact that it is impossible to distinguish between the reign of the moderates and that of the extremists? Would he refuse to see this social conflict as a revolution because of this; or would he see there instead an occasion to reconsider his typology of revolutions? Both options seem to be open to him and this most powerfully suggests the equivalence of the compulsion of language and that of experience in this kind of social and historical analysis. Hence, in both the case of the Marxist resistance against revolutions without a class struggle and that of revolutions disconfirming Brinton's typology of revolutions, we are thrown back on the question "What is a revolution?" When historians have to deal with this kind of question, issues of meaning and issues of empirical fact tend to become indistinguishable. This is, however, not a weakness of historical writing: for historical discussion is our only refuge if truth *de dicto* and truth *de re* intermingle. The attempt to decide these dilemmas by sacrificing one type of truth for the other would mean, first, the end of historical writing, and rob us, next, of an indispensable instrument for coming to a better understanding of the social world we are living in.

Even more illustrative is the following example. Barrington Moore, in his *Social Origins of Dictatorship and Democracy*, also develops a comparativist analysis of revolution, though it is an infinitely more profound one than Brinton's. In a most perceptive review, Theda Skocpol discusses Moore's concept of the so-called bourgeois revolution. She points out that for Moore the "bourgeois revolutions" are the Puritan Revolution in England of the 1640s, the French Revolution, and the American Civil War. Note that Moore, unlike Brinton, does not consider the American Revolution of 1776 to have been a "real" revolution and grants that honor (if that is what it is) only to the Civil War. In history what is ordinarily called a revolution may, for certain historians *not* be a revolution, whereas what is ordinarily not considered a revolution may be argued by some to have been one. Next, Skocpol observes that when Moore contrasts the bourgeois revolution to the fascist and the communist revolutions, he does so not by identifying some independent variable explaining why in some cases you would have to do with a bourgeois revolution (and in others with a fascist or communist revolution), but by merely looking at the results of the revolution in question. A revolution is a bourgeois revolution if a bourgeois state emerged from it, and a similar story can be told for the fascist and communist revolutions. In sum, revolutions are identified and named by what is caused by them. This is what he argues, and there is nothing necessarily wrong with this. However, if revolutions are given their names in this manner, the very notion of a bourgeois (or fascist and communist) revolution can no longer help us to explain the nature of the revolution in question (as Moore mistakenly thinks it could). For things can only properly be explained by their causes and not by their consequences. If this is lost from sight—as is the case with Moore—naming may start to function as a quasi-explanatory procedure. For we will then be tempted to believe that we are saying something deep and profoundly revealing about the nature of the kind of revolution in question when we label it as a bourgeois or some other kind of revolution—and that we have thus succeeded in explaining it in some way or other. What merely is a truth *de dicto* (because it is analytically and not empirically true that the French Revolution is a bourgeois revolution, if we have decided to fix the names of revolutions in agreement with what results from them) may under such circumstances deceitfully acquire the aura of being a truth *de re*. And Skocpol therefore correctly concludes that Moore's analysis "suffers from *interrelated* logical and empirical difficulties" (emphasis mine).[7] Even more outspoken is the Dutch philosopher of history Chris Lorenz (who is, by the way, no less sympathetic with regard to Moore's comparative method than Skocpol) when he writes that Moore's generalizations about "bourgeois revolutions" are *conceptual* rather than *empirical* truths.[8]

In agreement with the foregoing, I would like to emphasize that there is nothing necessarily wrong with Moore's approach. For in historical writing we will sometimes find ourselves (whether we like it or not) not being able to distinguish between truths *de dicto* and truths *de re*. At this juncture decisions are made that will determine to a large extent how we see the past. The kind of criteria that are decisive here are not reducible to questions of truth or falsity—for it is, essentially, a decision about what set of truths we shall prefer to some other set of truths when we are looking for the best account of the relevant part(s) of the past. Truth is here not the arbiter of the game but its stake, so to say.

We will then have to rely upon other criteria besides truth and falsity—it is an empiricist superstition to believe that no such criteria can be conceived of and that prejudice, irrationality, and arbitrariness are the only other options to the criteria of truth and falsity. For, as is suggested by the examples of Newton's law, the Renaissance, or the Enlightenment, the fact that Newton's law or statements on the Renaissance or the Enlightenment can be construed as being either empirically or analytically true does not in the least imply that we could not give good (or poor) arguments in favor of our views on Newton's law or for a specific conception of the Renaissance or the Enlightenment. Historical debate is sufficient proof of the fact that there *are* rational criteria, other than the truth criterion, that we can appeal to when we have moved to this level. It may well be that it is not so easy to identify these criteria for rational historical discussion, but it would be most "irrational" to see in this unfortunate fact sufficient reason for simply dropping the search for these criteria.[9] The empiricist's unwillingness to recognize other criteria than the truth criterion must therefore remind us of the blind man who argues that there could not be a table in this room since *he* is unable to see it.

Thus, as will have become clear from the foregoing, from whatever angle we decide to look at the linguistic turn it can never be construed as an attack on truth or as a license for relativism. For the linguistic turn does not question truth in any way but exclusively the standard empiricist account of the distinction between empirical and analytical truth. Hence, we should not follow the many historical theorists who are inclined to read into the linguistic turn an argument in favor of what they refer to as "linguistic relativism." As is made clear by the linguistic turn, the fact that there may be different "languages" for speaking about historical reality is no less an argument in favor of historical relativism than the fact that we can describe the world in English, French, German, or Japanese. Of course, it may well be that the meanings of words in these different languages do not always correspond exactly to each other—and though this undeniable fact may give rise to the difficult problem of translation from one language to another *salva veritate*,[10] it cannot be construed as an argument against the possibility of expressing truth in any of these languages. Such a conclusion would only be thinkable on the Russellian assumption that there is only one language—that is, the language of science—that would allow us to express truth. Nonetheless, it may well be that certain historical languages more easily give us access to truth than others. And it may be added that a discussion about the appropriateness of these languages is part of what goes on in historical debate, and that, as the foregoing has made clear, such discussions, to be situated on the level of "speaking about speaking," should not be reduced to the only level that the empiricist is willing to recognize. But the criteria of truth and falsity are useless in such debates.

We observed a moment ago that the linguistic turn has its significance for both the sciences and history, but it cannot be doubted that its significance is far greater for history than for the sciences. For the indeterminacy of truth by this compulsion of experience and truth by the compulsion of language will increase to the extent that it will be more difficult to pin down with precision what part of language corresponds to what chunk of reality. The less room there is for uncertainties in this correspondence, the less will we encounter the indeterminacy identified by the linguistic turn. Now, the success of the sciences is undoubtedly largely because of its unequaled capacity to manage reference; that is, to define the meaning of its words and concepts in experiential terms, or at least in terms of what investigated (physical) reality shows to be the case. Put differently, if we recall Frege's distinction between *Sinn* and *Bedeutung*, between meaning and reference, the sciences have can be said to have been eminently successful in excessively expanding the dimension of *Bedeutung* at the expense of *Sinn* (though even in the sciences the former dimension will or could never be wholly absent). It follows that in the sciences the ascendancy of the compulsion of experience over that of language will be far more pronounced than in the humanities. What happens on the level of language, what definitions are either explicitly or implicitly proposed there—the web of associations determining meaning—will contribute far more to knowledge in the humanities than in the sciences. Science has an elective affinity with the level of "speaking" and historical writing with that of "speaking about speaking."

But this does not in the least imply that we have any reason to be skeptical with regard to historical writing and discussion from the perspective of truth (as both defenders and detractors of the linguistic turn in historical theory are in the habit of arguing). The only legitimate inference permitted by the linguistic turn is that in history truth may have its origins in the compulsions of language no less than in those of experience. The empiricist tends to commit the mistake of being alarmed by the alleged relativist implications of the linguistic turn because he believes that the compulsion of experience is the only constraint on our way to true and reliable knowledge—and, indeed, if one embraces this prejudice (and this is nothing but a prejudice), then it would follow that historical writing floats aimlessly on the seas of relativism and of moral and political bias (just as the Cartesian arguing that reason is our only reliable source of truth is likely to condemn the empiricist's trust in empirical findings because it would deal the death blow to sound scientific inquiry). But as soon as we also make room for the compulsions of language, and for the constraints of a meaningful use of language, then there is no reason at all for such dramatic and overhasty condemnations of historical writing.

I am well aware that these optimistic comments on historical writing will be regarded by most people as profoundly counterintuitive. Surely, they will argue, truth is more easily attainable in the sciences than in historical writing with its endless disputes, its *dialogues des sourds*, its frequent misunderstandings, and its clumsy and often ill-focused discussions. They will see in these, admittedly distressing, features of historical debate both sign and proof of how much harder it is to arrive at truth in history than in the sciences. And, as it seems to follow, if the trajectory to truth apparently is so much longer and so much more arduous in history than elsewhere, what other conclusion is open to us than that the historian ordinarily lingers in places where truth is not to be found and in the doubtful company of the enemies of truth?

But though we have every reason to agree with this lamentation about the daily discomforts of historical debate, we should not accept the diagnosis on which it is founded. For truth is simply not at stake here. In order to explain this, we had best return to my example of the Renaissance or the Enlightenment. As the protagonist of the linguistic turn will argue, the debate on the Renaissance will mainly be a debate on how the Renaissance had best be *defined* (in terms of the description[s] that a historian may give of the relevant part and aspects of fourteenth- and fifteenth-century Italian civilization). And what is *then* said about fifteenth- and sixteenth-century Italian civilization is, admittedly, true *by definition*—but *true* it is. For the logical structure of such an account of the Renaissance essentially is that all, and only all the statements that a historian has been using for describing the Renaissance add up to the lengthy and complex manner in which the historian in question proposes to define the Renaissance. Put differently, *each* historical account of the Renaissance is true, since it can be derived logically from how the historian in question proposes to define the Renaissance.[11] And truth thus is not at stake in the disagreement about such definitions—what is at stake is what truths are *more helpful* than others for grasping the nature of the period in question. Similarly, we cannot use truth as the criterion that may enable us to decide whether we should define the human being as a featherless biped or as creature endowed with reason—and which of the two definitions is the more useful one will depend on what type of conversation about human nature we wish to engage in.

But I repeat, this does not in the least exclude the possibility of a meaningful discussion of how we could best define the Renaissance. A certain definition of the Renaissance may teach us more about what is of interest in Italian civilization in the relevant period than some rival definition. And one may have good and convincing arguments for preferring one such definition to other(s). Once again, the discussions that may arise with regard to the question of how best to define the Renaissance cannot be decided by having recourse to truth conditions. For, in a way, they are *all* true; and this may make clear why the truth criterion is so unhelpful here. Truth is not decisive here, but the question of what definition of the Renaissance is most successful in meaningfully interrelating as many different aspects of the period in question.

DESCRIPTION AND REPRESENTATION

We may rephrase the foregoing in terms of the distinction between description and representation. On the face of it the distinction between the two seems to have no real theoretical significance: both terms are suggestive of a true account of part of reality. And while this may invite us to see the terms "description" and "representation" as being more or less synonymous, if we look more closely some interesting differences will present themselves.

As I have discussed elsewhere,[12] the most notable logical difference between the two is the following. In a description such as "This cat is black," we can always distinguish a part that refers—"this cat"—and a part attributing a certain property to the object referred to—"is black." No such distinction is possible in a representation of the black cat, in a picture or photograph of it. We cannot pinpoint with absolute precision on the picture those parts of it that exclusively refer to the black cat (as is being done by the subject-term in the description) and those other parts of it that attribute to it certain properties—such as being black—as is done by the predicative part of the description. *Both* things, both reference and predication, take place in pictures at one and the same time.

And so it is with historical writing. Suppose, once again, that in a historical text about the Renaissance we are reading a chapter, a paragraph, or an individual sentence on Renaissance painting. Should we say, then, that this chapter, paragraph, or sentence refers to the Renaissance in the sense of exclusively picking out some historical object or part of the past to which elsewhere in the text certain properties are attributed? Or should we say, instead, that the chapter, paragraph, or sentence attributes a property to an object that has been identified elsewhere. And, if so, where and how has this object been identified? If so, what enables us to distinguish it from other closely related objects such as those of Mannerism or the Baroque? All questions that are impossible to answer. And this is not merely a matter of history being an inexact science in which absolute precision with regard to reference is unattainable. It is, rather, a matter of principle. And the principle in question is that in the writing of history, and in the historical text, reference and attribution always go together.

But this not yet all. It might be objected that the mere fact that reference and predication go together in (pictorial and historical) representation by no means excludes the possibility that reference and predication are both achieved by representation. Surely, a picture or photograph of this cat *refers* to this cat and also *attributes* to it the property of being black—and, similarly does not a book on the Renaissance *refer* to certain aspects of the past while, admittedly, at the same time attributing certain properties to it? The fact that both operations are being done at one and the same time by representation is certainly an interesting observation on the nature of representation, so the objection might go on, but this amounts to no more than the pedestrian observation that there is a regrettable vagueness in representation if contrasted to its more sophisticated counterpart, namely, description. But to make such an objection would be to underestimate representation and its complexities: representation is far more than a mere tentative and imperfect halfway station between an unstructured encounter with reality and the certainties of true description.

Let us for sake of the argument grant for a moment that a text on the Renaissance "refers" to the past. We should then ask exactly what past the text refers to. And here disagreement will arise. Different texts written by different historians will "refer" to different things. Burckhardt's Renaissance differs from the Renaissance that Michelet, Baron, Huizinga, Burdach, Goetz, Brandi, or Wölfflin had in mind.[13] And these differences are not mere uncertainties occasioned by the lack of precision peculiar to historical writing. For it is in these differences and these uncertainties that all historical thinking and all historical understanding articulate themselves. We could have no historical discussion and no progression in historical understanding if everybody knew what the Renaissance was and what the term did and did not refer to. Surely, there is a certain historical period, a certain civilization in a certain country that we will all have associations with when hearing the phrase "the Renaissance." But though this is a necessary condition, it is an insufficient condition for fixing reference.

In order to bring this out and to avoid confusion, we should therefore use an alternative term and avoid the term "reference" when discussing the relationship between the word "Renaissance" and that part of past reality we associate with it. I propose using the term "being about" instead, which would result in the following terminological distinction. Though both descriptions and representations stand in a relationship with reality, a description will be said to *refer* to reality (by means of its subject-term), whereas a representation (as a whole) will be said to *be about* reality. And where "reference" is fixed objectively, that is, by an object in reality denoted by the subject-term of the description, "being about" is essentially unstable and unfixed because it is differently defined by the descriptions contained by the text of each representation. That does not imply that we should be desperate about representation and lament the absence of the certainties of description and of reference. For "being about" gives us the "logical space" within which historical thinking and historical discussion are possible; where "reference" takes the place of "being about," historical understanding withers away and science takes over. The discussion of what set of descriptions (as embodied in a representation) would best represent a chunk of reality is then exchanged for a discussion of what predicates are true of reality.

This may clarify why the linguistic turn, as discussed in the previous section, is so essential for a correct understanding of historical writing. I referred there to Quine's notion of "semantic ascent," which was defined as a discourse in which the level of "speaking" and that of "speaking about" begin to intermingle. It is, as we have seen, in the fusion of these two levels that this indeterminacy of the "compulsion of language" and "the compulsion of experience" that so much interests the advocate of the linguistic turn announces itself. And it is precisely in this fusion of "speaking" and "speaking about" where historical understanding and historical debate should be located. For on the one hand the historical text contains the level of "speaking" (i.e., the level where the historian describes the past in terms of individual statements about historical events, states of affairs, causal links, etc.).

But on the other it *also* comprises the level where the discussion takes place about what chunk of language (i.e., what historical text) represents best or corresponds best to some chunk of past reality. This is the level of "speaking about speaking" and is where we may ask ourselves, for example, what *definition* we had best give of the concept "Renaissance" or "revolution" in order to come to an optimal understanding of a certain part of the past.[14]

Before proceeding further it will be helpful to answer an obvious objection. It may now be suggested that I have elevated in all this a merely practical problem into a theoretical one. The practical problem is that "things" such as the Renaissance or the French revolution are not so easy to identify as, for example, the Statue of Liberty or the Eiffel Tower. But this is a mere difference in degree and not in principle. And it would follow that there is no need to introduce fine logical distinctions when we move from *descriptions* of the Statue of Liberty to *representations* of, say, the Renaissance. For description and representation are similar from a logical point of view—and it is only because the Renaissance is such a far more complex object in the world's inventory than the Statue of Liberty that we happen to prefer the word "representation" in the former and the word "description" in the latter case. Moreover, so the objection may go, think of pictorial representation; for example, of the photograph or picture of the black cat that was discussed above. Is the represented, the black cat, not an objective given for us so that we can assess the adequacy of its pictorial representation in much the same way that we can decide about the truth or falsity of descriptions such as "This cat is black"? Is this in both cases not merely a question of correctly identifying the object of description or representation and of establishing, next, whether what is said about the object in question corresponds or not to what we see?

I shall not say that there is no truth in this view: in the next section I shall explain where it is right and wrong when discussing certain types of statements suggesting a kind of sliding scale between description and representation. But for the moment I wish to point out that even in the case of pictorial representation the issue may be more complicated than in that of the photograph of the black cat.

Think of portrait painting. When the painter paints a portrait, we tend to believe that the reality depicted is objectively or intersubjectively given to us (just as when the photographer makes a picture of the black cat). For the sitter presents to the painter a physical presence, and it may seem that no disagreement can exist about its exact nature. The sitter must seem the same to any painter, and to just anybody carefully looking. But observe, next, that if a person is painted by different painters, we will get as many different paintings or representations of the sitter as there were painters. Our initial reaction to this state of affairs will be that some paintings are more accurate and approach accurate description more closely than others. An intuition, by the way, that would most counterintuitively confer on photography the honor of being the ultimate touchstone of artistic excellence—already a warning about the foregoing conclusion. For we all know well that we do not judge portraits (exclusively) on the basis of their photographic accuracy. A good portrait should, before all, give us the personality of the person represented.

However, this personality is just as little an objective given as the nature of the Renaissance or of the French Revolution (i.e., the examples of historical representation we dealt with a moment ago). So, in both cases, in that of the portrait and in that of historical writing, we are faced with a movement from an (intersubjective) surface down into ever deeper layers of reality.[15] Our assessment of a portrait may well start with the criterion of photographic accuracy, but from there it will move on into ever deeper levels giving us access to the sitter's personality. And much the same is true in historical writing. As (a sum of) description(s) the historical text should be unexceptionable. This is the "surface," so to say. But a historical text giving us correct descriptions of the past is not sufficient: the text should also give us the "personality" of the period (or aspect of it) with which it deals. And, just as with the photograph, as soon as we have broken through the surface of what is intersubjectively given, and as soon as we have thus entered into the deeper levels of reality, there is no obvious (and intersubjectively given) mark where we should stop or, reversely, where we are invited to penetrate even deeper. Yet *somewhere* we will have to stop in the end: in both painting and historiography, from a certain moment further penetration will give us less instead of more. And, once again, this is a constraint that has its only origin and scope of action at the level of representation: reality itself does not provide us with criteria for this kind of representative consistency, nor for how to apply them.

The crucial implication of all this is the following. We should be wary of the common intuition that representation is a variant of description, a conclusion that suggests that the represented is intersubjectively given in exactly the same way to us all if only we take care to look in the right direction. The intuition is correct only for the "surface" of what we see. But as soon as we want to look more deeply into reality, it becomes opaque and multilayered; layers lose themselves in darkness and obscurity the deeper we go, downward from that reality's "public" or quasi-intersubjective surface. And this is not an ontological pronouncement about the nature of reality, but on how representation makes us perceive it. Representation makes reality unfold itself into this infinity of different layers; and reality itself meekly adapts itself accordingly. This insight into the nature of representation can be explained if we recognize that all representation has to satisfy certain rules, criteria, or standards for scale, coherence, and consistency; and these rules and so on all live their life exclusively in the world of representation and not in that of the represented. Only representations can be "coherent" or "consistent"; it makes as little sense to speak of a "coherent reality" as of a "true reality." But at the level of representation, these rules and so on are indispensable. For example, the figurative painter painting a landscape cannot paint the rind of individual trees into the greatest detail, while at the same reducing the staffage in the foreground to a mere suggestive smear. And, as Haskell Fain already most acutely observed, some thirty years ago, much the same is true for the writing of history.[16] The representation itself is tied to certain layers, so to say—the possibilities are accordingly limited.

Once again, this has nothing to do with truth. For a painting or historical text that ignores these rules, criteria, or standards for representative coherence and consistency does not invite us to hold mistaken beliefs about reality. A historian who begins by correctly informing his readers about the GNP of Britain in 1867 and then goes on to tell us about mental processes in Charles Darwin's mind in 1863 does not sin against the requirement to tell the truth about the past; we will accuse him, instead, of presenting us with an incoherent historical narrative. And a historical theory insensitive to this dimension of the writing of history and intimating that all theoretical problems about historical writing can ultimately be rephrased as problems about truth is as helpless and defective as an aesthetics arguing that photographic accuracy is all we need in order to assess the merits of the pictorial representation of reality we may admire in our museums.

The upshot of these considerations is that there exists in representation a correspondence between the represented and its representation that does not have its counterpart or equivalent in description. Description does not know these constraints of coherence and consistency that inevitably enter the scene as soon as we move from simple description to the complexities of representation. There is, thus, something peculiarly "idealist" about representation, in the sense that how we decide to conceptualize reality on the level of representation (of reality) determines what we will find on the level of the represented (i.e., on that of reality itself). This should *not* be taken, however, to mean that thought or representation actually "makes" or "creates" reality—as, admittedly, some extremist deconstructivists or narrativists are in the habit of saying—but only that a decision with regard to the former level will determine what we shall find on the second level.

Nevertheless, the suggestion of idealism is reinforced by the fact that reality (or the represented) will remain a chaos as long as no such decision has been made and no level of representation has been singled out for ordering this chaos. In this sense, and *only* in this sense can the pseudo-idealist claim be defended that representation determines the represented. Put differently, the contours of reality, though not reality *itself*, can only be defined if they are represented by a representation. To force a decision as to whether these contours have their origin in reality or in the mind is just as useless and misleading as the question of whether America existed before people started to use the proper name "America." In a certain sense, yes, but in another, no—and we should acquiesce in this ambiguity.

Finally, the linguistic turn is not only to be associated with a claim about the distinction between analytical and synthetic truths but also with a philosophical method. The philosophical method in question is that many, if not all, philosophical problems can be solved, or rather be dissolved, by a careful analysis of the language in which these problems were stated. In one word, language may mislead us and it is the linguistic philosopher's task to show where language has led us astray. From this methodological point of view, the linguistic turn has another lesson to teach us about the differences between description and representation and between "reference" and "being about." From a grammatical point of view there is no difference between the statement "This cat is black" and the statement "The Renaissance is the birth of the modern mind." And this has led many (empiricist) philosophers into mistakenly believing that the logic of these two statements is identical as well. However, in contrast to what grammatical similarity suggests, the logic of the latter (type of) statement is highly complex if properly analyzed. The statement is ambiguous and, further, each of its two meanings possesses different layers of meaning. Let me clarify this.

With regard to ambiguity, the above statement may in the first place refer to no representation of the Renaissance in particular, but merely express what is regarded as more or less the common denominator in what people will customarily associate with the phrase "the Renaissance." Let us assume—as is a reasonable thing to do—that there is such a common denominator. In that case the subject-term of the statement will refer to this common denominator and the question of whether the statement correctly describes this common denominator will decide its truth or falsity. Next, this common denominator is, obviously, a representation of part of the past (though probably a severely truncated one). As such it can unproblematically be said to "be about" the past (in the sense that I have been using this term). But this is not all. If there really is some such common denominator—hence a substantial overlap in how all speakers will use the word Renaissance (and that may be summarized in the view that the Renaissance gave us the birth of modernity)—the statement will be analytically true, since it merely expresses what is already part of the (accepted) meaning of the phrase "the Renaissance." This is, then, where the statement will differ from a synthetic truth such as "This cat is black," in spite of the grammatical similarities between the two of them. But on the other hand, it will now share with synthetic truth the capacity to "refer" to reality. For if all speakers will relate the same (set of) word(s) to the same aspects of reality, then the aspects in question will coagulate into the *thing* that we can "refer" to by means of this (set of) word(s).[17] So here "being about" will shade off into "reference"—but even *this* makes the statement not into a descriptive one. For whereas descriptions are synthetically true or false, this one is analytically true or false, depending on whether it has correctly expressed the (common denominator of the) meaning(s) of the phrase "the Renaissance," or not.[18]

In the second place, the statement "The Renaissance is the birth of modernity" may be the summary into one sentence of some quite specific representation of the Renaissance. The apodictic character of the statement will then reflect or express the speaker's agreement with this specific representation. In this way the statement expresses what Russell had somewhat enigmatically called the speaker's "propositional attitude": that is, the speaker believes that the representation of the Renaissance in question is a sensible, believable, or plausible one. Assuming that the speaker knows what he is talking about, the statement will be analytically true since in this case what is predicated to the Renaissance will be true on the basis of the meaning that the representation in question proposes to grant to the phrase "the Renaissance." It follows as a matter of course that in this case the subject-term of the statement does not "refer" to, nor is it even "about," (some part of past) reality. But the propositional attitude of the speaker is such that he believes the representation in question to be a sensible, believable, or plausible one (and he may or may not have good reasons for this belief—but that is not the issue in the present context). Or, put differently, he believes that the representation in question is the best way for coupling language (a text) to (a specific part or aspect of historical) reality. From this perspective the statement is to be situated on the level of "speaking about speaking": it is an (implicit) pronouncement on how we should speak about reality, about what chunk of language had best correspond to what chunk of reality. But all this can, of course, only be justified on the basis of what is said about the past on the level of "speaking," that is, on the level of what the individual descriptions contained by the representation in question assert about the past. In this way the statement in question involves both "being about" (i.e., the representational level that is to be identified with the specific historical text to which the statement's subject-term "refers") and "reference" (both insofar as the subject-term of the statement "refers" to a representation *and* insofar as reference is made to *past reality* by means of the subject-terms of the descriptions contained by the representation).

Now, all of these subtle but necessary distinctions are wholly lost when one brutally and bluntly lumps together (with the empiricist) description (and "reference") and representation (and "being about") on no other basis than the grammatical similarities of statements like "This cat is black" and "The Renaissance is the birth of modernity." All that makes the writing of history into the fascinating discipline that it is—and all, moreover, about which the discipline of history still has to teach contemporary philosophy of language a lesson or two—is then lost from sight. This will be elaborated in greater detail in the next section.

No less should one avoid the other extreme and project on descriptions what exclusively belongs to the nature of representation—as has recently been done by Berkhofer.[19] For then even the simplest descriptive statements are presented as having the same indeterminacy with regard to past reality as we have claimed for the level of representation. And the result ordinarily is a skepticism just as bottomless as it is absurd. But, as the foregoing will have made clear, we should steer a prudent middle course between, on the one hand, the empiricist's attempt to put all historical representation on the procrustean bed of description and, on the other hand, Derridean exaggerations. Certainly the empiricist is right in much of what he finds objectionable or even ridiculous in the orgiastic word cult of Derridian deconstructivism. Certainly the deconstructivist is right when arguing against the empiricist that language has its own contribution to make to historical understanding. Both are right, to some extent, and both are wrong as well. We should therefore invest our intellectual energy in exploring the *juste milieu* between the Scylla and Charybdis of empiricism and Derridian deconstructivism. And this we can do by granting both to description (and "reference") and to representation (and "being about") what is due to them, while at the same time recognizing the limitations of each. But unfortunately contemporary historical theory has a stubborn penchant for extremism that effectively bars the way for an intelligent and fruitful compromise.

Let me conclude this section by emphasizing that the indeterminacy that has been claimed for the relationship between historical language and historical reality does not in the least oblige us to cut through all the ties between both. In the individual descriptive statements of a representation, reference is made to past events, and so on; a representation, as a whole, "is about" part of a specific past reality. But "being about" must be distinguished from "reference," since the indeterminacy in the relationship between language and reality characteristic of representation is absent in the case of reference. And both should be distinguished from the formal correspondence between a specific historical representation (language) and what it represents (reality), which will be more closely investigated in the final section of this chapter. Lastly, above all one should avoid confusing "indeterminacy" with "arbitrariness," for all historical discussion—the very possibility of a rational argument about how best to link historical language to historical reality—both presupposes and requires the "logical space" opened up by this indeterminacy.

AGAINST THE EMPIRICISTS

In his excellent survey of contemporary historical theory, Munslow distinguishes between the reconstructionist, the constructionist, and the deconstructionist approach to historical knowledge. The reconstructionist maintains a "foundational belief in empiricism and historical meaning"; constructionism refers to the socioscientific approach to history; and the deconstructionist "accepts that the content of history, like that of literature, is defined as much by the nature of language used to describe and to interpret that content as it is by research into the documentary sources."[20] It will be obvious that the main difference between these groups of theorists is the degree to which they hold to (a variant of) undiluted empiricism. Deconstructionists (at least the more sensible among them) recognize that *both* the compulsion of experience *and* the compulsion of language have their roles to play in historical understanding, whereas the empiricists (either reconstructionist or constructionist) allow *only* the compulsion of experience. This situation implies that the onus of proof lies with the empiricists; they should demonstrate that all the cases where the deconstructionist will be likely to appeal to the compulsion of language are ultimately reducible to the compulsion of experience. So, instead of vociferously accusing the deconstructionist of an irresponsible irrationalism (by which the empiricists try to hide their theoretical nakedness), the empiricist had better make clear how the many theoretical and practical differences between history and the sciences can be explained without jeopardizing their empiricism.

A striking example of empiricist prejudice is the sentence with which Richard Evans ends his denunciation of what he indiscriminately lumps together as "postmodernist" historical theory. After having enumerated a few postmodernist authors (I have also been included in the list) and after having tied them to one-sentence summaries of their views, he goes on to write: "I will look humbly at the past and say despite them all: it really happened, and we really can, if we are very scrupulous and careful and self-critical, find out how it happened and reach some tenable though always less than final conclusions about what it all meant."[21] One is reminded here of the anecdote of Samuel Johnson's "rejection" of Berkeley's idealism, when he kicked a stone and then declared this to be the irrefutable proof that objective reality exists. But most striking in this final sentence of the book is its peculiar mixture of arrogance and modesty. On the one hand, it is arrogantly claimed that truth about the past is attainable (if only one is careful and self-critical), but on the other, in the same breath truth is most modestly declared to be unattainable with the casual and seemingly innocuous concession that one will reach always only "less than final conclusions." Evans is strangely insensitive to the harsh opposition between his confidence in our being able "to find out how it happened" on the one hand and our incapacity to reach "final conclusions about what it all meant" on the other—and that in one and the same sentence! Furthermore, he apparently never felt compelled to consider the intriguing problem of these endless disputes in historical writing, about such most peculiar "things" as the Renaissance or the French Revolution, that never go beyond "less than final conclusions."

What Professor Evans has probably never gathered from his short and perfunctory incursion into the strange country of historical theory is that here lies the inspiration of most, if not of all of historical theory. For this is precisely what has always fascinated the more serious and intelligent historical theorists: how is it possible that on the one hand we know so much about the past, whereas on the other historical writing is "a discussion without end," as Pieter Geyl famously put it? This is what the empiricist has never explained in a satisfactory way, nor even cared to try to explain.

Professor Evans's mixture of arrogance and modesty can also be discerned in more sophisticated empiricist attacks on the position that I have defended here. Though Professor Zammito may not consider himself to be an empiricist, since he speaks with much sympathy about hermeneutics, nevertheless it is an empiricist argument that he marshals against my position when commenting on the following quote from a text by Carlo Ginzburg:

Instead of dealing with the evidence as an open window, contemporary skeptics regard it as a wall, which by definition precludes any access to reality. This extreme antipositivistic attitude, which considers all referential assumptions as a theoretical naiveté, turns out to be a sort of inverted positivism. Theoretical naiveté and theoretical sophistication share a common, rather simplistic assumption: they both take for granted the relationship between evidence and reality.[22]

I must confess that I fail to see why the contemporary skeptic, as described by Ginzburg, should be guilty of an "inverted positivism"; but maybe I simply misunderstand what he means with this circumscription. But apart from this I find this a somewhat puzzling statement; it is unclear to me what bearing it could possibly have on the debate between "postmodernists" and empiricists. All that Ginzburg is talking about here is the relationship between historical reality and historical evidence. I cannot recall any discussion occasioned by "postmodernist" historical theory where this has or should have been an issue. Discussions always focused on the relationship between the historical language (or the text *tout court*) on the one hand and past reality on the other.

But perhaps Ginzburg wishes to take "postmodernists" to task for their neglect of the issue of evidence. If so, who would wish to disagree with him? For everybody can rightly be criticized for not discussing what they do not discuss (though following this strategy may easily turn intellectual debate into a most tedious and unproductive *dialogue des sourds*). But if it was Ginzburg's intention to criticize the postmodernist for irresponsibly framing the relationship between historical language and historical reality into something other than the relationship between evidence and historical reality, then I cannot agree with him. For the latter issue is largely irrelevant to the former one. The latter *could* only have any such relevance for the former on the assumption that historical evidence *dictates* what representation the historian should propose about the past. Only on the basis of this assumption it would follow that nothing of any interest happens on the trajectory from evidence to the text, whereas all that really matters takes place on the trajectory between past reality and historical evidence. This would oblige us to postulate a complete fusion of the level of evidence and that of representation. But that would amount to an empiricism so utterly primitive that I would only reluctantly dare to ascribe it to any person in his right senses. It would, for example, justify speculations about the possibility of computer programs that would reduce all of historical writing to a mere press on the button after all the relevant evidence has been fed into the computer. All this is too absurd to need further discussion.

Nonetheless one can understand why empiricists might feel attracted to this idea. For if one sees, with the empiricist, in historical writing only description and no representation, it may seem that evidence (that can be used for justifying true descriptions of the past) is all that there is to historical writing. And then one may be tempted to believe that the kind of relationship existing between true description and what is described is the logical matrix of the relationship between all of historical writing and the past.

Statements such as Zammito's "there remains a referentiality about which historical practice seeks to be lucid" or "while it is certainly the case that textuality always transmutes its referent, it does not follow that it annihilates it"[23] are then to be expected. And the result is the same peculiar mixture of arrogance and modesty that we already noted in Evans's account. For on the one hand there is a passive submission to what evidence may teach us about the past, while on the other it is arrogantly claimed or suggested that absolute and final truth can be attained on the basis of this evidence.

As we saw a moment ago, Ginzburg accused "postmodernism" of an intriguing "inverted positivism." The same criticism has been leveled against White and me by Chris Lorenz: "When we look at the metaphorical turn in narrative writing of history in its opposition to this brand of positivism we can observe an interesting feature: the type of narrativism defended by White and Ankersmit represents the simple *negation* or *reversal* of the traditional positivistic view."[24] This comes from a section in Lorenz's essay entitled "Narrativism as Inverted Positivism"; later on in the same section he writes, "empiricism also shows up in White's and Ankersmit's representation of historical research."[25] Now, to begin with, I was not a little disconcerted to find myself criticized in this way by a self-professed empiricist or positivist historical theorist. Apparently the empiricist philosopher of history is an opponent who is extremely difficult to please; for even if you agree with him, you should not expect this to make him happy; rather, you will be brushed aside with a cantankerous remark. I myself cherish a far more sunny attitude toward my discussion partners. So when Lorenz, after having lengthily explained how and why metaphor sins against his own empiricist standards, suddenly begins to sing the praises of metaphor at the end of his essay, I can only openly and unashamedly rejoice in this rapprochement between him and me.[26]

The inverted positivism of narrativism is explained by Lorenz as follows:

This opposition between literal metaphorical language—presupposed in positivism—is retained in "metaphorical" narrativism in an inverted form: now descriptive statements are treated as mere information, hardly worth the philosopher's attention, and metaphorical language is upgraded to the real thing. Consequently, epistemology and aesthetics trade places in philosophy of history as well: epistemology—up till then regarded as the bread and butter of analytical philosophy of history—is thrown out and aesthetics takes its place.[27]

There is a great deal of rhetoric in this quote: note the dismissive "mere information, hardly worth the philosopher's attention" that is ascribed to the narrativist, his alleged apotheosis of metaphorical language thanks to its being "upgraded to the real thing" and the narrativist's "throwing out" of epistemology. And on top of that, there are, of course, all the most regrettable things empiricists will immediately associate with (narrativist) "aesthetics" and that we are implicitly invited to project on the "postmodernist" position. The upshot of this rhetoric is to present the "metaphorical" or "narrativist" philosopher of history as an intellectual savage wildly throwing around the philosophical furniture so carefully constructed and cared for by the empiricist.

But there is no need for this rhetoric. My own interest in narrativism (I shall not venture to speak for Hayden White) has nothing whatsoever to do with a belittling of historical research, that is, with the process of gaining factual information about the past (to be expressed in true descriptions), with causal explanations at an elementary level, and so on. On the contrary, I am deeply impressed by the almost incredible achievements of archeologists, philologists, and of historians of science, and by how they have enlarged our knowledge of the past to an extent that previous generations of historians would have believed to be utterly unthinkable. However, the present popularity of narrativism has nothing to do with a haughty looking down upon historical research, but everything with the state of affairs in the historical theory of some thirty years ago. In those days historical theorists were mainly interested in topics such as the covering law model, the teleological explanation of human action, and so on. Though the discussion of these topics has undoubtedly been most useful and is an indispensable and most valuable part of historical theory, some theorists nonetheless felt that something important about historical writing was left out, namely the issue of how historical facts are integrated into the historical text. So these narrativist theorists tried to remedy this regrettable one-sidedness; consequently, their effort should be seen as a *supplement* rather than as a *replacement* of what was being done already.

This may explain what is wrong in Lorenz's view of narrativism as an "inverted positivism." He ascribes to narrativism an "either-or logic" which he defines as follows:

The either-or logic just referred to can be seen at work in the way narrative is analyzed in metaphorical narrativism: *either* the narrative of the historian is a simple by-product of research, as the "traditional," positivistic would have it, *or* it has nothing to do with research at all. *Either* the narratives of historians are empirically founded—as the "traditional" positivistic view would have it—*or* historical narratives have no empirical foundations at all and are the product of literary imagination.[28]

Now, this picture of an "either-or logic" exists only in Lorenz's mind: for what narrativists advocated was rather an "and-and" logic. Narrativists recognized that in the first place the historian's narrative had its foundations in the results of historical research. They observed, next, that these results had to be integrated in some way or other into a historical text, and then they began to wonder how this is achieved and in what way historical reality may guide (and correct) the procedure. This is how they hit upon the linguistic turn with its notion of the "semantic ascent," which can be used to conceptualize the problem of which chunk of reality best corresponds with which chunk of language. They were aware, moreover, that this was a problem different from, and not reducible to, the kind of problem the historian encounters on the level of historical research. And this is why they saw in historical writing an "and-and" (of historical research *and* of an integration of the results of historical research in the historical text), instead of Lorenz's "either-or" (of both these things).

If one asks oneself how Lorenz could perceive an "and-and" as an "either-or," the answer is not hard to realize. The key is his assertion that "at both levels [i.e., that of historical research and the level of narrativist integration] the establishment of truth and falsity is dependent on fallible, intersubjective conventions; the difference between individual statements and complete narratives is therefore a difference in *degree* and not in *kind*."[29] Surely, if one holds that there is no real difference between a and b (as Lorenz does with regard to [1] the level of individual statements and [2] that of complete narratives), it is a matter of elementary logic that "a and b" can be exchanged by "either a or b." For the conjunction "x and x" has the same truth value as the disjunction "either x or x." So much for an explanation of Lorenz's misinterpretation of what is the narrativist's position.

But that still leaves us with the issue of the plausibility of his own view that there should be a continuity between these two levels and that there is not a "difference in *kind*" between historical research and narrative integration. Of course, I could resort now to what has been said above about the distinction between description (the level of the individual statement) and representation (the level of complete narratives) in order to question this continuity. However, in order to prove my point I shall instead focus on a further inconsistency in Lorenz's own account. In the last phase of his argument Lorenz asks himself to what criteria we should appeal in order to assess the believability, truth, or plausibility of what the historian has written about the past. His answer is: "With this goal epistemology has developed *truth-tracking* criteria—to use Carroll's apt phrase—such as scope, explanatory power, comprehensiveness and so on and these are the criteria that really matter whenever we want to assess rival knowledge claims."[30] For a correct understanding of this quote it is important to observe that Lorenz recommends that we not confuse truth itself with "truth-tracking" criteria such as scope, and so on. For in a note (referring to Goodman's *Ways of Worldmaking*) Lorenz explicitly embraces the view that truth itself is of little help in science and in history ("truth, far from being a solemn and severe master, is a docile and obedient servant"). Hence, not truth, but scope, explanatory power, comprehensiveness, and so on are what we should consider if we wish to understand the rationality of historical debate.

I was no less disconcerted by this passage and this quote than by the passage that I referred to at the outset of the present discussion of Lorenz's historical empiricism. For in my book on narrative logic I had similarly argued that scope and not truth is the right criterion for the plausibility of historical narrative[31]—but Lorenz makes no mention of this here, though he does elsewhere.[32] So, just as in the case of the role of metaphor in historical writing, there appears to be far more agreement between Lorenz and myself than Lorenz is willing to recognize; so much so that, if I am allowed to paraphrase Lorenz's own accusation of narrativism as being, in fact, an "inverted positivism," I would feel tempted to characterize his own position as that of an "inverted narrativism."

Needless to say I am happy with Lorenz's embrace of the narrativist's scope criterion. But narrativism and the narrativist's scope criterion have their limits; at the level of historical research, truth and not scope is decisive. No sensible historian would appeal to scope, explanatory power, or comprehensiveness in a discussion about, for example, in what year Erasmus was born or about what the long-term interest rates were in the United States in 1887. Statements about issues like these are simply true or false— and scope and the rest have no role to play in this (however difficult it may in practice sometimes be to establish truth or falsehood in such cases). So, paradoxically, Lorenz's empiricist position is in need of an extra injection of empiricism. The paradox came into being since empiricists—as Lorenz explicitly states in the passage I quoted a moment ago—leave room for only *one* criterion of historical plausibility. So when confronted with the fact that historical writing comprises both description (truth) and representation (scope), they will have to make up their minds in what direction they will move, while downplaying the other. Lorenz decided to move as far into the direction of representation as his empiricism allowed him to do (and in my view beyond that). He even went so far in this direction that narrativists (like me) will start worrying about what is left of the descriptive component in his argument and insist that he should allow more room for (empiricist) truth, and all that, than he presently is inclined to do.

As we shall see in a moment, McCullagh opted for the other horn of the empiricist's dilemma: he reduced all representation to description and truth. But we should recognize above all that the dilemma is purely a production of empiricist ideology and that, in contrast to this ideology, (1) description ("speaking") and representation ("speaking about speaking") are *both* part of the historian's attempt to deal with the past, and (2) we should never be tempted into abandoning the one in favor of the other.

The gist of McCullagh's empiricist criticism, as expressed in his recent *The Truth of History*, can be found in the following passage:

One philosopher of history, F. R. Ankersmit, has argued repeatedly that general descriptions of the past cannot be true, because they do not refer to anything real in the world. He thinks that particular events are real, but that generalizations are just conceptual constructions, created by historians but referring to nothing real at all.[33]

Now, I never said such a thing and it is no coincidence that McCullagh does not refer to any passages in my writings where such strange assertions can be found. Nevertheless, it is not difficult to see how this caricature of my position could come into being. For McCullagh goes on to write:

Ankersmit first presented his reasons for denying that general terms refer to anything in the world in his book *Narrative Logic* (1983). In Chapter 5 of that book, he presents the following analysis of the use of such terms. Historians study available evidence and derive knowledge of many particular facts about the past; looking at these facts, they acquire an idea of one or more patterns in them, conceptual wholes which are sometimes referred to by general terms; they then describe these patterns in their writing. "For instance, terms like 'Renaissance', 'Enlightenment', 'early modern European capitalism' or 'the decline of the Church' are in fact names given to 'images' or 'pictures' of the past proposed by historians attempting to come to grips with the past." (p. 99)[34]

I pass over McCullagh's suggestion that, first, certain patterns (let alone "an idea" of those patterns) are discerned in the past which are, next, "described" with terms such as "the Renaissance."[35] For as I have always insisted, both in the book discussed by McCullagh and elsewhere, the word "description" can only meaningfully be used with regard to the past *itself* and not with regard to the patterns that the historian decides, or, rather, proposes to project on it. And this distinction is absolutely crucial to my argument: for it reflects the distinction between description and representation discussed above. It surely is no coincidence that McCullagh fails to recognize the difference: for it does not fit into his empiricist framework that has room for (true) description only.

Most striking, however, is that McCullagh describes terms like "the Renaissance" as "general terms." Indeed, *if* terms like "the Renaissance" or "the Enlightenment" were "general terms" such as "being large," "speaking robustly," "trial," "execution," and so on (these are McCullagh's own examples of general terms), *then* the views McCullagh attributes to me would be clearly nonsensical. For who would wish to deny that such general terms help us describe (past) reality (though I would resist the view that they "refer" to reality, though they may be true of reality).[36] But I have nowhere defended such a profoundly wrong-headed account of the status of such terms. Instead, I have always and consistently described them as the *proper names* of so-called narrative substances (i.e., of views or representations of the past or, as we have seen in the previous section, of a common denominator to be discerned in a number of roughly comparable representations) referring to those narrative substances or representations of the past. So there are not just *two* levels, the one of the past itself and the one in which the past is described in terms of properties that are attributed to objects in the past named by and referred to by the proper names mentioned in these descriptions. This is McCullagh's empiricist and descriptivist conception of historical language and of how it relates to the past. We should, instead, adopt a *three*-level model of how historical reality and the historian's language hang together. There is, first, the past itself; next there is the level of McCullagh's descriptions; and thirdly, that of (historical) representation. And since description and representations are logically different (see the previous section), we should resist the descriptionist effort to reduce all representation to description.

Let me elaborate on this. Exchanging the two-level for the three-level model implies that proper names can be found on both the second and the third level: a proper name can refer to an object in the past (second level) *and* to a representation of the past (third level). And (unfortunately) it can do both by making use of *one and the same* proper name. We shall recognize the indispensibility of recognizing the presence of a third level if we note the equivalence of (1) "Napoleon was a self-possessed person" (uttered by someone who just finished reading Caulaincourt's memoirs); and (2) "Caulaincourt's Napoleon was a self-possessed person." "Napoleon" in statement (1) is interchangeable with "Caulaincourt's Napoleon" in statement (2). In both (1) and (2) reference is made to a certain (i.e., Caulaincourt's) *representation* of Napoleon and *not* to the person of flesh and blood, who lived from 1769 to 1821 and was emperor of the French. We tend to forget this meaning of statement (1) because of its misleading resemblance to a statement like (3) "L'Empéreur n'était pas naturellement violent. Personne ne se maîtrisait comme lui quand il le voulait [The emperor was not violent by nature. Nobody was so much master of himself if he wanted this]."[37] and where Caulaincourt undoubtedly refers to Napoleon himself and *not* to a representation of him (though it is *part* of such a representation). Because of the grammatical similarities of (1) and (3) we tend to conclude that both statements are logically equivalent as well. However, statements about the past (second level) must be distinguished from statements about representations of the past (third level).[38] I remind the reader here of my admonition in the previous section that in the writing of history the most dramatic logical disparities may hide themselves under grammatical similarity. The point is most strikingly illustrated by the foregoing considerations, for we observe here how even statements may move from the level of description (statement 3) to that of representation (the statements 1 and 2). Statements may already be infected by the logic of representation.

What has happened is this: in the book McCullagh refers to I discussed historical representation (as defined above). Since McCullagh's philosophical dictionary does not contain this notion, but only variants of description, he felt compelled to search for the nearest equivalent in his own dictionary, which turned out to be the notion of the "general term." He probably felt that there must be "something" general about notions like "the Renaissance" or "the Enlightenment," since they can be related to some more or less "general" characteristics of the relevant historical periods. This is why he conveniently "forgot" that I always and consistently characterized those terms as proper names (of representations) and not as general terms. He then went on to observe (correctly) that general terms can be used for formulating true descriptions of the past and then concluded that my claim that such terms do not refer to historical reality must be wrong. But this is ignoring the essence of my analysis and certainly not an argument against it.

Let us now widen our scope and consider McCullagh's discussion of the uniqueness of the Renaissance or of the Enlightenment. His argument is that we can not only speak of "the Renaissance" or "the Enlightenment," but also of "the Carolingian Renaissance" and even of "renaissances" in the plural as a general classificatory term. McCullagh's view is that from a logical point of view the term "Renaissance" functions in much the same way as terms like "dog" or "chair":

> What Ankersmit seems never to have acknowledged is that different instances of general terms are always unique in detail, but that that does not prevent them from also being classified. He allows that there are really chairs and dogs. But chairs and dogs differ enormously. Indeed it is difficult to think of the general characteristics of all chairs. . . . Precisely the same is true of the general concepts used to characterize the past [i.e., concepts such as "Renaissance," "Enlightenment," and so on].[39]

As an example, McCullagh mentions in this context Haskins's *The Renaissance of the Twelfth Century* (1927)[40] and argues that this book demonstrates that history knows different periods that can all be "classified" as renaissances—just as different dogs can all be classified as dogs in spite of their sometimes impressive differences. He then concludes that "there is no doubt that some classificatory terms are quite vague, and their vagueness can sometimes lead historians to dispute their applicability."[41]

Now, Huizinga had already criticized Haskins's use of the term "Renaissance" to characterize the mind of the twelfth century with the following argument:

> The mind of the twelfth century, says Etienne Gilson, may seem to us to have been closer to that of the Renaissance then the mind of the thirteenth. The twelfth century is a century of preparation, preparation for the thirteenth, that is. If this

may seem contradictory to us, the mistake is ours, who are in the habit of considering the Renaissance as the culmination of the development of all of the Middle Ages. But in order to grasp the twelfth century, it should not be compared to the Renaissance but to the thirteenth.[42]

In sum, Huizinga criticizes Haskins's use of the term "Renaissance" for the twelfth century because it was inspired by a teleological conception of the past that makes us forget about the uniqueness of different historical epochs. Haskins knew about the Italian Renaissance of the fifteenth century and then decided to see renaissances wherever something happened that seemed to prepare the way for this Renaissance. It is as if you were saying that your years at secondary school were, in fact, already a university study since they prepared you for the latter—thus denying to your years at secondary school a status of their own. So Huizinga insists that one should resist the temptation (or at least be very careful about what one is doing) to discover everywhere renaissances and enlightenments after historians have characterized certain periods as "the Renaissance" or "the Enlightenment." Such an approach may be expected to create obfuscation, rather than clarification, since the exact meaning of such terms has always to be stipulated by everyone using them and is never part of the normal use of language.

Much to my surprise McCullagh presents himself a striking example of this systematic instability of the meaning of historical terms or concepts—an example that seems to me absolutely devastating for his own thesis. For he discusses a book by George Holmes on the Florentine Renaissance, entitled *The Florentine Enlightenment*. So here the Renaissance is "referred" to with the "classificatory term" "Enlightenment"! I would now like to ask Professor McCullagh what he would say when he was living in a world of language users where one and the same thing can be characterized by some as a dog and by others as a chair. Wouldn't this strike him as a little odd or, at least, unusual and in need of clarification? So does not his own example make perfectly clear that classificatory concepts such as "dog" and "chair" obey a different logic than typically historical concepts such as "the Renaissance" or "the Enlightenment" and that the latter therefore require a separate handling by the logician?

I think that McCullagh's theory of historical concepts—classificatory or not—is vitiated by a lack of understanding of how language and reality are related in historical writing. He seems to have two theories on it. He refers here, first, to Wittgenstein's well-known language game theory, which claims that no sufficient and necessary conditions can be given for the correct use of words. And he then goes on to defend the theory that "there are criteria for the application of most general terms"[43]—hence precisely the theory that Wittgenstein wished to discredit with his language game theory. Now, I shall not bother McCullagh with this inconsistency, but ask him instead what authority we have for the correct application of words to reality. The later Wittgenstein's answer was, essentially, that "the meaning is the use" and the whole scandal of his theory was that there are no criteria for justifying the use. There is just the use, and that is all there is to it. But what about the *use* of terms like "the Renaissance" or "the Enlightenment"? Is there such a generally accepted use—as in the case of terms like "dog" or "chair"? Apparently not, if some historians will characterize a certain period as "the (Florentine) Renaissance" and others, such as Holmes, as "the (Florentine) Enlightenment." And there will, perhaps, even be historians with a penchant for compromise arguing that it was both (for was the Renaissance not also a period of enlightenment?)—thus making us imagine a people made up of three categories of language users where the first category calls a certain type of thing a dog, a second category calls it a chair, and then you have still a third category saying that it is *both* a dog and a chair. It is to be expected that verbal communication will be quite a challenge for this people and that they will have to spend a disproportional amount of their time and energy on the meaning of words. As, indeed, not coincidentally, is the case in historical writing.

Now, of course we do have such an authority: this is historical debate as it gradually evolved in the history of historical writing. But in the course of this debate disagreement is never decided by an appeal to the meaning of words. One does not say to Haskins, "Well, we all know what the word 'Renaissance' means and now you have (in)correctly applied it to (part of) the past," nor would we argue that Holmes is sadly ignorant of the meaning of both the words "Renaissance" and "Enlightenment" because of his use of the terms in question. Instead historians will quietly wait and see what a historian *does* with these words in his book or article. That is, when introducing or using these terms in an unexpected and novel way, historians will ask themselves whether this new use may make us aware of something of the past that we had not noticed before and whether it may make us see connections that are new to us. Questions like these are decisive—and not whether a term has been correctly applied (or not). Historical debate is a semantic quarrel not about the exact meaning of words, but about the past.

And it is precisely in terms of *different* meanings given to terms like "the Renaissance" or "the Enlightenment" that historians settle this kind of dispute. Or, to put it provocatively, it is not the *overlap*, but *difference* in meaning that does all of the work in the practice of historical debate. That is why these concepts are, and even ought to be, "essentially contested," as Gallie put it half a century ago already.[44] And whoever (like McCullagh) relies on what is common in different uses of historical concepts, relies on what is pure dead weight and irrelevant in historical practice. So if there would actually exist theories of history capable of "murdering history" (to use Windschuttle's alarmist phraseology)—which is most unlikely, though—the dangers will come from doctrinaire empiricists like McCullagh (and Windschuttle himself) rather than from their liberal-minded narrativist opponents.

I come to a final remark. McCullagh fights his battle under the banner of historical truth. "Truth" is for him the highest and most sublime aim of all of historical writing. And he is in the habit of throwing historical truth as a kind of argumentative hand grenade in the direction of anybody whom he (rightly or wrongly) suspects of cherishing relativist or similarly unhealthy sympathies. Now, truth surely is supremely important and everything begins with truth, though (and there I would disagree with McCullagh) it does not end with it. This is already the case in the sciences. One may fill libraries with true observations on physical reality but without ever adding a iota to our understanding of it. Decisive in the development of the sciences over the last two hundred years has not been truth, but the talent for identifying those truths that really count and that may deepen our understanding of the nature of physical reality. This is what distinguishes important new theories from those that are not, and great scientists from their merely mediocre colleagues. And so it is in history. It may well be that the historian who advances a poor view of the Renaissance never sins against the commandment to tell the truth and nothing but the truth. It may even be that all the truths unveiled by him had never been noticed before—and yet his colleagues may cast aside his work as not significantly adding to our understanding of the past. In our itinerary through the past, truth should always be our companion, but never our guide—for the simple reason that it *could* never be our guide; neither is it in the sciences.[45]

One of the advantages of the linguistic turn is that it may enable us to understand this. We have seen that, in agreement with the linguistic turn, we will not always be able to distinguish between the "compulsion of language" and the "compulsion of experience." The implication is that we may often hold true beliefs—I emphasize: *true beliefs*—about the past that have their origin in the language used or proposed by the historian rather than in established empirical fact. Once again, truth is not at stake here: the historian who uses an impoverished, conventional, and unimaginative language need never be found guilty of violating truth because of this. His truths are simply uninteresting, trivial truths that we would rather not waste our time on. In sum, the linguistic turn teaches us that we may discern in language, and more specifically in the concepts, the vocabulary and the metaphors that we use, our guide to avoid the uninteresting truths and to get on the track of those truths that will deepen our understanding. And, as Gallie emphasized already (see note 44), recognizing the limitations of truth does not in the least imply that we are now the will-less playthings of prejudice, arbitrariness, and irrationality. It can be shown that the double requirement of scope-maximalization and of originality (by the way, a requirement that is surprisingly similar to what theorists such as Karl Popper have developed for the sciences) can both explain and justify what is decisive in historical debate. The rationality of historical debate can be explained in terms of these two requirements, and truth has no role to play in this.[46]

LITERARY THEORY AND HISTORICAL THEORY

I started this chapter with the well-known fact that Hayden White's *Metahistory* of 1973 completely changed existing historical theory. Old questions lost much of their previous urgency and new questions now demanded the attention. I tried to explain the nature of the change in terms of the linguistic turn. I did so because the linguistic turn is the best key for getting access to the nature of these changes in recent historical theory. But I should add that, when doing so, my account is not in agreement with the facts of how these changes actually came about. In *Metahistory* the linguistic turn is never referred to—and if I'm not mistaken, neither has White ever paid attention to it in his later writings. The explanation is that White found his main source of inspiration not in the philosophy of language, but in literary theory. In *Metahistory* and in his later works, Northrop Frye, Auerbach, Barthes, Jakobson, and so on, are the theorists White most frequently refers to, whereas he is less interested in philosophers, whether they had accepted the linguistic turn or not. Even an author such as Richard Rorty, whose views are so close to his own, seems never to have provoked his interest. And this is true not only of White, but of most of later historical theorists, such as Kellner, LaCapra, Gosman, Rigney, Shiner, Carrard, and Linda Orr, whether they followed White or arrived independently at conclusions similar to White's. And though we should be profoundly grateful for what they achieved in their writings, we unfortunately have at the same time no fewer good reasons for deploring their failure to relate their enterprise to what has happened in contemporary philosophy. This may explain the complete disregard, or even outright contempt of philosophers (of language) for contemporary historical theory.

So this raises the question of the relationship between the linguistic turn and literary theory; and, more specifically, the question of whether both come down to much the same thing—as most historical theorists seem to believe without ever arguing their belief—or whether there are some differences between the two that we should take into account.

Now, obviously, there are important similarities. Both the linguistic turn and literary theory emphasize that language is not a mere "mirror of nature" and that all our knowledge and all our linguistic representations of reality bear the traces of the linguistic medium in which they are formulated. One might call this the "linguistic Kantianism"[47] that is shared by both the linguistic turn and literary theory—language functions in both cases much like the Kantian imagination and the Kantian categories of the understanding. However, there are no less important differences between the two. Of course it is difficult to generalize over such a complex discipline as literary theory, but whether one thinks of formalism, of structuralism, of deconstructivism, of reader-response theories, of psychoanalytic theory, or of Marxist criticism,[48] the literary text always is the object of research, hence the investigated *reality*. This is, in fact, less trivial and innocuous than it may at first seem to be. For the implication is that literary theory does not really problematize the language/reality gap, as this is done in epistemology and in the philosophy of language in general. It follows that for a literary theorist there is absolutely nothing revolutionary or even interesting in the statement that a text is a "thing" or an "object," which is part of (empirical) reality. For him or her the assertion is no more sensational than when we would tell the biologist that flowers and bacteria are part of reality. So he freely talks about language as if it were no less part of reality than flowers and bacteria; and he will see no more theoretical and philosophical problems in doing so than when the biologist discusses his bacteria and his flowers (though, of course, he will discover all kind of fascinating problems in the *linguistic* or *textual reality* investigated by him).

But this is quite different for the philosopher, for whom the reality/language gap is where all the secrets of reference, meaning, and truth originate. The literary theorist "naturalizes" language, whereas the philosopher of language will always "semanticize" language and its relationship to the world.[49] For the philosopher, there is, on the one hand, reality, and, on the other, language, and crossing the gap between the two means covering the trajectory where all the topics of research can be situated. So the philosopher will immediately cast aside the suggestion that language is an object or a thing—for then there would be no difference between the beginning and the end of the trajectory under investigation. It is true that some philosophers[50] say that language is a thing, but when they do so they are well aware that they are proposing a most revolutionary and provocative thesis. They may argue with the pragmatist, for example, that language is just one more instrument enabling us to make sense of the world and, as such, similar to microscopes, maps, or watches, whose causal interactions with the world leave no room for doubt about their wholly unspectacular ontological status. Or they may argue—as I have been doing here—that though statements belong to the domain of language, texts can properly be said to belong to reality again. But though the former pragmatist kind of argument may succeed in naturalizing semantics and in reducing philosophical questions about the relationship between language and the world to cognitive science, this option will not be open to us when we adopt the latter argument. For then all those difficult semantic problems of reference, truth, and meaning (accompanying the reality/language gap) will reappear when we move from the level of the statement to that of the complex (historical) text.[51] These, obviously, are the issues that we have investigated in the previous sections of this chapter. In sum, the assertion that language is a thing is, for the philosopher, a far more problematic statement—and one that is badly in need of far more clarification and qualification—than for the literary theorist.

Of course, the problems that provoke the philosopher's professional interest would all reappear when we would ask about the relationship between the text (as the literary theorist's object of research) and the language used by him to express the results of his research. But *this* trajectory is *not* investigated by the literary theorist. He investigates texts and not the epistemological problem of how *his* language is related to the (textual) reality studied by him.

Hence, for all their agreement about language not being a transparent medium in its relationship to reality, the philosopher defending the linguistic turn has something different in mind about it than the literary theorist. For literary theorists, the recognition of this fact amounts to the identification of a new, and hitherto unnoticed part of empirical reality—that is, the (literary) text—that can, next, be investigated empirically just like any other aspect of reality. For philosophers, however, the nontransparency of language has its implications for how language (co)determines the *true beliefs* that we have about reality (more specifically, the fact that we cannot always discern between "the compulsion of language" and the "compulsion of experience." For literary theorists this insight has no relevance—it would acquire relevance only if they started thinking philosophically about how the language that they use is related to the language and the texts investigated by them. But why should literary theorists be interested in this? Similarly, why should physicists be interested in epistemological problems? The problem is irrelevant for the kind of research they do. So it follows that, in fact, one can be a literary theorist without ever needing to embrace the linguistic turn—and vice versa.

It follows from the foregoing considerations that there certainly is common ground in what the linguistic turn and literary theory must imply for historical theory. And from that perspective it is understandable that historical theorists didn't worry too much about potential differences in these implications. But, as we now must recognize, such differences should be expected to exist and conceptual clarity requires us to carefully scrutinize these differences. For this may enable us to say something about what is good and bad in contemporary historical theory, as far as it draws its inspiration from literary theory.

The crucial difference is that the linguistic turn puts on the agenda the transition from reality to language. This is not the case with literary theory, since (1) it deals exclusively with language or texts, and (2) literary theory does not formulate a specific view about the epistemological relationship between its own theories and its object of investigation. One tends to forget about the latter issue because literary theory always discusses how we should read and interpret texts—and this *seems* to involve the epistemological relationship between reader and text. But this is a delusion. For we must distinguish between what goes on in the relationship between the reader of a literary text and the literary text, on the one hand, and what happens between the theoretical text of the literary theorist and those aspects of literature discussed in the theoretical text, on the other. Only at the latter level will the epistemological problems be discussed that we may encounter when investigating the epistemological or interpretative problems encountered on the first level.

To put it in one phrase: indeed, literary theory is a theory about texts, but not about its *own* texts. Take, for example, deconstructivism: it is a recommendation to the reader to deconstruct literary text read by him, but not a recommendation to deconstruct deconstructivism. And even if one would try to apply deconstructivism to its own text—as undoubtedly some authors, such as Derrida and Rorty, who see in the (con)fusion of levels their main contribution to theory—we would be faced with an endless regress. For then consistency would require us to do the same with the results of the deconstruction of the deconstructivist text, and so on ad infinitum. And it follows, that one should suspect all attempts (such as Rorty's)[52] to effect a fusion of philosophy and literary theory. For such attempts will inevitably founder in an endless regress—as we may expect when we try to solve philosophical problems with nonphilosophical means.

It will, by now, be clear what historical theorists can and cannot expect of literary theory. It may help us to read and to properly understand the historical text; it will make us aware of the fact that the historical text is a highly complex "machine" for the generation of textual meaning, and that we have hitherto been blind to many of these complexities. It may inform us about the hidden meanings of a text, meanings that have not been intended by the author and in many cases not perceived by their readers. To be sure, the significance of these hidden meanings cannot reasonably be doubted. Think, for example, of the affinities of the nineteenth-century realist or naturalist novel on the one hand, and the realist style of much of historical writing down to the present day that have been pointed out by authors such as Roland Barthes, Hayden White, Hans Kellner, Lionel Gossman, or Ann

Rigney.[53] Here the discovery of hidden meaning amounted to the identification of nothing less than a historical *style*. And in literary theory the identification of style is one of the most important keys to the secrets of the text. It is no different in (the history of) historical writing. For an analysis of the history of such historical styles may show us the most general features of how different periods conceived of their past. Think of how White distinguished between the ironical style of Enlightenment historical writing, the metaphorical and organicist style of romantic historical writing, and the metonymical style of its socioscientifically inspired contemporary counterparts. And it may even be, as White's tropological model suggests, that there exists a hidden stylistic logic that leads from one style to a later one. Hence, no one who intends to write the history of historical writing can afford to ignore the lessons taught be literary theory. And indeed, since White's *Metahistory* historiography, that is, the history of historical writing, has undergone a complete metamorphosis. In fact, a wholly new and fascinating kind of historiography came into being and there can be no doubt that this is a lasting contribution to the historical discipline that no future generation will ever abandon. Indeed, the books written by the authors I mentioned above resemble in virtually no respect the books by a Fueter, a Meinecke, a Srbik, or an Iggers—though I would certainly not wish to imply that the work of these historians of historical writings has been superseded by "the new historiography." In the future we will need both variants of historiography.

But literary theory is far less helpful when we have to deal with the central problem of historical theory, that is, the problem of how the historian accounts for or represents past reality. It is a theory about where we should look for the meaning of texts but not about how a text may represent a reality other than itself and about the relationship between the text and reality. Certainly the problem of the meaning of a text is part of the problem of that relationship. How could we say anything sensible about that relationship if we did not know what we were reading when reading a text? So we may surmise that in order to determine the relevance of literary theory for historical theory it will in the first place be necessary to examine how problems of meaning and problems of historical representation interfere with each other in the practice of historical writing.

In order to deal with this preliminary question, let us take as an example the historical debate on the Renaissance. Needless to say, if historians of the Renaissance are to have a fruitful debate, a minimal condition is that there should be sufficient agreement about the meaning of the different works that have been written on that topic. Equally obviously, literary theory has the pretension to be able to deal with this problem. Less obvious is how this will work out in practice. Suppose a deconstructivist literary theorist intervenes in the debate on the Renaissance and argues that the meaning of *X*'s book on the Renaissance differs from what one or more of the participants in the debate have always believed its meaning to be. For example, the deconstructivist might take as a point of departure Burckhardt's famous picture of how during the Renaissance the veil was blown away under which during the Middle Ages both sides of human consciousness still lay hidden. And then the deconstructivist might plausibly argue that this was for the human individual not in the least the liberating gain that Burckhardt wished to see in it, but was, in fact, a tremendous loss and a tremendous impoverishment of the self; a loss comparable to the trauma that each human individual undergoes when moving from a solipsistic identification with the world (i.e., the mother) to being a puny and miserable individual apart from and opposite to all of the outside world. When regarded from the perspective of the world outside, one loses the whole world by becoming oneself; and when regarded from the subject's perspective, the Renaissance discovery of the self was the first step in the direction of the nakedness of the later Cartesian and Kantian transcendental self. It was only the organicism of romanticism that would restore to the human individual a small part of the treasures lost by the Renaissance. Small wonder that romantic authors so much liked to idealize the Middle Ages.[54] Proceeding further from there, the deconstructivist might go on and see in the apparent triumphs of the Renaissance a poor compensation for the loss of all its trusted and traditional supports. Was the free and emancipated individual of the Renaissance not also a pitiable solitary in a hostile world that continuously had to muster all of its available energies in order to keep at bay the unnamable and unspeakable dangers that threatened it? Was this not precisely the message of Machiavelli's claim of the endless fight between the Goddess Fortuna and *virtù*? And the deconstructivist would conclude by saying that we have always noticed only half of Burckhardt's text and that there is a darker undertone in his text as well, and that to fully comprehend Burckhardt's amazing genius we must recognize the presence of *both* meanings in his text, instead of only its surface meaning.

Well, this is merely an example of the unnerving things that literary theorists could do with historical texts.⁵⁵ And there can be no doubt that insights like these in the hidden meanings of the historical text might immensely complicate historical debate. It might be inferred that we need first consult the literary theorist before entering on any serious historical debate. The obviously uninviting implications of this complication of historical debate will undoubtedly have contributed to historians' disgust of literary theory and their conviction that its introduction into the practice of history might well amount to "the murdering of history" (Windschuttle again). And this might also explain why historians tend to be so doggedly dogmatic about authorial intention:⁵⁶ it seems to be the only reliable brake upon a dissolution of historical debate into the mists of radical textual ambiguity. Hence, whereas the abandonment of authorial intention provides the literary theorist with his daily bread in the academic world, it seems to deprive the historian of his.

But are things really so serious as the historian fears? Not incidentally did I take deconstructivism as my example of what literary theory might do to history and to historical theory. For even deconstructivism with its alleged fascination for subversion, irrationality, and inconsistency—which makes it so hated and feared by the Windschuttles and the Evanses—is no real threat. As my example may have made clear, there are two sides to the deconstructivists' intervention. In the first place, they discover hitherto unsuspected meanings in historians' texts and by doing so may make us better aware than we were of what is of interest in the text. What could possibly be wrong with this? Second, by doing so deconstructivists suggest new ways of looking at the past—without, however, pronouncing about the plausibility of these new views of the past from the perspective of professional historians. This is left to them—and so the net result seems to be a gain rather than a loss.

Nevertheless, the historian's fears are not wholly groundless. For whereas in the example mentioned just now the distinction is carefully respected between linguistic meaning and historical meaning, between what we owe to language and what we owe to the world—so that language does not become experience's rival *in the latter's own domain*⁵⁷—this may, at times, be different. White's tropology provides us with a good example. For on the one hand it is a purely formal system derived from relevant suggestions that White had found in the writings by Vico, Frye, Pepper, and Mannheim. As such it may at first sight seem to be devoid of material implications. But if we take a closer look, this initial impression appears to be mistaken. Thus the historian's account will, according to the tropological grid, always and inevitably be either a comedy, a tragedy, a romance, or a satire, and so on. Surely, these are all narrative forms, but still they are forms with a more or less specific content, as White liked to emphasize himself by speaking about "the content of the form" (not coincidentally the title of one of his books). Undoubtedly, this is where most resistance against White's system felt by historians originates and where the resistance is surely legitimate. Historians now felt like painters who are told that, wittingly or unwittingly, they are all either impressionists, expressionists, fauvists, or cubists—and that every effort on their part to escape these four representational forms is doomed to failure. Understandably historians now tended to see tropology as a system providing them with four speculative philosophies of history dictating a large part of what they wished to say about the past. The fact that they were allowed to choose between four different speculative philosophies they saw as an only meager improvement on the exclusivist pretensions of traditional speculative philosophy of history. In sum, in contrast to deconstructivist openness, White thus placed the historian in a closed world of fixed forms. If White's system had been more flexible so that it could adapt itself to each conceivable historical content, it would undoubtedly have provoked the historian's ire far less than presently is the case. And the problem was further aggravated, since White never offered a kind of "transcendental deduction" for his list of tropological forms. His tropology is "à prendre ou à laisser."

The linguistic turn, as expounded above, will show us our way out of this predicament. For when we cannot discern between the compulsion of language and that of experience, we could not possibly ever be justified in saying that formal constraints strain historical evidence. Hence the lesson we may learn from the difficulties occasioned by White's tropology is that formalism should at all times avoid foisting forms with a more or less fixed content on the potential richness of historical writing. When this happens the claims of the linguistic turn have been illegitimately transgressed. Language would then no longer merely be a potential source of truth irreducible to what reality shows to be the case, but would now start to interfere with the compulsion of experience. It would begin to dictate what experience may and may not discover in reality by being hospitable to certain contents offered by experience while being hostile to certain others—just as cubist formalism is hospitable to the straight line and the square angle and hostile to the circle or the ellipse.

It might now be objected that the requirement is an impossible one, at odds with the very nature of all formalism. For formalism always imposes certain forms on reality (or on how we perceive it); so a formalism completely respecting the historian's freedom of representation seems to be a *contradictio in terminis*. It is as if one began by leaving to each historian a complete freedom to do as he pleases, and then to solemnly confer on each narrative the honor of exemplifying a certain form that fits this narrative only and no other. Surely, this is the *Liebestod* of formalism.

But in the writing of history there is nothing odd or objectionable about this anarchistic kind of formalism. In order to clarify this, I would like to refer to my example of how to apply the linguistic turn to historical writing. We observed there how a linguistic form, that is, the meaning of a concept such as "the Renaissance," was devised by the historian in order to give form and meaning to a specific part of the past. Here we find that a perfect fit between form and content and its perfection is a priori demonstrable. For the *form* is here exclusively defined by its *content*, and each different content would automatically give rise to a different form. But why still use the term "form" in order to describe *this* specific content; what does it add to the possession of mere content? Why would we need the notion? Is it anything more than Wittgenstein's "wheel that can be turned though nothing else moves with it," and that is, therefore, not part of the machine? The answer is an unambiguous "no," since only *form* can give coherence to what was hitherto *mere content*; only thanks to *it* a chaotic mass of data about the past is organized into a recognizable *whole*. Only if endowed with a form as intended here can historical content be processed in the practice of historical research and of historical debate. The formal "skin of the form" is, and ought to be, infinitely thin, since it should add nothing to what is within it,[58] but even so it is sufficiently strong for performing the job it is expected to do. So we should be grateful to White for having made us aware of this formal "skin," but his tropological skin is still too "thick" and too "leathery," so to say, to adapt itself with complete ease to each individual content.

In order to properly grasp the nature of its job, I recall to mind the view that there is no represented without its representation. If we apply this insight to the present context, we shall recognize that this symmetry of a representation and what it represents had best be (re)formulated in terms of *form*. Or, to be more precise, forms denote those aspects of (a) *represented* (reality), that correspond to the nature of a certain representation as denoted by a certain historical concept. To put it in one formula: concepts are the linguistic counterparts of forms in reality. But these forms do not logically and temporally antedate representation. When accounting for reality in terms of (aesthetic) representation, representation projects its own forms on reality—thus endowing it with the property of being a represented reality. And the paradox is that, on the one hand, representation does not (or rather, should not) add anything to reality, nor even to our knowledge of it, while, on the other hand, it adds all that we need for our being able to find our way around in the world. It is, therefore, in the interaction between concept and form that language and reality come closest to each other—and this is why representation brings us closer to the world than description. We tend to forget this because representations are often compositions of descriptions—which seems to confer a logical priority upon the latter. But we need only think of painting in order to realize ourselves that representation without description is possible. And it is, in this context, no less instructive to observe that representation is intimately related to (the forms enabling us to) "find our way around in the world." Representation is practical; description is theoretical and abstract. Animals and babies, not (yet) having the use of language, do have the capacity to recognize forms in reality and, thus, of *representing* it, though they are not yet able to *describe* it. Or, put differently, when we ascend with historical writing from the level of description to that of representation, we move, in fact, backward to a most elementary level in our encounter with the world.

THE DANGERS OF LITERARY THEORY FOR HISTORICAL THEORY

By taking my point of departure in the linguistic turn, I have tried to draw up an inventory of what we may expect from literary theory for a better understanding of historical writing. The linguistic turn is an extremely useful instrument for doing this, since, just like literary theory, it problematizes traditionalist conceptions of the relationship between language and reality. The linguistic turn does so by making us aware of the fact that the use of language is not restricted to our speaking about reality but that it sometimes also surreptitiously and unnoticedly resorts to a speaking about this speaking about reality. Language then becomes a kind of "instant epistemology," that is, an epistemological claim for how in a *specific* case language and reality had best be related. Grammar does not warn us when this shift takes place—and this (partly) explains why empiricists tended to ignore this dimension of our use(s) of language.

If we are ready to recognize in historical writing this dimension of "instant epistemology," the question of what we may expect from literary theory is not hard to answer. For no compartment of literary theory addresses the problem of the epistemological gap between language and the world. Literary theory is an investigation of literary language, and although it does so by transforming language into a part of the world, this should not tempt us to think that it can teach us anything of value about how (historical) language relates to the world. For insofar as this problem (might) reappear in literary theory, it would only do so in the guise of the problem of how its own results relate to its object of investigation (i.e., the literary text). And this (epistemological) problem is *not* investigated in literary theory—neither is it in any way relevant to its purposes.

It follows that literary theory can be most helpful as an instrument for analyzing historical texts—and as such it presently is correctly perceived to be the historiographer's main auxiliary science. Whoever wants to write the history of historical writing can no longer afford to ignore literary theory. But literary theory is wholly useless as a theory of history: it has not said and could not possibly have anything of interest to say about the issue of how the historian succeeds in representing the past. It is true that *some* historical theorists have derived, either implicitly or explicitly, from literary theory claims about the relationship between the past and its textual representations. But, as we have seen when discussing White, this results in speculative philosophies of history. The explanation is that this use of literary theory will drag along in its wake a material content to the forms that the historian discerns in past reality—thus adding to our view of the past elements whose introduction can only be justified on the basis of the claims propounded in the preferred literary theory, but not on the basis what the past has actually been like.

In sum, let us restrict the uses of literary theory to the writing of the history of historical writing—where it is immensely valuable—and never admit it to the quite different field of historical theory.

2

IN PRAISE OF SUBJECTIVITY

Since antiquity, historians have recognized that the historian's political and moral convictions strongly determine the nature of his accounts of the past. In the second century Lucian urged the historian, just as Ranke would do some two millennia later in exactly the same words, "to tell the past as it has actually been"; again like Ranke, this primarily meant to him that the historian should write like an impartial judge and avoid all partisanship.[1] The kind of intuitions behind this recommendation to avoid political and moral partisanship are too well known and too obvious to need further elucidation here.

However, there is a less obvious aspect to these intuitions that demands our attention. The words "subjectivity" and "objectivity" themselves will prove to be our best clue here. These terms clearly suggest that historians should at all times be "objective," since their possible "subjectivity" would make them add to the "object" investigated by them, that is, the past, something that belongs exclusively to the "subject," that is, historians themselves. And in this way the historian would distort the past itself by projecting something on it that is alien to it. This, obviously, is the picture that is suggested or implied by the two words "subjectivity" and "objectivity."

When we think this over, it must strike us as odd, in fact, that the historian's subjectivity has always been so exclusively linked to his political and moral values. Why is this so? we may well ask ourselves. For it might be argued that the historian's subjectivity—his presence in his own writings—

may just as well be due to many other factors. A certain historian may have a preference for a specific kind of historical topic, have a specific style of writing or argument, belong to a specific historical school, or simply demonstrate in his writings a stupidity that is characteristic of his well-attested lack of intellectual capacities.

But why, again, have these other causes of subjectivity so rarely been associated with the problem of subjectivity? The explanation cannot be that the traces of these other factors would be so much less obviously present in historical writing than political and moral values. For example, one need only open the kind of book written some thirty years ago by a disciple of the Annales school in order to recognize immediately the scholarly affiliations of its author, whereas it would probably be hard to find any identifiable political or moral commitment in it. Nevertheless, no reviewer in his right mind sense would criticize the book as "subjective" merely because it is so conspicuously a product of the Annales school—even if the reviewer in question happened to hold the Annalistes in very low esteem.

And there is more occasion for wonder. For to be the disciple of a certain historical school, to write in a certain style, to be characteristically stupid, and so on: these are all things that are far less part of the historical past investigated by the historian than our political and moral values, which will almost always be most intimately tied up with the vicissitudes of the historical process itself. Political and moral values have most importantly contributed to what the past has been like: they truly are an important component of the historian's "object" of investigation. So, if one were to use the term "subjectivity" in a sense close to its etymological origins, one would more accurately call the Annaliste historian "subjective" than the historian whose socialist or liberal values are clearly present in his work. There truly is something "objective" about political and moral values that is wholly absent from disciplinary affiliations, historical style, or sheer personal stupidity.

But perhaps this *is* precisely why historians tend to be so extremely sensitive to the influence of political and moral values. Perhaps they intuitively feel that these influences are so far more dangerous, and a so far more serious threat to historical truth because of their quasi "objectivity" than these ostensibly so much more "subjective" factors. Or, to put it differently, perhaps political and moral values are perceived to be such a threat to historical truth *not* because they are so *remote* from it and do belong to such an entirely different world, but precisely because they are, in fact, so *close* to historical truth that the two can often hardly be distinguished from each other. Moral and political values belong to the world of the object rather than to that of the subject—and the so-called subjective historian therefore obeys the world of the *object* (in the way required by objectivism) rather than what constitutes his own *subjectivity* and what is personal to him. Or, to put it differently, the problem therefore might well be that political and moral values are ways in which historical truth may sometimes manifest itself, and vice versa.

This, then, will determine the plot my argument. I shall start with an exposition of some traditional views on the subjectivity-versus-objectivity problem and attempt to show that these views fail to recognize that the problem arises from the logical proximity of truth and value. After as much has been established, it obviously follows that we shall have to look much harder for the exact nature of their relationship than has been done up till now. Precisely because (historical) truth and value are so extremely close to each other, we should look for the best philosophical microscope we can find in order to accurately investigate the interaction of historical truth and value.

What we shall see in the end through our microscope will prove to be most reassuring: for it will become clear that "truth" determines "value," and not vice versa, and hence that we need not fear value as much as we have traditionally been taught to do. On the contrary, it may be argued that value often will often be a useful or even indispensable guide on our difficult way to historical truth.

TRADITIONAL OBJECTIVIST ARGUMENTS

My thesis—that we should not worry so much about subjectivism as most of the handbooks advise—admittedly has its antecedents in historical theory. A good starting point is William Walsh's observation that nothing need necessarily be wrong with the indisputable fact that different historians, when writing about one and the same historical event—say the French Revolution—will always present us with different accounts of that event. The handbooks often already saw in this an occasion for relativist despair, because the fact seemed to suggest that an intersubjective account of the past acceptable to all, or most, historians, is an unattainable ideal. But Walsh points out that this is an overhasty conclusion. Relativism only becomes an option to be considered if these accounts should all be mutually incompatible and if, next, we had no means at our disposal to decide which of them is right and which is wrong. But nothing as bad as that will necessarily be the case when we are presented with different accounts of, for example, the French Revolution. For most often these accounts will complement rather than contradict each other. An account focusing on the intellectual causes of the French Revolution and another one on its economic causes can peacefully coexist together. It would require a most naive and unsophisticated conception of the notion of "cause" to presume incompatibility here. If you say that your car hit another one because the road was slippery, this explanation can unproblematically coexist with the alternative one that you had been driving too fast. Both can be right (or wrong, of course). And to the extent that the descriptive component of historical accounts tends to outweigh their causal component, incompatibility becomes even less likely. The statement that a chair has four legs is not in the least contradicted by the statement that it was made by Hepplewhite. Similarly, a political history of France in the eighteenth century does not contradict, but complements, an economic history of France in that same period. And we may agree with Walsh that this simple and pedestrian observation will already solve most of the problems that so often and so needlessly have driven relativist historians to despair.[2]

Yet Walsh is prepared to admit that in some cases there actually may be incompatibility—and I note in passing the remarkable fact that it will be far from easy to find convincing examples of this, for outright conflict is astonishingly rare in the history of historical writing. But an example would be the conflict between the Marxist thesis that the French Revolution served bourgeois interests and Alfred Cobban's argument a generation ago that the revolution was reactionary and hurt rather than furthered capitalist bourgeois interests. Here, indeed, we have a conflict, and the conflict undoubtedly had its origins in the fact that Cobban held political values other than those of the Marxists.

But Walsh remains undeterred by even this kind of example, arguing that even here conflict is merely apparent. Conflict disappears, as he goes on to say, as soon as we recognize that a liberal might agree with the Marxist if he were prepared to consider the French Revolution within the framework of *Marxist* values, while the Marxist, in his turn, would be ready to see Cobban's point after having embraced *his* set of moral and political values.

But I expect that most historians would find this an impossibly Arcadian view of historical debate; and they would probably object that in this way history would be emptied of meaningful debate. For all that would now be required is the readiness of the historian to temporarily and dispassionately accept the values of his opponents—and then all disagreement would disappear like snow under a hot sun. However, if debate and disagreement could really be banned in this way from historical writing, the same would be true for historical truth as such. For if there were no longer anything to disagree about, the search for historical truth would have become an illusion and then there would be no room for truth anymore. Similarly, the search for something that is white is unworkable in a world in which everything is white.

We may observe in this later part of Walsh's argument this tendency (that I mentioned a moment ago) to so completely separate truth and value that the two could never come into real conflict with each other. And I would now agree with the historian's conviction that this would be a most naive simplification of the role of values in historical writing—though, admittedly, at this stage of my argument I am not yet in the position to present a convincing argument for my agreement with the historian. This I can only do after having shown how closely truth and value are really related in historical writing.

A similar strategy for explaining away the problem of historical subjectivity by putting truth and value miles apart can be found in the well-known "reasons versus causes" argument. The main idea in this argument is that we should always clearly distinguish between what *caused* a person to hold a certain opinion (such as his moral convictions) and the rational arguments or *reasons* that this person may have, or fail to have, in favor of this opinion. And since these are completely different things, thus the argument goes on to say, it may well be that certain political or moral values cause people to have certain beliefs, but this fact alone is completely irrelevant with regard to whether the belief in question is right or wrong. For example, three decades ago a person may have believed that Mao's China was an awful mess simply because his conservative values caused him to believe so; nevertheless, the belief was completely correct. Hence, even if we can explain what values have caused people to hold certain opinions, these opinions may well be correct and true to actual fact. Or, as Arthur Danto once so succinctly put it: "there are few more pernicious beliefs than the one which suggests that we have cast serious doubts upon an opinion by explaining why someone came to hold it."[3]

This surely is a most effective way of dealing with the problem of subjectivism; but it shares with most knockdown arguments of this type the disadvantage of being, in practice, a bit too effective. For, as each historian will be able to tell you, this philosophically so neat and convincing distinction between causes and reasons will simply not work in practice. In actual historical debate the arguments in favor of or against certain views of part of the past cannot be carved up into what belongs to the world of political and moral values on the one hand, and what belongs to the world of fact and of rational argument on the other. What is objective truth to one historian may well be a mere value judgment in the eyes of another historian. Hence, as was already the case in Walsh's argument, the fatal weakness of the reasons-versus-causes argument is that it fails to take into account how close historical truth and political and moral values actually are to each other.

HISTORICAL REPRESENTATION

For a more detailed exploration of the interconnections between historical truth on the one hand and political and moral values on the other, it will be necessary to start with a few general observations on the nature of historical representation. I am intentionally using here the term "historical representation" instead of alternative terms, such as "historical interpretation," "description," "explanation," or "historical narrative." For as will become clear in a moment, the relevant secrets of the nature of historical writing can only be discerned if we see the historical text as a *representation* of the past in much the same way that the work of art is a representation of what it depicts—or, for that matter, in the way that Parliament or Congress is a representation of the electorate.

Presently, the most widely accepted theory of aesthetic representation is the so-called substitution theory of representation.[4] According to this theory—and in agreement with the etymology of the word "representation"—a representation essentially is a substitute or replacement of something else that is absent. Obviously, precisely because of the latter's absence, we may be in need of the substitute's "re-presenting" it. To take the example made famous by Ernst Gombrich—one of the most influential proponents of the substitution theory—a hobbyhorse may be a representation of a real horse for a child, because it may function in the child's eyes as a substitute or replacement of a real horse. Similarly, because the past is past, and therefore no longer present, we are in need of representations of the past; and we have the discipline of history in order to avail ourselves of those representations of the past that may best function as a textual substitute for the actual, but absent, past.

There is one feature, or implication, of this account of aesthetic and historical representation that especially deserves our attention within the present context; namely, that a representation aims at being, from a certain perspective, just as good as the original that it represents. To be more precise: in the first place, the representation attempts to be such a believable and effective substitute or replacement for what it represents that differences between the represented and its representation can safely be disregarded. Yet, in the second place, there *will* and always *must* be such differences. For as Virginia Woolf so aptly summarized the nature of artistic representation: "Art is not a copy of the world; one of the damn things is enough." Representation is paradoxical, in other words, in that it combines a resistance to difference with a love of it. This is a paradox that can be solved as soon as we recognize the logical affinities between the notions of representation and of identity: just like representation, identity somehow attempts to reconcile sameness and difference (by change through time) and is required to do just this—since things may remain the same thing, and thus retain their identity in spite of their having different properties at different stages of their history.[5]

Three conclusions follow from these considerations. In the first place, though language may be used for representing reality (as will typically be the case with the historical text), the opposition between the represented and its representation by no means coincides with the opposition between reality and language. Even more so, if we think of works of art, of political representation, of representation in legal contexts, the represented and its representation will share the same ontological status. For both will belong to the world, both will unproblematically be a part of the inventory of reality. And, as we saw in the previous chapter, when language is used to represent historical reality it also takes on the logical features that we normally attribute to things (in objective reality) and withhold from the language we use for making true statements about things. If, then, we conventionally define epistemology as the philosophical subdiscipline that investigates the relationship between cognitive language and reality, it follows that epistemology is of no help to us if we wish to know more about the relationship between the represented and its representation. Epistemology ties *words* to *things*, whereas representation ties *things* to *things*. And it follows that the historical theorists who attempt to develop a brand of *historical epistemology* that will explain to us how historical narrative and historical reality are or should be related to each other are like those philistines who try to explain artistic merit in terms of photographic precision. In both cases, the merits of relevance and importance are recklessly sacrificed to those of precision and accuracy. History cannot be understood on cognitivist assumptions only—though undoubtedly these also will always be involved in any account of the past. Cognitivism clearly gives us access to part of the historian's intellectual activities, but the nature of these activities could never be completely reduced to it.

Secondly, and most importantly, an explanation can be given for why representation is so little inclined to satisfy the cognitive desires of the epistemologist. The crucial insight here, as Arthur Danto has shown, is that the represented only comes into being, or to be more precise, only gains its contours, thanks to its being represented by a representation.[6] An example from the writing of history may be helpful here. Suppose a historian is writing a history of the labor movement. This phrase "a history of the labor movement" suggests that there exists in historical reality some unambiguously identifiable thing like Karl Marx or Friedrich Engels that is named or can be referred to by the phrase "the labor movement"—and whose history we can subsequently describe by following it on its admittedly quite complex path through space and time. And this picture suggests, furthermore, that when historians disagree about the history of the labor movement, they will be in the fortunate position of being able to settle their disagreements by simply looking at the labor movement's path through space and time, in order to establish who is right and who is wrong. But if this is to work, we must ask ourselves what exactly *is* this labor movement whose history the historian wishes to write? In the case of a historical individual such as Marx, the answer is simple enough. But what *exactly* is the thing in historical reality that *this* phrase purportedly refers to?

Indeed, in a case such as Marx's we have, on the one hand, the *individual human being* who lived from 1818 to 1883, while, on the other, we have the *histories* that have been written about him by historians such as Franz Mehring or Isaiah Berlin. But when we consider the labor movement, we have only the latter and we then make the rather amazing discovery that discussions about what the labor movement *is*, or *was*, and what the phrase may be thought to *refer* to, will prove to be completely identical with the kind of discussions that historians have about its *history*. Disagreements about what the labor movement is or was will be settled in terms of accounts of its history and vice versa. Things (that are represented) then coincide with their histories (i.e., with their representations)—as nineteenth-century historicists such as Ranke and Humboldt have already taught us.[7] And this is where things like the labor movement will differ essentially from less problematic things such as Karl Marx or Friedrich Engels. So we must recognize that we actually have *two* categories of things in past reality: on the one hand, there are things that we can unproblematically identify without taking their history into account; but on the other, there are things where identification depends on the histories or the historical representations that we have of these things. And we can therefore truly say of this latter category of representable things in the past that they have no contours in the absence of the representation that has been proposed of them. If there is no representation, in other words, then there is no represented as well. Self-evidently, in the case of cognitive language the situation is completely different: here things exist independently of the true statements that we can make about them. And language is not required for our becoming aware of them.

It might be objected now that this is true only of historical representation and that things will be different already in the case of the artistic, pictorial representation of reality. Think, for example, of the portrait painter. Is it not the case that the represented, the sitter, is given to us first, so that his portrait, the representation of the represented, can be painted later? But this objection fails to do justice to the challenges of portrait painting, since it identifies the represented exclusively with those physical features of the sitter that may correspond to a good and clear photograph. However, if we consider Titian's famous portrait of Charles V, it is not photographic precision that makes us admire this representation of the emperor. We admire Titian's portrait because it so strikingly presents us with the emperor's personality and his state of mind after the immense political struggle that had consumed all his energy and vitality. And *this* is a feature of the emperor that is by no means unambiguously and unproblematically given to us; it is a feature as elusive and as impossible to accurately define as those features of historical reality that the historian of the labor movement attempts to narrate. From this point of view, the represented of the portrait painter is no less dependent on how it is represented than the past that is represented by the historian.

To put the same point differently, the physical appearance of the sitter for a portrait as presented by a photograph (i.e., what is depicted by a photograph) is a mere "shadow," a mere "abstraction," so to speak. We will recognize that it is such an abstraction, and not (contrary to common-sense opinion) what is immediately given to us, since it corresponds to what all representations of the sitter, as produced by various artists, may have in common. For all these representations will succeed—supposing that the artists in question possess the technical skills required for accurately painting what they see—in presenting us with as good a likeness as we may expect from a photograph. But this is not where they do begin: painters do not begin by first painting a good likeness of the sitter in order to add, next, a few more details representing the sitter's personality. They just paint; and do both things at one and the same time. And then we, as spectators, may come along and divide up these paintings into what is a good likeness, on the one hand and, what the paintings suggest about the sitter's personality, on the other. But this is a pictorial logic that we project on these paintings and that is part neither of the process nor of the nature of (pictorial) representation itself. We then project on representation what belongs to a postrepresentational stage in our relationship to the world.

In the context of this discussion it may be helpful to recall Roland Barthes's characterization, in his *La Chambre claire*, of photographs as "messages without a code." The painter may have a specific style, he may show his affiliations with a certain period in the history of art—and this is why we will discern in his paintings a certain code, that is, a certain system for how to translate what is given to us, in experience, into a representation. The photograph seems to be without such a code. We will even be prepared to say that the photograph could not possibly have such a code since it is the product of a purely mechanical process: it is the result of how light rays pass through a system of lenses and effect certain chemical changes in the material of the film, etc. This is also why we tend to see a painting as a "subjective" and the photograph as an "objective" representation of the world.

Or, to go one step further, this is why we tend to believe that the photograph brings us closer to what the world really is like than the painting. For does the photograph not show reality itself to us, whereas the painting only, or at least primarily, shows us how the artist experienced reality?

I would not wish to deny that there is some truth in this view. But it is also mistaken in a fundamental way—and the Barthesian notion of the code may explain this. The crucial datum is that we tend to confuse (1) our not being aware that codes determine how we represent the world with (2) the absence of codes. If the codes do not make themselves felt, if their activity or role in the representation of the world is not clearly manifest to us, we will feel inclined to infer from this that we are dealing with "messages without a code"—as typically will be the case if we look at a photograph. Furthermore, if we ask ourselves why we so easily yield to this temptation, the answer is, self-evidently, that the intersubjectivity of codes will make us oblivious of their existence and functioning. If you, I, and everybody else apply the same codes for representing the world, these codes will no longer be perceived as such, but will, instead, be experienced as part of the world itself. Codes, or ways of seeing the world, have then been transformed into one more set of properties of the world.

We will now be able to see what is wrong with the intuition that the photograph should bring us closer to the world than the painting could do. For precisely because paintings are messages with a code, paintings make us aware that we always apply codes for the translation of our experience of the world into representations of the world. And it is precisely the wide variety of codes that have been used by artists all throughout the history of art that will continuously and inexorably remind us of the presence of these codes and of what they do on the trajectory from the world itself to our representation of the world. It follows from this that painting will draw our attention to the trajectory from the world itself to representation and to all that happens on that trajectory, whereas the photograph will take this trajectory for granted and be interested, instead, in what inferences are justified by what we see on the photograph, in how it relates to what we may have seen on other photographs or to certain theories that we had developed on the basis those other photographs. And, obviously, the former trajectory must involve us with reality itself more intimately than the latter one. Put differently, painting is epistemological, it focuses on how we see the world and can only do so by "opening up," so to speak, this trajectory between the world and our representation of it, whereas the photograph is cognitive and will ignore, or take for granted the existence of this trajectory.

This, then, is what art puts on the agenda of philosophy. More specifically, it will require us to add a new and extra dimension to epistemology as we know it since Descartes, Kant, and since contemporary philosophy of language. Traditional epistemology is "the epistemology of the photograph," so to speak; it is the epistemology of our knowledge of a world that is shared by us all, and that we seem to share since the codes we apply for representing it are the same for all of us. But precisely this renders this epistemology largely irrelevant; for it is true, we can just as well forget about the codes that we all share and that we all take for granted. Far more interesting is the kind of epistemology suggested by art, the kind of epistemology recognizing the many different ways, and codes, that we may apply for representing the world. Or, rather, even if one truly wishes to come to grips with the kind of issues that are being addressed by traditional epistemology, one can only responsibly do so within the framework of an aestheticist epistemology. For only after we have discovered the secrets of aestheticist representation can we move on to the subsidiary question of why and how we may represent a world that is shared by us all and of which we may gain knowledge thanks to representational codes that we all share as well. So the epistemologist should start with abandoning the idea of a world that is the same for all of us, and he can only do so by recognizing that this shared world is, in fact, an abstraction produced by the codes of the photograph paradigm. This is what Hegel had in mind when he argued in the *Phenomenology of Mind* that reality is an abstraction, whereas the Idea (or, in my terminology, pictorial representation) gives us access to the Real. Or what the Foucault of *Les Mots et les choses* wished to demonstrate when making us aware in this book of the arbitrariness of how we cut up the world into (hierarchies of) individual types of things. We tend to forget this since we are no longer aware of how routine compels us to process and to codify the manifold of representations into an intersubjectively accessible and public reality. Nevertheless, think of how the (still uncodified) representations that a newborn baby (without speech, without words for naming things, and without any conception of what the world contains) will finally crystallize out into an inventory of the things in the world. In this sense we all begin by being great artists (as babies) before losing our artistic skills when growing up and when making our entrance into a publicly shared reality. We then have no need anymore for that supreme artistic achievement of the synthesis of the manifold of experience to be projected on the world. This is the process making philistines of the majority of us. So only the artist may still remind us of the baby that we once were. And this is why we may well agree with the interest of theorists like Paul Ehrenzweig in his *The Hidden Order of Art* in the drawings made by children. In sum, this is where this deceitful objectivity of so-called objective reality may so dangerously mislead us (especially when we tend to be empiricists). For representations are truly basic, whereas the things of "objective reality" are mere constructions, abstract truncations of concrete representations. Hence, as in the case of the narrative representation of the past, pictorial representation and what it represents logically depend upon and owe their existence to each other.[8]

Thirdly, it follows that precision, in the sense of an exact match of words and things, will never be attainable in artistic representation, historical writing, or, for that matter, in how the state represents the electorate. Precision can only be achieved if we have at our disposal some generally accepted standard or scheme determining how words are or ought to be related to things. But such epistemological standards or schemes will typically be absent in the case of representation. At most, each representation could be seen as a *proposal* for such a rule to be generally accepted—I shall return to this in the next section. And this should not be interpreted as some regrettable shortcoming of representation, if compared to situations in which such standards *are* available—as paradigmatically will be the case with singular true statements such as "The cat lies on the mat." For the absence of such epistemological standards is precisely what makes representation so useful, if not positively indispensable to us. Here we are still at liberty to make our *choice* of those standards, and this will most rigorously be applied at a later stage, when strict conventions are needed for meaningful and effective communication. Put differently, representation offers us language in its presocialized or natural state, so to speak; in its representational use, language still is essentially a "private" language. And those eighteenth-century philosophers, such as Rousseau, who where so passionately interested in the origins of language would have been well advised to focus on language in its representational use, instead of on the socializing dimension of language. For from a logical point of view this Rousseauistic dimension of language really belongs to a later stage.

Hence, the indeterminacy of the relationship between words and things is not a defect but the supreme virtue of all representational use of language. And those historians who regret the lack of precision of their discipline distrust their discipline precisely for what is its greatest merit and its greatest interest. For here language is born from what was *not yet* language.

NARRATIVE VERSUS COGNITIVE AND NORMATIVE DISCOURSE

In the previous section, we discussed some logical features of representation in general and applied our conclusions to the historian's representation of the past. Put differently, we moved from a variant of representation that is not necessarily linguistic to one that is exclusively so. One aspect of this transition deserves our special attention. Namely, that precisely this strategy will permit us to attribute to the narrative use of language properties that have no necessary connection with language as such. For, from the present perspective, (narrative) language is just one more variant of the representation of reality. Here we are not relying upon previously observed properties of language in order to derive from those properties knowledge about language's narrative or representational use—our strategy has been exactly the reverse, a strategy, that is, that uses insight into the nature of representation as the basis for a clarification of (the narrativist use of) language. Language here is the dependent variable, so to speak, instead of being the origin and source of all true philosophical insight—as ordinarily has been the case in most twentieth-century philosophy.

The important insight to be gained from this can be summarized in the following paradox. On the one hand, there are no independent standards on the basis of which the link between the represented and its representation can be justified, explained, or verified—and from this perspective we may observe here an indeterminacy in the relationship between language and reality that has no counterpart in the uses of language that have customarily been investigated by epistemologists. On the other hand, the relationship between language and the world is, in the case of representation, far more intimate and direct, since *this* narrative representation has with the utmost care been devised by the historian in order to most convincingly account for precisely *this* represented part of the past. So there are two different ways in which language and the world may be connected;

where the one is strong, the other is weak. Representation is strong in the sense that it most intimately and exclusively connects one representation to one represented only, but weak in the sense that no formal epistemological schemes can be relied upon to justify this so special and unique connection, schemes that could demonstrate that this really is the "correct" connection. The relationship between the singular true statement and reality, on the other hand, is weak in that many other true statements may connect language to this specific part or aspect of reality just as well, but it is strong in the sense that formal epistemological schemes will successfully decide about the truth or falsehood of any of those statements. Therefore, we can either trust representation to bring us to the heart of reality—but then we will inevitably be vague and imprecise—or we shall have to sacrifice relevance and insight and get the precision and accuracy of the true statement in return. All our use of language must inevitably oscillate between these two extremes—and never will we succeed in combining relevance with precision, or insight with accuracy. This, alas, is our predicament as language users.

What has been said just now about the difference between representations and true statements can be rephrased in terms of the difference between proposals and rules. We may make a proposal for a specific action under a specific set of circumstances; and though the proposal in question may be as specific and as well adapted to these specific circumstances as we like, alternative proposals will nevertheless always be conceivable. Thus proposals share with representation this peculiar combination of uniqueness or specificity with a tolerance of alternatives. Because of this shared feature, we may well see historical representations of part of the past essentially as *proposals* for what specific piece of language could best be tied to a specific part of the past. And other historians may then disagree with this proposal and present, in their turn, other proposals for how best to link language and historical reality for this specific case. But none of these proposals for how best to represent the past could ever be justified by an appeal to some specific general rule for how language and reality are to be related. Nevertheless, life tends to repeat itself and the contexts in which we have to think and act may often be sufficiently similar to allow for generalization. If this happens, the same proposal we made on previous occasions may also be considered to be the appropriate one for other, similar occasions. And in this way, what originally has been a mere *proposal* intended for a particular occasion may become a general *rule* for a certain type of situational context. Representation is then reduced to the level of language-use that is investigated by epistemologists—insofar as epistemology attempts to formulate general rules for how words and things are related.

Two remarks are relevant at this stage. In the first place, against the background of the notion of representation we will now recognize that the attempt to formulate such a general account of the relationship between words and things may take two different forms: it may focus *either* on the nature of the relationship itself *or* on what is most generally true of the things that are related by the relationship. And the differences between these focuses should be kept in mind. For if x is in the relation R to y, an investigation of R is not necessarily identical to an investigation of what makes x and y stand in this relationship R to each other. The former investigation is *internal* to R, so to speak, whereas the latter is *external* to it. And we may say that aesthetics, as a general theory of *representation*, focuses preferably on the internalist aspects of this relationship, whereas epistemology as a general theory about *how things are related to words* has almost exclusively been interested in its externalist aspects. It has been the perennial myopia of epistemology to believe that only the latter sort of investigation can further philosophical insight into the relationship between language and the world.

A second and more important remark concerns the *logical hierarchy* between these two accounts of the relationship between words and things. When we consider this issue, we should notice that without there first being *proposals* for how to relate words to things, these proposals could never crystallize into *rules* for this relationship. And this justifies the inference that from a logical point of view representation is prior to the true statement. Or, to put it differently, aesthetics precedes epistemology and it is only against the background of aesthetics that we may discern what is, and what is not, of value in epistemology. We may well agree, therefore, with the postmodernist attack on epistemology that was inaugurated by Rorty's *Philosophy and the Mirror of Nature* (1979), with the all-important qualification that aesthetics—a theory of representation—should guide us in this attack and show us, firstly, what precedes epistemology and, secondly, what parts of epistemology can be rescued (or how it should be supplemented) after we have learned to see it as a mere offshoot of representation.

This latter remark is all the more important since it has its counterpart in ethical discourse, which attempts to present us with *general* rules for action given certain types of circumstances. Ethical discourse will typically have the nature of statements such as "Given a situation of the type *S*, one ought to perform an action of the type *A*." This differs from political discourse in that political decisions ordinarily concern issues for which no general rules are, as yet, available. In this way there is, as has often been observed, a truly most intimate and direct relationship between history and politics. And the notion of the proposal may help us to explain this relationship. The historian will make a proposal to us for how best to see part of the past, whereas the politician will do much the same with regard to an aspect of contemporary political reality and how to act in response to it. And such proposals may indeed result, at a later stage, in general rules for how to relate language to words, or for how to act under a certain general type of circumstances, but in neither case are such general rules presupposed.

Here, then, may we discern the wisdom of Machiavelli when he so strongly opposed politics to ethics and when he warned us against the now so popular fallacy which derives politics from ethics; *if* there is any relationship between the two at all, it is precisely the reverse.[9] Although political decisions should not be based on ethical considerations, it is nevertheless the case that, just as representation may ultimately become codified in epistemological rules for how to relate things to words, political experience may ultimately become codified into ethical rules. And, surely, there is an interesting historical connection between the origins and claims of epistemology on the one hand and of those of ethics on the other. For both came into being after Descartes withdrew the self from the complexities of the real world into the quiet sanctuary of a Cartesian *forum internum*—thus dealing the death blow to the Aristotelian weltanschauung that was still shared by Machiavelli and his humanistic contemporaries. This Cartesian self was henceforth considered to be the source both of all true knowledge of the world and of an exact science of morals—as most paradigmatically would be the case within the architecture of Kant's first two *Critiques*. After the withdrawal of the Machiavellian human individual from all the complexities of social and political life into this cognitive and normative *forum internum*, history and politics were automatically and inevitably reduced to the lowly status of impure, tainted, and uncertain derivatives of epistemology and morals—instead of being recognized as logically prior to these. This is why a high prestige was granted to both cognitive and moral discourse in most of Western intellectual history, whereas history and politics have had to pay dearly for the triumphant successes of their rivals over the last few centuries.

TRUTH AND VALUE IN HISTORICAL WRITING

On the basis of the foregoing, a preliminary account can be given of the relationship between fact and value in the narrative representation of the past (and in the next section we shall see how the account given in this one has to be supplemented or corrected). We have seen that narrative representations should be conceived of as proposals of what could be seen as the best (textual) substitute or replacement of part of the past. And then the decisive question will be—as Gombrich's theory of representation indicates—what could best *function* as such a textual substitute? If we wish to come to a decision about this, much, if not all, will depend on the kind of circumstances within which we shall have to consider our decision. We can only adequately evaluate a proposal when we take into account the specific kind of circumstances to which the proposal is related. The proposal to put up an umbrella obviously makes sense if it is raining, but, equally obviously, not if the sun is shining. An important consideration is directly connected with this. Proposals can be neither true nor false in the way that statements can be so: the proposal to put up an umbrella when the sun is shining is "stupid," "silly," or "inappropriate" (or whatever other adjective one might prefer) but could not possibly be said to be "false." However, the fact that proposals cannot properly be said to be either true or false does not in the least exclude the possibility of rationally discussing the merits of proposals. Hence the fact that narrative representations of the past are, from a logical point of view, proposals does not automatically place historical writing outside the reach of rational debate.

In any discussion of the rationality of narrative representations, two sets of circumstances will primarily demand the historian's attention. In the first place, each proposal made by a historian in order to account for part of the past will have to be compared to other, rival proposals that historians have already made for that specific purpose or that could be sketched, or roughly outlined, on the basis of already existing knowledge of the past. Here the "circumstances" under which the historian presents his proposals can be identified with the present state of the art in historical writing about some historical topic. And, self-evidently, when we think of *this* kind of circumstance we evaluate historical representations from a perspective essentially independent of normative, ethical, or political considerations. For example, the debate about the contribution made by the Dutch state to the economic and political success of the Dutch republic in the seventeenth century would involve no obvious or necessary commitment to the historian's moral or political standards.

In the second place, however, these circumstances may (also) include the social and political realities of the historian's world. For example, the discussion of the totalitarian state during the Cold War period, and the proposals made by historians for how best to see this phenomenon, cannot possibly be isolated from the East/West conflict of that time. And this is not merely because of the difficulty of distinguishing between the purely historical and the political dimensions of the debate, but because these proposals were simply *intended* to be both a historical account *and* suggestions for a purely political standpoint. Furthermore, obviously histories of tragedies such as the Holocaust would fail to meet even the most elementary standards of taste and appropriateness if they were to observe a complete moral neutrality and impartiality regarding the unspeakable atrocities that were committed against the Jews.[10]

When we consider these two types of circumstances under which historians may formulate their proposals for how to see the past, we will agree that a clear distinction between them will be difficult to make in the practice of historical writing. Most if not all historical writing will have to be located somewhere between the situation in which only the former set of circumstances or only the latter set will have to be taken into account. Next, most often each individual work of history will in certain stages of its argument move closer to one set and further from the other—in either direction. The history dealing with the state of the seventeenth-century Dutch republic that I mentioned a moment ago may, in certain stages of its argument, either explicitly or implicitly, express or imply a political philosophy about the ideal relationship between the state and civil society. Furthermore, a history of the Holocaust will always require a basis in solid documentary research. So even the extremes presented in the previous paragraph will ordinarily already present us with a mixture of fact and value. And the attempt to completely separate the two is unrealistic because no historian can isolate completely one set of circumstances from the other. The belief that such a clean separation is or ought to be possible has its only basis in our post-Humean and post-Kantian conviction that fact and value are logically distinct domains, but decidedly not in the actual realities of historical writing (or of human life in general, for that matter).

Consider the following theoretical explanation of this continuity between fact and value. A historical representation of the past may contain only true statements about the past, yet these statements may have been selected and arranged by the historian in such a way that they strongly suggest a certain (political) course of action. For example, nineteenth-century nationalist historical writing may occasionally have been wholly unobjectionable from a purely factual point of view, and yet have functioned in contemporary political discussion as a historical justification of expansionist purposes. In this way historical representation truly presents us with the much sought-after *trait d'union* between the "is" and the "ought." We begin with merely a set of true statements and move then, automatically and naturally, toward an answer to the question of how to act in the future. The transition is completely natural, and at no stage can we identify a point where pure knowledge becomes pure action. Our search for such a point has no other justification than the a priori dogma that there somewhere *should* be such a point. It may well be true that a dissociation between the "is" and the "ought" will make sense if we ask ourselves how we ought to act given a certain *type* of situation. But as soon as we have to do with the unicity and the concreteness of individual historical contexts, this continuity between fact and norm immediately takes over, and the distinction between the "is" and the "ought" then is an artificial and unrealistic a priori construction.

These considerations may explain why truth and value can come so infinitesimally close to each other in the practice of historical writing—as we had already observed at the beginning of this chapter. In representation and metaphor "fact" and "value," the "is" and the "ought," are merely the extremes on a continuous scale. Another conclusion would be that all of the traditional and well-known worries about the historian as helpless victim of moral and political standards are justified after all. For, if there is this continuity between facts and value, if these two come so close to each other—and even shade off into each other to such an extent that we cannot say with precision at what point "fact" becomes "value," and vice versa—what resources are then left to the historian in order to successfully resist the political and moral prejudices of the day?

However, as we shall see in the remainder of this chapter, there is no occasion for despair about the rationality of historical writing and historical debate. For we shall discover that aesthetics will provide us with the means for rescuing historical writing from the twin threat of relativism and irrationality.

IN PRAISE OF SUBJECTIVITY

This brings us to the last stage of my argument in this chapter. There will be general agreement that we may discern in the historian's narrative of the past all of the three variants of discourse that were mentioned above. First, it presents us with a *representation* of the past; second, this representation will consist of *true statements* embodying its cognitive pretensions; and third, though this may take different forms and may be more prominent in some cases than in others, *ethical rules and values* will codetermine the historian's account of the past.[11]

Most accounts of historical writing (and of its "subjectivity") have focused on the interaction of the cognitive and the moral dimensions of historical writing, and on how the two might get in each other's way. That these two should ordinarily obstruct each other need not surprise us, for the same philosophical regime that reversed the Machiavellian relationship between historical and political discourse, on the one hand, and cognitive and moral discourse, on the other, also gave us the distinction between the "is" and the "ought." The intimate interaction of thought and action, of what was to become, at a later phase, the cognitive and the normative, now broke apart into one formal and epistemological scheme for thought and quite another one for the science of ethical action. Even for Kant, the distinction between the "is" and the "ought" was an indisputable truth, although his love of philosophical symmetry inspired him more than any philosopher living either before or after him to discover as many parallels as possible between the two schemes. Anyway, the realm shared by history and politics was now divided between the social sciences on the one hand and ethics on the other.[12] For the post-Kantian philosopher, the potential conflict between cognitive and normative discourse had to be the most obvious source of worry connected with thinking about historical writing. And indeed, as we all know, the neo-Kantians at the end of the nineteenth century and at the beginning of the twentieth century saw in this potential conflict even the single most important and most urgent problem of all of historical theory. Thus, the reversal of the Machiavellian relationship between historical and political discourse, on the one hand, and cognitive and normative discourse, on the other, has strongly contributed to the low esteem of historical and political discourse in the modernist intellectual climate. Just as Belgium was the hapless terrain where France and Germany used to fight their wars, so history now came to be seen as the preferred domain for the never-ending war between fact and value. Obviously a place where nobody in his right senses would wish to live. So much the worse, then, for the poor historians who unsuspectingly chose to reside in this strife-ridden area.

But this perception requires us to set matters straight again. That is, we should realize that narrative discourse and its representational proposals have a logical priority over cognitive and normative discourse. Consequently, against this background, this private war between cognitive and normative discourse—which so much interested the neo-Kantians—is of a mere subsidiary significance. What truly counts is that the aesthetic criteria that enable us to evaluate historical representations logically precede the criteria we apply for evaluating cognitive and normative discourse. Narrative representation should not be evaluated by an appeal to these criteria of cognitive and normative discourse—on the contrary, the aesthetic criteria of representational success will enable us to evaluate the contribution of cognitive and normative discourse to historical representations. In my *Narrative Logic: A Semantic Analysis of the Historian's Language* (1983), I have tried to define the nature of these aesthetic criteria. Firstly, there is no a priori scheme in terms of which the representational success of individual narrative representations can be established; representational success always is a matter of a decision between rival narrative representations. It is a matter of comparing narrative representations of the past with *each other*, not of comparing individual narrative representations with *the past itself* (i.e., the kind of situation with which the singular true statement presents us). An implication is that the more representations we have, the more successfully they can be compared to each other and the better we will be equipped to assess their relative merits. If we were to possess only *one* representation of part of the past, we would be completely helpless to judge its scope. Next, the decisive question to ask about such a set of comparable narrative representations of the past will be: which one has the largest scope, is capable of subsuming the greatest part of reality? Secondly, the narrative representation that is most risky, most hazardous, and most unlikely to be the right one on the basis of existing historical knowledge—but that can nevertheless *not* be refuted on that same basis—is the representation with the largest scope. I emphasize that this set of criteria for the evaluation of historical representations contains no *normative* elements: in no way is an appeal made to ethical norms or standards.

It must strike the reader to what extent these aesthetic criteria resemble Popper's view of how to evaluate scientific theories. Popper convincingly attacked the logical-positivist view that the best scientific theory is the one that is most likely to be true, the one with the greatest probability—since such an approach would make statements such as "tomorrow it will rain, or not rain" into the very ideal of scientific truth.[13] However, precisely because of its probability, precisely because it could not possibly be refuted by whatever happens tomorrow, this "theory" lacks all "empirical content" and gives us no useful information whatever about the world. Hence, only if one is prepared to take risks with one's theories, to move *away* from probability—only then can "empirical content" be maximized and meaningful information about the nature of empirical reality be gained. "Hypotheses are nets: only he who casts will catch," as Popper quotes Novalis in the epigraph of his famous study. Obviously, then, much that Popper has written about how scientific theories may maximize their empirical content can, *mutatis mutandis*, also said to be true of how we should evaluate historical representation of the past.[14]

So from this perspective the criteria of representational success in the writing of history may seem at first sight to be closer to those of cognitive truth than to those of aesthetic perfection (or of ethical rightness). But since even in the sciences we move at this level beyond the sphere of cognitive truth in the proper and original sense of the word—since scientific theories cannot properly be said to be "true," but "plausible," or "better than rival theories," or, at most, to "approximate the truth"—one might surmise that an account of the evaluation of scientific theories as proposed by Popper belongs to the realm of aesthetics rather than to that of cognitive certainty. But in the end it is in all likelihood a matter of philosophical strategy, rather than of ineluctable philosophical truth, as to how we should decide about this. Indeed, one may decide to move from (the) cognitive truth (of the singular true statement) as far as possible in the direction of scientific plausibility—and this is the strategy that has almost universally been adopted in both philosophy of science and in historical theory. But one may just as well try the opposite tack that is advocated here, to see how far we may get in the attempt to account for both the plausibility of scientific theories and for representational success in the writing of history from the perspective of aesthetics. To see aesthetics with just a little more respect than we are accustomed to do is all that would be needed in order to make the latter strategy worth trying. And if we embrace this strategy, it may well prove to be a plausible assumption that the realm of aesthetics is where science and history finally meet each other.

Within the context of the present chapter, however, I shall refrain from further discussion of the aesthetic criteria of representational success. It is of more interest for my argument here to recognize that these criteria (however defined and spelled out in detail) logically precede the criteria we might adopt for the evaluation of cognitive and of normative discourse, and that they do not depend on these. And this brings me to the main thesis that I wish to defend in this chapter, namely, the uncommon thesis that narrative or historical discourse is what we had best rely upon when we wish to decide what moral and political standards we had best adopt. To put it differently, the procedure for finding out what should be our most recommendable moral and political values is as follows. We must begin by collecting a large number of historical texts that have clearly been written from different moral or political points of view and let us take care, furthermore, that more or less the same historical phenomena (such as the French Revolution, the Industrial Revolution, the modernization of the West, and so on) are discussed in all these texts. We should observe, next, what has been the verdict in the history of historical writing on all these texts. Or to express it more solemnly, what will the application of the essentially aesthetic criteria used for assessing the merits of historical representations tell us about the qualities of these texts? Which of these texts satisfy these aesthetic criteria best? If we have ascertained as much, we should ask what moral and political values are dominant in the preferred set of historical texts. These, then, will be the moral and political values we should adopt and use as our compass for our present and future individual and collective action. For example, few historians will doubt that Tocqueville's account of the French Revolution is superior to the one that was presented by Michelet. In precisely this datum we may find a strong argument in favor of the liberal individualist values present in Tocqueville's account and against the leftist liberalism exemplified by Michelet's *Histoire de la Révolution Française*. If, moreover, the comparison of other historical texts would further confirm this picture, we are justified in seeing in this a convincing and decisive argument in favor of liberal individualism and against leftist liberalism. Aesthetics (the criteria that obtain in historical discussion) thus decides about ethics—and it can do so since aesthetics has a logical priority to ethics in the logic and the practice of historical writing.

Hence, it is in historical writing, not in rationalist, a priori argument of whatever variant, that we will find our most reliable gauge for choosing political and moral values. Historical writing is, so to speak, the experimental garden where we may try out different political and moral values and where the overarching aesthetic criteria of representational success will allow us to assess their respective merits and shortcomings. And we should be most grateful that the writing of history provides us with this experimental garden, since it will enable us to avoid the disasters that we may expect when we would have to try out in actual social and political reality the merits and shortcomings of different ethical and political standards. Before starting a revolution in the name of some political ideal, one had best begin with assessing as accurately and as dispassionately as possible the merits and shortcomings of the kind of historical writing inspired by this political ideal. A striking illustration of how history may confirm or refute ethical or political standards would be the anti-Americanism of the so-called revisionist account of the Cold War. A revisionist such as Gabriel Kolko finally decided to abandon his revisionist anti-Americanism because, however unwillingly, he had to acknowledge that the traditional view of the Cold War proved in the end to be the more convincing one, the one with the greater scope. Here we may see, as embodied in the thought of one and the same historian, how aesthetic criteria of representational success necessitated the abandonment of one set of political standards in favor of an alternative set. Here, clearly, aesthetics triumphed over ethics. And so it *is* and *ought* to be.

This is, lastly, why we should praise subjectivity and not demand that historians lay aside all their moral and political commitments when they write history. In the first place, such a commitment to moral and political values will often result in the kind of historical writing that is of greatest use to us for our orientation in the present and toward the future. We need only think, for example, of the histories written by authors like Jakob Talmon,

Isaiah Berlin, or Carl Friedrich, which were so obviously inspired by a devotion to liberal democracy and by an uncompromising rejection of totalitarianism, in order to see that subjectivity is not in the least under all circumstances a fatal shortcoming of historical writing. It may equally well be that all truly important historical writing will require the adoption of certain moral and political standards. "No bias, no book," as the British historian Michael Howard once so forcefully put it.[15]

But even more important is the fact that any historical writing that has successfully eliminated from itself all traces of moral and political standards can no longer be of any help to us in our crucial effort to distinguish between good and bad moral and political values. Having knowledge of the past surely is one thing; but it is perhaps no less important to know what ethical and political values we should cherish. So both our insight into the past and our orientation in the present and toward the future would be most seriously impaired by historical writing that tries (however vainly) to avoid all moral and political standards. And, thus, instead of fearing subjectivity as the historian's mortal sin, we should welcome subjectivity as an indispensable contribution both to our knowledge of the past *and* to contemporary and future politics.

I end this section with a final note on politics as defined in the previous sections and the political values that were discussed in this one. In the previous section politics was closely related to history: for as we have seen, both are essentially proposals, from a logical point of view. On the other hand, I have been speaking fairly indiscriminately of moral and political standards in this section, thereby suggesting that political discourse should rather be associated with the kind of cognitive and moral discourse that I had previously opposed to history and politics. The explanation of this ambiguity is that politics combines an affinity with the discourse of history and an affinity with ethics. For on the one hand, the politician has to find his way in a complex political reality in much the same way that the historian has to look for the best grasp of the complexities of some part of the past. And the kind of representational synthesis that the historian aims for is also the necessary prerequisite of all meaningful political action. Without such a minimally adequate grasp of the historical context in which the politician has to act, political action can only result in utter disaster.[16] On the other hand, the politician will observe or apply certain moral values in political action, as inspired by political ideology. For example, the value that he should further the cause of political equality or the interests of a certain segment of civil society may govern much of his behavior and most of his individual decisions as a politician.

Now, these ideologically inspired political and moral values may, as we all know, also play an important role in the writing of history. Think, for example, of socioeconomic history as inspired by Marxist or socialist ideologies. But whereas such values will be used *normatively* by the politician, the historian will make a *cognitive* use of them—he will discern in them an additional instrument for understanding the past. Once again socioeconomic history (or the history of one's nation, to take another example) may exemplify how such values can cognitively be exploited by the historian. Hence, when the role of cognitive discourse was discussed above, we associated cognitive discourse here primarily with how political ideologies suggest how historical realities should be tied to historical narrative. For this is the way in which the epistemological concern of how to tie things to words will customarily present itself when we investigate the writing of history.

Obviously, this does not substantially alter the picture given in this section of the logical hierarchy of narrative or representational discourse versus normative discourse and the specific variant of political discourse discussed just now. Narrative representational discourse, and the aesthetic criteria we rely upon for its evaluation, may be expected to be just as successful in assessing this variant of political values as they have been seen to be in ethical discourse untainted by political considerations.

I come to a conclusion. At the beginning of this chapter we established what the real problem is with historical subjectivity. The problem is not, as is ordinarily believed, that the introduction of ethical and political standards in historical narrative amounts to the introduction of something that is wholly alien to its subject matter and thus can only occasion a gross distortion of what the past has actually been like. The real problem is precisely the reverse: historical reality and the historian's ethical and political values may often come so extremely close to each other as to be virtually indistinguishable. Two conclusions follow from this. In the first place, just as a construction line in geometry, after having deliberately been made into a part of the geometrical problem itself, may well help us to solve it, so ethical and political standards, because of their natural affinity with the historian's subject matter, may often prove to be a help rather than an obstacle to a better understanding of the past. I would even not hesitate to say that all real progress that has been made in the history of historical writing in the course of the centuries somehow or somewhere had its origins in the ethical or political standards that were, either knowingly or unwittingly, adopted by the great and influential historians of the past.

But, as we all know in our age of automobiles, of TV sets and transistor radios, what may be a blessing under certain circumstances may easily be worse than a curse under others. And so it is with ethical and political values in historical writing. They may at times have contributed immeasurably to the advancement of historical learning, but on other occasions they have proven to be the most effective and insurmountable barrier to historical enlightenment. And it is precisely because ethical, political (and, even more obviously, cognitive) values are so inextricably tied up with historical writing that they could have led to what is both the best and the worst in the discipline's past. In order to preserve the best and discard the worst, it will be necessary (as I have argued) to develop a philosophical microscope that will enable us to see what exactly goes on where the finest ramifications of historical discourse and of ethical and political discourse meet, and where they get entangled with each other. As we have seen, a theory of the nature of historical representation will present us with the required philosophical microscope.

Looking at historical writing through this microscope of historical representation, we discovered, first, the logical priority of the aesthetic criteria of representational adequacy to criteria of what is right from an ethical and political point of view. The reassuring insight to be derived from this has been that we may trust the discipline in how it will, in the long run, succeed in dealing with ethical and political values and in making them subservient to its own purposes.

We discovered, second, that we may safely assign to history the most important and responsible task of distinguishing recommendable from objectionable moral and political values—obviously a task that history can adequately perform only if we are not scared off by the manifest presence of these values in historical writing. And we need not be scared off by this presence, since aesthetics is the stronger partner in the interaction between the criteria of aesthetic success and those of what is ethically, politically, or cognitively right. Though there is one all-important exception to this rule: aesthetics can only perform this function if freedom of speech and of discussion about the past are completely and unconditionally guaranteed. So *this* moral requirement is the *conditio sine qua non* of all that I have argued in this chapter. But the supremely important role that is played by *this* moral value is not in contradiction with what I have been saying about the regime of the aesthetic versus the cognitive and the normative: for though this value guarantees the indispensable *multiplication* of narrative representations, it does not tell us how to *evaluate* them.

PART II

HISTORICAL CONSCIOUSNESS

3

GIBBON AND OVID:
HISTORY AS METAMORPHOSIS

"Many experiments were made before I could hit the middle tone between a dull chronicle and a rhetorical declamation: three times did I compose the first chapter, and twice the second and the third, before I was tolerably satisfied with their effect."[1] Thus Gibbon in his *Autobiography* about the genesis of his *Decline and Fall of the Roman Empire*, the book that would assure him his fame as a historian down to the present day. Indeed, few historians have paid more attention to their style and the "effect" that it might have on the reader than Gibbon did. Gibbon had the habit of reciting his sentences aloud in order to test the rhythm of his language, he fully exploited all the possibilities of suggestion and persuasion given by alliteration and he saw to it that the majestic flow of his prose would be experienced by the reader as a textual mimesis of the immeasurable grandeur of the course of the events that he chose to narrate in his book. Like many other eighteenth-century historians, Gibbon was fully aware that style is not merely a matter of presentation but also determines the content of narrative.[2] "The style of an author should be the image of his mind,"[3] wrote Gibbon in a way that may call to mind Buffon's well-known dictum; that is to say, style expresses the personality of the historian and the nature of his personality will define his conception of the past and so the content of his story.

Not surprisingly, therefore, Gibbon's style has been much discussed by historiographers. One may distinguish between two approaches to Gibbon's style. The more customary approach is to focus on his irony. In fact, almost all studies devoted to *Decline and Fall* consider the all-pervasive irony of Gibbon's writing to be an important clue to the secrets of his texts. An example is Peter Gay's perceptive essay on Gibbon, where he demonstrates how the figure of irony links style and content in Gibbon's historical writing.[4] Hayden White's influential *Metahistory*—to take another example—likewise argued that style, more specifically, the tropes favored by the historian, give expression to his most fundamental assumptions about the nature of historical reality.[5] Elaborating this assumption for Gibbon, White also came to the conclusion that irony is Gibbon's master trope. And Gibbon's most recent biographer, David Womersley added that "Gibbon is famous as an ironist; but it should by now be apparent that, even when one can discern no ironic *tone*, the prose of volume 1 of *The Decline and Fall* tends to be ironic in its creation of a disingenuous relationship between writer and reader."[6] Here Gibbon is the eighteenth-century gentleman, expatiating on the crimes and follies in the history of mankind with the tongue-in-cheek irony in which only the Enlightenment historian could and so much liked to indulge.

However, there is another, less conventional approach to the historian's text that urges us to concentrate on the nature of narrative—its genre, focus, voice, and so on—rather than on matters of style. Leo Braudy, for example, has brilliantly shown that Gibbon, whose admiration for Fielding was as deep as it was sincere,[7] saw in the latter's novels a model worthy of imitation for the narrative organization of his own history. "Fielding's benevolent judge, and Fielding's whimsical but controlling novelist-historian"[8] fascinated Gibbon so much that, when writing *Decline and Fall*, he tried, insofar as his subject matter would allowed it, to write from the same kind of perspective as did the narrator of *Tom Jones*. Such is the essence of Braudy's argument.

Like Braudy I shall not discuss in this chapter Gibbon's tropology, but concentrate on the narrative structure of *Decline and Fall* and, more specifically, on the features that it shares with a classical author whom Gibbon admired just as deeply as Fielding: I want to demonstrate in this chapter the similarities between *Decline and Fall* and Ovid's *Metamorphoses*. I hasten to add that I do not claim that Gibbon actually took the *Metamorphoses* as his literary model: though Gibbon was a no less eager reader of the *Metamorphoses* than so many of his contemporaries, there is no evidence that Gibbon ever seriously considered it an appropriate model for his own scholarly enterprise. My thesis is merely that a comparison of Gibbon and Ovid may illuminate some characteristics of Gibbon's text that will remain obscure as long as we are unaware of what these two authors have in common. Comparisons like these can be enlightening even when imitation was not deliberately intended by the author whose work we wish to understand, and ever since Barthes it has often been argued that reference to an unnoticed stylistic *basso continuo* may sometimes give us access to deeper levels of meaning than if we merely would restrict our analysis to the manifest literary intentions of an author.

NARCISSUS'S FATE AND THE FALL OF ROME

I shall begin with a material similarity. No doubt the story of Narcissus, if only because of its role in contemporary psychoanalysis and, more generally, in our contemporary "culture of Narcissism," is one of the best known of all the metamorphoses that are related by Ovid in his book—though the metamorphosis of Daphne or Midas may also come to mind here. Anyway, we all know the sad story of how the nymph Echo fell in love with the beautiful youth and how she was handicapped in her effort to reveal to Narcissus the true nature of her feelings. For, like the historian, Echo could only echo what had already been said, and, once again like the historian, Echo was condemned to repetition and inaction and because of this found herself effectively prevented from a union with the object of her strong desire. Repetition and imitation (and we might add inaction to the list) are both the grandeur and the inevitable shortcoming of history; they are what we expect historians to achieve, but precisely their success in being echoes of the past irrevocably puts the past beyond our reach. For the more the historian's story is an acceptable substitute for the past itself, the less reason do we have to value the past itself. Good substitutes, good "echoes," tend to make us oblivious of that for which they are substitutes. Echo's unhappy fate is therefore an invitation to reflect on the historian's predicament in his relationship to the past. Moreover, this theme of the misfortunes of imitation and representation is reiterated in the story of Narcissus's falling in love with his own image. From this perspective it surely is no coincidence that it was Echo who fell in love with Narcissus, and we may admire Ovid's wisdom in presenting Echo as Narcissus's adorer in this metamorphose. For the misfortunes of both originated in the treacherous traps of imitation and representation: Echo was incapable of any initiative since she could only repeat (represent) the words of others while Narcissus's misfortune originated in his desire of himself via a representation of himself. And we may say that historians always have to discover the right balance between merely echoing the past (like Echo), and the other extreme of becoming fascinated by their own image as it is reflected by the past (as was the case with Narcissus). The story of Narcissus is therefore, apart from its other meanings, also an allegory of the problems occasioned by historical writing, and so this metamorphosis is particularly relevant to a comparison of the *Metamorphoses* to *The Decline and Fall of the Roman Empire*.

When Narcissus was born his mother asked the prophetic seer Tiresias whether the boy would live to a ripe old age, and the latter replied: "Yes, if he does not come to know himself"[9]—which, as we know, he did. Wishing to quench his thirst with the clear water of a spring, Narcissus fell in love with the reflection of his own face in the water and at the same time realized the impossibility of satisfying this love:

"My distress is all the greater," he sighed, "because it is not a mighty ocean that separates us, nor yet highways or mountains, or city-walls with close-barred gates. Only a little water keeps us apart. My love himself desires to be embraced: for when I lean forward to kiss the clear waters he lifts up his face to mine and strives to reach me. You would think he could be reached—it is such a small thing that hinders our love. Whoever you are, come out to me. Oh boy beyond compare, why do you elude me?"[10]

Unable to bear this torture any longer, and incapable of living with this love doomed to eternal frustration, Narcissus now gradually wasted away "as golden wax melts with the gentle heat, as morning frosts are thawed by the warmth of the sun."[11] So in this most peculiar manner Tiresias's prophecy was fulfilled. And it was precisely at the moment of his metamorphosis into the flower bearing his name that Echo, who had closely watched all that happened with desperation, became unusually explicit: "Woe is me for the boy I loved in vain," was Narcissus's last sigh—and for the first time Echo could properly express her own feelings by fully echoing Narcissus's exclamation. Hence, only at the moment that the object of her love becomes unattainable forever does she succeed in repeating Narcissus's lamentations from beginning to end. Similarly, historians can only be articulate and adequate to their task when the object of their story is no more and when their "echoes" can therefore become more real than the past itself.

In fact, this is a near to perfect parable of Gibbon's account of the causes contributing to Rome's fall. Assessing the reign of Diocletian, Gibbon observes:

Like the modesty affected by Augustus, the state maintained by Diocletian was a theatrical representation; but it must be confessed, that of the two comedies, the former was of a much more liberal and manly character than the latter. It was the aim of the former to disguise, and the object of the other to display, the unbounded power which the emperors possessed over the Roman world.[12]

This passage suggests what was, in Gibbon's opinion, the *vitium originis* of imperial Rome. Rome became a "theatrical representation," a reflection or copy of its original self. It was Augustus who had been the first to transform Rome into a political construction that carefully respected all the outward appearances of republican Rome, and who therefore initiated the process that would gradually transform Rome into a lifeless representation or imitation of its own former self. Augustus and his successors, precisely the best and most perceptive among his successors, looked into the spring of republican Rome and fell in love with the self-image that they discovered on the surface of its waters. Like Narcissus, Rome, in the successive persons of its most constructive emperors, was fascinated by its own image, and it was Rome's love of itself that destined it to the same fate as Narcissus. For owing to this lust of imitation, all authenticity disappeared, "the fire of genius was extinguished and even military spirit evaporated."[13] From then on Rome was no longer inspired by the republican virtues, from then on "men of their own accord, without threat of punishment, without laws, [no longer] maintained good faith and did what was right"—to borrow from Ovid's description of the Golden Age in book 1. Rome had become a mere construction with which the citizen could no longer identify himself. The citizen "sunk in the languid indifference of private life" and the pleasures of private life were now valued above the participation in public and political debate.[14] If republican Rome had almost naturally sprung from the "patriotism" inspiring its citizens, from Augustus onward an elaborate administrative machinery was gradually developed—and had to be developed—in order to substitute for this evanescence of patriotism and republicanism.

The infatuation of Rome with its own image, the desire to save Rome in its most difficult predicaments by the desperate attempt to breathe life and energy into a mere representation of republican Rome, would reach its culmination point in the reign of Julian the Apostate. No emperor was more intent upon restoring Rome to its former greatness, and no emperor was more serious in his attempt to resuscitate the traditional, "manly" virtues of pre-Augustan, republican Rome—and yet his reign was disastrous. Precisely this explains why Gibbon found it so hard to present his readers with a well-balanced final judgment of Julian's short career as emperor, why he wrestled with the story of this emperor more than any other, and why his account of Julian's reign became far longer than that of any other emperor. Gibbon's story of Julian is, in fact, what Paul de Man would have described as "the point of indecision" in his account of Rome's fall. For on the one hand, Gibbon admires republican Rome no less than Julian did, but on the other hand, he is well aware that no "theatrical representation" can actually replace what it represents. This becomes clear when we see how Gibbon applies the representation metaphor to Julian. Discussing Julian's plans to reform Rome, he writes: "But if these imaginary plans of reformation had been realized, the forced and imperfect copy would have been less beneficial to Paganism, than honourable to Christianity."[15] It is ironic that imitating republican Rome, far from resulting in a return to republican purity, would instead only benefit Christianity, that archenemy of what Gibbon throughout his book describes as "the Genius of the Empire." And the disasters with which Julian's short reign ended prove the soundness of this view. The paradox, therefore, is that Julian was the worst of the Romans precisely because he was the best of them, precisely because he had best understood the nature of republican Rome and because his love of these virtues was most sincere. Insofar as we can see the emperor as the incarnation of the empire, Julian's empire had, just like Narcissus, fallen in love with itself. This was the symbolic and disastrous culmination point of the Narcissistic love that was characteristic of Rome's history from Augustus onward. Tiresias's prophecy that Narcissus would die of self-knowledge found its historiographical counterpart in Gibbon's view of the causes of Rome's fall. Narcissism, Narcissus's and Rome's infatuation with their own self-image, effected in both cases a "Spaltung der Persönlichkeit und Verlust der Identität [splitting of the personality and a loss of identity]"[16] that eliminated the possibility of all meaningful and purposive action.

Thus we may say that the cause of Rome's fall can be attributed to the propensity of some of the best Roman emperors to become, so to speak, the "historians" of republican Rome and to try to "reenact" in actual reality their historical appreciation of the ancient republic. In the attempt, a distance between Rome's original identity and its mimesis was inevitably created, and it may be argued that this distance is the source of Rome's (self)-destruction. Gossman gives us the following comment on Gibbon's conception of history:

History and civilization are in themselves a process of alienation and dispossession [hence the title of Gossman's book], by which an original, closed and self-contained being—a being that can never be found in history, however, since it is already divided by the very fact of being historical—extends outwards, multiplies, enters in contact with others, and is altered by this contact.[17]

In other words, according to Gossman, Gibbon sees in history a permanent propensity toward a Narcissistic mimesis of a previous original world, where each mimesis (or signifier) is always an alienation and a corruption of the signified in which it has its origin. And the arbitrary distance between signifier and signified allows room for all the abuses that may bring about the fall of a nation or civilization—as actually was the case with Rome. Hence, a theory of language and of the signifier's necessary inadequacy as a substitute for the signified is Gibbon's ultimate, "Narcissistic" model for his explanation of the fall of Rome.

This raises, of course, the interesting question of whether historians, and not only the Roman emperor assuming their role—are susceptible to the same kind of Narcissistic delusions as these architects of Rome's downfall. If so, that would imply the Nietzschean conclusion that all writing of history is inevitably a corruption of both historians themselves (or the historical consciousness they exemplify) and of the historical reality that is described by them. If so, historians will invariably be a kind of Narcissus, and generate in culture this same kind of "Spaltung der Persönlichkeit und Verlust der Identität" that we observed a moment ago and that had led to Narcissus's death and that had been the principal cause of Rome's destruction.

OVID'S AND GIBBON'S RESISTANCE TO TRAGEDY

There is, however, one more interesting parallel between the *Metamorphoses* and *Decline and Fall*. Galinsky draws our attention to the peculiarly "untragic" character of Ovid's *Metamorphoses*:

Most metamorphoses deal with the changing of a person into something else such as, for instance, a tree, a stone or an animal. Regardless of the way they are brought about such transformations often are not capricious but turn out to be very meaningful because they set in relief the true and everlasting character of the person involved. . . . The physical characteristics of the personages may change but their quintessential substance lives on.[18]

Thus Ovidian metamorphosis is quite unlike historical change or development: it is a return to or the revealing of an origin, rather than a development of it.

If we take the Narcissus story as an example, it is true that Narcissus's life comes to a premature and sad end (though, of course, he lived on as a flower). Nevertheless, the story does not invite us to lament Narcissus's fate or to meditate on the tragedy of the human condition as exemplified by it. We are moved by the story, but sadness is not what it effects in us. Part of the explanation lies in the purpose of the book. Ovid wishes to inform his readers what transformations the things in our world have undergone, "from the earliest beginnings of the world, down to my own times."[19] Hence, Ovid's aim is to instruct rather than to evoke pity or even to impart a moral message to his audience. The result is a peculiarly "untragic manner of narration."[20] Indeed, Ovid's narrative is playful, ironic rather than tragic, and the many stories related by him seem to take place in an idyllic and, on the whole, harmonious world that is singularly devoid of drama and pathos.

It is here that Ovid's emplotment interestingly differs from the best-known metamorphosis that has been written in our own time: Kafka's *Verwandlung*. On the one hand Gregor Samsa's tragic end seems to be foreordained right from the beginning of the story: the reader is immediately made aware of the unbridgeable gap that Gregor's metamorphosis into a beetle has created between himself and his world. A compromise between Gregor and his world is obviously unthinkable, and the reader realizes that his ultimate destruction will only be a matter of time. On the other hand, there also is something peculiarly playful and untragic about the story: Gregor does not seem to be aware of this gap, and his recognition of his metamorphosis does not rank any higher in his self-consciousness than his awareness of the weather on the fateful day of his metamorphosis or of his failure to be on time for the train he has to catch. And this is where Gregor's metamorphosis most significantly differs from those related by Ovid, despite their initial similarity. For if there is something "untragic" about the metamorphosis of Ovid's subjects, this is because their metamorphoses seem to be the logical and satisfactory fulfillment of their manifest destiny;

Gregor Samsa's metamorphosis, however, is presented by Kafka as "untragic" since this metamorphosis (and all that follows from it) seems to have nothing whatsoever to do with the person he is, nor with his deepest feelings. Gregor's personality seems to lie in a quasi-autistic self that remains completely unaffected by his metamorphosis and thereby effectively robs it of the dimension of the tragic. Nothing was lost, simply because there never was anything to lose; in Ovidian metamorphosis, however, nothing is lost because a potentiality (that had always been there) has now in fact been realized. Thus in both cases, though for entirely opposite reasons, all sense of tragedy can properly be said to be absent.[21]

We encounter the same propensity for "untragic" narrative in Gibbon's *Decline and Fall*. Needless to say, there is enough tragedy in the more than one thousand years of history that are related by Gibbon, so that if Gibbon had wished to convey to his audience the tragedy of the self-destruction of a political edifice that he himself admired so much, he would have had ample material. But just like Ovid's *carmen perpetuum*,[22] Gibbon's calmly flowing prose is free from the cataracts and whirlpools in which the dimension of the tragic manifests itself. His aversion to decisive and dramatic caesuras is illustrative; historical events are never presented by him as radical beginnings or endings in the *carmen perpetuum* of his narrative. The way he deals with the fall of the Western empire in 476 is characteristic. As Gibbon's biographer Patricia B. Craddock observes, the event "is passed over almost parenthetically"[23] and certainly does not mark the end of the third volume, as one might have expected. Rather, that volume ends with a sketch of the rise of the new kingdoms in the West, therefore effectively mitigating the tragedy of Rome's fall with the construction of new political entities. Histories overlap, and what is destruction from one point of view is construction from another. Therefore, nothing ends in 476 A.D. that had not yet ended already, and nothing began in that year that had not begun already—such is the message of Gibbon's narrative. Moreover, Gibbon's resistance to dramatic incisions induced him to give to his narrative the form of a *set* of stories rather than the unified story of one nation (e.g., Rome). For one of the most striking features of *Decline and Fall* certainly is that it so successfully avoids the temptation to see the world only from the point of view of Rome. Just as Ovid most artfully weaves together some 250 separate stories into his *Metamorphoses*, so Gibbon's history is, in fact, an intricate web of many individual stories that partly overlap and that partly have their own autonomy and are never forced into one scheme. Both Ovid's *Metamorphoses* and Gibbon's *Decline and Fall* are a *carmen perpetuum* rather than a *carmen unum*.

METAMORPHOSIS

Expounding "the teachings of Pythagoras" in the fifteenth book of the *Metamorphoses*, Ovid explains what we may consider to be his own view of change and of metamorphosis:[24] "nor does anything retain its own appearance permanently. Ever inventive nature continuously produces one shape from another. Nothing in the entire universe ever perishes, believe me, but things vary and adopt a new form."[25] Hence, the world as we presently know it is the result of an infinity of metamorphoses of an infinity of substances all functioning as the unchanging substrate of morphological change. Nothing is ever essentially (or substantially, to use the right word) new; we only encounter new forms (the new external envelopes of a substance) as the result of metamorphosis. It is quite characteristic that when Ovid discusses in book 1 how the world came into being, he makes it clear that no creation in the true sense of the word was involved but that creation was, instead, a process of separation. Initially there was a chaos in which "everything got in the way of everything else," but this strife was

finally resolved by a god, a natural force of a higher kind, who separated the earth from heaven, and the waters from the earth, and set the clear sky apart from the cloudy atmosphere. When he had freed these elements, sorting them out from the heap where they had lain, indistinguishable from one another, he bound them fast, each in its separate place, forming a harmonious union.[26]

There is no true genesis and no real change, in the sense that something develops out of something entirely different; all the "substances" out of which the world is built up have been present forever. It is only that they may present themselves in the guise of different "metamorphoses." Change—and history—only affects the external, peripheral, and contingent features of the substance.

The same picture is suggested by Ovid's account of the Four Ages, illustrative of which is his use of negations when describing the Golden Age: "no penalties to be afraid of," "no bronze tablets were erected," "no judges," "no helmets and no swords," and so on.[27] Obviously, the Golden Age can only be characterized by having recourse to the world as it presently is (that is, by negating it) and in that sense the present is already present in that remote past, and vice versa. That Ovid's world is a world whose inventory is fixed once and forever is also clear from the fact that there is no real development through the Four Ages; it is rather as if a big wheel is turning before our eyes so that different parts of the eternal and unchanging properties of the wheel gradually become visible to us from our fixed perspective. But the wheel remains as it has always been. "All things change, but nothing dies,"[28] as Ovid makes Pythagoras say; and where nothing dies, nothing is really born either. Ovid in all likelihood owed this undramatic conception of change to Posidonius, a Stoic who had quite a following in the Rome of Ovid's days. The part of Posidonius's teaching that is relevant in this context is his view that neither our physical quality nor our soul constitute our real character but that our actual substance is an unchanging nature behind these more peripheral manifestations of a person's identity.[29] Hence, Ovidian ontology presents us with a universe consisting of substances that eternally remain the same, despite the fact that their outward appearance may be subject to dramatic changes.

We encounter much the same picture in *Decline and Fall*. As in Ovid's initial chaos, all the elements that will play a role in Gibbon's narrative are there right from the beginning. It is true that the first three chapters of *Decline and Fall*, in which Gibbon presents his readers with an account of the empire in its happy days under the Antonines, is the Gibbonian equivalent of Ovid's Golden Age rather than of the initial chaos with which the latter began his story. Rome in the second century A.D., writes Gibbon, "is marked by the rare advantage of furnishing few materials for history; which is, indeed, little more than the register of the crimes, follies and misfortunes of mankind."[30] Ovid's negative characterization of the Golden Age repeats itself here in Gibbon's characterization of Rome under the Antonines in terms of the absence of the crimes, follies, and misfortunes that constitute the substance of human history.

But beneath this apparently harmonious surface lies a more complex account of the political reality of second-century Rome that announces itself already on the first page of the book. Gibbon confronts his readers there with the provocative paradox that Rome's "peaceful inhabitants enjoyed and abused the advantages of wealth and luxury."[31] In peace, harmony, the cultivation of the arts and sciences—where we would least expect them—lay the seeds of destruction, or such is his suggestion. More than any other of

Gibbon's modern commentators, Pocock has made us aware of the importance of the theme suggested by this paradox. In his magisterial *The Machiavellian Moment in the Atlantic Tradition* (1975), Pocock analyzed eighteenth-century political discourse in terms of the opposition between "court" and "country." The republican "country" tradition required the transparency of the political domain; that is to say, the active participation of the citizen in matters of government was considered essential for preventing its corruption. The state must be transparent with regard to the will of the free and politically active citizen. Freedom is thus political, positive freedom—and this freedom is the pillar on which the state rests. In fact, the state can be said to be nothing but that "pillar": the state has, or ought to have, no existence outside the minds of the citizen, inspired by republican virtue. The "court" tradition, on the contrary, is prepared to accept the autonomy and the nontransparency of the political domain; it favors representative government and recognizes the State as an entity *sui generis*, which cannot be reduced completely to the free will of the individual citizens. Within this political matrix, the adherents of the "country" tradition (called this way since it had had its most active and most characteristic supporters in the seventeenth-century gentry) saw in the "court" tradition the source of corruption, greed, and political dependence on debilitating luxury—in short, of all the evils that the good society ought to avoid.

There can be no doubt that Pocock is right when he places Gibbon firmly in the "country" tradition.[32] Indeed, it is not hard to find statements in *Decline and Fall* that confirm Pocock's view. Gibbon's adherence to the "country" tradition is illustrated by his assertion that "public virtue," called patriotism by the ancients, "is derived from a strong sense of our own interest in the preservation and prosperity of the free government of which we are members." And a loss of freedom is to be expected as soon as "war [is] gradually improved [N.B. Gibbon's irony!] into an art, and degraded into a trade."[33] And elsewhere he laments the dependency, the passion for self-enrichment, and the corruption that invariably is the consequence of the disappearance of civic, positive freedom:

Under the Roman Empire, the labour of an industrious and ingenious people was variously but incessantly employed, in the service of the rich. In their dress, their table, their houses, and their furniture, the favourites of fortune united every refinement of conveniency, of elegance and of splendour; whatever could soothe their pride or gratify their sensuality. Such refinements, under the odious name of luxury, have been severely arraigned by the moralists of every age; and it might perhaps be more conducive to the virtue, as well as the happiness of mankind, if all possessed the necessaries, and none the superfluities of life.[34]

This is, in a nutshell, the political message of the "country" tradition that Gibbon explicitly embraces in this passage.

In other words—and this is the intellectual challenge that the "country" tradition had to face and was unable to answer—all that contributes to Roman civilization, as to any other civilization, is also what contributes to its decline and its corruption. Part of Rome's greatness lay in the achievements of Roman culture, its arts and sciences, but these achievements are the no less unmistakable signs of its decline. We may observe a similar paradox in Ovid when he carefully avoids the Augustan theme of the eternity of Rome, as we find it, for example, in the beginning of the *Aeneid*, when Virgil has Jupiter declare: "his ego nec metas rerum nec tempora pono; imperium sine fine dedi [to Romans I set no boundary in space or time; I have granted them dominion, and it has no end]."[35] An equally indicative example of Ovid's reticence with regard to the Augustan age is his rejection of the topos, common in his days, of equating that age with the Golden Age: and

What else could be concluded from this than that this is an expression of Ovid's dissatisfaction with his own time. True enough, there are also places where Ovid fully embraces his time. But he then has in mind its culture and standard of life and never its moral and political condition.[36]

So both Gibbon and Ovid (and here they are in agreement with several other classical historians) are aware of the dangers of culture and of the fact that the arts and sciences may fatally weaken a civilization.

STOICISM AND METAMORPHOSIS

Having finally arrived at this stage, we may begin to reap the fruits of our comparison of Ovid and Gibbon. Above all, we should realize that Gibbon did not write the *Bildungsroman* of Rome; such would be the past's model only for the German historist historians of a later generation, who typically wanted to present their readers with the edifying picture of the gradual development and the gradual unfolding of a nation or culture. Gibbon's narrative is free from the kind of substantial change that was always at stake in historist historical writing: Gibbon presents us with the *metamorphoses* that Rome underwent in the course of more than one thousand years of history. That is to say, in contrast to historist historical writing, the essence, or the substance, of the subject of his *carmen perpetuum* invariably remains the same in spite of all the dramatic changes that transformed Rome from the world's master into a Byzantine empire that was to go through a protracted agony of some thousand years. We have every reason to be surprised by the suggestion that such a sad deterioration can take place without substantial change; but don't we have even more reason for wonder that the metamorphosis of human beings into stars, trees, and rivers involves no substantial change?

Perhaps we may even discern here the unparalleled narrative potential of the metamorphosis as a literary form; and if at first sight we now consider Gibbon's narrative to be unconvincing, it is primarily because the triumph of historist, evolutionist narrative has made us forgetful of the powers of the literary convention that preceded it. More specifically, we can only dream now about the historical accounts that might be given of Western history if they were modeled on Ovidian and Gibbonian metamorphosis. "The return of the repressed" that is so much a feature of contemporary European history and that does not fit within historist, evolutionary models could be plausibly accounted for within the Gibbonian model. Historist models of historical change, by contrast, will not permit the idea of the persistence of an unchanging essence that remains untouched by even the most dramatic historical metamorphoses, and they will leave us empty-handed when we wish to account for them. Generally speaking, the literary model of the metamorphosis is ideally suited for rendering justice to both the synchronic and the diachronic aspects of the past. Here lies its decisive advantage over the kind of historical writing to which we have become accustomed. One might argue that it was precisely this fact that made the Burckhardt of *Die weltgeschichtliche Betrachtungen* (1905; Force and freedom: Reflections on history) see in the past a continuous metamorphosis in the relationship between state, church, and culture, rather than the modernist metanarratives that are presupposed by historist historical writing. And if we would agree with Gossman that Burckhardt seems both to anticipate and transcend the tensions between modernism and postmodernism by sidestepping the polarization between past and present presupposed by both positions, we have in our "post-postmodernist" age every reason to be interested in Ovidian metamorphosis as a model for historical change.

The structural similarities between Ovid's and Gibbon's narratives can be explained by their shared Stoicism. Though Ovid had no philosophical pretensions and the philosophy that is implied by the *Metamorphoses* has correctly been described as "a mixed bag,"[37] we can certainly agree with Galinsky's claim that Ovid's metamorphoses in several respects betray the Stoic influences of Posidonius. Stoic panlogism, with its conception of the *logoi spermatikoi*, the unchanging rational principles that constitute the essence of the cosmos in its many manifestations, is undoubtedly the ontology that is suggested by the *Metamorphoses*. Next, with regard to Gibbon, we should recall that Gibbon, as an exponent of Enlightenment historical writing, accepted without reservation the weltanschuung of natural law philosophy. And as has been pointed out by many historians since Dilthey, seventeenth- and eighteenth-century natural law philosophy can well be seen as a continuation of Stoic ontology. Thus the conception of a universe consisting of entities essentially remaining the same during change is the ontological intuition that is shared by Stoicism, the stories that Ovid tells us, and lastly, by Gibbon's narrative of the history of Rome.

FINALLY: ONTOLOGY AND TRUTH

Moreover, there is a striking similarity between the ways that Ovid and Gibbon adapted Stoic ontology in order to make it fit their narrative purposes. In both cases external, peripheral causes effect a change in the substance so that its true nature can reveal itself. In Ovid the cause of the metamorphosis is typically merely accidental and could, in principle, be exchanged for another cause (a striking exception, as we have seen, is the encounter between Echo and Narcissus). Yet, it is as if these accidental causes "trigger" an internal, substantial cause that determines the nature and the outcome of the metamorphosis. The same causal pattern is found in Gibbon's *Decline and Fall*. Having come to the end of his work, Gibbon observes: "in the preceding volumes of this history, I have described the triumph of barbarism and religion."[38] Undoubtedly barbarism and Christian religion are presented in his work as the causes of Rome's fall; yet we must note that these causes are external in the sense that they did not originate within Rome itself, but only affected it, so to speak, "from the outside." And this certainly is part of Gibbon's analysis—no one could plausibly disagree with this summary that Gibbon himself gave of his work.

However, in the "General Observations" that conclude chapter 38 Gibbon reflects as follows on the deeper causes of Rome's destruction:

> The rise of a city, which swelled into an Empire, may deserve, as a singular prodigy the reflection of a philosophic mind. But the decline of Rome was the natural and inevitable effect of immoderate greatness. Prosperity ripened the principle of decay; the causes of destruction multiplied with the extent of conquest; and as soon as time or accident had removed the artificial supports, the stupendous fabric yielded to the pressure of its own weight. The story of its ruin is simple, and obvious; and instead of inquiring *why* the Roman Empire was destroyed, we should rather be surprised that it subsisted so long.[39]

After having been touched by a magic wand as it were—by barbarism and Christian religion—Rome underwent a metamorphosis that would reveal its true nature. Thus in a certain sense the ultimate truth about Rome *is* its more-than-thousand-year-long agony—including the history of the Byzantine empire—and it is only befitting that Gibbon decided to tell us *that* history and not, for example, the history of the triumphant republic. No less to the point is Gibbon's statement that the question of *why* Rome fell is, in the end, less interesting than the question of how Rome could subsist so long. For the fact of Rome's metamorphosis is, in itself, sufficient explanation of its fate; and as always with metamorphosis, the only enlightenment we may expect from historians is simply the *story* that they can tell us of the metamorphosis. More that that one cannot do—and it is all we need.

But this can be elaborated. We need not be satisfied with the insight that prolonged agony is the final truth about Rome. The true statement inevitably creates a gap between itself and what it is about. When discussing the similarities between Ovid's story of Narcissus and Gibbon's story of Rome, we found that for Gibbon, this distance, this gap between the sign and the signified (in Gossman's terminology), between truth and what it is true of, is the gap in which republican virtue and Rome's greatness were lost. It was self-knowledge (as Tiresias had prophesied) that decided Narcissus's death; likewise, the search for truth about Rome (as best exemplified by Julian) occasioned an alienation from truth and what truth is true about, and in this alienation all the evils originated that would lead to Rome's destruction. So, in the final analysis, historical truth is what this chapter has been about all along, and in this "metamorphosis" of the topic of my exposition we may situate the affinities between Ovid and Gibbon.

4

THE DIALECTICS OF NARRATIVIST HISTORISM

> Historism is not just a bright idea, it is not a fashion, it is not even an intellectual movement, it is nothing less than the foundation from which we must consider our social and cultural reality. It is not an artificial contrivance, it is not a program, but the organically grown basis, the *Weltanschauung* itself that came into being after the dissolution of the medieval religious conception of the world and of its secularized Enlightenment successor with its notion of an eternal and time-transcendent reason.[1]

According to historism the nature of a thing lies in its history. If we wish to grasp the nature of a nation, a people, an institution, or an idea, the historist requires us to consider its historical development. And it is no different with historism itself. Discussions about the nature of historism therefore tend to turn into discussions of how historism developed out of Enlightened historical writing. Two accounts are given of this genesis of historism. According to the first account, historism is the result of a historicization of the ahistorist conception of social and political reality that was adopted by eighteenth-century natural law philosophy. This is the account ordinarily proposed by historists themselves and codified in Meinecke's *Die Entstehung des Historismus* (The rise of historism) and in the brilliant essay on historism that Mannheim wrote in 1924.[2] In the other account, it is pointed out that during the Enlightenment historical writing was seen as "literature," that it was taught by professors of rhetoric and that historism reacted to this literary conception of historical writing by advocating a *Ent-rhetorisierung und Versachlichung des historischen Denkens* ("substitution of rhetoric by fact in historical thought")—to use Rüsen's terms.[3] This alternative account was originally developed by Anglo-Saxon theorists such as White, Reill, Gossman, Bann, and Megill, and now also inspires a good deal of contemporary German debate about the genesis of historism.

We thus have two alternative accounts of the genesis of historism that are so entirely different that we cannot believe that both could be true. What separates the two accounts is their picture of Enlightened historical writing and its theoretical assumptions. What could natural law philosophy, with its love of rational argument, of proceeding *more geometrico*, and its affinities with what we now know as the social sciences, possibly have to do with rhetoric and literature? Surely, one of these two accounts *must* be profoundly mistaken. I want to demonstrate, however, that the two accounts *are* compatible and that the recognition of this compatibility furthers our insight not only into the nature of historism but also into what is at stake in the contemporary theoretical debate that in many ways continues the debate between historism and Enlightened natural-law philosophy. My argument to that effect will proceed in three steps. In the first place, I shall propose an abstract, rational argument in favor of the compatibility of the two accounts; in the second place, I shall resume in a few, necessarily short remarks the analysis that was presented in the previous chapter about Gibbon's *The Decline and Fall of the Roman Empire*, the book that may well be seen as the supreme achievement of Enlightenment historical writing. In the third place, I hope to show the relevance of my argument for contemporary theoretical debate.

THE STATEMENT AS MODEL FOR ENLIGHTENMENT HISTORICAL WRITING

If we wish to grasp the nature of Enlightenment historical writing, we must realize that it took the true statement as its model; the ontology presupposed by Enlightened historical writing is the ontology suggested by the true statement. The true statement consists of two parts: the subject-term, which typically refers to an object in reality, and the predicate-term attributing a property to that object. The ontology that is suggested by the statement is therefore that of a world consisting of a totality of objects, all more or less remaining the same, while acquiring or losing certain properties in the course of their histories. Two consequences follow from this account of the ontology of the statement. First, the model of the statement invites us to accept the kind of substantialism that we find in natural-law philosophy;

that is, the assumption that reality is made up of entities essentially remaining the same in the course of time. We may think here of our notion of a universe consisting of things like mountains, rivers, stones, chairs, or pieces of organic material. These things may change in the course of time because of causes external to them. So the ontology of the statement by no means excludes change, even radical change. Only, when change occurs, we should always be able to identify, as is also the case, an unchanging subject of change to which change can be ascribed. As we have seen in the previous chapter, this was feasible even in the case of the dramatic metamorphosis of a beautiful adolescent into a flower.

Second, change can be explained with the help of the language of causality. For the language of causality always presupposes an object whose changes are the effects of causes external to those objects themselves. In sum, accepting the ontology of the statement will give us the substantialism characteristic of natural-law philosophy and will, secondly, predispose us to use the language of cause and effect. And this is, in a nutshell, how Enlightened historical writing conceived of the historical world.

But this is only part of the story. We may well wonder where to draw the demarcation line between what belongs to the substance of an object and its contingent properties changing in the course of time. Even more so, as Locke already realized, all our intuitions about what still does belong and what no longer belongs to the substance will in the end prove to be arbitrary.[4] And here we may discover what one might call the dialectics of Enlightenment historical writing. This dialectics has a double origin. First, as Locke's own argument suggests, there is no fixed demarcation line between the substance itself and what is merely contingent to it, and we shall, in practice, be unable to tell where the substance ends and where what is merely peripheral begins. Second, within the ontology expounded just now, cause and effect are restricted to what is merely peripheral to the substance itself. Moving a chair or spilling ink on it can be explained with the language of cause and effect but remains peripheral to that chair itself, or its "substance." However, the most eligible cause will always be the cause that is *least* peripheral and *closest* to the substance: peripheral causes will tend to remain mere necessary conditions, whereas causes close to the substance can claim to become sufficient causes. For example, if we decide to have the chair reupholstered because of the ink that was spilled on it, the relevant actions of the upholsterer are a more satisfactory explanation (i.e., an explanation in terms of sufficient rather than merely necessary causes) of its partial metamorphosis than our decision to take the chair to the upholsterer. If, then, we combine these two facts about the ontology of natural-law philosophy, we will understand that within this ontology there will be a permanent and persistent urge to invite causal language to invade the domain of the substance. For it is only in that domain that "deeper" and not merely peripheral causes can be given for the phenomena studied by the historian.

However, if one actually surrenders to this dialectics of Enlightenment historical writing, if the historian is actually tempted to enter the domain of the substance, we will have moved outside the domain where the language of cause and effect can properly be used. As soon as cause and effect enter the domain of substance, the substance is no longer the passive substratum separating causes from their effects and thus enabling us to tell them apart; effects now become part of their causes, and vice versa, and since both have now lost themselves in the substance, the substance may now present itself as the cause of its own effects and, hence, of its own history.

Two further conclusions can be derived from this. First, if effects have become part of their causes, and vice versa, each attempt to separate them will have become arbitrary. And this means that the consistency of the use of causal language has its guarantees no longer in a (historical) reality outside language, but only in the historian's language itself. Not facts about the past, but the rhetorical vigor of the historian's text is now the exclusive basis for the consistency of that text. This, then, may show us why these two accounts of what is involved in the transition from Enlightenment to historist historical writing, which I contrasted in the Introduction, can both be correct despite their apparent incompatibility.

The second conclusion is that we can be more specific about the nature of the kind of rhetoric to be favored by Enlightenment historical writing. If the regime that customarily governs the language of cause and effect is abrogated—as is the case here—we will enter a world that is defined by the trope of irony. For it is essential for irony to ironize our intuitions about the relationship between cause and effect. Irony is therefore the master trope of Enlightenment historical writing.

We find all this, as it were in a pure culture, in Gibbon's *Decline and Fall*, that undisputed *chef d'oeuvre* of Enlightenment historical writing. To begin with, we must observe that the story of the history of a "substance" will be a narrative without beginning or ending and without incisive caesuras. The permanent presence of the unchanging substance excludes origins, terminations, and radical discontinuities. And precisely this is what determines the structure of *Decline and Fall*. The three opening chapters give a description of the empire in the second century A.D., its military power, its prosperity and its constitution in the age of the Antonines. Two features of this way of beginning the book must be observed. First, this is not the beginning of a story informing us about some development in historical time: the argument here is synchronic and not diachronic. It might be objected, however, that no historical narrative can be convincing that does not start with some such sketch of the background against which the story will unfold itself. But if this narrative strategy is adopted and is to succeed, the background must be related to the story itself in the way we may relate a plant to the soil from which it grows. And that brings me to my second observation: this is precisely what Gibbon wishes to avoid. Discussing the reign of Antoninus Pius, Gibbon comments: "His reign is marked by the rare advantage of furnishing very few materials for history; which is, indeed, little more than the register of the crimes, follies and misfortunes of mankind."[5] The happy days of the empire under the Antonines are thus, so to speak, "lifted out" of the history that Gibbon wishes to tell us: they are placed outside the realm of (narratable) history in the proper sense of the word and for that very same reason we have no beginning in the proper sense of the word.

A similar story can be told for the end of *Decline and Fall*. As every new reader of *Decline and Fall* finds out to his surprise, the book does not end with the fall of the Western empire, or even with the reigns of Theodoric and Justinian, but only with the fall of the Eastern empire in 1453. Yet, as Gibbon repeatedly emphasizes, the nature of his account of the decline and fall of the Roman empire suggests nowhere the necessity of including the history of Byzantium in his enterprise. Thus Gibbon himself candidly states in his *Autobiography*: "So flexible is the title of my *History*, that the final era could be fixed at my own choice: and I long hesitated whether I should be content with the first three volumes, the fall of the Western empire, which fulfilled my first engagement with the public."[6] But even the year 1453 does not fix the end of Gibbon's narrative. Not only are there many substantial references to the history of the West in the fifteenth and the sixteenth centuries; more importantly, the books ends with a history of the city of Rome from the twelfth century.[7] Lastly, if Gibbon's narrative avoids beginnings and endings, it no less resists the effort of periodization that ordinarily structures historical narrative and even seems a condition for its very intelligibility.[8] No reader of *Decline and Fall* can fail to be struck by Gibbon's provocative minimization of the significance of the deposition of Romulus Augustulus as the last emperor of the Western empire in 476 A.D. (that was already mentioned in the previous chapter). On the one hand, in agreement with a periodization already generally accepted in Gibbon's time, he observes that Romulus's reign marked "the extinction of the Roman empire in the West,"[9] but on the other, the event is presented as just one more of the tedious *faits divers* of that chaotic epoch. Moreover, Gibbon skillfully discourages our inclination to assign any historical significance to the event by demonstrating the relative successes of the reign of Odoacer, "king of Italy," whose victories seemed to repeat, at least to a certain extent, the triumphs of republican Rome.[10] And in the contextualization of this period Gibbon carefully avoids suggesting any alternative periodization of the more than one thousand years of history that he is telling us.

Let us now turn to causality. Two levels must be distinguished here. On the first and more superficial level we find the causal explanation of the fall of the empire that is best summarized by Gibbon himself when he writes in the last chapter of his book: "In the preceding volumes of this history, I have described the triumph of barbarism and religion."[11] "Barbarism" and "Christian religion" are presented here as the kind of external, "peripheral" causes that we may expect in a history sharing the substantialist assumptions of the Enlightenment. However—and this is crucial for my argument—when asking himself in his "general observations" added to chapter 38 what is to be seen as the *deepest* cause of Rome's fall, Gibbon writes that the key for answering this question is to be found in Rome itself.[12] It is true that Rome was destined to conquer the world, but it was no less true that this would also mean its death. For though Rome succeeded in vanquishing all its enemies and rivals, it was incapable of mastering itself. The greater it became, the less it succeeded in controlling its ever growing empire, and the more imminent its death became. So in the end it was crushed under the very burden of its own conquests. Success thus contained the seeds of decay, prosperity the seeds of decline, virtue the seeds of corruption and of moral disintegration, and artistic excellence the seeds of degeneration. So each step Rome made toward greatness was, at the same time a step in the direction of its ultimate destruction. Both, greatness and destruction, were indelibly inscribed and most intimately tied together in the heart—or rather, in the *substance*—of that greatest of all empires.

Obviously, in agreement with the relevant tendencies of Enlightenment historical writing, Gibbon enters here the domain of the substance:[13] Rome is presented here as being the cause of its own decline. The empire succumbed to the pressure of its own weight, and the conditions of its rise were also the conditions of its ultimate fall. This may also explain Gibbon's puzzling statement that we should not ask why the empire was destroyed but rather focus on the subsidiary question of the date of its ultimate demise: Rome's fall is part of its "substance" and the really interesting question is when and why this potentiality was to be activated. Neither should it surprise us that Gibbon's explanation of Rome's fall is the same as the one given by his Enlightened predecessor, Montesquieu,[14] nor that both Montesquieu and Gibbon appealed to the strangely helpless metaphor of a "poison" that was introduced "into the vitals of the empire."[15] For in both cases the search for the "deepest" and ultimate causes of Rome's fall resulted in an invasion of the domain of substance by the language of cause and effect and in the peculiar conclusion that in the use of that language Rome's rise and greatness becomes indistinguishable from its decline and dissolution.

The paradox of Rome having been the cause of its own fall will explain the propensity for paradox, irony, and ambivalence that is so clearly present in Gibbon's rhetoric—as in most of Enlightenment historical writing. As soon as the language of cause and effect enters the domain of the substance, there will be nothing, outside the text itself, that can govern or check its use. Gibbon was aware of this himself, as may become clear from an annotation that he wrote a few years before his death in the margin of his own copy of *Decline and Fall*: "Should I not have deduced the decline of the Empire from the Civil Wars, that ensued after the fall of Nero or even from the tyranny which succeeded the reign of Augustus? Alas! I should: but of what avail is this tardy knowledge? Where error is irretrievable, repentance is useless."[16] Cause and effect can now roam more or less freely through the whole of the history of the Roman empire since their cooperation is presented as part of the unchanging *substance* of the empire; and what has been a cause of Rome's greatness can now equally be seen as a cause of its decline. As a result, the relation between the actions of historical agents and their results is now systematically ironized. The apparent saviors of the empire in its most difficult predicament, emperors like Augustus,

Diocletian, Constantine, and Julian the Apostate, can now be presented as its most effective grave diggers as well.

FROM THE ENLIGHTENMENT TO HISTORISM

We now have obtained a vantage point that is ideally suited for assessing what was at stake in the transition from Enlightened to historist historical writing—a transition that has determined to a large extent the nature both of historical writing and of historical theory down to the present day. We have seen in the foregoing that the ontology of the statement is a good heuristic instrument for comprehending why natural-law philosophy and rhetoric were and had to be so intimately related in Enlightened historical writing. On the one hand, the constative statement and the kind of knowledge expressed by it may seem hostile to metaphysics. The statement gives us empirical knowledge of the world, and this is why it may seem that the constative statement gives us knowledge of the world not tainted by metaphysics. And this is why contemporary protagonists of a "scientific historical writing," of "Geschichte als Sozialwissenschaft," have often felt a nostalgia for Enlightenment historical writing and why they were tempted to characterize the birth of historism as a *Verlustgeschichte*, a history of loss, to quote Rüsen.[17]

On the other hand, as Nietzsche already surmised and as was demonstrated by Strawson in his *Individuals: An Essay in Descriptive Metaphysics*,[18] the constative statement suggests the metaphysics of a universe consisting of unchanging entities whose properties may vary in the course of time—in short, the kind of metaphysics that was embraced by natural-law philosophy. In Enlightenment historical writing this paradox of an antimetaphysical metaphysics was resolved by rhetoric. Language and its rhetorical potentialities were now enlisted to reflect the processes of historical change that effectively defied the parameters of the ontology of the statement. And precisely this was Gibbon's paradoxical predicament when he wanted to explain to his readers how the substance or, as he called it himself, the "genius" of the Roman empire at one time or another disappeared from the inventory of historical entities. Rhetoric had to fill the void created by the gradual disappearance of that particular substance.

The ontology of the statement is a no less useful heuristic tool for measuring the achievement of historism and for appreciating the intellectual courage displayed by the first historians. What historism effected was a historicization of the substance. For the historists, historical change could not be restricted to what is merely peripheral; indeed, "substantial" change was seen as the true domain of historical research and in this way Gibbon's aporia was now provocatively transformed into historism's most cherished and valuable insight. Within this new and more comprehensive conception of historical change, the ontology of the statement is no longer adequate. We can now no longer trust that what the subject-term in the constative statement refers to will "substantially" remain the same object during a process of historical change. Thus, contrary to what the logical structure of the statement may suggest, the subject-term in one statement on the Roman empire may refer to a "substantially" different entity than a statement on the Roman empire at a different phase of its history. So instead of a set of statements all sharing a subject-term referring to the same entity, we now have a set of statements whose shared subject-term should never tempt us to believe that in all cases reference is made to one and the same historical entity. What we have now is, in fact, a set of statements with different subject-terms (if we recognize that the literal sameness of the subject-terms is misleading); in short, a set of statements in principle as disjunct as any set of statements arbitrarily put together. This may explain why, in the transition from Enlightened to historist historical writing, coherence, or *Zusammenhang*, suddenly became an issue of such great urgency and importance for both history and historical theory. Coherence and *Zusammenhang* now had to provide the historist historian with a substitute for the coherence that was still unproblematically granted to the historian accepting the assumptions of natural law philosophy.

Notions like "the Roman empire" now became deeply problematic: Can we use it, for example, only to refer to republican Rome? Or perhaps it refers only to the period before Diocletian? And the framing of such questions will depend on whether the unity suggested by the term can still be supported by a coherent narrative of the relevant part of the past. The rhetorical power of Gibbon's narrative was now exchanged for the coherence of narrative. Admittedly, the historist constitution of narrative coherence is an addition to the mere recital of fact no less than Enlightenment rhetoric had been; but what the historist makes historical language do is significantly different from what Enlightenment historians (such as Gibbon) did with language. What Enlightenment historical language adds to the facts of the past could never go beyond language itself; it will always remain a mere rhetorical play of language with language. There is, hence, no real interaction between the historian's language and the past. But the historist use of language also involves the substance of the past itself in how it represents the past by historicizing substance and by thus making historical substance itself into an issue in (rational) historical debate. Historical language here truly becomes a (linguistic) instrument for exploring, explaining, and clarifying the past. Historism succeeded in bringing about this most remarkable feat thanks to a movement that we could best summarize as a *reculer pour mieux sauter*: first language is crippled, so to speak, by robbing it of its (apparent) capacity to fully and adequately describing the world by lying it on "the cross" of the constative statement's subject- and predicate-term. As a result of this initial movement all suggestions of how the world is or can be divided into individual things (corresponding with a statement's subject-term) and their properties (corresponding with its predicate-term) are temporarily suspended and put into question. A kind of primordial chaos thus comes into being. But order is then restored again by how the historist's historical language may enable us to discern new identities and, at a later stage, individual things in the past, that is, things that we had not previously included in our inventory of the world. In this way the historist use of historical language possesses a problem-solving capacity exceeding by far the capacity of Enlightenment historical language.

THE PROBLEMS OF HISTORISM AND HOW TO SOLVE THEM

But the historist's proposal to make coherence do the job that was performed by substance and rhetoric in Enlightenment historical writing was not without its own problems. Let us note, first, that historicizing the substance only makes sense if one is prepared to accept the "substantial" differences in the several manifestations of a historical entity in the course of its history. Even more so, it will be part of the historist program to emphasize these differences as much as possible. But this suggests a conclusion that is diametrically opposed to the historist thesis that the essence or nature of a historical entity lies in its history. For the more we emphasize the difference between the individual phases of an entity's history, the less plausible it will be to go on considering it one and the same thing through all the phases of its development. Put differently, the suggestion of *diachronicity* that is implied by the definition of historism adopted here will have the effect of ungluing the successive phases through which a historical entity passes in its history, and thus result in *syn*chronicity.

This unpleasant dialectics can actually be observed in the writings of historists like Ranke. On the one hand, Ranke writes about the nations whose histories fill the many volumes of his stupendous oeuvre: "States and nations are the product of a creative genius, not of individual persons, nor of an individual generation—just as little as one could say this about language; they are the product of a totality and of many generations."[19] Like languages, nations are the product of the creative genius of many generations; their nature can never be grasped if one narrows one's view to merely one generation, but only reveals itself if we carefully follow the whole of their histories. This is how I defined historism at the beginning of this chapter and here we find historism's diachronic face. On the other hand, we have Ranke's well-known *dictum*, "Jede Epoche ist unmittelbar zu Gott [Each epoch is immediate to God]," which emphasizes the unique character of each phase of a historical entity's development. And this gives us historism's synchronic face. As long as the historist historian paints a relatively large and impressionist painting of the past, this Janus face of historism may not yet manifest itself. As long as our understanding of the web of history is still vague and incomplete, the diachronic and the synchronic approach can retain so much overlap that we may not notice their intrinsic opposition and divergence. But to the extent that the past is more intensively and closely researched—as has obviously been the case in the two centuries separating us from the birth of historism—that tension between diachronicity and synchronicity has increased continually. When our historical knowledge becomes more precise, both tendencies will inevitably articulate themselves at the cost of each other, and as a result the overlap will gradually lose content. In the end, the subject of historical change completely evaporates and all that is left to us is a mere jumble of fragments stubbornly resisting each effort to relate them in a meaningful way.[20] Because of this dialectics of historism, what could initially still be conceived as a continuous historical process would inevitably disintegrate into its many components. It thus became ever more difficult to meet the requirements of coherence and *Zusammenhang* that had to be satisfied after the dissolution of the Enlightened conception of the past—and insofar as one was still successful in this, cohesion became ever more "local." This dialectics of historism already announced itself in Burckhardt's conception of history, in which the different phases of historical evolution tend to become independent of each other.[21] And its victory over the historist's demand of unity and coherence would be indubitable with the advent, in our time, of postmodernism openly embracing fragmentation and dispersion.[22]

I will not investigate here whether the historists were themselves aware of this inconvenient dialectics in their historism. I will focus, instead, upon the technical concept by means of which historians, either knowingly or unknowingly, succeeded in obscuring this dialectics from sight. This was the notion of the "historical idea," or *historische Idee*, which is, in my opinion, the most fruitful concept that has ever been developed in the history of historical theory. The historical idea manifests itself in two ways, wrote Humboldt,

> on the one hand as a creation of energies which affects many particulars, in different places and under different circumstances, and which is initially barely perceptible, but gradually becomes visible and finally irresistible; on the other hand, as a creation of energies which cannot be deduced in all their scope from their attendant circumstances.[23]

The features ascribed by Humboldt and Ranke to the historical idea can be summed up as follows: (1) the historical idea embodies what is unique to both a historical entity and a historical period; (2) by embodying the unique, it gives us access to what is essential to that entity of period; (3) when becoming acquainted with the idea of an entity or period, we have in a theoretically crucial sense of that word "explained" it; (4) though social-scientific laws may help us to ascertain the nature of the historical idea, it can never be reduced entirely to the kind of knowledge expressed by these laws; (5) the historical idea embodies the coherence of the many properties of a historical entity or period, so that in debates about the merits of several proposals of how to conceive of a historical idea, the decisive criterion will be which proposal is most successful in giving coherence; and (6) the historical idea cannot be defined aprioristically as Fichte or Hegel had hoped to do, but only on the basis of unbiased historical research.[24]

From the point of view of historical practice, the historical idea effectively solved the problems that had been created by abandoning the Enlightened notion of the unchanging substance of historical entities; but from a theoretical point of view, the solution is not satisfactory. The problem already announces itself quite clearly in Humboldt's essay. Humboldt states: "It is, of course, self-evident that these ideas emerge from the mass of events themselves, or, to be more precise, originate in the mind through contemplation of these events undertaken in a truly historical spirit." A little later in this text he writes about the historian: "Above all, he must take great care not to attribute to reality arbitrarily created ideas of his own, and not to sacrifice any of the living richness of the parts in his search for the coherent pattern of the whole."[25] Statements like these raise the issue of where the historical idea must be situated: is the historical idea part of the inventory of the past itself, or is the historical idea, as the term itself suggests already, merely a construction by the historian?

At this junction we can discern where historism and contemporary narrativism agree and disagree with each other. Narrativists agree with their historist predecessors that it is the historian's task to see coherence and *Zusammenhang* in the past, and they will readily acknowledge the immense value of the notion of the "historical idea." But where the historists—with the sole exception of Droysen[26]—thought of the historical idea as an entelechy present in the past itself that had to be "mirrored" by the historian's language, narrativists believe that the historian's language does not *reflect* a coherence or *Zusammenhang* in the past itself, but only *gives* coherence to the past. And this narrativist point of view is not inspired by the philosophical fashions of today—instrumentalism, nominalism, antirepresentationalism, and so on—though it shares the epistemological asceticism of these positions. Rather, narrativism accepts here the consequences of surrendering the Enlightenment's attachment to the unchanging substance. For as soon as we give up the ontology of the *single* statement for the ontology of the *set* of statements whose subject-terms no longer refer to one and the same entity in extralinguistic reality, coherence is no longer guaranteed by the coherence of that objective entity, but by whatever coherence and unity the set of statements may possess. There is no third possibility: coherence has its source either in reality or in the language we use for speaking about it; and if the former option cannot satisfy the consistent historist historian's requirements, the latter is the only choice left. Substance must not be conceived as being part of historical reality, but as originating in language, in the historian's narrative. The post-Enlightenment historian's substance is, therefore, a *narrative substance*,[27] and its coherence is not *found*, but *made* in and by his text (though the historian will always see the past as his best guide for how to construct these narrative substances). Simply put, narrativism, as a historical theory of the narrative substance, is a historism that is stripped of all its metaphysical accretions and of the last remnants of Enlightenment substantialism that historians like Humboldt and Ranke (unlike Droysen) still retained in their notion of the historical idea.

This, then, will enable us to demonstrate how Enlightenment historical writing, historist historical writing, and narrativism are related to one another. The Enlightenment accepted the notion of substance and situated the substance, as is at first sight the obvious thing to do, in the past itself. But this option had the unintended result of surrendering historical writing to rhetoric when the historian addressed topics, like the fall of the Roman empire, that clearly involve the fate of a historical substance. Historism was, from this point of view, both revolutionary and reactionary. It was revolutionary since it resolutely situated itself precisely where Enlightenment historical writing was inadequate: that is, where substantial change occurs. Gibbon's *Decline and Fall* was from an historist point of view indeed a book on substantial change; it seemed to attempt to do what historism had been invented for, namely to account for how a historical entity may undergo changes that involve even its very substance—as typically will be the case in an account of the ultimate dissolution of such an historical entity. But Gibbon undertook to achieve this so very historist program with the means of the Enlightenment; hence the paradox of an unchanging substance, whereas, on the other hand, this unchanging substance was paradoxically expected to explain the dissolution of this substance itself. Historism eliminated this paradox by historicizing substance by means of the notion of the *historische Idee* and by allowing that a thing may substantially differ at one stage from what it was, or will be at other stages of its evolution. But at the same time historism as reactionary was well. For by derhetoricizing historical writing and by restricting the aesthetic dimension of historical writing to what merely is a matter of presentation, it revoked the role that the Enlightenment had unwittingly assigned to language—a role that was so superbly fulfilled by the powerful flow of Gibbon's majestic prose. Historism could do so by situating substantial change in the past itself in the sense that these substances were believed to come into being, to grow and die in the past itself, just as we can say this of plants, animals, and individual human beings. Hence, according to the historist, the historian merely has to passively register this evolution of substantial change. And, indeed, this meant a return to an even more pronounced substantialism than that of the Enlightenment, insofar as the Enlightenment was aware of the power and the inescapability of historical rhetoric. And this may explain why the ideal of an "objective" and "scientific" history was even more plausible within historism than in the parameters of its Enlightenment predecessor.

Narrativist historical theory, lastly, is the *juste milieu* between Enlightenment and historist historical writing. With historism, as opposed to the Enlightenment, it allows of substantial change and of the recognition that the ontology of the true statement is less appropriate for furthering our understanding of the past (though not wholly inappropriate). With the Enlightenment, and as opposed to historism, it has no wish to people the inventory of the world with the substances that historism was tempted to situate in the historical past itself. For the narrativist these substances lead their life exclusively at the level of language: they are narrative substances. However, as such they do introduce at the level of language some of the properties that we would normally attribute only to things and not to language. Indeed, for the narrativist, the narrative substance is a linguistic thing that satisfies all the ontological requirements of thingness. In this way narrativism retains what is good and rejects what is bad in both the Enlightenment and the historism paradigm—and when doing so makes us aware of a kind of relationship between language and the world that is characteristic of most of our daily use of language while, at the same time, it was neither noticed nor analyzed by philosophers of language before. So this is where we may expect philosophy of history to add a new dimension to existing philosophy of language.

The feature of narrative of language relevant in this context is that it creates the split between "speaking" and "speaking about speaking" that we discussed in Chapter 1. The distinction between language and the world is, so to speak, repeated and transfigured at the level of language. We may speak about a table, but the table itself will not make its appearance in the language we use to that effect. Similarly, we may speak about narrative substances, enumerate their properties, discuss their merits or demerits, and so on, but in spite of being a linguistic thing the narrative substance itself will, like a chair or a table, always remain outside that language itself. In all such discussions, the narrative substance will be mentioned *referentially* and not as a syntactic component of the statements in which such reference to a narrative substance is made.[28] That the narrative substance is a thing from a logical point of view (albeit a *linguistic* thing) enables us to ascertain what rhetorical figure will be favored by both historism and narrativism. There is, on the one hand, historical reality itself, which is the historian's object of investigation; on the other hand, there are linguistic things (narrative substances), in terms of which the historian tries to make sense of the past. In other words, one (linguistic) thing is used for understanding another thing (that is part of historical reality). And this is how metaphor works. In the metaphor "the earth is a spaceship," for example, two *things* are compared, while one of the two things is not part of the other (that would give us either synecdoche or metonymy). So whereas irony is the natural trope of Enlightenment historical writing, historism has a natural affinity with metaphor.

Though I cannot do justice here to the many present discussions on metaphor,[29] the following remarks may suffice. By inviting us to see one thing from the point of view of another thing, metaphor effects an *organization* of our knowledge. Thus the metaphor just mentioned organizes all the knowledge we have of our earth and of spaceships in such a manner that our present and future ecological problems are highlighted by that organization. The organization of knowledge (paradigmatically expressed in constative statements) thus brings about a hierarchization of our knowledge; it suggests what is important and what is unimportant, and by means of this chiaroscuro succeeds in giving us the contours, and even a "picture," of the part of reality that is at issue in the metaphor. This is one of the reasons that metaphor is the preferred rhetorical tool for both historists and narrativists. Secondly, metaphor also allows us to answer the difficult question of to decide between rival accounts of the past. If historical insight is essentially metaphorical, it follows self-evidently that the best account of the past must be the most metaphorical one. The historian is thus required to think of the strongest metaphor in terms of which he invites us to see the past. Semantic deviance is what makes metaphor into what it is; the best metaphor is, therefore, the metaphor in which semantic deviance is most pronounced without the metaphor becoming incomprehensible— which, as we observed in Chapter 2, means that the historian should aim at the most courageous and risky narrative, and avoid what seems to fit most easily within accepted historical conventions. We saw the parallelism with Popper's critique of logical positivism when he argued that the strongest theory is not the most probable, but, on the contrary, the most *im*probable theory, the one that maximizes its empirical content by "forbidding" the greatest number of possible states of affairs. This is, in a nutshell, how we can rationally decide between alternative representations of parts of the past and what may convince us of the rationality of historical writing and of historical debate.[30]

Precisely this similarity to Popper's criterion for scientific acceptability justifies the hypothesis that the historist historian's metaphor has a function in historical writing analogous to that of theories in the sciences. I would therefore agree with Rüsen that the opposition that was created between the historist's narrative interpretation of the past and *Strukturgeschichte* or *Geschichte als Sozialwissenschaft* ("history as a social science") has been much exaggerated and ignores the essential continuity existing between the two.[31] Indeed, narrativism provides with an optimally convincing justification of Kocka's definition of theory as it functions in *Geschichte als Sozialwissenschaft*: "Theories are explicit and consistent conceptual systems that cannot be derived from the historical sources themselves, but that may make possible the identification, discussion and explanation of historical objects."[32] Metaphor organizes our knowledge by seeing one thing from the perspective of another, and no thing has the capacity to determine itself the perspective from which it will, has to, or can best be seen. Metaphor thus respects and explains the independence of theory from data about the past itself required by Kocka's definition, thanks to the separation between perspective (or point of view) and what is seen from that perspective. Narrativism is the up-to-date theoretical legitimization of historism and of its latter-day variant of *Geschichte als Sozialwissenschaft*.

Hence, if we are looking for a fruitful way of periodizing contemporary historical writing, we should not situate historism and *Geschichte als Sozialwissenschaft* on opposite sides of a caesura. Admittedly, there is a difference in subject matter and often in ideological inspiration, but narrativism will make us aware of the far more fundamental similarities.

THE DIALECTICS OF NARRATIVIST HISTORISM

If this chapter had been written some twenty to thirty years ago, this would have been the appropriate place to wrap it up. By then, it had been shown how historism grew out of Enlightenment historical writing and thinking; to what extent the historist paradigm still determines the practice of historical writing; and finally, that historical writing's explanatory ideals should be clarified and justified on the basis of the ontological and epistemological presuppositions of historism. In the past twenty to thirty years, however, new variants of historical writing—such as the history of mentalities, *Alltagsgeschichte* ("the history of daily life"), and the "microstorie"—have come into being that seem to deny the basic tenets of historism. I say "seem to deny" since it is doubtful whether these new variants should be considered to be a radical break with historism. Whereas historism always aimed at the achievement of coherence and synthesis (and we have seen that this belongs to the heart of historism), these new variants rejoice in the fragment, the small detail, and in the revelation of an unsuspected and fascinating find, be it a source or a captivating sign of the past's strangeness. Authenticity and a direct link with the past, or at least the suggestion of such a direct link, have taken here the place of the overarching syntheses that historism used to see as its highest goal.

Nevertheless, in spite of this apparently outright opposition to historism a continuity can be observed; or rather, it can be argued that there is a dialectic intrinsic to historism provoking this shift from synthesis to fragmentation. In the previous section we saw how the tension between diachronicity and synchronicity inherent in historism stimulated a turning away from unity toward fragmentation. From this perspective the present embrace of the fragment is a movement *within*, rather than *against* historism. But this does not yet explain the desire of authenticity and of this direct link with the past that I mentioned just now.

In order to explain these additional features of contemporary historical writing, nothing is more instructive and appropriate than a discussion of Hugo von Hofmannsthal's "Der Brief des Lord Chandos." The Austrian poet and prosaist Hofmannsthal (1874–1929) wrote this letter after having gone through a deep mental and intellectual crisis in the years 1900 and 1901—a crisis which, in one way or another, was experienced by many poets of that period, such as Rainer Maria Rilke and Stéphane Mallarmé, or the Dutch poets Herman Gorter and Lodewijk van Deijssel. The crisis can best be characterized as a "language crisis," that is, a period of profound despair of the possibility of language to establish contact with reality. Naturalism and realism had promised—and in their view, failed—to do this. And so the question arose of whether language can really capture the world in words, or whether it will always remain a poor substitute, more conspicuous by its shortcomings than its successes in rendering reality. It is no coincidence that philosophy of language came to fascinate philosophers at about the same time. And we need only recall the books by Janek, Toulmin, and Carl Schorske on the intellectual atmosphere of *fin de siècle* Vienna to recognize that Wittgenstein was certainly sensitive to the language crisis experienced by the best poets of the age.[33] The fate of philosophy and of poetry were intimately related at the time (and so much the better for both of them, I would venture to say).

"Der Brief des Lord Chandos" is Hofmannsthal's fictitious letter written in the persona of Lord Chandos to the seventeenth-century statesman and philosopher Sir Francis Bacon. Chandos begins by ruefully recounting to Bacon his former natural and wholly unproblematic relationship to the world and his former complete confidence in language to discover and adequately express the secrets of the world. Reality was for him a coherent totality in which each object was a clue to all the others: "It was to me as if everything was a likeness of, as if each creature was a key to all other things. I was confident that I was capable of obtaining a secure grasp of one thing after another and of forcing them to open themselves up to other things as far as possible."[34] He conceived of the world as if it was an encyclopedia in which all things were metaphors for each other and where knowledge thus seemed to guarantee its own proliferation. It was in this mood that he confidently conceived of the ambitious plan of writing a history of the reign of Henry VIII and of a classical mythology. He did not doubt the power and the efficacy of the language and the general concepts that would enable him to perform these tasks successfully. But then a peculiar intellectual paralysis set in: "It gradually became impossible for me to discuss any abstract and general theme and to unproblematically use for this the words that other people would spontaneously employ for doing so. I felt a peculiar kind of discomfort when pronouncing words like 'mind,' 'soul,' or 'body.'"[35] Language, and more specifically, the kind of general concepts that we unproblematically use in ordinary language—and hence in the writing of history—became for Chandos a most unreliable instrument. When he heard words being used in even the most trivial social context, Chandos felt compelled to look at what they seemingly referred to from an "uncanny proximity," as if he were seeing the objects of daily reality through a magnifying glass. As a result, everything disintegrated into its constituent parts, and those parts disintegrated into their parts, until nothing could be grasped anymore by means of language and its concepts. And this was not because Chandos no longer understood the meaning of the concepts in question: rather, he understood them *too well.* It was precisely because of the clarity and transparency of his concepts that what was expressed by them seemed to him "so unprovable, so untruthful, so partial as anything could possibly be."[36] Having gained this state of clairvoyance with regard to the prism of language, language became an unusable instrument for him. It is as if language can only function as a means for communication as long as there is a collective acceptance of its fuzziness and its uncertainties. Language socializes us as language users, thanks to its imperfection, but the quest for a perfect language—as is suggested by Chandos's experience—encloses us within the frontiers of solipsism.[37] And one need only concentrate for some time on one's own name to recognize the uncanny vertigo that was experienced by Lord Chandos when he considered language from a position outside language itself.

But Chandos's linguistic paralysis was compensated for by a new awareness of reality: at certain moments there was a directness in his access to reality that language always seemed to prevent:

"It will not be easy for me," Chandos writes to Bacon, "to make clear to you the exact nature of these felicitous moments; words once again fail me. For it really is something wholly unknown and unnamable when, at such moments, some object of daily reality suddenly presents itself to me as if it were a cask ready to be filled with an overwhelming flow of higher life. I cannot expect from you to understand me without any example, and must apologize for the ineptitude of my examples. A jug, a harrow left abandoned in the fields, a dog in the sun, a poor churchyard, a crippled beggar, a needy homestead—all these things may become the cask of my revelation."[38]

And the sublimity (to use the most appropriate term in this context) with which these insignificant objects of daily reality may suddenly reveal themselves to Chandos obliterates the distance that language always created between itself and the reality described by it. A direct access to reality now became possible that Chandos described as "an unprecedented capacity of participation, or of flowing over in these objects; or the feeling that a veil of death, of dreaming or of being awake has been cast over them."[39] Linguistic paralysis thus stimulated Chandos's capacity to experience reality with an intensity that, sometimes, gave him the impression of a "flowing over" into the objects of daily reality that had suddenly caught his attention. It is as if these objects were little punctures in the infinitely thin but nonetheless impenetrable foil separating language and reality.

The experience that Hofmannsthal attributes to Lord Chandos is an exact parallel of what has happened in historical writing in the transition from historical writing aiming at synthesis and coherence to the variants of the new cultural history that were mentioned at the beginning of this section. The objects of the world were, for Lord Chandos, all signs of each other; together they formed a world in which he could completely feel at home, a world that was familiar to him and that happily adapted itself to all the meanings he wished to give to it. Each object was ready to serve as a metaphor for another, and language was the self-effacing medium in terms of which these metaphors could be expressed. In this overbold confidence in the powers of language he conceived of his plan of writing a history of Henry VIII and of classical mythology. But the very ease with which language seemed to perform all the tasks it was required to do made Chandos suspicious. Should we not expect the translation of the world into language to meet with some resistance now and then? For does not reality make itself felt only in and thanks to such resistance? Is it not only at such occasions that we can become aware of reality *itself*, as possessing an autonomy of its own? Have we, therefore, no good reason to doubt language precisely because of its perfection? Is not language of this kind like a person who is everybody's friend and precisely for that reason nobody's friend? Considerations like these made Lord Chandos distrust language and fear that language may put us at a distance from reality exactly when it seems to bring us closer to it. Cassirer once expressed the same idea with a wonderful metaphor: "Language may be compared with the spear of Amphortas in the legend of the Holy Grail. The wounds that language inflicts upon human thought cannot be healed except by language itself."[40] Language both wounds and cures thought and the world—and we shall never be sure when it wounds and when it cures.

And so it is with historical writing. A similar confidence in the powers of language had inspired historist historical writing: however complex the past, however variegated its elements, however tragic or comic the course of historical events, the capacity of the historian's language and of metaphor to do complete justice to it was never doubted for a moment. There seemed to be no limits to the historian's language, to the concepts used in it, nor to its narrative and explanatory potential or its capacity to evoke the past and capture its uniqueness. No part of the past was so strange or so remote, so sublime or so majestic that it could effectively call into question the powers of language to represent it.

And even now, after the Holocaust has compelled both historians and historical theorists into "probing the limits of representation" (Friedlander), few will insist that there are parts or aspects of the past that truly are beyond representation. At most, one will be prepared to concede that certain extraordinary forms of representation will have to be appealed to in order to deal with the terrors of a past like the Holocaust. Such is the position, for example, of Hayden White when he recommends that we consider the middle voice, or a notion like "the modernist event," as the probably appropriate stylistic means for speaking and writing about the Holocaust.[41] And to the same end, Dominick LaCapra requires us to think about the notion of trauma because of the problems occasioned by the effort to account for traumatic experience.[42]

But it may well be that one should not primarily think of the Holocaust (and of similar catastrophes) if one ask oneself where and how the "language crisis" has announced itself in history. For we should recall now that it was not unspeakable horror or a vast historical panorama that made Lord Chandos aware of the limitations of language. Instead, his inhibition had its source in the most banal and trivial of things—objects like a tankard, a harrow left in the fields, a dog in the sun—in which reality "revealed" itself to him and that made him realize where reality succeeded in transcending all that we can say and write about it. None of which should surprise us. For language is the vehicle of meaning, and it is therefore to be expected that reality as the antipode of language will preferably manifest itself in what had hitherto only been seen (if at all) out of the corners of one's eyes and in what was until now believed to be meaning*less* and not worthy of observation. We may indeed become aware of such forgotten corners of our world when we notice an object that has, so to speak, curled up inside itself. And we will certainly not find this in an event such as the Holocaust, which is more completely saturated with meaning than any other event in history.

In the preface to his magnificent book on experiencing Waterloo, Verdun, and Auschwitz, Eelco Runia observes:

If in historical writing a change of form is the truly adequate and creative response to "the becoming reality of what was hitherto inconceivable," the question immediately arises of what way the writing of history since the Holocaust has been changed *by* the Holocaust. But remarkably enough this has hardly been the case. . . . If this observation is correct, it can mean either of two things. Either the Holocaust has not been the event transgressing all bounds that we always take it to be, or there is something special about the relationship between history and historical writing after World War II.[43]

Dismissing the first option as obviously nonsensical, Runia then opposes the effects of the French Revolution on historical writing with those of the Holocaust. The crucial difference, in his view, is that the French Revolution invited, above all, many different proposals for how to situate it in the course of history, whereas historical writing on the Holocaust tends to remain focused on the Holocaust itself. Though especially the German historians of the so-called Deutsche Sonderweg thesis have wrestled intensively with the question of how to locate the Holocaust in German history at least since Luther, I nonetheless tend to agree with Runia. And this propensity of the writing of the history of the Holocaust to focus on the Holocaust itself, instead of on its historical antecedents, has undoubtedly much to do with the fact that its meaning is so very obvious. For what else can it mean than that this has been the unprecedented low in all of Western history and that this must *never, never* happen again? Each historical account of the Holocaust (and of World War II) that fails to come to this conclusion about its meaning, as obvious as it is inevitable, has been blind to the enormity of the crime and has to be condemned for both historical and moral reasons.

This, then, may explain why representational innovation is not, and even ought not, to be expected from the Holocaust, and why innovation can be found instead at the opposite end of the historical spectrum, where the historian is confronted with what hitherto had been meaningless and that had hitherto remained unperceived.[44] Historical innovation will be achieved where historians encounter the historical equivalents of Hofmannsthal's abandoned harrow, his dog in the sun, or his decrepit farmhouse— not coincidentally the kind of object around which the interest of the historians of *Alltagsgeschichte* tends to cluster. Hence, if we think of what is called "the new cultural history,"[45] of contemporary history of mentalities, of *Alltagsgeschichte* or of what has become known as "micro-storie," we will encounter there the kind of paradigm change that *Geschichte als Sozialwissenschaft* did not provide. I shall assume that the reader is sufficiently acquainted with these new forms of historical writing and therefore restrict myself to an enumeration of the major differences between the traditional historist or narrativist paradigm and the newer one.[46]

In the first place, in agreement with its metaphorical character, historist historical writing is panoramic, in the sense that it wishes to provide its readers with as wide a panoramic survey of the most important developments in our history as the historian can achieve. These new forms of historical writing, by contrast, have an amazing fascination for the small and apparently insignificant detail. They are no longer interested in history on the grand scale. Second, traditional history often aimed at defining our historical identity, at describing the historical process that has made us into what we are; *Identitätsstiftung* surely lay at the heart of historist historical writing. The new forms of historical writing, however, have surrendered all the ideological and emancipatory pretensions of their historiographical predecessor. History is more depoliticized even than in cliometric economic history. To be more precise, the new form of historical writing exemplifies the politics of depoliticization, and could from that point of view properly be seen as the counterpart in historical writing of the victory of democratic individualism that we may observe in so many Western countries and that has so surprisingly effected the evanescence of the collective will that used to legitimate the state and its actions. The historical agent living in the past is no longer presented as being part of the same historical process of which we are also a part, and a kind of "democratic" or even "anarchical" independence of the elements of the historical process (including the present) is achieved. Third, all historical writing has its raison d'être in the difference between the past and the present. Historist historical writing was an attempt to bridge the gap between the past and the present and to make the past accessible to us in this way. The historian's language, the (metaphorical) technical concepts used by the historian and the (socioscientific) theories in which these concepts are often defined, have traditionally functioned as such bridges between the past and the present. One may think here of concepts like "revolution," "social class," "industrialization," "intellectual movement," "Enlightenment," or "Romanticism"—we should not forget that history has technical concepts just as much as the sciences! These bridges are almost entirely absent in the newer forms of historical writing, with important consequences. For, pursuing the metaphor of the bridge for a moment, we should note that bridges enable us to *overcome* a distance or difference but at the same time also *mark* that distance. However, in the new forms of historical writing the paradox of the bridge is absent, and thus the past is both more distant from and more close to us.

Thinking over these three major differences, we might conclude that we encounter here a movement of both decontextualization and an increasing directness and immediacy with which the past is presented to us. "Decontextualization," since the reassuring context of a historical development connecting all the many different phases of our history has been given up. Fragments of the past present themselves without the larger context of which they were formerly believed to be a part. "Directness and immediacy," since the intermediary of the conceptual bridges has disappeared. We now encounter the past with the same directness anthropologists experience when they enter a strange and mysterious part of the world. "Hans Medick and the representatives of historical anthropology in general," writes Iggers in his recent book on twentieth-century historical writing, "emphasize precisely the strangeness of each object of historical investigation, not only of the non-European natives, but also of the inhabitants of a Württemberg village in early modern Europe."[47] And the fascination for anthropology that is so clearly present in these new forms of historical writing need no longer surprise us.

I began my story with two apparently incompatible accounts of the origins of historism. From the point of view of contemporary narrativism, the two accounts are complementary rather than incompatible. Indeed, both accounts presuppose one another and, once again, narrativism shows us why this is so. Narrativism thus complicates our picture of what was at stake in the transition from Enlightened to historist historical writing. However, this does not result in a blurring of the boundaries between the Enlightenment and historism, but, on the contrary, in an increased awareness of the intellectual daring and revolutionary newness of historism. The old cliché *is* true: historism *did* give us historical writing as we know it down to the present day. And if we recognize to what extent historism revolutionized historical thought, we will also recognize that much of the resistance against historism—as exemplified, for instance, by structuralist or socioscientific historical theory and writing—does not really transcend the parameters of historist historical thought. These centers of resistance can without much difficulty be integrated within historism.

Such a paradigm change may, however, be observed in the newer forms of historical writing I referred to above. For two reasons this paradigm change can be characterized as a movement from "language" to "experience." Firstly, as is emphasized by Iggers, "experience" became the new subject matter of the historian:

This emphasis on the subjectivity of individual human beings requires a new conception of historical writing, which complements the traditional "centristic and unilinear" perspective adopted by social history and its "systematic logic" with a "logic that focuses on the life-world and respects communication and experience" (Habermas).[48]

But there is also a second, no less important, "formal" reason: historism relied upon the historian's language to give coherence to the past, whereas these newer forms seem no longer interested in coherence, and in viewing the past from the perspective of a coherence-making center.

But was this not what historism had always seen as its supreme goal? Did not the historist always invite us to leave behind the familiar present and to enter the strange and alien world of the past? And to do all this by giving us an idea of "the feel of the past"? So, once again, historism quietly awaits us at the end of the route we had chosen in our attempt to escape from it. Historism is and will be our fate, whether we like it or not. And we had better try to like it, for as long as we stubbornly resist historism, we will be capable of understanding neither the nature and the rationality of history nor the many metamorphoses that historical writing has undergone during the last two centuries. And in the metamorphosis of historism—as is always the case with metamorphosis—the substance remains the same.

5

THE POSTMODERNIST "PRIVATIZATION" OF THE PAST

Until far into the nineteenth century, history was seen as being essentially the result of the actions of kings, statesmen, generals, and other dignitaries. Readers expected the historian to explain the actions of such people; this was the measure of the historian's success. Furthermore, it was generally believed that common sense was all that is needed for the historian to be able to give such a plausible and convincing account of the actions of kings and statesmen. And since common sense is, in Descartes's well-known view, the most justly distributed good, since nobody complains about having too little of it, there was no need for the historian to have any specific abilities as a historian. The only talent that was needed, beyond mere common sense, was the historian's ability to write a sufficiently coherent and convincing narrative. Rhetoric was the discipline that taught the historian how to be such a successful storyteller—hence, history was conceived as a branch of (applied) rhetoric rather than as a discipline in its own right.

This changed in the beginning of the nineteenth century: history was now seen as the result of all-encompassing historical and social forces, rather than of the actions of individual kings or statesmen. The French Revolution had dramatically illustrated how far the actual course of history might be removed from the intentions of its main actors. All the lofty ideals that had initially inspired the revolution ultimately resulted in the guillotine and in the Law of 22 Prairial, on the basis of which anyone might be sent to the scaffold because "one was suspected of being suspect." It was now recognized that the past was to a large extent governed by forces transcending the will and power of individual actors and history; the object of the historian became now primarily identified with the unintended results of intentional human action. As a result, common sense and the capacity to empathize with the actions of statesmen and generals could now no longer be considered sufficient qualifications for writing history. Henceforth, the historian had to be acquainted with the workings of these supraindividual forces and with speculative philosophies like those of Hegel and Marx. Also, in a later, more positivist phase, the theories that were developed in the social sciences provided historians with the proper background knowledge for how to deal with the relevant aspects of the past. One now discovered in the past secrets that could only be adequately investigated by the historian who was properly trained to identify the workings of these large impersonal forces. In short, history became a discipline that had to be taught in history departments, that required the establishment of specialist journals and of scientific debate if it was to produce a reliable and scientifically convincing account of our past.

Consequently, if history as an academic discipline came into being in the course of the nineteenth century, it was founded on the following assumptions. Predisciplinary historical writing saw no essential difference between past and present, since there is no essential ontological and epistemological difference between the kings and statesmen of the past and the historian of the present. Hence, there was not an object of knowledge that was truly and essentially historical. Nineteenth-century disciplinary history, however, separated past and present from each other in terms of large supraindividual social and political forces (the development of the nation, scientific and technological progress, the social class as the maker of the past, etc.), and the workings of these forces provided historical writing for the first time with an object of investigation that successfully demarcated historical writing from other disciplines. Hence, there now was a specific *historical reality* existing independently of the historian and functioning as an objective given that all historians of past and present, in spite of all their differences of opinion, can discuss, while being certain, at the same time, that the results of their historical research will be commensurable in terms of this "objective," or, rather, intersubjective, reality, according to which all historical interpretations can meaningfully be compared, criticized, and judged. This commensurability, in its turn, justified the faith in the cumulative character of all the research that is done by historians. For if there is a background enabling us to define the merits and shortcomings of individual historical interpretations, this background also enables us to establish where each historical interpretation has significantly contributed to our knowledge of the past. Hence, history as an academic discipline presents us with a community of historians in which all historians cooperate in one common enterprise and where each historian does his or her bit in building the cathedral of our knowledge of the past.

The notion of history as an enterprise in which all historians participate defines history as an academic discipline and permits us to see each individual historian as a representative—or, to put it in a more ceremonious way, as an "emanation"—of the knowing subject that is embodied in the discipline as a whole. Thus, insofar as all historians speak roughly the same language, use roughly the same methods, have roughly the same conceptions of what is important and unimportant, and are trained in a way that more or less guarantees that they have all this in common, we may speak of a quasi-Hegelian "subjective mind," incorporating the joint effort of historians to penetrate into the secrets of an objective, historical reality. In this way, the notion of an objective past as a unity in itself had its counterpart, on the side of the object, in the notion of a quasi-collective knowing subject that is embodied in the discipline as a whole.

THE DE-DISCIPLINIZATION OF HISTORY

Arguably the most important development in our contemporary, postmodernist time has been the abandonment of the notion of the past as an object that is governed by large, supraindividual forces that embody the essence of the past. The past is no longer conceived as being divisible into essence and contingency, but rather, in contemporary historical writing each aspect of the past can be both. As a consequence, historians can no longer meaningfully ask themselves how the individual results of their research fit into a picture of history as a whole; the past is no longer conceived as a map of the globe with a number of white spots that will duly be filled in by future research; it is no longer seen as an already sketched rough outline of large impersonal forces that needs only more further work by historians to fill in the details. Instead, the past has become a huge and formless mass in which each historian may dig his own little hole without ever encountering colleagues (either from the present or the past) and without knowing how the results of individual labor relate to "history as a whole" (insofar as that is still considered a meaningful notion at all).

Hence, history as a cathedral to which each historian contributes a few bricks for the greater glory of the common effort has given way to history as a metropolis in which everybody goes their own way and minds their own business without caring much about what others do. The disintegration of the past as a unity in itself, however complex, thus prompted the dissolution of the quasi-collective knowing subject as embodied by the discipline. Ontological disintegration was followed by epistemological disintegration. This loss of clarity and of an organizing center from which we can grasp and act on the world is generally seen as a loss of bearings, as a loss of utopia in political thought, and of our capacity to distinguish between the important and the unimportant, the relevant and the irrelevant, in social and historical thought—an incapacity that was laboriously exploited, and with unmistakable delectation, in the writings of Derrida and his many deconstructivist followers on either side of the Atlantic.[1]

If history no longer has this quasi-Hegelian "subjective mind," doing for the discipline what the transcendental self had always done for the individual in Kantian epistemology, history has irreparably lost what made it into a discipline. To a certain extent this meant a return to the situation in which historical writing found itself in the nineteenth century prior to the disciplinization of historical writing. In the writings of Gibbon, Carlyle, Macaulay, and the great French romantic historians of the beginning of the last century—Augustin Thierry, Tocqueville, or Michelet—we find the indelible presence of the historian's self instead of the universal, disciplinary self of post-Rankean "scientific" historical writing. These romantic historians have aptly been described as "me-first" historians by Linda Orr:[2] they wrote history for a quite personal purpose, however much they tried to convince their audience of the urgency of their views and of their indispensability for an adequate understanding of their own age. They all had a most personal relationship with the past and found precisely in this personal relationship their main, if not their exclusive inspiration. They would have dismissed Ranke's "Ich wünschte mein Selbst gleichsam aus zu löschen [I would like to wipe myself out, as it were]" as intellectual cowardice and as a shameless forsaking of the historian's moral obligations to his own time and audience.

However, the recent de-disciplinization of history meant a rehabilitation of the historian's self in his relationship with the past, at the expense of the former, universal disciplinary subject, does not mean a resurrection of the romantic historical consciousness. For the self of romantic historical writing, either deliberately or unwittingly, aimed at the exclusion of other, "competing" historical selves. One might compare the "predisciplinary state" of historical writing to the state of nature as described by the natural law theorists of the seventeenth and eighteenth centuries. In both cases only individual selves were recognized and not the collectivity. Just as Rousseau, in his *Contrat social*, required the individual to surrender all natural rights to the sovereign community, so did history become a discipline thanks to the readiness of nineteenth- and twentieth-century historians to renounce the romantic self and to merge into the single, disciplinary subject of historical knowledge and writing. But as democracy is different from both the state of nature and the prototatalitarian kind of society that was envisaged by Rousseau, so is the postmodernist historical consciousness different from both romanticism and from the demand that the historian unreservedly accept the disciplinary matrice(s) prominent at a given moment in the history of historical writing. Just as in a properly functioning democracy the only justification for central institutions is to guarantee the safety and the freedom of the citizen, so the postmodernist historian still recognizes the institutional functions of disciplinary historical writing only insofar as they serve the freedom of movement of the individual historian. And only to that extent is the individual historian prepared to acknowledge their indispensability.

Thus, much of history in its nineteenth- and twentieth-century disciplinary form is wholeheartedly accepted even by postmodernist historians, in the sense that institutional frameworks such as journals (each with their own standards for the acceptance of papers), history departments, national and international networks, and so on, have even now lost little of the importance that they used to have under the previous dispensation. But this should not make us forget that, within these traditional and trusted frameworks, a "democratization" or "privatization" of the past has begun such that there no longer is one or more self-evident disciplinary center from which knowledge of the past is organized. Our relationship to the past has become "privatized" in the sense that it primarily is an attribute of the individual historian and no longer of a collective disciplinary historical subject. To complete this political metaphor, it is as if in history the "positive" freedom of its disciplinary phase has had to give way to the "negative" freedom of contemporary historical writing that has its origin in its defiance of the "center" of traditional, disciplinary historical writing. And here historical writing is in agreement with developments in the contemporary political world of Western democracies, where negative freedom has become so overwhelmingly more important than positive freedom and the willingness of the citizen to identify with the state or the nation.

This democratization or privatization of the historical subject, this transition from history as a common enterprise to history as written by the individual historian, is best exemplified by the sudden predominance of the notion of memory in contemporary historical consciousness. Until recently, "memory" referred to how we remember our personal past as individuals, whereas the notion of history was traditionally reserved for our collective past. It may even be argued that the word "memory" can only properly be used for what we can remember to have experienced ourselves.[3] For it is a matter of logic that I can never have your memories, even if the content of *your* memories is completely identical with that of *mine*. Hence, making the word "memory" mean what was formerly meant by the word "history" is a sure sign of a personalization or privatization of our relationship to the past. "History" corresponds to the study of the past by a collective, transindividual subject and has, therefore, a natural affinity with national history, social history, economic history—in short, with those topics in which a collective history is expressed. "Memory," on the other hand, corresponds to what has been marginalized in the past by the collectivity. In the words of Patrick Hutton,

> One could argue that postmodern historians are not rejecting the traditions of modern history, but are only appealing to others that have been too long neglected or forgotten. In opposition to the official memories enshrined in modern historiography, they contend, postmodern historiography poses new lines of historical inquiry in the guise of counter-memories.[4]

"Memory" stands for all that was repressed, ignored, or suppressed in the human past and therefore by its very nature could never attain to the public sphere of what is collectively known and recognized—that which has always been the proper domain of "history" in the traditional sense.

"Memory" as a key to the postmodernist historical consciousness is intimately related to the history of mentalities. As Hutton observes: "But the time of the memory topic was about to come, as scholars began to see its relationship to the history of collective mentalities."[5] The explanation is that the history of mentalities has eliminated from historical writing the supraindividual forces to which historical writing owed its development into an academic discipline. We should note here the paradoxical role played by these forces in historical writing. On the one hand, the past was defined by and became accessible thanks only to these forces and the historical concepts that referred to them—concepts like the state, the nation, social class, or even "France," "Germany," and other nations. These notions placed the past at a distance from the present, though they also provided historians and their readers with a bridge enabling them to approach it. For that is what bridges generally do: they mark a distance *and* help us to overcome that distance.

We can now understand that if much contemporary historical writing, especially the history of mentalities, dispenses with notions like these, then the past is at once closer to us and, at the same time, stranger.[6] For there is no longer the age-long development of the nation or of the social class, both separating the present from the past and yet successfully inviting us to identify with it, as was the case in nationalist and in liberal or socialist historical writing; we now stand face to face with our own past, as if we are confronting a former, alienated alter ego. And in this new relationship to the past we feel both challenged to identify with that alter ego and prevented from effectively getting hold of it, in the same way that memory may both remind us of a forgotten part of our own past and at the same time emphasize its ultimate unattainability. The postmodernist past is, therefore, a past that is at the same time more concrete and more alien than was the past of disciplinary historical writing.

THE TWO FACES OF MEMORY

If contemporary historical theorists raise the issue of (collective) memory, they will refer to the writings of Maurice Halbwachs (1877–1945). The reader of Halbwachs's *Les Cadres sociaux de la mémoire* (1925) is amazed to find that this sociological study begins with a lengthy digression on what we believe to be most private in the human individual: dreams. Halbwachs agrees with Freud that our dreams are memories that give us access to a remote and forgotten past and that the content of dreams is not restricted to the present part of our life.⁷ And, like Freud, Halbwachs is convinced that dreams more often than not present us with a distortion of memory but that this distortion is often quite meaningful and no less revealing than the event itself that is remembered in the dream. But where for Freud the dream is "the royal road" to the secrets of one's personality, Halbwachs sees in dreams a reflection of the social order of which we are part: "We will, in all likelihood, come to a better understanding of the nature of these distortions of the past that are effected by dreams, if we recall that even when our imagination reproduces the past, it can never escape the influence of the existing social environment."⁸

However, Halbwachs's main target is not Freud but his former teacher Henri Bergson. For Bergson, *durée* (duration)—the succession of mental states of an individual—is the primary source of how we experience ourselves and the world in which we live. *Durée* is, therefore, for Bergson also the basis of our memory. And, since *durée* can only be ascribed to the individual, it follows that our relationship to our past and how the we remembers our past must necessarily have a logical priority over collective memory. Even more so, in the individual's memory, or experience of *durée*, we will find the memory of all kinds of recurring phenomena that are publicly observable, like the succession of day and night or of the seasons. It is the individual's memory of such recurring phenomena that serves as the basis for the notion of intersubjective time in which the collectivity orders its history. In general, not reality itself, but the memory of individual human beings (and similarities in these memories) is the ultimate source of our knowledge of such recurring phenomena.⁹ And thus we cannot avoid the conclusion that the individual's memory is the ultimate basis for collective memory and not the reverse.¹⁰

Halbwachs rejects this account of memory, however much it may seem to be in agreement with all our intuitions about memory. He has several arguments for extolling, in opposition to Bergson, the essentially collective character of memory. First of all, for our memories to be accessible to us at all, we have to be able to put them into words, and since language and the meaning of words are socially determined, the same must be said about memory. But if one were to object to Halbwachs that general concepts, concepts that we possess thanks to being part of a community of language users, may successfully identify and describe what is purely individual, one will see that Halbwachs has more strings to his bow. He now argues that memory is something more than pure description. For memory always is a construction in his view; and for the construction of memory we will inevitably make use of the social and collective categories that structure our world and our communication. Put differently, memory has nothing around which to crystallize as long as the individual is enclosed within a solipsistic, presocial world. Hence, there is no "pure," individual, solipsistic memory, determined exclusively by the objects that were given to us in our perception; memory is always codetermined by the social categories that determine the selection and communication (even if only to ourselves) of memory and what we unwittingly project on our memories. Halbwachs concludes that there is no such thing as a purely private memory; all our memory is, to a larger or lesser extent, "collective memory."

We fail to recognize this, Halbwachs argues, for two reasons. First, we are deluded by the complexity and the fullness of our memories, since we falsely see this complexity and fullness as expressive of the concreteness of our individual life as opposed to the abstractions of the social order. But the reality is precisely the reverse: this complexity results from the individual's life being an intersection of the myriad social forces constituting the collectivity. Not society, but the individual is an abstraction. Second, there is the strange paradox that we have the illusion of being a completely free and autonomous being, precisely if we uncritically accept what is suggested to us. But it is precisely then, in fact, that we are subject to our *Umwelt*. And that is why we remain unaware of most of the social influences that determine our life. It is exactly the same with memory. Collective memory is most powerful precisely where we most sincerely believe to be in an unmediated, pure contact with our innermost self and our most private past.[11] Only what we consider merely contingent or irrelevant in our lives, if anything at all, could be associated with our individuality.

The implications of Halbwachs's amazing account of (collective) memory and his near complete reversal of our intuitive conceptions of it, can best be characterized by figuring out the losses and the profits it involves if we allow ourselves to be convinced by it. What we will lose, needless to say, is the strictly private world of our personal past that was still granted to us by Bergson and somewhat more hesitantly by Freud (think of how the collectivity also penetrates into the sphere of the individual in terms of the Freudian superego). But the profit compensating for this loss is an amazing enlargement of the range of memory. While for Bergson (and for our intuitive conception of memory), memory can never exceed the boundaries of our individual life; and while for Freud, our collective past can only be part of the life of the individual in the guise of "the eternal recurrence of the repressed" (think of what Freud tells us in *Totem and Taboo* about the origins of society); Halbwachs's collectivization of memory permits us to speak of our individual memory of the historical past of the society of which we are part. For him there are no longer insurmountable barriers between our personal and our collective past; hence, there is no a priori reason for rejecting the possibility that we may remember, in the proper sense of that word, something antedating our own biological life. And if we recognize this, we will no longer be astonished when Halbwachs informs us that he had still felt, and in a way still could "remember," the last vibrations of the romantic movement that had died out about half a century before his own birth. In other words, thanks to the notion of "collective memory," we get a direct access, an access that is not necessarily mediated by the general historical concepts and notions that were discussed in the previous section, to a past that we had hitherto believed to be irrevocably dead and beyond our reach. And indeed, if we think of the amazing resurgence of nationalist feelings that we had believed were crushed by decades of communist rule in Eastern Europe, we may discern in that phenomenon a convincing empirical confirmation of Halbwachs's thesis of the persistence of history deep in the minds of individual human beings. Furthermore, since this is a past that has always been felt or experienced rather than objectified or exteriorized, it seems fairly obvious that the history of mentalities, the historical genre that is most resistant to the historian's urge for abstraction, will be the best instrument for grasping the content of this collective memory.

Although Halbwachs was, mainly, a sociologist and his argument intended to serve a sociological purpose, it will be clear that his view of (collective) memory has its philosophical implications. We should note, then, that it will not be difficult to find support for Halbwachs's views in contemporary philosophy. What is, in the end, at stake in Halbwachs's account of memory concerns the question of whether we are, as individuals, in the possession of some inner sanctuary to which we have, through introspection, a privileged access. Halbwachs's socialization of memory resists the belief in the existence of such an inner sanctuary; and this is in agreement with the attack on Cartesian notions of the self that abound in contemporary philosophy of the self. As is well known, this attack was begun by Gilbert Ryle in his *The Concept of Mind* (1949). When we say that a man has a memory of his nursery, we are tempted to construe this remark, Ryle says, as if he is contemplating some kind of immaterial picture of his nursery; "moreover, this paperless picture is in a gallery which only he can visit. And then we are inclined to say that the picture must be in his mind, and that the 'eyes' with which he contemplates it are his mind's eyes."[12] Whereas, in fact, according to Ryle, this statement should be taken to be a prediction about some publicly observable phenomena, such as that the person in question will be able to correctly answer some questions about his nursery or to draw a rough map of it.

Though he may not share Ryle's behaviorism, William Lyons agrees with this "disappearance theory of introspection" as he calls it. And, like Ryle, he concludes that when we believe we speak about what is "given to us in our memories," this "is often more like the formation or reference to some already formed, stereotyped, culture-tinged model or version or rationalization of what we believe to be our inner cognitive and appetitive processes in particular circumstances."[13] Hence, where the Cartesian (and Bergsonian) conception of the mind would present memory as a stepping-stone into a sanctuary that is only accessible to ourselves, Lyons sees precisely the reverse, namely a past that is only accessible thanks to the "stereotyped" and "culture-tinged models" that we use for describing it. It should be added that the so-called antifoundationalist, Rortyan attack on Cartesian and Kantian notions of knowledge and the self—which is often associated with postmodernist patterns of thought—has further contributed to this philosophical conviction that we should not postulate the existence of such a never observed entity as the individual's memory, behind or below the range of publicly observable phenomena, in order to explain memory. Hence, Halbwachs *and* these authors agree that memory is an essentially social phenomenon without foundation in some presumed, publicly inaccessible, and ultimately private reality.

To conclude this section it must be observed that we can interpret the arguments of Halbwachs (and of Ryle and Lyons) in either of two ways. We might say—and this is where the emphasis lies for each of these authors—that these arguments make public what used to be private. The individual is shown to consist of "social stuff." But if we think of how Halbwachs dramatically extended the past that the individual can properly be said to remember as his own past, we might just as well speak of a "privatization" of the past, in the sense that what used to be an exclusively collective (national, political, or social) past now becomes a private past that can be privately remembered. For as soon as we erase (with Ryle, Lyons, and Rorty) our unquestioned assumptions about what is private and what is public or social, we can both socialize the private and privatize the social. In the remainder of this chapter, I want to argue that the latter interpretation best captures the contemporary, postmodernist, historical consciousness. It is here that my account differs from the "modernist," sociological approach that is still characteristic of Halbwachs's writings on collective memory. I shall discuss, to that end, the recent debate on the representation of the Holocaust, and to what extent the present cult of commemorations exemplifies our contemporary privatization of the past.

THE REPRESENTATION OF THE HOLOCAUST

We should ask ourselves, above all, why the Holocaust suddenly acquired such a central place in historical theory some fifty years after it took place. The explanation lies in an increased awareness of the limitations of "the linguistic turn" that dominated historical thinking during the last two decades. We must recall that the linguistic turn taught us that language is the condition for the possibility of all historical knowledge and insight, and that therefore an understanding of the properties of the historical (narrative) text is required for an adequate understanding of the nature of historical knowledge. From this point of view, the linguistic turn can well be seen as a twentieth-century variant of Kantian transcendentalism; what Kant ascribed to the categories of the understanding was now ascribed to language.[14] And the mainly structuralist account of the nature of the historian's narrative text could be compared to Kant's transcendental deduction of categories like causality, relation, quantity, quality, and modality. Most of the theorists whose names have been associated with the linguistic turn could therefore be seen as proposing a twentieth-century, linguistic variant of transcendentalism, even when these theorists often saw themselves as critics of Kantian transcendentalism. But we need only recall Gadamer's (Heideggerian) thesis that Being can be understood as language; Foucault's view that discourse is the principal (political) agent in the formation of historical reality; Derrida's "il n'y a pas dehors texte"; Richard Rorty's "language goes all the way down"; or, for that matter, Hayden White's tropology, in order to realize to what extent all these most influential advocates of the linguistic turn presented a variant of Kantianism. And as Kant's critical philosophy almost imperceptibly developed into Fichte's and Schelling's idealism, so the structuralist analysis of (the historian's) language quickly evolved into a linguistic idealism (as was recognized by Rorty in spite of his own contribution to this evolution).[15] In both cases, a most welcome and indispensable critique of more or less naive variants of empiricism, or of what has come to be called "the myth of the given," gradually developed into a philosophical disregard of the constraints upon truth and knowledge that lie in reality itself.

It need not surprise us, from that perspective, that the Holocaust was recognized as the greatest challenge to this linguistic transcendentalism: for no event in the whole of human history tolerates less its obfuscation behind the veil of text and language less than the Holocaust. Nowhere has the historian greater responsibilities, both from a cognitive and from a moral point of view, to the past itself in its, so to speak, "noumenal" quality than in the case of the Holocaust. And it was therefore to be expected that the linguistic turn in historical theory would encounter its nemesis in the problem of the representation of the Holocaust.

In an illuminating essay, Hans Kellner has correctly identified the nature of the problem. We understand the past by giving to the data of the past a meaningful narrative order, by fitting it into a literary model that enables us to make sense of these data. But what literary model can explain this monstrous and unspeakable crime? Hence, "a writer about the holocaust will either be seen as adding what does not belong, or omitting something that does,"[16] and in either case the writer's shortcomings seem to call into question both scholarly capacity and moral integrity. Most contemporary debate, therefore, deals with what formal requirements must be met for a responsible representation of the Holocaust. This is why Berel Lang argues that the inevitable defect of literary language is that its poetic dimension invites language to place itself between us and the Holocaust, and that for this reason an account that remains as close as possible to the facts is to be preferred;[17] this is why the discourse of *Alltagsgeschichte* is considered by some incapable of representing the real dimensions of the Holocaust, and why others argue that it is precisely thanks to this kind of discourse that we will be able to recognize both "the banality of evil" and the ease with which "ordinary men"[18]—people like ourselves—can be brought to commit the most horrendous crimes. This is also why, according to Jean-François Lyotard, the Holocaust confronts us with a perplexity similar to the Kantian sublime and why this notion may help us to overcome the paradox of representing the unrepresentable of the Holocaust. Finally, this is also why, for Geoffrey Hartman "our *sefer hashoah* will have to accomplish the impossible: to allow the limits of representation to be healing limits yet not allow them to conceal an event we are obligated to recall and to interpret, both to ourselves and those growing up unconscious of its shadows."[19]

But we can take one further step and not merely ask ourselves what formal requirements a representation of the Holocaust should satisfy but focus instead on the more straightforward question of what content such a representation is in danger of leaving out or even of obliterating. An answer to that question is suggested by Gadamer, who, despite the linguistic transcendentalism that is advocated in his opus magnum, was not entirely insensitive to the limitations and shortcomings of language. Thus we cannot fail to be struck by Gadamer's surprisingly frank admission that "we know what it means for the mastery of an experience if one tries to put it into words. It is as if its threatening and striking directness has been removed in the distance, reduced to manageable proportions, as if this directness has been made communicable and been eliminated by precisely this effort."[20] Hence, what is destroyed by language and the text, what is "domesticated" and "appropriated" by the transcendentality of language, is the preverbal experience that we have of reality. And, in fact, Gadamer's own work is the best illustration of his own insight: though Gadamer's subject is our experience of the work of art and of history, we see that it is the major purpose of his work to exchange the category of experience for the text describing a *Wirkungsgeschichte* ("effective history"). The experience of historicity is abandoned for the historicity of experience and of the language in which it is expressed.[21]

Therefore, the dimension of experience is what is most likely to get lost in representation, and we may conclude that it is the experience or the reexperiencing of the Holocaust that makes us confront the limits of representation. An exploration of these limits thus urges us to consider "testimony" and what we ordinarily associate with that word: for does not testimony give us a representation of a person's deepest and most significant experiences? And should we not agree that to the extent that the experience of the Holocaust can be represented in language, language will have to take the form of testimony? Is it not in the testimony of the survivors that we can come closest to the unnamable horrors of the K.Z. (concentration camps)? And is not the most impressive language about the Holocaust, like Celan's "Todesfuge" (Death fugue), written in the form of a testimony? Surely testimony is the only way of giving expression to the experience and reexperience of the Holocaust.

Let us consider, then, the book in which Felman and Laub describe how the survivors of the Nazi regime remember the Holocaust—and whose title *Testimony* is the very best and most appropriate one they could possibly have given to it. Shoshana Felman gives the following meaning to the word:

> To testify before an audience of speakers or spectators—is more than simply to report a fact or an event or to relate what has been lived, recorded and remembered. Memory is conjured here essentially in order to *address* another, to impress upon a listener, to *appeal* to a community. . . . To testify is thus not merely to narrate but to commit oneself, and to commit the narrative to others.[22]

The language of testimony thus goes beyond the limitations of narrative language as it is customarily used by the historian, in which an impersonal, intersubjective voice addresses a similarly impersonal and intersubjective audience. Felman comes to this conclusion about the shortcomings of conventional historical prose in considering the cooperation of Claude Lanzmann with the historian Raul Hilberg, when the former was producing the film *Shoah*. In this film, where testimony is the exclusive form of representation, Lanzmann "does embrace the historical insights of Hilberg, which he holds in utter respect and from which he gets both inspiration and instruction, while the film also places in perspective—and puts in context—the discipline of history as such, in stumbling on (and giving us to see) the very limits of historiography."[23] Thus, according to Laub, it is by using the language of testimony that *Shoah* transcends the limits of conventional historiography. For the testimony is addressed to us, as individual, moral human beings, and that effectively prevents us from hiding behind the morally neutral screen of historical objectivism; it suggests, so to speak, a direct confrontation with the utterances of the testifier; it is a direct line from the voice of the testifier to us, and thus cuts short the whole circuitry of historical questioning—thereby "putting historiography in its proper context," as Laub wrote, and at times even correcting it.[24]

But even more significant is the following. Massive trauma is what is recollected in the testimonies discussed by Felman and Laub in their book. And trauma determined the character of these testimonies. Trauma results when experiences have been so horrendous and unspeakable that they cannot be accepted and admitted to consciousness. In the interviews that the psychoanalyst Laub had with the survivors of the K.Z., the unspeakable past was made present again in the most literal sense of the word. Thus Laub describes the "testimony" by an older lady in the following words of a concentration-camp experience: "A dazzling, brilliant moment from the past swept through the frozen stillness of the muted, grave-like landscape with dashing meteoric speed, exploding it into a shower of sights and sounds."[25] When speaking about what she suddenly remembered for the first time, in her testimony, she saw "the unimaginable taking place right in front of her own eyes."[26] Speech and experience became mere aspects of each other, and the barriers separating them were temporarily obliterated, in the act of speaking about the traumatic event, in the event of the testimony in which the shell that enclosed the traumatic past was broken. A historical *reality* took on the form of *testimony*, that is, of *words*—and vice versa. And it has been argued that if we really encounter reality itself, cold and naked reality itself, stripped of all the soft narrative and linguistic cushions that we have placed between us and it, we could not help but be traumatized.[27] It is in moments of awe and horror that we face reality itself, and there are no moments of supreme ecstasy to compensate for this; reality exclusively is the source of pain and trauma. Hence Laub's surprising argument, "it is thus genocide, and genocide alone, that can give one the right to feel as *real* and as *lasting*."[28] It is genocide that confronts us with reality in its primordial, noumenal nakedness, and it is in the trauma effected by the experience of reality that all the complexities of representation finally unfold.

Therefore, only to the extent that the history of the Holocaust is "personalized" or "privatized"—that is, in the testimony of the traumatic experiences of the survivors and in our recognition that their testimony is addressed to us as individuals—can the inexorable law dictating the limits of representation momentarily be defied. Probing the limits of representation, testing the limits of the "linguistic turn" and the textual appropriation of the past, as we are required to do by the Holocaust, thus inevitably effects the personalization or privatization of the past.

COMMEMORATION

If the preceding section presented us with the most tragic and intensely experienced aspects of human history, I now turn to its opposite part in the spectrum of our relationship to the past. If the history of the Holocaust transfigures the meaning of every word used for describing it, we will now deal with the *degré zéro* with which the past presents itself to us— that is, in commemoration. I do not want to say that the commemorated past cannot be a most dramatic past; one only need think of the commemoration of the French Revolution or the commemoration of the Holocaust (as opposed to testimonies of the Holocaust). I wish to emphasize, rather, that whereas testimony obliterates the barriers between us and past reality, commemoration does the opposite, since the whole raison d'être of commemoration is the celebration of a past of fifty, one hundred, or two hundred years ago. Commemoration originates in the time barrier, deliberately places the past at this distance of decades or centuries, and thus deemphasizes *sui generis* the drama of even the most dramatic events. The past is here really very much "past." Furthermore, testimony is pure experiential content, whereas commemoration is ritualistic and happily extols all its ceremonial formalisms. Testimony is content, commemoration is form.

If we wish to grasp how commemoration privatizes the past, we should take into account that commemoration always combines a primary movement of decontextualization with a secondary one of *re*contextualization—and it is the latter that enables commemoration to privatize a hitherto more generally shared past. With regard to the movement of decontextualization, the simple but crucial datum is that, in commemorations, our relationship to the past is generally determined—and the very oddity of this observation brings us to the essence of the matter—by our preference for numbers that are a multiple of five. That is to say, we commemorate the discovery of America, not in 1990 or in 1976, but in 1992, when the event took place exactly five hundred years ago. Hence—and that is the upshot of this trivial observation—the relationship between the commemoration itself and the commemorated past does not have its origin in the precise historical nature of either of the two or in the nature of the historical evolution connecting them (as always was the case in historism where the past was studied precisely because we see ourselves as a product of that historical evolution), but in the contingent fact that we happen to have five fingers on each of our two hands. To conclude, the commemoration does not have its real origin in the nature of the past itself: our relationship to the past is determined here by extrahistorical and purely arithmetical considerations.

It even seems likely that this high-handed subjection of the past to arithmetical schemes is precisely what attracts us so much in commemoration. And, indeed, there certainly is a deeper meaning in this attraction; the commemoration, if seen from this perspective, convincingly testifies to our complete mastery of the past. For here the past is ruthlessly forced into schemes that are so alien to it that it could never effectively itself protest against our decisions with regard to commemoration. Here the past is completely helpless with regard to ourselves, to the commemorator. Perhaps we may even discern here the real motivation of the recent increased need to commemorate the Second World War and the Holocaust: perhaps this is how we, subconsciously, try to rid ourselves of this most oppressive and still largely undigested part of our past. And if there is some truth in this conjecture, commemoration can clearly be seen as the very opposite of testimony as it was discussed in the previous section. For testimony is a Michelet-like "resurrection of the past," whereas commemoration is the ultimate attempt to master the past and to render it innocuous forever.

But this movement of decontextualization is only half of the story. The human mind is associative and feels an irresistible need to connect, to associate and to contextualize. Arguably this is what secured man's success in his Darwinian struggle for survival. There are few things that require of us such a tremendous and apparently unnatural effort as the effort *not* to relate something to something else (which is, perhaps, why mathematics and logic are so unnatural and therefore so difficult for most of us)—so much so that our need to contextualize is almost always victorious. We may also recall here that if the mind is really left completely to itself, as paradigmatically is the case when we dream, pure patterns of contextualization are replayed and recreated again and again, while what is contextualized itself loses all autonomy to these patterns of contextualization. All meaning in the dream is contextual meaning, as Freud has taught us.

This fact about the human mind may deepen our insight into the nature of commemoration. Let me explain this with the help of the following simile. Compare our memory to a slate. Most often the slate will be completely covered by the memories that we have been scribbling all over it in a more or a less remote past. And if new memories present themselves, they have to be written over and across other memories, so to speak—and precisely this is how these contextualist patterns of memories, which I mentioned a moment ago, come into being. Within this metaphor decontextualization—as effected by commemoration—could best be compared to a wiping clean of a small corner on the slate. As a consequence, not only what is remembered in commemoration itself, but also the accidental *circumstances* under which commemoration takes place, will tend to be written down on the place that was wiped clean. And the crucial result is that a purely accidental but nevertheless very strong link is created between the commemorated past and the relevant features of the present of the commemoration itself. Hence the commemoration makes it possible to link all kinds of "macro-events" with a historical and political significance to those "micro-events" of our daily life that happened to take place during the commemoration. We may therefore agree with David Lowenthal when he writes about commemorative memory: "Memory converts public events into idiosyncratic personal experiences."[29]

Something similar could be said about statues—which are no less paradigmatical examples of Nora's *lieux de mémoire* than commemorations. We will often find statues in the busy centers of our large cities, where little, if anything, actually reminds us of the person or the event that is commemorated by the statue. The result of this contextlessness of the statue is that the public, insofar as it is aware of the existence of the statue at all, will tend to subsume the statue in its own daily routine without ever asking itself pertinent questions about the historical personality or the event that the statue commemorates. The statue is like a part of the past itself that rather helplessly stretches out in the present and that is unable to defend itself against all unseemly things that we might wish to project on it. As Diderot saw, the statue is, because of its imperturbable contextlessness, an object that readily adapts itself to even our most bizarre and untoward desires for contextualization. "Diderot himself had great reverence for statues," writes Banville;

he thought of them as living somehow: strange, solitary beings, exemplary, aloof, closed on themselves and at the same time yearning in their mute and helpless way to step down into our world, to laugh or to weep, know happiness and pain, to be mortal, like us. "Such beautiful statues," he wrote in a letter to his mistress Sophie Volland, "hidden in the remotest spots and distant from one another, statues which call to me, that I seek out and encounter, that arrest me and with which I have long conversations."[30]

This willingness to go along in our conversation and to share our present preoccupations—a willingness that statues share with commemorations—can, needless to say, be exploited for present aims and purposes. To mention one example: When the French government in 1880 introduced the celebration of July 14, it also decided to start school vacations on that date. Obviously in this way an indissoluble link was established between the political freedom promised by the Great Revolution, in terms of which the Third Republic wanted to legitimate itself, and the prospect of being free from homework and oppressive classrooms for a period of two months. Pavlov wouldn't have arranged things differently. Here lies the practical political function of commemoration and of statues, a function for which a quickly increasing interest exists since the publication of Nora's vast collection of studies on what he referred to as the *lieux de mémoire*.[31] In this way, an initial movement of decontextualization is followed by a recontextualization that stimulates the identification with the state, its history, and its ideological inspirations. We might speak here—and I shall return to this again—of a "democratization" of the past, in the sense that the past, as re-presented by the commemoration or the statue, serves the "democratic" purpose of making all citizens feel members of one nation with one shared history.

However, this play of decontextualization and recontextualization is not without its ironies, and from the perspective of the "privatization" of the past (in contrast to the "democratization" of the past, mentioned just now) these ironies require our attention. Indeed, human memory constitutes itself, thanks to contextualization, within the ever changing webs of our associations. The anonymous author of the *Ad herennium*, the treatise that has determined Western thought about memory for almost two thousand years, was well aware of this aspect of our memory and looked there for an answer to the question of how to optimize our capacity to remember. "Constat igitur artificiosa memoria ex locis et imaginibus [artificial memory is constructed from places]"—hence Nora's *lieux de mémoire!*—and images, says this author.[32] That is to say, by relating certain events we wish to remember to the places where they occurred (or to those that we deliberately decide to associate with them), we will succeed best in shoring up our defective memories. We remember the place—and then the event itself is inevitably produced by our memory, because we have learned to associate it with the place in question. The crucial datum here, however, is that association is the "anti-elitist" function par excellence of our mind: association does not link (at least not necessarily so) what is "equal in rank," as is the case with reason, but has, on the contrary, a perverse fancy for *mésalliances*. Reason is aristocratic and association is democratic. Association is, as Freud has taught us, the great mental leveler which, without any respect for what we respect, does not hesitate to link the most superb and the most sublime to the most banal and most trivial. This constant destabilization of the "aristocratic" patterns that were laboriously constructed by reason is truly one of the most fascinating effects of our associative mind. In his associations the dullest neurotic can therefore be no less interesting than the greatest artist or scientist—and this was, obviously, another lesson from Freud.

Another example: We all know the question, "Do you remember where you were when you heard of the murder of Kennedy?" This question may effect, in an interesting way, in the link between place and memory, a shift from what is remembered to the place where we happened to be at the moment when we heard of Kennedy's murder. That is to say, we become intrigued by the fact that we happened to be at a particular place at the moment in question, rather than by the event that we associate with that place (in my case the buffet at Utrecht station). Hence, this support of memory, pointed out in *Ad herennium*, becomes stronger than what is remembered, and the past itself is now at the mercy of the one who remembers it. Or, to put in the terms of this discussion: what is commemorated loses its logical priority to the commemoration. Bearing this in mind, let us go back to our previous example of the beginning of the school vacations that coincided, in the France of the Third Republic, with the commemoration of the fall of the Bastille on July 14. We should observe, then, that the conflation of contexts that was effected by this arrangement could work out into either of two ways. Surely, the prospect of a vacation at the beach at Deauville or at the Basin of Arcachon could give a quite specific aura to July 14 and what happened on that date—and this "democratization" of the Great Revolution was undoubtedly what had been intended by the Ferry government in 1880, when it decided to present itself in this way as heir to the ideals of July 14. But this conflation of contexts can equally well work out in the wrong direction. That is to say, not in the sense of elevating summer vacation to the sublime level of one of the major events in French history, but, on the contrary, by demoting the latter to the trivial level of a vacation near the sea. Just as in the Kennedy example, the historical thus gets infected by the small pleasures and disappointments of daily life. Commemoration then no longer places the life of the individual against the background of national history; it no longer democratizes the past, but places, instead, national history against the background of the banalities of the individual's life. A shared, national past then becomes privatized within the petty domain of the small pleasures and disappointments that make up our daily life.

Even more so, this perverse effect of commemoration was not only recognized, but often exploited right from the start with as much relish as all the patriotic and nationalistic potentialities of commemoration. In Pascal Ory's discussion of the celebration of the one hundredth anniversary of the outbreak of the Great Revolution (which would give to Paris, by the way, the Eiffel Tower), Ory discerns, besides the need to commemorate the Revolution, "un volontarisme célébratif" that saw in the commemoration little more than a suitable occasion for presenting the triumphs and the successes of nineteenth-century science and technology. The obvious objection was, of course, that nineteenth-century science was being celebrated rather than 1789—an objection that was actually made at the time and countered by the peculiarly hypocritical argument that nineteenth-century science had only become possible thanks to the revolution. Apparently, proponents of the celebration had conveniently forgotten the revolutionary slogan (invented by Lavoisier's detractors) that "la Révolution n'a pas besoin de savants." Though they may sincerely have tried to find in 1889 the *juste milieu* between commemoration and celebration (in Ory's sense of these two terms), it cannot be denied that a first step was now taken toward the privatization (in contrast to the democratization) of the history and memory of the Great Revolution. And this would merely be the first step. As time went on, July 14 gradually degenerated into a welcome occasion for a free day, some collective amusement, drinking a glass too much, and ending the day in someone else's bed. The date lost the capacity to revive a historical event, with all its political implications: "Having become pure routine, the ritual is celebrated each year in a touristic ambiance that seems already a priori to be devoid of any political militancy and party affiliation." Thus Christian Amalvi in his history of the commemoration of July 14.[33]

All the evidence indicates a contemporary preference for the privatization of the past by commemoration, rather than for its democratization. Pierre Nora developed a surprising thesis about this evolution. It is paradigmatic, according to Nora, that the state no longer is the natural focus of interest in commemoration. This is most clearly evident from the many local commemorations that we see daily announced in the papers and in which often an only thinly concealed resistance to whatever we may associate with "the center"—and that is, paradigmatically, the state—clearly announces itself. Even more so, quite often the commemoration is consciously intended to extol a local community at the expense of other communities, and, most specifically, of the state as the paramount community. As Nora observes, the commemoration "has become, for all groups involved, an isolated thread in the social texture and that will permit to each of them a short-circuited relationship with a past that is definitely dead and gone."[34] The merely "patrimonial," the heritage of a local or "private" past, gets the better of the traditional historical consciousness that saw in the history of the nation the course of history and the self-evident center for each meaningful relationship to the past. Commemoration no longer serves those centripetal forces that made the nation in the previous century into the most important social and historical agent, but the centrifugal forces that are generally considered to be the defining characteristic of postmodernism. Contemporary commemoration and the return to memory that is expressed by it were both born on the grave of the state as the center of all creative politics. And we may therefore agree with C. S. Maier, when he expresses his uneasiness about the present popularity of "memory," and what is to be associated by it, as follows: "The surfeit of memory is a sign not of historical confidence but of a retreat from transformative politics."[35]

Hence, the peculiar paradox is that our contemporary culture of commemoration, which is, on the one hand, a product of Halbwachs's "collective memory," is, on the other, an exponent of our increased unwillingness to identify ourselves with that paramount collective entity, the state. Of course we still have commemorations on a national scale, perhaps even more than ever before, but as we saw with July 14, they have become the mere lifeless simulacra of what they once used to be. Nowadays, commemoration has all its force and all its authenticity in what is indissolubly linked to the local, to the region, the city, the village, or, speaking more generally, to whatever a community recognizes as its difference from the rest of society or of the nation. Commemoration now aims at exclusion, not inclusion. From that perspective, commemoration can well be seen as the counterpart in Western countries of that resurgence that we have observed over the last few years in the former Eastern European countries. And in both cases we have to do with a privatization of a formerly collective domain, rather than with its democratization.³⁶

Perhaps the most striking symbol of this shift from the democratization of memory toward its privatization is the so-called counter-monument. Gillis describes the first example of this kind of monument as follows:

> In 1986 the first of the counter-monuments was erected in Harburg, a lead-sheathed obelisk dedicated to the victims of Nazism that invited the public to inscribe their names and message on its surfaces. As these were filled, the obelisk was lowered gradually into the ground, where it eventually disappeared, leaving as its only trace the living memory of those who visited the site previously."³⁷

How far are we removed here from the paradigm of the "unknown soldier" in whom, lying beneath his eternal flame and surrounded by all the splendors expressing the nation's grandeur, each relative of each victim fallen in war can recognize his or her husband, father or brother. The unknown soldier is the commemorative counterpart of the state, abstract and general, the very incorporation of the nation's history and the center to which all personal memories are expected to gravitate. In the case of the counter-monument, on the other hand, each inscribes his own personal memories on the monument; it is a work of art that is made by the whole community as separate individuals and that carefully respects their individuality. It thus becomes a monument that reflects to each only his own personal memories; and in order to emphasize and to symbolize this privatization of memory, the monument is buried, so that, as a matter of fact, personal memories are all that is left to us. And yet, how effective and moving is the counter-monument: it is here that commemoration and testimony seem to be solemnly shaking hands over the whole of history and the sadness that it caused in the hearts of millions of individual human beings.

No reader of Hegel's philosophy of history will ever forget his elegiac description of the destruction of Greek morality by Socrates, surely is one of the most moving passages that ever to be written by a Western philosopher. What Socrates did to the Athens of his time is described by Hegel as follows:

> In a former time laws and customs were valid unconditionally; human individuality formed a unity with the universal. To honor the gods, to die for one's fatherland was a universal law and everybody fulfilled this universal content as a matter of

course. Then, however, humanity started to inquire whether one should really wish or comply with this content. The awakening of this thought brought about the death of the gods of Greece and of natural custom [*die schöne Sittlichkeit*]. Thought makes its appearance here as the principle of destruction, that is, as the destruction of natural custom; for because it knows itself to be an independent principle it establishes principles of reason standing in a critical relation to existing reality and in opposition to the limitations of natural custom. The former Greeks were perfectly well aware of what custom required them to do under each condition; but that man ought to discover the answer to such questions in himself—that has been Socrates' point. Socrates has made man aware of his inner self, so that man's conscience could become the measure of what is right and morally true [*Moralität*]. This is the contrast between the natural customs of a former time and the moral reasoning of a later time; the former Greeks had no conscience. Socrates is famous as a moral teacher; in truth, however, he has been the discoverer of morals.[38]

Hegel's account of "das Verderben der Griechischen Sittlichkeit" is, in fact, a most suggestive allegory for the fate of historical writing and historical consciousness over, roughly, the last two centuries, and for the contemporary privatization of the past discussed in this chapter. If the nineteenth and twentieth centuries were the heyday of historical consciousness in the history of Western civilization (perhaps only paralleled in this respect by the sixteenth century),[39] it was because there was generally felt to be a natural link between the fate of the individual and history. Just as Hegel's pre-Socratic Greeks accepted the existence of the gods, the obligation to die for one's country, and so on, as a matter of course—with the result that a momentary and aesthetically most pleasing harmony between the individual, morals, society, and the state became possible—so we have been able over the last two centuries to recognize ourselves in the majestic stories of the Western past, which were related to us by historians, of the nation, Western culture, or the struggle of social classes for political and economic emancipation. But just as Socrates destroyed the unparalleled harmony of the Greek state by introducing the domain of subjectivity into a situation where once subjectivity and objectivity had been in a subtle and perfect but precarious unity, so the no less precarious equilibrium of history and of the individual citizen's perspective is now gradually being destroyed by the gravitational forces of subjectivity—of the "private," to use the term that has been used in this chapter. This certainly does not mean, of course, that we shall soon witness the end of all historical writing as we have known it since the nineteenth century. It does, however, mean two no less significant things. In the first place, we may expect that the fascination for the domain of the private that is so characteristic of the history of mentalities, of the micro-stories, of *Alltagschichte*, and so on, will be with us for the foreseeable future. It means, in the second place, that histories on the grand scale, as they were produced in the nineteenth and twentieth centuries, will undoubtedly still be written and admired in the future, but that this great tradition will tend to resemble an impressive and seemingly impregnable stronghold that is, however, slowly but surely abandoned by its former occupants. It will no longer satisfy an urgent intellectual need of Western civilization—just as composers lost touch with the needs of civilization somewhere between Brahms and Schoenberg, with the result that contemporary music became an innocuous playground of marginal cultural significance, of interest only to a few snobs and a select little group of musicologically highly sophisticated individuals.

But let me try to be more specific and to narrow down somewhat these rather grand and sweeping claims. In this chapter I have contrasted testimony with commemoration. Each can be situated on either side of the spectrum of how we relate to the past. Testimony gives us the most intimate and intense relationship to the past and, as we have observed in the case of trauma, it may even take the form of a revival of the past in the proper sense of the word. On the other hand, nowhere is our relationship to the past less intense, less determined by the nature of historical evolution itself than in the case of commemoration. Not history but arithmetic is decisive here. History and historical writing, as we know it, are always somewhere in between these two extremes: in "normal" historical writing the past is never so dramatically present as it is in testimony; on the other hand, the past will be far less helpless and have considerably more autonomy than it may have in commemoration. Bearing this in mind, we should take note of two more facts. Firstly, as has been argued above, in both cases, in both testimony and in commemoration, the past becomes privatized in a way that would have been unthinkable in the days of traditional, disciplinary historical writing and the reign of the disciplinary historical subject that traditionally was history's epistemological backbone. Secondly, both testimony and commemoration have become the much preferred matrices for our relationship to the past. Thus Felman and Laub characterize our era "as an age of testimony,"[40] whereas William Johnston sees a "véritable industrie de la commémoration,"[41] and Nora unreservedly speaks about "le modèle mémorial qui l'a emporté sur le modèle historique."[42] If we take into account these three data, we cannot but conclude that traditional history, wedged as it is between testimony and commemoration, will gradually tend to yield to the pressure of the privatization of the past. And this would result, in the first place, in the gradual dissolution of history as a discipline, and in the second, in a greater tolerance for the presence of historians themselves in their writings. The changes that have been taking place at "the borders" of contemporary historical consciousness, and that have been discussed in this chapter, cannot fail to transmit themselves to what lies enclosed within these borders.

A more theoretical consideration can be added to the latter claim. "History as a discipline" always required the elimination of historians from the story they were telling, yet at the same time the very impossibility of this self-defeating demand was always emphasized. The argument took a most interesting form in structuralist theories of history. If we think of what Barthes meant by "myth," arguably the paramount example of the impasse disciplinary history had created for itself, the structuralist argument always required an undistorted, "objective" account of the past in order to permit any similar characterizations of the historical text. Without this curiously paradoxical ideal, without the idea of a past *an sich* that is distorted by "myth," the structuralist's characterization of the historical text would simply have made no sense. Hence, the elimination of the historian's self was presented as both a necessity and an impossibility. Whatever opinion one may have of the "privatization of the past" that is so openly and warmly embraced within postmodernist historical theory, it has at least the advantage that it no longer requires us to satisfy the epistemological acrobacy that was demanded by structuralism.

6

REMEMBERING THE HOLOCAUST: MOURNING AND MELANCHOLIA

Writing about the Holocaust has its own specific difficulties. Ordinarily it is sufficient for the theorist to respect the truth and be intelligent—though, as we all know, that is hard enough. But writing about the Holocaust requires, beyond that, tact and a talent for knowing when and how to avoid the pitfalls of the inappropriate. Every discussion of the Holocaust runs the risk of getting involved in a vicious circle, where misunderstanding and immorality mutually suggest and reinforce each other. And it is only an aesthetic category—the essentially aesthetic category of the appropriate—that may enable us to avoid here the impasses to which the search for the merely true and the ethically good invariably will lead. Hence, when confronted with the ultimate challenge—accounting for the Holocaust—it is aesthetics, and not the categories of the factually true and the morally good, to which history should appeal. The ultimate challenge for both historical writing and the historian is not factual or ethical, but aesthetic.

As we saw in the previous chapter, a good deal of recent historical theory has become involved in this issue of tact and of what is the "appropriate" kind of discourse for speaking about the Holocaust. The conflict of opinions about this issue can be charted in several different ways. In the present context, however, it will be most illuminating to describe this conflict as one between "history" on the one hand and "remembrance" or "memory" on the other. This issue could be summarized as follows. Some historians and theorists, such as Berel Lang, argue that one should adopt the "discourse of history" when speaking about the Holocaust. Their argument is that the historian's objectivist and detached language best satisfies the requirements of tact and appropriateness, whereas, for example, the novelist's language will inevitably appear as a blunt and self-assertive intrusion into a world that should be left untouched. It is, thus, precisely the aesthetics of the historian's language rather than that of the novelist that will enable one to deal as respectfully as possible with the realities of the Holocaust. Others, however, urge an abandonment of the discourse of history for that of memory, since only the language of memory can give us the aesthetics of authenticity that we ought to use when speaking about the Holocaust. And, together with the authors discussed at the end of the previous chapter, one might single out the language of testimony within the larger domain of the language of memory as being most appropriate.

Now, what is basically at stake in this debate? History and the discourse of history aim at describing and explaining the past—that is preeminently what we expect the historian to do. The historian typically realizes this aim by reducing what was initially strange, alien, and incomprehensible in the past to what was known to us already; that is, by showing what was strange in terms of what is already understood. This is what makes historical writing essentially metaphorical. Think, again, of the example of the Enlightenment: we are all acquainted with the reality of a room that is suddenly illuminated by a lamp or a candle. And we are then invited to relate the realities of eighteenth-century thought to that reality in a meaningful way. In this sense we can assert that metaphor is the foundation of historical writing and the source of its essential aesthetic properties.[1]

However—and this brings us to the alternative aestheticist position—is this feasible or even possible in the case of the Holocaust? Is there an already known reality to which we can reduce or in terms of which we can clarify the Holocaust? Is there an already well known and well established pattern of human behavior from which we can derive the Holocaust? Obviously not. When we refer to the Nazi crimes as "unnamable" or "unspeakable" we wish to express by these adjectives that there are no realities or concepts in terms of which these crimes can properly be described or represented. The Holocaust brings us to "the limits of what can be represented" by the historian, to paraphrase the title of Saul Friedlander's well-known collection that is devoted to the issue. This, then, is why the aestheticist awareness of the high demands of the "appropriate" has convinced some historians and theorists that one should exchange the discourse of history for that of memory in order to "appropriately" account for the Holocaust.

Their argument is that memory is free from the element of appropriation and intellectual possession so typical of the metaphorical and reductive language of the historian. Memory refers to the direction of our gaze rather than involving an identification of what we see in that direction. Characteristically, the strongest form of memory—nostalgia—is always accompanied by an intense and painful awareness of an unbridgeable distance to the object of nostalgic yearning.[2] Memory and nostalgia always endow their object with the aura of unattainability. And this is why the discourse of memory better respects these unnamable realities that we associate with the Holocaust than the discourse of the historian. The discourse of memory recognizes that we can never appropriate them and that each attempt to do so would be "inappropriate."

In a most perceptive essay, Jonathan Webber associated the Holocaust with a *tel olam*, the "biblical term for a place whose physical past should be blotted our forever."[3] That is to say, the Holocaust should remain to us forever an "empty place," a place that we can never hope to possess or actually occupy in the way that the historian hopes to appropriate or to come into the possession of the past with the help of his metaphors. The discourse of memory is "indexical," it points to or indicates the past, it encircles the past—but without ever attempting to penetrate into it. One is reminded here of how the Dutch poet Armando presents the Holocaust: not by simply and directly referring to the atrocities committed in the camps, but by incriminating the landscape, the trees surrounding the K.Z.'s, and the soil that witnessed these atrocities, and that thereby in a certain sense became accessory to the crime.[4] Access to the Holocaust is here indexical and metonymical rather than metaphorical. Metonymy favors mere contiguity, respects all the unpredictable contingencies of our memories, and is, as such, the very opposite of the proud metaphorical appropriation of reality. Metaphor has the pretension to go right to the heart of the matter, metonymy makes us simply move on to what happens to lie next to it—and so on, ad infinitum. Metonymy ties together a web of associations depending upon our personal experiences and a host of contingent factors, instead of forcing (past) reality within the matrices of a metaphorical appropriation of reality. That is also why metonymy—and not metaphor—is preeminently the discourse of psychoanalysis. For in psychoanalysis we do not move straight toward the metaphorical essence of our mind but retrace the route to our mind by abandoning ourselves to the unpredictable and quasi-Brownian movement of association.

The essentially indexical nature of memory—and where memory should be contrasted to the referentiality of history—is most clearly expressed by the monument. The monument does not tell us something about the past, in the way that the (metaphorical) historical text does, but functions rather like a (metonymical) signpost. Put differently, the monument functions like an index: it requires us to look in a certain direction without specifying what we shall ultimately find in that direction. Even more so, by being content with its mere indexicality, the monument not only leaves us free, but strongly invites us to project our own personal feelings and associations on that part of the past indicated by it. The monument generously accepts and respects all our feelings and associations and does not demand us to divide them into those that go right to the essence of the matter (supposing that there *is* such an essence) and those that avoid this pretension. This is where the monument and memory so conspicuously differ from history and from the written historical text. And this is also the dimension of the monument that is so subtly and ingeniously exploited by the so-called counter-monument.[5] As explained at the end of Chapter 5, the counter-monument is made to disappear underground in the course of time, so that a mere empty place, a *tel olam*, so to speak, remains that now exists in our memory only. In this way the counter-monument subtly requires us to internalize its essential indexicality.

Now, indexes may take many different forms. They do not share the aspirations of language, whose only purpose is to hide itself behind the reality that it refers to and which, therefore, ideally has one form only: namely that of the world described in it. The monument is, in the end, a work of art, and is granted the same broad range of self-presentation that we grant the work of art. The monument may, therefore, be just anything between the work of art that wholly absorbs our attention at the cost of the represented and the counter-monument discussed a moment ago that effaces itself completely by its wish to be nothing but a mere index or signpost.

YAD VASHEM

When considering the many varieties of the monument and the many different ways in which the monument may function as such a signpost to the past, nothing could be more instructive than Yad Vashem. Yad Vashem is Israel's official monument dedicated to the memory of the Holocaust. As early as 1942, when the first reports about the Holocaust reached Israel, Mordechai Shenhavi of the Kibbutz Mishmar Ha'emek proposed to commemorate both what he called "the Shoah of the Diaspora" and the participation of Jewish fighters in the Allied armies. Shenhavi also suggested the name "Yad Vashem," which literally means "a monument and a name." The name has its inspiration in the Bible book of Isaiah, where God announces how he will remember his covenant with the Jewish people: "I will give them, in my house and within my walls, a monument and a name, better than sons and daughters. I will give them an everlasting name that shall never be effaced."[6] All that Nora would associate many years later with the notion of the *lieux de mémoire* is thus present already in this name Yad Vashem. After an official act was passed by the Knesset in May 1953, Yad Vashem gradually developed into an elaborate complex of memorials, all commemorating the unspeakable crimes committed by the Nazis against the Jewish people.

There are several things about Yad Vashem that may strike the new visitor. In the first place, unlike the eternal flame under the Arc de Triomphe in Paris, unlike the monuments along the Mall in Washington or the monument of the victims of the World War II in Amsterdam, Jerusalem's Yad Vashem is located not in the center, but in the outskirts of the city. Whatever may have been the actual reasons for situating it there, there is something deeply symbolic about this location. It is as if in Paris, Washington, Amsterdam, and in so many other places, the already existing center of the city could only successfully endow the monument with the prominence it is supposed to possess in the heart of the nation, whereas Yad Vashem is not in need of such a situational support: the heart of the nation is with Yad Vashem and Yad Vashem creates a center of mourning wherever it is.

Moreover, walking along the paths and monuments of Yad Vashem one sees in the distance, on the hills silhouetted against the sky as on one of those quasi-surrealist frescoes by Fra Angelico, the white houses of the new

Jerusalem. These outskirts of Jerusalem, because of their silent serenity and their shining whiteness against the blue sky, seem to become part of the monument itself, or in a deeply meaningful way even to complete it. It is as if an atonement of the unnamable horrors of the past to be remembered at Yad Vashem is expressed by the mute, self-absorbed whiteness of this new Jerusalem. Here we are far from the old center, so heavily laden with a Jewish, Christian, and Muslim past and all the struggle and human suffering that have tainted these pasts; here we have come to a space truly between heaven and earth, where a new city of God could be built. In this way Yad Vashem seems to absorb in itself, and give a meaning to, the silent landscape surrounding it.

But there is more that provokes meditation. It is a common experience of those visiting Yad Vashem for the first time that one loses one's way again and again on the site. Though the terrain on which Yad Vashem is located does not exceed some ten to fifteen acres, and though shields clearly indicate the location of the different monuments, there is something peculiarly labyrinthine about the whole complex. It is as if it is reluctant to yield up the traumatic secrets of the past that it commemorates, as if these secrets can be revealed only one by one to the visitor, so that he can better realize their enormity. In a way the labyrinth of Yad Vashem thus seems to mimic the intricacies of two thousand years of Jewish history and the confusions into which it threw the Jewish people. The intricacies of the layout may also remind the visitor of the seemingly endless labyrinthine journeys that the Jews from Saloniki, France, or the Low Countries had to make before finally arriving at their dismal destination. And, lastly, the erratic path followed by the visitor may also bring out to him or her the paradox that the road to this greatest crime in human history could afford to be so tortuous and backward a road—so utterly unlike the nearby Via Dolorosa (that was seen by the eyes of the world and of history)—and yet reach its destination with a deathly precision.

Following the paths of the labyrinth of Yad Vashem, the visitor passes along the numerous monuments that were placed there—in fact, rather haphazardly—since 1953. Most of them were, of course, originally devised for Yad Vashem, such as Fink's *Soldiers, Ghetto Fighters, and Partisans*; Schwartz's twenty-one-meter-high, stainless-steel pillar dedicated to the heroism of those who rebelled in the camps and the ghettos; or Sakstier's deeply moving *Korczak and the Children of the Ghetto*, commemorating the teacher who did not want to abandon the orphaned Jewish children in his charge and preferred to die with them in Treblinka. Other monuments replicate those standing elsewhere, such as Nathan Rapoport's monument for the Warsaw Ghetto Uprising, or the replication of the monument *Dry Bones*, which Nandor Glid had made for Dachau.[7] This terrifying monument, where barbed wire and crying and distorted human bodies seem to have become each other's metamorphosis, and whose skeletal forms stand bleakly out against the sky of which they gradually seem to become a part, calls to mind lines from Celan's "Todesfuge":

> er ruft streicht dunkler die Geigen dann steigt ihr als Rauch in
>   die Luft
> dann habt ihr ein Grab in den Wolken da liegt man nicht eng
>
> he calls out more darkly now stroke your strings then as smoke
>   you will rise into air
> then a grave you will have in the clouds there one lies
>   unconfined[8]

The visitor, not familiar with the experience of so many different monuments, all so close together, feels overwhelmed and confused by the feelings and associations provoked by each of them. Why so many monuments? one asks oneself. For is there not something essentially exclusivist about the monument, in the sense that each monument suggests a perspective on or functions like a prism for what it commemorates? Is it not only thanks to this tactful exclusivism that the monument can disappear, by a logic of its own, behind what it commemorates, and why it can actually achieve a resurrection of what is remembered at the place vacated by its evanescent self? Put differently, does not the simultaneous presence of several monuments invite us to focus on the fact that they are all attempts to commemorate something, with the result that we only see *ways* of commemorating the past instead of *what* is commemorated? And does this not invite the danger that the monument becomes a kind of screen *separating* us from the object of commemoration instead of bringing us *closer* to it?

However, it is one of the strangest experiences of the visitor to Yad Vashem that precisely the opposite is evoked. Indeed, the flame of the Unknown soldier in Paris, or London's memorial to those who fell during the First World War will tend to become part of the city's furniture; these "solitary" monuments will start to interact with their surroundings and to become the helpless fetish on which we can project anything we like[9]—indeed, as the embodiment of the coalescence of the private and the public, of the history of the nation *and* of the individual citizen, it may remind the widower or the orphan of the husband of the father they lost during the war, but no less the young couple of that warm and sunny day when they first met in its shadow. As authors like Diderot and Musil already knew, monuments are, so to speak, quite sociable beings that like to talk to us and to address us in the language that we daily use and that enables us to reduce the world within the limits of our own preoccupations. They are only too ready to abandon what they represent for a participation in our daily life.

Yad Vashem, however, by the sheer multiplication of monuments, prevents us from domesticating it; the number of monuments and the differences between them enhance the monuments' autonomy with regard to their surroundings and each other in a kind of monumentalist "intertextuality"—and never is Yad Vashem degraded to the pitiful status of becoming a mere display of the several ways in which the Holocaust can be remembered. Why is this? Why do the many different ways in which this past is remembered and represented here not occlude and obscure a remembered and represented reality? Is it because of the immense weight of the remembered past that will always dwarf each representation, and that will always loom like a dark shadow far above each representation of it? Is it because each of the monuments testifies to another aspect of the nameless suffering and of the crimes they commemorate? Is it because the Holocaust will always go beyond the limits of representation? Is it because the Holocaust seems to stand outside narratable and representable history, so that the monuments commemorating it are reduced to the status of mere signs, like numbers or helpless syllables, unable to carry a meaning and to be anything more than pure and naked reference? Hence, can the Holocaust monument *never* properly be said to be a commemorative representation of the Holocaust because no Holocaust monument could ever add meaning to pure and naked reference? Is this, then, the secret of Yad Vashem?

Asking these questions brings me to how Yad Vashem can help us to understand the commemoration of the Holocaust. In order to make clear my intentions, I want to contrast Yad Vashem's two most spectacular monuments: the Hall of Remembrance and the Children's Memorial. For between these two monuments we may discern the whole spectrum expanding from meaning to pure reference and the experience of the meaningless referent I referred to a moment ago. I shall start with the Hall of Remembrance and follow with the description given by James Young:

> The floor panels of the Ohel Yiskor—literally, Tent of Remembrance—bear the names of twenty-two of the largest concentration camps and are arranged in rough geographical order. In one corner, directly beneath an open skylight, an eternal flame flickers amid a sharp-pronged sheath of bronze, which seem to open up like the petals of a black flower. It is bathed in a smoky beam of light from the opening above it and set just behind a white granite slab which covers a pit holding the ashes from the death camps. . . . It might be regarded more literally as a collective matzevah for unknown victims, a crypt.[10]

It is this which makes the Hall of Remembrance into the official monument of the State of Israel to the victims of the Holocaust, and this is the sense in which this monument is not unlike the monuments erected in so many countries to honor those who have fallen for the nation—though certainly, it is the names of the camps that effectively place this monument apart from all its counterparts in other countries. What can even remotely resemble the horrors we associate with those terrible names: Sobibor, Treblinka, Majdanek, Chelmno, Stutthof, and, above all, Auschwitz-Birkenau? These are names having such a deep and profound resonance in our minds that we even have difficulty in believing that places actually existing on our globe correspond to them—so that, when we see in Lanzmann's *Shoah* railway stations with the place names of Treblinka or Sobibor, we initially tend to react with the same disbelief as when someone might inform us that hell (or heaven) has recently been discovered by explorers in some remote part of the globe.

Precisely the kind of associations that are evoked by these terrible names permit the Hall of Remembrance to be the kind of monument that it is and that assure it its "effectiveness." The monument, so to speak, mobilizes all that we have heard and know about the concentration camps, about what six million Jews, half of them Polish Jews and the other half ethnic Jews, and so many from so many other nations suffered there, so that we become aware, once again, of the proportions of the crime. As a lens may concentrate the light in its focus, so the monument concentrates our feelings, associations, and knowledge of the Holocaust into a moment of awareness of the Holocaust as close to its actuality as we can come. It is this that makes the Hall of Remembrance into the kind of monument for the Holocaust that is most suitable for a generation that is still fairly close to the

Holocaust and for which the Holocaust has not yet receded into a past containing other horrors like (the often forgotten) genocide of the Aztecs and the Indians, the Thirty Years' War, the seventeenth- and eighteenth-century slave trade, or all that followed the French Revolution. The monument *presupposes* our memories, associations, and knowledge are already *present* in one way or another; without knowledge about the Holocaust, the Hall of Remembrance would be to us a mere list of strange and foreign names.

It is different with the Children's Memorial (commemorating the one and a half million Jewish children that were killed during the war), whose contrast with the Hall of Remembrance can deepen our insight into the commemoration of the Holocaust. Let me start my argument with a short description of the relevant details of the Children's Memorial. The monument was commissioned by an American survivor of the Holocaust, Abraham Spiegel, whose son Uziel perished in Auschwitz, and was designed by the Israeli architect Moshe Safdie. One may discern three levels in the memorial. With regard to the first level, outside the memorial are some twenty square pillars of increasing height, all roughly hewn off at the top. The artist's intention is undoubtedly to suggest in this way the truncated lives of the children that were killed in the ghettos and the camps, while the whiteness of the pillars symbolizes their innocence. The suggestion is most ingeniously reinforced by the fact that an inclined plane connects the tops of the pillars—and this seems to express that children of different ages were all killed by one and the same historical cataclysm. The second level we find in the foreroom of the memorial, where we are shown the three-dimensional photos of several of the children whose fate the memorial commemorates. But the true heart of the memorial is the third level. From the foreroom we descend a few steps into a darkened, narrow, but high octogonal corridor around a similarly octogonal central pillar. Both sides of the corridor are covered with mirrors behind Plexiglas. Five *ner neshama*, or memorial candles, are the only light in the corridor; the mirrors make the candles infinitely multiply into galaxies of lights, before, behind, above, and beneath the visitor of the monument, each of them symbolizing the soul of one of the children. Soft music, though rather more a groaning than music, is heard in the background while an apparently endless list of the names of the children killed by the Nazis is recited in all European languages.

The effect is both stunning and deeply moving. Unlike the Hall of Remembrance, we need no prior knowledge or memory of the Holocaust here in order to feel confronted with its horrors and the unimaginable proportion of the crime. This memorial does not *channel* our already existing feelings and emotions, but, in a way, succeeds in *creating* them. It therefore effects or produces what is the *ingredient* in the kind of remembrance of the past we may associate with the Hall of Remembrance. Or, to put it differently but more interestingly, we *experience* the Children's Memorial and what it commemorates rather than having our experience *organized* by it as is done by the Hall of Remembrance. The Children's Memorial ends, so to speak, where the Hall of Remembrance begins—and, as I shall argue, precisely this is why for future generations the Children's Memorial is a more appropriate memorial to the Holocaust than the Hall of Remembrance.

THE AMBIVALENCES OF "KITSCH"

For a proper understanding of the Children's Memorial it will be best to start with a criticism of it. In the *New York Review of Books* Avishai Margalit accused the memorial of being of being "kitsch."[11] Though this is certainly not how I myself feel about the memorial, I can nevertheless imagine that the accusation may make sense in the eyes of the survivors of the Holocaust themselves, or at least of some of them. For all *they* need and, arguably, can support is the mere tactful (metonymic or indexical) *reference* to their experiences (as by the Hall of Remembrance), instead of seeing the memory of their experiences contaminated by an essentially surrogate experience—an experience that can only caricature their own sufferings and can even be considered an attempt to give to these sufferings a meaning that could and will never coincide with what the Holocaust still means to the survivors. But, as will be my argument, this is exactly why the Children's Memorial is the memorial for those who either by place or date of birth will remain outsiders to the Holocaust, in contrast to those who were its victims. Whereas the Holocaust itself already ties the survivors together with a bond forever indissoluble, such a bond (though, admittedly, an infinitely weaker one) can only be created for a later generation by a monument like the Children's Memorial.

Let us consider how to react to Margalit's accusation that the Children's Memorial is "kitsch"? In answering that question, I shall take Margalit's accusation more seriously than it was probably intended—and begin by taking a closer look at the notion of "kitsch." Kitsch is, in fact, a most interesting aesthetic category that is most intimately related to what, in the final analysis, all art and aesthetic experience are about. As we shall see, an elaboration of this insight may take away most of the sting of Margalit's condemnation. Initially we associate with "kitsch" terms like "vulgar," "banal," "pretentious," "ranting," "sticky," "showy," "affected," "coquettish"—glossy terms all having as their common denominator the notion of "inauthenticity."

Now, "inauthenticity" is a peculiarly paradoxical accusation within the world of aesthetics. For of *all* art, of *all* aesthetic representation of reality, we could justifiably say that it is "inauthentic," that it is an inauthentic copy of the "real thing." That is why so many philosophers since Plato and Rousseau have profoundly mistrusted art and advocated a "decay of (aesthetic) lying," to paraphrase Oscar Wilde. And, in a certain sense, this criticism of art is irrefutable, for this is how one can, without inconsistency, conceive of art. One might put it as follows. Suppose that there has been a moment in history that the first work of art was created and everybody was aware of what was going on. At that stage everybody must have seen that first work of art as an essentially inauthentic copy of the real world. Hence, at that moment reality *itself* momentarily became a work of art, while this first work of art was its showy, banal, pretentious, and "kitschlike" imitation. So, if we go back to the origin of art, *all* art is inauthentic. But right after this first work of art had been accepted, reality lost its aesthetic character, became reality again, and the category of kitsch was now reserved for distinguishing between good and bad art—while, strangely enough, the latter, kitsch, was criticized for being what all art essentially is. To put it in one word, all art is *originally* kitsch, and what we now call kitsch reminds us of this origin and nature of all art.

In a paradoxical way this truth is presented in Hermann Broch's fierce and uncompromising attack on kitsch. Thus Broch writes: "the essence of kitsch is the exchange of an ethical for an aesthetic category; kitsch does not want to function in a morally good way but to please aesthetically, it is only interested in having a nice effect."[12] And elsewhere Broch is even more explicit: "the goddess of beauty in art is the goddess of kitsch."[13] In one phrase, precisely what is aesthetic in art may make art into kitsch. Hence, when attacking kitsch, Broch paradoxically criticizes kitsch for what, in his own opinion, art *itself* essentially *is*.

And this may help us clarify the relationship between the Hall of Remembrance and the Children's Memorial, and between the kind of experiences these two monuments may evoke in the visitors of Yad Vashem. We can now understand why at least some of the survivors of the Holocaust will see the Children's Memorial as a kitsch manipulation of their experiences of the horrors of the camps. They will prefer the Hall of Remembrance because it leaves their terrible memories intact and refrains from manipulating them. But as all art has its origin in this manipulation of reality, has its very raison d'être in this manipulation, and in this way may represent a reality for those who have not actually experienced it, the survivor's accusation of kitsch is proof of the "eloquence" of the Memorial as a memorial of the Holocaust for those who belong to a later generation and did not experience the Holocaust themselves. Put differently, if, as we saw with Broch, this supreme moment of the transition from reality to art and to the representation of reality will evoke in us sudden associations with kitsch, Margalit's accusation stamps the Children's Memorial as the memorial of the Holocaust for those who can only know the Holocaust through its representation. Hence, what the survivor of the Holocaust may object to in the Children's Memorial is precisely what will bring a later generation closest to the Holocaust.

THE NECESSITY OF NEUROTIC REMEMBRANCE

Let us return to Broch once again. Since kitsch, being the essence of art, depends on "schönen Effekt," on aesthetic effect, Broch concludes that kitsch is a neuroticized form of art, aimed, like all neurosis, at the repression of reality.[14] And, in agreement with the foregoing, we might add that this argument implies that all art, being such a repression of reality, is essentially neurotic. Of course, this association of art and neurosis belongs to the heart of Freud's later theory of culture and human civilization. Thus Freud writes in *Totem and Taboo*:

The neuroses show a striking and profound resemblance to the great social products of art, of religion, and of philosophy, but at the same time they may seem to be distortions of them. One might venture the assertion that a hysteria is the distortion of an artistic creation, that a compulsion neurosis is the distortion of a religion, and a paranoid delusion is a distortion of a philosophical system.[15]

And Freud's argument is much the same as the one given by Broch: art is an "illusion," a mere aesthetic "effect" completely devoid of "transference in the realm of reality."¹⁶ There is an "incongruence" between reality and art that reflects the closely similar incongruence between reality and how it is perceived by the neuroticist.

This incongruence can be defined with more precision if we compare Broch's and Freud's speculations about art with one of the four main definitions of the beautiful given by Kant in his *Critique of Judgment*. This very well known definition states "that the beautiful has as its foundation the judgment of a purely formal purposefulness, that is, of a purposefulness without purpose."¹⁷ It will not be necessary to enter here into all the technicalities of what Kant refers to as the subjective and reflective judgment of taste, since the intuition behind the definition is fairly straightforward. For suppose that we hold a rose in our hand and that we think the thing to be beautiful. We then think it to be beautiful, suggests Kant, because it is to us (I emphasize to us) as if all the components of the rose have been arranged for some purpose, while obviously we could not possibly say what this purpose might be. For what is the purpose of a rose *as such*—and not as, for example, a gift to our beloved? And that is why we can say that its beauty lies in its being purposeful but without a purpose.

And, indeed, Kant's definition may help us to clarify how one should conceive of the neurosis that Broch and Freud associated with art, and, more specifically, that we might associate with that particular subcategory of works of art that is constituted by monuments and memorials. For here this dimension of "incongruence," mentioned just now, is most conspicuously present. Think of the strange relationship between the monument or memorial and what it commemorates. What could a structure of stones, a flame, a steel column, and so on possibly have to do with the cruel death of millions of young men in a war, or with the murderous genocide of an entire nation? If we had been asked to give examples of objects fitting the Kantian definition of the beautiful, objects that are purposeful but yet without a purpose, what better examples could we have thought of than monuments and memorials?

At this stage, however, one might wish to object that monuments and memorials obviously all have the purpose of commemorating the major events of our collective past—and therefore certainly are "purposeful *with* a purpose." Of course, in a certain sense this objection is true, but it forgets one central feature of monuments and memorials: namely, that this purpose of commemoration can only be achieved by the purposelessness of the monument. For it is precisely because the monument is an open receptacle to our memories and associations that it can function as such. It must, so to speak, create or embody an "openness," a quasi-sacred void in our public space, in order to properly fulfill its functions. And it creates this "openness" by fitting Kant's definition of art as being "purposeful without a purpose." For, as we noted a moment ago, because of its incongruency in relationship to the commemorated, the actual monument *as such* has, just like the beautiful rose, no purpose: it gives us no shelter, we cannot live in it, it cannot be used for anything—it is *just there*, and its purpose precisely lies in being devoid of any purpose.

The most staggering illustration of this truth is Auschwitz-Birkenau itself. For recall that Auschwitz-Birkenau was the most deadly killing machine man has ever devised, even dwarfing the atomic bomb in its capacity to realize purposeful killing. But take away this purpose, and exactly the same place, with its buildings and so on, can undergo a metamorphosis into a monument to the Holocaust. These buildings perpetrated the Holocaust (or contributed to its perpetration), they are the deadliest buildings that have ever been erected by man, but can, nevertheless, become a monument to the Holocaust at the very moment that this purpose has been removed. Within the immeasurable distance or difference between the camp with and without its original purpose, the ultimate memorial commemorating the Holocaust has come into being. For this immeasurable difference conveys, symbolizes, and comes closest to being a representation of the Holocaust.

I want to argue that this purposefulness without a purpose and this neurosis that we must associate with the monument are not shortcomings of the monument, as one might have thought, but precisely its justification. To express it in a paradox: there are things in our collective past that we may *never* assimilate, that should cause a *perpetual* and never-ending illness or neurosis in us. There are aspects to our past of which one can justifiably say that being cured of them, of allowing the emptiness they created in our collective mind to be reclaimed again by so-called normal life, of being able to live with these aspects again, will change us into people whose future is in danger of becoming a repetition of our dismal past. There are wounds with which we should never cease to suffer, and sometimes, in the life of a civilization, illness is better than health.

MOURNING AND MELANCHOLIA

Once again I start with a reference to Freud. In his essay "Trauer und Melancholie," Freud distinguishes between two reactions we may have to the loss of a beloved person, or of deeply cherished abstractions or ideals like freedom or the ideal of humanism, to take an example suggested by Rüsen.[18] One reaction is described by Freud as that of "mourning," or *Trauer*. As Freud emphasizes, though mourning may cause the most disquieting deviations from normal behavior, we will not presume something pathological there that would require the attendance of a physician or psychologist. Mourning is the fundamentally "healthy" way of overcoming a great loss, with an emphasis on "overcoming." The loss is finally, though after an often extremely difficult period, accepted by the mourner, which will enable him to continue his life unmutilated by the loss. And this is what a monument like the Hall of Remembrance may help the survivors of the Holocaust to do: being the memorial lens that it is, it will focus the memories of the Holocaust on one place so that, by their sheer intensity, these memories may ignite into a holocaust of memory itself, thus transforming memories from an insupportable burden into the air one breathes and that gives us life. "Indeed the self will become free and uninhibited again," writes Freud, "after the completion of the process of mourning."[19] In this way, the Hall of Remembrance is the memorial for those who witnessed the Holocaust itself.

All this is different with melancholia—a psychological notion rarely occurring in Freud's writings, but with a profoundly interesting past going back to the dawn of civilization.[20] Freud discerns in melancholia two elements that are relevant to the present discussion. Firstly, Freud points out that in melancholia the libidinal investment in the loved object is not liberated so that it can be invested in new and other objects—as is the case in mourning—but is pulled back into the self. And, Freud continues, "it did not have an arbitrary use there but served the purpose of an identification of the self with the abandoned object. The shadow of the object thus was cast over the self, so that this self could now be condemned by some instance, just as had been the case with the abandoned object."[21] It is as if the loss of the beloved object left a psychological scar on the self, while this scar is experienced by the self as a metamorphosis of the beloved object—with the result that the loss becomes, so to speak, a real component of the self that will die, in the end, only with the self. In this way melancholia, unlike mourning, effects a kind of stasis, a kind of chronic psychological disease, a permanent neurosis of the self for which no cure can ever be devised.

The second aspect Freud attributed to melancholia is closely related to this. "The melancholic displays one more thing that is absent in the case of mourning, namely an extraordinary degradation of the concept of the self, a tremendous impoverishment of the self.... He has lost the respect for his own self and must have good reasons for this."[22] And Freud emphasizes that this loss of self ordinarily takes the form of a "moral displeasure with the self,"[23] a moral displeasure of the self with itself. And the explanation given by Freud is no less interesting in this context. He argues that the melancholic person has a permanent awareness of having irreparably *failed* with regard to the loved object that is lost. So, taking these two aspects of melancholia together, what melancholia stands for is a feeling of moral guilt, a feeling that has become permanent since it is in the self a copy of the openness or void caused by the loss of the loved object. In a way, this openness or void in ourselves is the counterpart of the openness or void that is created by the monument and the memorial.

This brings me, finally, to the question of how the Freudian account of melancholia may help us explain the kind of experience that is evoked by the Children's Memorial and, more specifically, why this is the kind of memorial for the Holocaust that will best fulfill the task of commemorating the Holocaust for future generations. First, the experience evoked by the memorial is not an experience *of* the past (in the way that those who have directly experienced the destruction of European Jewry can be said to have had an experience of the Holocaust, or to have their experiences reactivated by a monument like the Hall of Remembrance), but an experience *about* the past. But, as such, the experience evoked by the memorial and by its singular capacity to deeply move us, may attain the highest degree of experience *about*. Yet, like all art originating in the mimesis of reality, there is in the experience *about* inevitably an element of unreality. Experience *about* can never be the experience of reality that is given by experience *of*. And this is why the Children's Memorial is unrelated to mourning, trauma, and the assimilation of trauma to which the Hall of Remembrance may contribute. Experience *about* presents us with neurosis and melancholia rather than with trauma. Next, as Freud's analysis of melancholia has made clear, the feelings evoked by melancholia stimulate a vague but persistent awareness of a moral failure on our part with regard to the object of memory or of commemoration.

This is precisely what the Holocaust memorial must be for future generations. It must not aim at an overcoming of the past, nor at a reconciliation with the horrors of the past. The memory of the Holocaust must be an illness, a mental disorder from which we may never cease to suffer. Not only because of the crimes themselves that were committed against the Jews, but also because genocide will remain forever a possibility in future human history. For we must never forget the paradox that the greatest crimes always meet with least resistance, precisely because they are most successful in transcending the barriers we have erected in the course of time against human cruelty. We can prevent, to a certain extent, what we can more or less foresee, since it is on our list of potential evils to be avoided—but who could foresee the Holocaust? And because we can not foresee excesses of this order, they may, under certain circumstances, take place overnight. This is the lesson we must learn from the writings of Hannah Arendt, Berel Lang, or Zygmunt Bauman.

Modern society, as it came into being with the French Revolution, has a natural affinity with the crime without a heart, without a center, and without an author—the kind of crime that may for this very reason transcend even the most depraved and bloodthirsty imagination. The worst tant in human history will always be a mere angry child in comparison to this crime without a heart. The melancholic, neurotic remembrance of the Holocaust may and must help us to prevent another discharge of these terrible potentialities of modernity. This is what Auschwitz and Yad Vashem must mean to us.

PART III

THEORISTS

7

WHY REALISM? AUERBACH ON THE REPRESENTATION OF REALITY

Mimesis, Auerbach's *opus famosum*, has neither foreword nor introduction and has only a short and perfunctory epilogue. And the epilegomena that Auerbach wrote some six years after the publication of *Mimesis* were clearly not intended to compensate for this lacuna.[1] Apparently, Auerbach did not believe that his study would justify some general conclusions with regard to realism in Western literature and its history, or he believed such conclusions to be so very obvious that no further clarification would be required. Anyway, whatever Auerbach's views may have been, we readers are now obliged to ponder the book's implications for ourselves. So we should ask ourselves what we can we learn from *Mimesis* about the nature and evolution of realism and, more specifically, about the philosophy of realism that is suggested by Auerbach's brilliant and powerful exposition.

AUERBACH AND HISTORISM

It is not immediately clear from Auerbach's book what strategy it is going to adopt for dealing with realism. The subtitle of the English version of the book—*The Representation of Reality in Western Literature*—suggests that it will give us a history of how different writers, from Homer to Virginia Woolf, each in their own way, have attempted to give, as well as they could, a representation of reality. The suggestion is that realism can only be defined by means of a *history* of realism—and this would certainly be in accordance with Auerbach's self-professed historism,[2] and that he welcomed historism as "the 'Copernican discovery' in the field of historical studies."[3] Furthermore, Auerbach was quoted as saying, "My purpose is always to write history,"[4] and writing history meant to him, first, the constitution of a *historische Topologie*, that is, a list of what must be considered to be "the most significant works of art," and second, an analysis of "the conditions of their origin and the direction of their influence."[5] Obviously, this Kantian definition of the historian's disciplinary goal is in perfect agreement with Gadamer's well-known and authoritative characterization of classical historism as developed by Ranke, Humboldt, or Dilthey.[6]

Indeed, there is a profound structural similarity between Auerbach's *Mimesis* and a paradigmatic product of historist historical writing such as Friedrich Meinecke's *Die Entstehung des Historismus*, which is only ten years older; in both cases we are given what Meinecke called a *Gratwanderung durch das Gebirge*,[7] in other words, a trail over the impressive mountain peaks in the intellectual history of either the historist or the realist representation of reality. It need not surprise us, therefore, that Auerbach approvingly cites Meinecke's *chef d'oeuvre* several times in his own.[8] No less characteristic of Auerbach's historism is his historical relativism, and, together with Meinecke (and Huizinga), he belonged to that select group of wise and sober-minded historians who saw in historist relativism no reason for epistemological panic and despair.[9] Like Meinecke, he did not fear a radical historicization of thought and knowledge; on the contrary, he agreed with Meinecke that such historicization is the condition of all understanding in and of the history of thought. Indeed, as a good historist Auerbach primarily wants to understand and not to recommend or to condemn. He therefore is ready to discern a sincere and original realism in an impressive variety of literary works culled from three thousand years of efforts to depict what the world and the human condition is like. And this is, perhaps, the explanation of why neither in this book nor in any other publication did Auerbach attempt to develop some general insights into the nature of realism. Realism only exists for him in the many variants in which it has shown itself in the course of the long history investigated in this book; all that we can meaningfully do is tell the narrative of its history.

Obviously, Auerbach's historist approach to realism as sketched just now must also have its implications for the present exposition. Since Auerbach presents us with variants of realism, rather than with a general theory

Why Realism? 199

of literary realism pretending to be valid for all times, my exposition should respectfully reflect Auerbach's historist prudence. Consequently, in the remainder of this chapter, I hope to show that at least five variants of realism can be discerned in Auerbach's writings. Nevertheless, at the end of this exposition I hope to demonstrate that Leibniz's monadology can be seen as the common denominator of all five of these variants. In fact, this conclusion need not surprise us, since Leibniz's monadology has often been considered to be the metaphysics associated with the historist weltanschauung.[10]

FRENCH CLASSICISM AND ITS DISCONTENTS

Nevertheless, with the French classicists such as Corneille or Molière, and above all Racine, the limits of Auerbach's relativist tolerance have apparently been exceeded.[11] And since we can get a glimpse of the historist's own opinions when he begins to fail to satisfy the standards of his historist relativism, we have every reason to be interested in why these French classicists so much aroused Auerbach's unhistorist wrath. However, for a proper grasp of Auerbach's impatience with the French classicists it will be helpful to start with some comments on Cervantes, whose *Don Quixote* is discussed in the chapter immediately preceding the one on the French classicists.

According to Auerbach, Cervantes' main inspiration for writing his *Don Quixote* was to present his readers with "an attitude—an attitude toward the world, and hence also to the subject matter of his art—in which bravery and equanimity play a major part. Together with the delight he takes in the multifariousness of his sensory play there is in him a certain Southern reticence and pride."[12] But obviously, if the presentation of this typically Spanish attitude of a mixture of "bravery and equanimity" truly is the secret of *Don Quixote*, it will have become impossible to explain the book's immediate popularity all through Europe, or why, as Auerbach himself wrote a moment before the passage I quoted just now, each generation down to the present day can enjoy it so much and discover something new in it. The novel's eternal "newness" suggests that it addresses an aspect of human existence that we will lose sight of if we tie the novel exclusively to sixteenth-century Spain, as Auerbach is inclined to do.

To understand this perennial fascination of *Don Quixote*, we should note that there is something truly universal about the fate of Don Quixote. What is so striking about Don Quixote is not that he is mad or deluded—

for as Auerbach himself observes, the intriguing paradox of the book is precisely that Don Quixote is basically as normal as anybody else[13]—but that he so systematically misreads the signs that reality presents to us: he sees giants where other people see windmills or a noble lady in a boorish peasant girl. Don Quixote's mind is excellent, but something often tends to go wrong en route from reality itself to his perception of it. Or, as Foucault so famously and convincingly made clear, Don Quixote's confusion is not psychological but epistemological. He is to be compared to that cognitive self presented in Descartes's *Meditations*, desperately trying to distinguish between dreams and reality and ultimately deciding that it can only be certain of its own existence as *res cogitans*. Indeed, epistemology since Descartes has always attempted to deal with the kind of problem in which Don Quixote became entangled, the problem of how we can be sure that the windmills that we seem to see really are windmills and not, for example, giants—and that may give us at least part of the explanation of why the book continued to amuse an audience that, down to the present day, is inclined to take seriously such epistemological worries about the reliability of our knowledge of reality.

As was so brilliantly suggested by Foucault in *Les Mots et les choses*, *Don Quixote* announced a new dispensation in the relationship of word and world, in terms of which new standards for truth and realism had to be formulated. The theater of the French classicists with all its rules for how to represent reality realistically on stage clearly exemplified this new dispensation. From this perspective, then, the French classicists seem to deserve a more honorable place in the history of realism than Auerbach is prepared to grant them. Of course we may now laugh at, or rather be bored to death by Racine's lifeless tragedies. But, as Auerbach explicitly pointed out himself,[14] we must not forget that both for Racine himself and his audience, this was truly what reality is like. *Ressemblance*, plausibility, and credibility were considered the most urgent requirements in the theater, precisely the requirements that actually resulted in the shackles of the unity of time, place, and action and that have been criticized so heavily and so ritually since the late eighteenth century as the very acme of an absurd unrealism. In short, where we see a lack of realism, Racine and his contemporaries (and even such a supremely intelligent nineteenth-century observer as Tocqueville)[15] saw the *ne plus ultra* of realism. As Cervantes' successors in dealing with the problem of realism, Corneille, Racine, and Molière were the Cartesians of the theater: where Descartes constructed an epistemological scheme that would give us access to reality, so the French classicists developed their no less rigid formalism for how to represent reality in the theater.

THE THREE STYLES

Now we should ask ourselves: why did Auerbach, in spite of his historism, so harshly condemn these French classicists? Of course he could rightly criticize them for having an amazingly poor and ideological conception of the realities of the human psyche and of sociopolitical reality. In the same vein we may rightly criticize Descartes for his many mistakes and bad arguments but without thereby discrediting the enterprise that Descartes had put on the philosopher's agenda. Thus, the historist's attitude toward the French classicists should rather have been that, like Descartes in the domain of philosophy, they were the first to be profoundly aware of the nature of the problem of realism, and of the true proportions of this ultimate challenge to the whole of Western thought—the problem of how to properly represent reality in language or thought. And though their first groping attempts to deal with it may seem singularly inept and ineffective from our present point of view, it would be arrogant Whiggism to take them to task for that. Instead, we should praise both Descartes and the French classicists for the intellectual courage and originality so amply displayed by them.

Self-evidently, Auerbach's not being able to muster this historist generosity in support of the French classicists must be because he has a normative definition of realism in mind, against which the Corneilles and Racines fatally sinned. As every reader of *Mimesis* knows, according to this definition realism has its basis in a mixture of styles. But before turning to a discussion of this mixture of styles, there is a minor problem occasioned by Auerbach's position that requires our attention. In the rightly famous opening chapter, the elevated style of Homer, the style appropriate to the sublime and the tragic aspects of human experience, is contrasted with the low style in which the Old Testament presents to the reader Abraham's sacrifice of Isaac. The genius of the writers of the Old Testament was that they succeeded in weaving the dimensions of the sublime and tragedy into the contingencies and seemingly insignificant details of human existence. Or, to take an example from a later chapter of *Mimesis*, St. Peter's betrayal of

Christ takes place under the most sordid and pedestrian historical circumstances, and yet the Evangelist perfectly succeeds in rendering all the tragic grandeur of St. Peter's despair.

Now, the problem to which this gives rise is whether there are two or three styles. Do we have the elevated style of Homer next to the "realist" (which is not Auerbach's terminology!) style of the Bible, in which a sublime transfiguration of the commonplace is effected? Or should we agree with the French classicists that there are three styles:[16] the elevated style for tragedy, the low style for comedy, and the middle style for rendering that social reality in which Molière liked to situate his plays? On the basis of Auerbach's text, the two-styles thesis is no less plausible than the one involving three styles.

More important is that Auerbach's notion of the mixture of the styles as a condition of realism explains Auerbach's disgust with the French classicists.[17] For in their Cartesian conviction that reality will only disclose itself to us on the condition that we possess and apply some neat formal schemes in our approach to it, the French classicists were obviously in outright opposition to Auerbach's conviction that realism is only possible on the basis of this mixture of styles. Cartesianism and all that we might associate with it are therefore Auerbach's natural enemy. I shall return to this at a later stage of my argument.

Taking this into account we now will also comprehend why Auerbach's *bêtes noires* are not openly antirealist literary theories and practices, such as we may find in legend, in Chrétien de Troyes's habit of idealizing reality, in medieval allegory,[18] or in symbolism and surrealism (that are not even mentioned by Auerbach), but rather realist theories and practices that clash—as in the case of the French classicists—with Auerbach's own definition of realism as a mixture of the two or three styles. As a consequence, Auerbach's book is not a book about the triumphs of realism over nonrealist literature and about how to account for these triumphs; rather, it examines the struggle between the different proposals that have been made over the past three thousand years for how to represent reality. He looks at realism and its history from the inside, as it were, and not from the outside.

Recognizing this may clarify another, at first sight puzzling, feature of Auerbach's book. For surely most of Auerbach's readers will initially be surprised by his presentation of Dante's *Divina Commedia* as a high point in the history of realist literature.[19] Suppose that such paradigmatic realist novelists such as the Goncourts or Zola would present themselves on a tour through heaven and hell under the guidance of Virgil.[20] We would surely conclude that they had now completely abandoned their realist attempt to give us *une copie exacte et minutiueuse de la vie humaine*, as Zola once put it,[21] and started to do something entirely different. However, as will be suggested in the next section, from the perspective of Auerbach's normative definition of realism Dante can correctly be seen as one of the virtuosos in the history of European realism.

FIGURA

This will become clear if we consider what Auerbach wrote, both in *Mimesis* and on other occasions, about the notion of *figura*. *Figura* is defined by Auerbach as follows: it

> establishes a connection between two events or persons in such a way that the first signifies not only itself but also the second, while the second involves or fulfills the first. The two poles of a figure are separated in time, but both, being real events or persons, are within temporality. They are both contained in the flowing stream which is historical life, and only the comprehension, the *intellectus spiritualis*, of their interdependence is a spiritual act.[22]

Several comments may help to clarify this notion of *figura*. In the first place, one cannot fail to be struck by the similarity of *figura* to what Louis O. Mink referred to as "configurational comprehension." Mink had in mind here an aspect of historical writing that he considered to be the essence of all historical understanding. According to Mink the historian's task is mainly a "seeing together"—hence the term configurational comprehension—of what is separate in chronological history itself. He likens the procedure to the effort of finding the most suitable point of view for comprehending within one glance different parts of one and the same river. "But in the configurational comprehension of a story which one *has followed*," says Mink,

> the end is connected with the promise of the beginning as well as the beginning with the promise of the end. To comprehend temporal succession, means to think of it in both directions at once and then time is no longer the river which bears us along, but the river in aerial view, upstream and downstream seen in a single survey.[23]

If, then, there is, as I believe, much truth in Mink's contention, and if, next, history can justifiably be said to aim at the most realist representation of historical reality,[24] the obvious similarities[25] of Auerbach's *figura* and Mink's "configurational comprehension" will strongly reinforce our belief that Auerbach was basically right in his thesis of the realism of *figura*. No less interesting is Auerbach's philological analysis of the word *figura*, suggesting the close affinity of the notions of *figura* and form.[26] According to neo-Kantian historical theory (and influential individual authors such as Huizinga) the historian's task is the identification of the "forms" of historical reality. Auerbach's notion of *figura* might well have been proposed by the neo-Kantians instead of the notion of "form": both notions require us to discover a pattern or *gestalt* in a variety of historical phenomena. A difference, though, is that *figura* can only articulate itself if we have at least two comparable historical phenomena, while the notion of "form" is free of this requirement.[27] But it might well be argued that this precisely is why the notion of *figura* is better suited to the practice of history than the neo-Kantian notion of "form."[28]

Moreover, Auerbach himself gave us an additional and interesting argument in favor of the realism implied by *figura*. Though the argument is nowhere stated clearly and succinctly, its structure is not hard to reconstruct from his treatment of *figura*: we shall always have to look at some specific event in historical reality itself in order to discover there the true meaning of the figurative announcement or fulfillment of some other historical event. Thus, only a close and detailed scrutiny of an actual, concrete historical event can give us access to the meaning of the other event to which it is "figurally" related.[29] The secrets of reality must therefore be discovered in reality itself, and the level of a transcendent eternity is only a mirror that inexorably sends us back to reality again, thereby strangely emphasizing and reinforcing the claims of the real. And it will now also become clear why, for Auerbach, in opposition to the Cartesianism of the French classicists, the mixture of the styles is the condition of the realist representation of reality. For it is only thanks to this moving backward and forward between the level of the lowly and earthly events and the sublime level in which these events mirror themselves that the ("figural") meaning of reality can be grasped. Put differently, "verticality," and thus the mixture of the low and the elevated styles in which this "verticality" can articulate itself, is the condition of our effort of successfully relating what belongs to the "horizontal" level.[30]

But there is a further aspect to the mixture of styles that must be noted. The point of departure here is the at first sight strange characterization that Auerbach gives of the realism of the late Middle Ages: "This realism is poor in ideas; it lacks constructive principles and even the will to attain them. It drains the reality of that which exists."[31] Apparently this is meant to be a criticism—and then we must ask ourselves whether "constructive principles" and being rich in ideas is not *sui generis* at odds with realism. For should not realism present us with what reality actually is like, while avoiding as much as possible the introduction of "ideas" and "constructions" of the mind? And would therefore its being "poor in ideas" not precisely be a virtue in late medieval literature instead of a shortcoming?

But here again the lessons of the mixture of styles and of *figura* are most helpful. For we should realize that it is precisely the Cartesianism of the French classicists that wants to divide the world into neat compartments such as "ideas of the mind" or "reality itself" that should be carefully kept separate if we wish to see these things "as they really are." The requirements of *figura* and of the mixture of the styles, however, teaches us that these are artificial schematisms and that it is exactly one of the most essential features of human reality that the comic and the tragic, the low and the sublime can coexist in the closest proximity. "Reality" and the "idea" are often even aspects of each other, as was so clearly the case in the episode of St. Peter's history referred to above.

AUERBACH'S HEGELIANISM

It is here also that the Hegelianism of Auerbach's notion of *figura* reasserts itself. Hegel wrote the following about the *Divina Commedia*:

Here all that is individual and particular in human interests and aims disappears in order to make room for the absolute greatness of the final aim and goal of all things; but at the same time what is transient and fleeting in human existence presents itself here in its epic fullness and as fathomed objectively down to its essence, assessed in its value, or lack of it, by the most powerful grasp, i.e., by God.[32]

It is likely that Auerbach's interpretation of Dante originated in statements like these by Hegel.[33] And in this way Auerbach's notion of *figura*, of the mixture of styles and of realism, refers us back to the heart of the Hegelian system. For, as we all know, it was the main aim of Hegel to effect in his system a reconciliation of the universal and the individual in what he called "the concrete universal," in which the categories of the individual and the universal are transcended.[34] And one might add that this is also why realism and science are intimately related: in a host of sordid and puny little details, science succeeds in discovering eternal scientific truths. We might even wonder whether the scientific treatise therefore exemplifies the same mixture of styles that, according to Auerbach, characterizes the realist novel.

Lastly, Hegel's notion of the concrete universal is also suggestive of the political implications that Auerbach liked to derive from his literary criticism. As a victim of Hitler's Nazi regime, acutely sensitive to the latent totalitarianism reflected or to be associated with the texts he studied, Auerbach often indicated to what extent the separation of the styles can be used for elitist conceptions of society. Similarly, the mixture of styles and the notion of *figura* have an elective affinity with democracy, liberalism, and universal suffrage.[35] Realism, as defined by Auerbach, is the literary style of democracy, and the freedom to move through the hierarchy of styles is the literary analogue to the freedom of a society that respects democratic equality.

REALISM AND THE SUBLIME

Should we conclude, then, that Auerbach's conception of reality and realism is ultimately Hegelian? To a certain extent this conclusion would be right, I believe, but it would fail to do sufficient justice to another important strain in Auerbach's thought. The crucial datum here is that, for Auerbach (in a way curiously reminiscent of Aristotle),[36] the mixture of the "styles" should not be reconciliation or transcendence of the styles, in the way that for Hegel the concrete universal is a transcendence of the individual and the universal or the Absolute Mind a reconciliation of the objective and the subjective mind. For example, when describing Flaubert's realism, Auerbach admirably makes it clear that the secret and newness of *Madame Bovary* lies in Flaubert's presentation of Emma as neither tragic nor comic; there is both something deeply tragic about her fate and something comic in her "silliness, immaturity," and in the resulting "disorder of her life."[37] Put differently, Flaubert's narrative makes us reach for the two mutually exclusive categories of the tragic and the comic, while, at the same time, revealing the inadequacy of these two categories. And the purpose of the novel seems to be to effect precisely this, to show where the categories in terms of which reality normally discloses itself to us demonstrate their shortcomings. But it is and remains the presence of both the tragic and the comic, and not of a *third* category transcending both, that constitutes the novel's realism.

Now, aesthetics provides us with the category of the sublime for conceptualizing such a conflict of schemes without reconciliation or transcendence. Thus the Kantian sublime[38] is not a transcendence of reason and understanding and the entry to a new and higher order reality, but can only be defined in terms of the inadequacy of both reason and understanding. The sublime is, so to speak, a comment on these two faculties of the human mind, and therefore requires a prior awareness of both in order to be aware of their insufficiency at a later phase. Similarly, it is only by way of the positive numbers that we can get access to the realm of negative numbers; and gaining this access does not in the least imply the abolition or transcendence of the realm of the positive numbers, but a continuous awareness of their existence as well.

This association of realism with the domain of the sublime is no mere speculation of mine, but is in close agreement with Auerbach's own writings. For the intimate relationship between realism and the sublime was developed by Auerbach in his brilliant short essay on the poem entitled "Spleen" in Baudelaire's *Les Fleurs du mal*. We should recall, first, that "spleen," *ennui*, or "melancholia" traditionally expresses the awareness that reality escapes our effort to discover it or to give a satisfactory meaning to it: reality assumes here the sublime proportions of a world ridiculing each attempt to reduce it to the categories of the known (or of Kantian "phenomenal") reality. We feel excluded from reality because all the categories, such as the Kantian categories of the understanding, that used to give us access to it, clearly show their radical inadequacy. In short, "spleen" or "melancholia" is a paradigmatic form of the experience of the sublime[39] and arguably even an ingredient in all experience of the sublime. And so it is with Auerbach: for him, Baudelaire's "Spleen" is an expression of "gray misery" (*das graue Elend*): "this sort of desperate terror has its traditional place in literature; it is a variant of the sublime; it can be found in the writings of many tragedians and historians of Antiquity, and of course also in Dante; it possesses the highest dignity."[40] Moreover, though the sublime may well have had its traditional place in literature since the tragedians of antiquity, it is with realism that the sublime truly became the dark angel of literature—or its *fleur du mal*. In "Spleen," Baudelaire evokes a terrible reality—*eine fürchterliche Wirklichkeit*, as Auerbach puts it—and decisive here are the harsh and painful paradoxes by means of which this evocation of a sublime reality is effected: "Decisive is the force of the evocation, and in this sense Baudelaire's poem is of an unsurpassable realism."[41] The sublime is the real; codified, categorized, "phenomenal" reality can never be more than its mere shadow.

REALISM

We should note then that when the real presents itself in its sublime manifestation, this will necessarily be a terrible reality, a *fürchterliche Wirklichkeit*, in Auerbach's words. There never is anything pleasant or reassuring about it. The explanation is that the sublime always confronts us with a reality that does not fit the categories we use for appropriating the world; hence, the sublime—and therefore reality "as such"—will always be experienced by us as alien, threatening, and beyond our grasp. Thus, when the realist novelists since Flaubert, especially the Goncourts and Zola, took so much interest in the sordid, the ugly, the pathological, and in all that causes in us a profound "feeling of moral discomfort,"[42] this is not because these novelists felt a morbid fascination for these less redeeming aspects of human existence, nor because of a pessimistic conviction that this is what human life is ultimately like,[43] nor even because the mixture of styles requires the introduction into the novelist's narrative of the degrading dimensions of life—though all this is also part of the truth—but above all because this is how life presents itself when seen in the light of the sublime.

Two other features of Auerbach's history of realism can now be clarified. First, since we arrive at the sublime when confronted with the bankruptcy of our traditional categories for understanding the world, our first impulse will be to devise new categories that are suggested by the sublime object of experience itself. We will try to speak, as well as we can, the new and strange language of the sublime itself in our hope to be able to enter into a dialogue with it. The implication is that in adequate speech about the sublime object of experience (insofar as this speech can be realized), form and content will come as close to each other as possible. Formal categories will have their sole justification in the specific content of that object of sublime experience, since the object will escape us as soon as we rely on other categories. We can now understand why Auerbach sees the realism of Gregory of Tours in his "visually vivid narrative," where Gregory's prose truly becomes a mimesis of the things he had witnessed himself.[44] Similarly, Gregory's primitive and inadequate Latin seems to reflect the primitive society he was living in and where normal and rational behavior seemed to have become a rare exception. In this way, content and form coalesce and reality "speaks itself," so to say. And the same is true when Auerbach, several chapters later, praises Boccaccio's realism in speeding up or slowing down the pace of his prose in agreement with the actions that are narrated in it.[45]

Secondly, from the perspective of the relationship between realism and the sublime, we can explain the notion of the "creatural" (*Kreatürlichkeit*, in German) and its prominent role in Auerbach's analysis. The "creatural" refers to our bodily functions, to our mortality, to the inevitable disintegration of the human body and mind, in general to all these humiliating and degrading logistics that are inevitably part and parcel of human life. However much we may try to stylize and to beautify our lives, the sublimity of these nightmarish aspects of life will never cease to announce themselves. This is the realism of the *danse macabre* of the late Middle Ages, of the coarse antics of Rabelais,[46] of the humiliating degradation of Shakespeare's King Lear and the realism that would almost completely overtake the nineteenth-century realist novel. For the social classes described in most of these novels, the "creatural" is ordinarily the all powerful, arbitrary, and unsparing despot; so by focusing on this, the realist novel gave its complacent bourgeois readers an uneasy inkling of the brute and dark forces hidden in the depth of their own souls. Whatever abject or pathological individuals might people the realist novel, and however much exact information they might present about a world that the readers of the novel would never enter themselves, they were so eagerly read because of the recognition, both thrilling and unnerving, of a *fabula de te narratur*. What was normal and simply how life was lived for the brutal protagonists in these novels took the form of the sublime "creatural" in the eyes of its middle-class readers. And in this way, the realist novel has immensely contributed, perhaps more than any other individual factor, to the psychologization of twentieth-century man and to his readiness to embrace a democratic political order based on the assumption that all people are equal. The same dark psychological forces operate in all of us, whether we are the descendant of an illustrious, centuries-old family or of mere simple workers. The nineteenth-century realist novel has been one of the major moral educators of humanity in the history of the West and we must praise it for that.

REALISM AND EXPERIENCE

But there is a still more important aspect to this intimate relationship between realism and the sublime that requires our attention in the present context. I have in mind here Auerbach's tendency to closely associate realism and experience. Not only is Auerbach convinced of the deep truth that "the writing of history is based on one's own experience of the past,"[47] not only is it, in the words of DePietro, Auerbach's "own presence—the subjective 'I' of personal experience—which carefully selects from the enormous amount of potential non-textual evidence the data relevant to a given text or to the movement of historical periods."[48] More suggestive still is Auerbach's qualification of Dante's realism as "a direct experience of life."[49] And much the same is true of his obvious sympathy for such peculiar authors as Ammianus Marcellinus and Gregory of Tours because these authors had, according to him, a natural talent for retaining all the richness and vividness of experience in their prose. Auerbach praises the "sensory vividness" of Ammianus's account of how the governor Leontius courageously confronted the Roman mob, of the sordid masquerade of the election of the Emperor Procopius, or of the dowdy physical appearance of the ill-fated Emperor Valens. In Ammianus this results in a prose "in which the gruesomely sensory has gained a large place, a somber and highly rhetorical realism that is totally alien to classical antiquity."[50] Similarly, in Auerbach's analysis of Gregory of Tours the adjectives "concrete," "sensory," and "sensible" appear again and again. It is Gregory's talent for preserving all the freshness of his own experience that gives to his history a realism that really makes us see what he has seen: "but this brutal life becomes a sensible object; to him, who would describe it, it presents itself as devoid of order, but tangible, earthly, alive."[51]

Now, experience is always a matter of the moment. It is not repeatable in the way that an experiment is. It is uncompromisingly direct; we undergo it and are totally absorbed by it in the same way that the sublime leaves no room for cool objectivity—in both cases we find ourselves truly in a momentary union with reality. The customary boundaries between the self and reality have dissolved for a moment and the realism of experience is an immersion in reality rather than an effect in or of the mind. The moment is therefore the closest that we can come to reality. But the moment, contrary to what we might have thought, is not an infinitesimally thin and small slice of life, but precisely where the greatest complexity in our relationship to reality can manifest itself. And the further we move away from experience, the more abstract our awareness of reality will become, the larger the rips in its texture will be, and the more schematic and poorer its content. This may explain why Auerbach's *Mimesis* ends with a high-pitched eulogy of the random moment: in its last chapter Auerbach writes that the genius of Virginia Woolf was

> to put the emphasis on the random occurrence, to exploit it not in the service of a planned continuity of action but in itself. And in the process something new and elemental appeared: nothing less than the wealth of reality and depth of life in every moment that we surrender ourselves without prejudice. To be sure, what happens in that moment—be it outer or inner processes—concerns in a very personal way the individuals who live in it, but it also (and for that very reason) concerns the elementary things which men in general have in common.[52]

In experience, or rather in the random moment of experience, both Auerbach's highest literary and political desiderata obtain their fulfillment. Reality is given to us, and at the same time we now recognize, with Montaigne, "que chaque homme porte la forme entière de l'humaine condition."[53] Or, put differently, there is a reality which is fundamentally our own most personal reality, and yet at the same time this is a reality we share with all of humanity. This fusion of the most authentic self and what is radically alien to the self is, and always has been, the supreme goal of all of literary realism. Only when the novelist succeeds in achieving this union can the barriers to realist representation be taken away.

MONADOLOGY AND REALISM

On the face of it, this is a most paradoxical enterprise. And we might therefore conclude that we should not take the requirement completely literally, but rather as a somewhat dramatically formulated injunction to the realist novelist dictating the unattainable ideal that he should nevertheless try to approximate as much as possible. However, in the conclusion to this chapter I hope to demonstrate that this demand on the realist novelist is less paradoxical than we might initially suppose. In order to see this, it is best to return once more to Auerbach's essay on Baudelaire's poem "Spleen." At the beginning of his essay Auerbach says of Baudelaire's poem that "the conception of reality evoked in it was certainly intended symbolically, but it also concretizes most penetratingly a dreadful truth, a terrible reality—even when the control by reason is capable of establishing that this is not a reality corresponding to experience."[54] And at the end of the essay we will find the following comment on Baudelaire: "The nakedness of the most general and most concrete existence of an epoch was expressed in a new way and most completely by the poet whose personality and life have been so extraordinary."[55] We may discern in these statements the same paradox that I referred to a moment ago: for Auerbach wishes to say here that Baudelaire succeeded in presenting the reality of his *age* precisely by presenting the most *personal* experience of it that one may think of.

Of special interest is Auerbach's assertion that we can be sure that Baudelaire did not give us "a reality corresponding to experience" (*eine erfahrungsgemässe Wirklichkeit*), whereas Auerbach nevertheless describes the poem as being of "an unsurpassable realism" (see the end of section above, "Realism and the Sublime"). Auerbach expresses here the absolutely crucial insight that the reality that is at stake in the realist novel is not the intersubjective reality that empiricists have always talked about; it is not a reality that is "lying between us," so to speak; it is not the trivial reality of the chairs, houses, and trees that we all perceive in more or less the same way; it is, rather, a reality "lying at the intersection" of all the different ways in which we experience the world. And this should not be taken to be a new and mentalized form of Cartesianism, in the sense that we have here to do with the shared *perceptions* of objective material objects instead of with these objects *themselves*, for Auerbach's notion of reality is true of all that goes on both in the world and in the mind of the subject of a novel (or of Baudelaire's poem), regardless of whether this is a reality that Descartes would see as part of *res extensa* or of the world of *res cogitans*. It is a reality having its true counterpart, not in "the idea," but in what is "unrealistic."

But this description of what the realist reality is like is obviously insufficient to guarantee that such a reality exists or that the notion of such a reality is not inconsistent. And because of the paradoxes that seem to be part of this reality, our worries about this inconsistency are surely not baseless.

However, Leibniz's monadological universe provides us with a model of reality that is both free from inconsistencies and yet in agreement with Auerbach's apparently self-contradictory requirements of realism. Leibniz effects this tour de force by granting to the monadological point of view a logical priority to what is seen from it. And actually this is reasonable enough: we can only see the world if we observe it from a certain point of view, and there is not an observable world without points of view (which, needless to add, does not in the least entail the idealistic thesis that there should be no world outside the point of view). Next, reality itself is not covered by boundaries demarcating what falls within the scope of individual points of view. The important implication is, then, that a common, objective reality is the *result of,* rather than that it is *presupposed by,* the monads and their points of view. First there are points of view, and only next an intersubjective reality arising out of the interaction of all the points of view. As Leibniz formulated this insight himself: "Just as the same city viewed from different sides appears to be different and to be, as it were, multiplied in perspectives, so the infinite number of simple substances, which seem to be so many different universes, are nevertheless only the perspectives of a single universe according to the different points of view of each monad."[56] Leibniz's monadology can account for reality's intersubjectivity—there is only one city though we may see it from different perspectives—while at the same time this intersubjective reality is logically and ontologically wholly dependent on the complete subjectivity of the monadological perspectives.

An interesting problem concerns the fate of Leibniz's thesis of the preestablished harmony of the monads and their perspectives, if his monadology is applied, as I am suggesting, to the modernist novel.[57] This problem is especially interesting since it suggests a distinction Leibniz did not take into account when he formulated his monadological ontology. The distinction I have in mind is that between how God conceives of the monadological universe and how it is conceived by the monads contained within it (e.g., human individuals). For the monads require Leibniz's argument in favor of preestabishled harmony (or any alternative to that argument) in order to *explain* the observed agreement of all that is seen from their different points of view. And this is how Leibniz dealt with the issue. But for God, or, more generally, for anybody outside the monadological universe, there are only points of view, and the possibility of a conflict between points of view and what is seen from them (i.e., the world) simply does not arise. Only when one moves from God's position to that of the individual monad does the gap between point of view and the world open up—and it is only then that Leibniz's problem comes into being. For one has to be part of the monadological universe in order to be able to differentiate between points of view and what is seen from them—and to become entangled in this problem about their (eventual) harmony. Or, to put it differently—and in terms closer to Leibniz's own thinking—for the monads *in* the monadological universe the world is the realm of the a posteriori (i.e., of the a posteriori discovery of the harmony of the monadological points of view), while the world is for God, or for anybody *outside* it, the domain of the a priori (i.e., of the a priori impossibility of a clash between points of view and the world).

On the basis of this analysis, the writer or reader of the modernist novel is on a par with God rather than with the monad, since both of them do not participate in the world within the novel. That world is presented to them, or presents itself to them as a reality outside themselves—as is also true of the world in its relationship to the Leibnizian God. And that means that the problem of preestablished harmony does not arise for the writer or reader of the novel; or, to be more precise, the problem has no meaning from *their* perspective.

MODERNIST REALISM AND MONADOLOGY

With Leibniz's monadology—I shall be the first to admit it—we have moved into the domain of the most abstract speculation. It is therefore all the more satisfactory that the famous chapter of *Mimesis* dealing with modernist literature enables us to put flesh and muscles on the naked skeleton of Leibniz's ontology.

The literary device paradigmatic of modernism is the *monologue intérieur*, in which almost everything stated appears by way of reflection in the consciousness of the dramatis personae. The narrative progresses according to what is going on in the mind of the novel's characters, and at all times, therefore, *their* point of view, rather than what is seen from it, is the decisive factor. Most of the defining characteristics of the modernist novel can be derived from the notion of the interior monologue. In the first place, presenting the world in terms of it results in "obscuring and even obliterating the impression of an objective reality completely known by the author."[58] For the suggestion that such a reality exists and is accessible to both novelist and audience would put, so to speak, the interior monologue within parentheses, objectifying and thus reducing it to a mere *quote* from a *dialogue intérieur*. Next, and most importantly, "there actually seems to be no viewpoint at all outside the novel from which the people and events within it are observed, any more than there seems to be an objective reality apart from what is in the consciousness of the characters."[59] As I indicated at the end of the previous section, point of view in the modernist novel is consistently locked within the novel itself; just as, in Leibniz's monadology, no point of view can be attributed to God, so the writer and the reader of the modernist novel write and read without possessing or suggesting an Archimedean point of view from which all of the elements of the novel's text have been integrated. To realize this God-like absence of point of view has been the supreme achievement of the modernist novel. And the paradox is that the *ne plus ultra* of objectivity (as defined by God's position with regard to the world) is the condition of the *ne plus ultra* of subjectivity (the exclusive identification with the monadological world of the interior monologue).

Obviously, it is here that Auerbach's analysis of the modernist novel so strongly suggests an appeal to Leibniz's ontology: reality does not *precede* from but *derives* from the point of view, without becoming an "idealist" construction of the point of view. For the characters of the modernist novel do not live in a reality that is idealistically constructed by themselves; on the contrary, the tendency of most modernist writing and art, no less than of nineteenth-century realism, is to show how little we are the masters of our own fate and how much we are carried along by forces beyond our cognition and influence.

The Leibnizian and monadological nature of the reality of the modernist novel most clearly announces itself in its treatment of time. Time is here not the time we find indicated on our clocks and in our agendas; it is no longer the objective time preceding and organizing our experience of the world. Time is here a function of what goes on in the mind of the novel's characters. Here time is not a Kantian intersubjective a priori intuition;[60] it has become a posteriori, in the sense of being a mere product of the random chain of associations in the mind of the novel's character. The objectivity of the Kantian universe has given way here to the subjectivism of Leibnizian monadology. A subjectivism that is so radical that it even transcends the remnants of objectivism still present in all idealism: after all, idealism is not a theory against the possibility of objective knowledge but about how and where objectivity originates (namely, objectivity does not have its source in a reality "out there," as naive realists believe, but is to be found in the workings of our own mind). But in agreement with its Leibnizianism, the modernist novel refuses to make any such categorical claim about the ontological locus of objective reality. This is most clearly brought out by Auerbach's following observation: the essential technique represented by modernism "is that we are given not merely one person whose consciousness is rendered"—that would still be compatible with idealism—"but many persons, with frequent shifts from one to the other." And "the multiplicity of persons suggests that we are here after all confronted with an endeavor to investigate an objective reality"[61]—and that gives us Leibnizian monadology, where we do have an objective reality, though one that is preceded by perspectivism.

Lastly, because of the web of internal relationships weaving together all the monadological perspectives into one objective, "realist" reality, nothing has priority to anything else. Everything will give us access to everything else, in the way that even the humblest of the Leibnizian monads is a mirror of the whole universe. Obviously, this truth is most dramatically demonstrated by suggesting how the most insignificant of events can give us access to the structure of the novel's universe. As Auerbach writes: "The important point is that an insignificant exterior occurrence releases ideas and chains of ideas which freely cut loose from the present of the exterior occurrence and range freely through the depths of time. It is as though an apparently simple text revealed its proper content only in the commentary on it, a simple musical theme only in the development section."[62] The synthesis is here part of the detail and not the detail part of the synthesis—or, as Auerbach writes a little later: "There is confidence that in any random event plucked from the course of a life at any time, the totality of its fate is contained and can be portrayed."[63] And all this explains the deep truth of Montaigne's assertion, mentioned above, that each individual human being contains within himself or herself the whole form of the human condition, and why and how the familiar and the alien do not exclude each other but live in a perfect symbiosis.

In spite of Auerbach's historist equanimity with regard to how reality has been represented since the days of Homer, we may discern in his book no less than five normative conceptions of realism that are concealed beneath this factual description of the history of realism. First, there is the notion of the mixture of styles; second, the notion of *figura*; third, there is Auerbach's Hegelianism; fourth, the sublimity of realism is emphasized; and fifth, reality preferably presents itself in experience as defined in this chapter.

At first sight, it would not seem easy, either in theory or in practice, to find a common denominator for these five different proposals for how to define literary realism. And this might make us believe that Auerbach's *Mimesis* is basically inconsistent. However, I hope to have shown that a theoretical reconciliation of the five definitions can be achieved on the basis of Leibniz's *Monadology*. Lastly, as far as practice is concerned, the modernist novel as exemplified by Virginia Woolf satisfies the five definitions reasonably well, though a complete specification of these agreements would still have to be given. But in order to avoid becoming predictable and pedantic, I shall leave these technical details for what they are.

8

DANTO ON REPRESENTATION, IDENTITY, AND INDISCERNIBLES

According to Georges-Louis Buffon's maxim "le style c'est l'homme même," our style makes us into the kind of person that we are. Our behavior, our beliefs, our character, in short our whole personality, is a matter of form and style rather than of content. And it is no different with the philosopher: the philosopher without a style of his own, the philosopher ready to sacrifice style on the altar of philosophical truth, may surely achieve results that we will admire and respect from a technical point of view, but he will never introduce us to a wholly new domain of philosophy. As we all realize, the style of writing of Hume, Kant, Schopenhauer, Nietzsche, or Wittgenstein is an inextricable part of their philosophical thought and of the kind of philosophies that they so successfully practiced and advocated. There simply are no great philosophers without quite specific style of their own, a style that we immediately recognize and that is impossible to detach from the content and the matter of their thought. The authors of textbooks on the history of philosophy would therefore be well advised to add to their expositions a few short but characteristic specimens of the kind of philosophical prose written by the philosophers expounded in their textbook. Nothing could be a better introduction.

For both an explanation and exemplification of these remarks on (philosophical) style, we had best listen to what Arthur Danto wrote about the issue:

It seems to me that what we mean by style are those qualities of representations which are the man himself, seen from the outside, physiognomically. And the reason that there cannot be knowledge or art for style, though there can be for manner, is that the outward aspects of representations are not commonly given to the man whose representations they are: he views the world through them but not them. . . . Thus to be his style they have to be expressed immediately and spontaneously. And something of the same sort is true for the historical period considered as an entity. It is a period solely from the perspective of the historian, who sees it from without; for those who lived in the period it would be just the way life was lived. And asked, afterwards, what is was like to have lived then, they may answer from the outside, from the historian's perspective. From the inside there is no answer to be given; it was simply the way things were. So when the members of a period can give an answer in terms satisfactory to the historian, the period will have exposed its outward surface and in a sense be over, as a period.[1]

Let us focus, first, on the style of Danto's eloquent comment on style. In doing so, what will strike the reader above all is the curious opposition between the profundity of the insight itself and the simple and unpretentious words that were used for expressing it. A gap has been deliberately created in this passage between the transhistorical and sublime point of view from which, on the one hand, style is discussed, and, on the other, the absence of all drama and sublimity in the prose itself.[2] Put differently, on the one hand Danto's prose is suggestive of the kind of mood we will be in after all has been said and done and we sit down to meditate quietly what final, and ultimate insights we may derive from all the bustle. Here we are required to adopt the Olympian perspective. But on the other hand, the unpretentious and deliberately untechnical language, the repeated "ands," "sos," and "thuses," the easy flow of the sentences, the way their strong and intimate interconnections present themselves as if they were the result of a mere afterthought, all this seems to wish to pull the august and sublime level of the insight down to that of unpretentious and straightforward matters of fact.

And the reader, even if equipped with only a minimum of sensitivity to matters of style, will realize that the extraordinary power of this passage should be located in this opposition of the sublime and the prosaic and the so curiously elegiac tonality resulting from it. If Auerbach was right in arguing that literary realism, the style that brings us closest to reality itself, requires an opposition between the high and the low style, this may explain why Danto's words will strike its reader with the same intensity and directness as a confrontation with reality itself. If each new form of philosophy is an encounter with philosophical reality, surely Danto's philosophical elegy provokes such an encounter.

The passage I quoted from Danto's *Transfiguration of the Commonplace* could only have been written by a philosopher who is intensely aware of the power of style, that style and argument should intimately go together if new avenues of philosophical thought are to be fruitfully explored. And indeed, no reader of Danto will doubt for a moment that he belongs, together with Wittgenstein, Quine, Searle, or Rorty, to the great stylists among recent philosophers. Their writings are like music: just as we need to hear only a few bars to recognize Mozart, Schubert, or Berlioz, so we need to read only one or two pages taken at random from their work to recognize their signature.[3] And it is their "musicality" that makes them into the fascinating philosophers that they are and that invites us to return to them again and again.

ON HOW TO READ DANTO

But let us focus next on the substance of Danto's statement on style. Two elements can be discerned in his argument. In the first place, Danto states that style is expressed immediately and spontaneously: style differs from manner in that it is not the result of a conscious decision by the artist. Style is naive in a certain sense: it can only originate in a sincere and unreflected effort to present the world as it is and in the belief that this effort may be successful.[4] Yet—and this brings us to the second element in Danto's argument—only *afterward*, when a new historical phase in the representation of the world and a new way of looking at the world has come into being, shall we be able to recognize both the naivete of the effort and the style of the work of art resulting from it. Historical sophistication then reveals the style of a previous way of thinking about and of presenting the world: what was "naive" has now become "sentimental," to use Schiller's terminology.[5] The long and unending chain of the history of our representations has then unmasked what was believed to be an immediate contact with the world as merely one more way of experiencing and seeing it—though the deep respect with which Danto speaks about style strongly suggests that he would heartily agree with Schiller about how essential this aesthetic naïveté is.

It must now strike us that Danto's argument about style is remarkably consistent with the description of his own style of writing that I proposed in the previous paragraph. For this curious opposition between the complete absence of any emphasis in his prose on the one hand and the sublime, transhistorical level of the substance of his thought on the other has its exact counterpart in his argument that style originates in an opposition between the immediate and the spontaneous, on the one hand, and the (trans)historical perspective that we need in order to notice style, on the other. If, then, the agreement of form and content, of style and substance, is a fairly reliable criterion for distinguishing between philosophers (artists, historians, and writers in general) who really tell us something new and interesting, we can no longer be in doubt about to which category Danto belongs.

And this also suggests how we should read and study Danto's writings. Three remarks are relevant in this context. First, a philosopher's style is his *way of dealing* with philosophical problems: as we all know, the literary style of the *Philosophical Investigations* shows what method we should adopt according to the later Wittgenstein in our attempt to deal with philosophical problems. Second, if the relationship between form and content enables us to distinguish between the interesting and the uninteresting philosopher, it follows that this relationship is what we should focus on if we try to understand the writings of an interesting philosopher. In the case of the uninteresting philosopher, this relationship will be more or less random and no valuable insights can then be expected from investigating it. Third, it need not surprise us that in the case of an interesting philosopher, like Arthur Danto, it is easy to discover where we should look for this relationship between content and form, substance and style. For as was already perceptively pointed out by Mark Rollins in his introduction to a collection of essays devoted to Danto's work: "Two major features stand out in Danto's efforts, the significance of which goes beyond the role they have played in his aesthetics. One is an abiding concern with *the concept of representation,* the other is the *method of indiscernibles.*"[6] Hence, if we decide to focus on the relationship between substance and form in Danto's philosophical oeuvre, our question must be how the concept of representation and the method of indiscernibles hang together in his work. The first will give us its substance or content, the second its style, method, or form.

So this will be the plot of my story: I shall first focus on Danto's account of representation; next on the method of the indiscernibles; and last, ask the question of how the two are related. Danto's philosophy of history will prove to be most helpful for answering that question.

REPRESENTATION: RESEMBLANCE AND SUBSTITUTION

If we allow ourselves to be guided by the etymology of the word (a dangerous strategy, I admit), we are likely to define "representation" as the making "present" "again" of what is "absent"—or, put differently, it is the task of a "representation" to function as a *substitute*, or *replacement* for a represented that is absent for whatever reason. Consequently, we could call this view of representation the substitution view of representation. In his book on the sublime and the beautiful, undoubtedly one of the greatest texts in the history of aesthetics, Edmund Burke was, as far as I know, the first to have openly defended the substitution theory: "But *descriptive* poetry operates chiefly by *substitution*; by the means of sounds, which by custom have the effect of realities. Nothing is an imitation further than as it resembles some other thing; and words undoubtedly have no resemblance to the ideas for which they stand."[7] The following comments on this theory are in place here. Firstly, and most importantly, Burke explicitly dissociates the notions of representation and of resemblance. By doing so, he anticipates Nelson Goodman's well-known argument that representation and resemblance each obey a logic peculiar to themselves.[8] In this way, Burke's view of representation is an implicit rejection of the view that a representation should resemble what it represents. Certainly, much is to be said in favor of the resemblance view of representation: especially in the case of the relationship between a figurative painting and what it represents, an "iconic" resemblance (in the Peircean sense) can ordinarily be observed between the represented and its representation. But, as Burke aptly points out, if we wish to use the notion of representation with regard to texts as well, we shall have to abandon the resemblance theory: words do not "resemble" in any noncircuitous way what they "represent." Or, rather, whoever wishes to maintain this view contrary to better judgment will have to rob the word "resemblance" of all meaning and significance.[9]

So, if we are looking for a satisfactory theory of representation capable of accounting for both pictorial and textual representation of the world (and for political representation, for that matter),[10] the substitution theory is to be preferred to (variants of) the resemblance theory of representation.[11] All the more so, since the substitution theory is compatible with the resemblance theory, if the latter is reduced to the more modest role of accounting for certain (naturalist) traditions or conventions of pictorial representation. For there is no inconsistency in saying (1) that all representation is substitution and (2) that in pictorial representation resemblance is sometimes (or perhaps even customarily) relied upon in order to achieve a believable substitute for the represented. On the other hand, one cannot do the opposite and assert (1) that the resemblance theory is correct and (2) that texts, nonfigurational art, or parliaments "represent" a represented. Hence, the resemblance theory fails to account for instances of representation that unproblematically fit within the substitution theory while the reverse does not hold—and, obviously, this datum alone already counts strongly against the former.

Another, more theoretical disadvantage of the resemblance theory is its tendency to reduce problems of representation to those that are traditionally investigated by epistemology. To put it more precisely, resemblance tends to function within the resemblance theory as the representational analogue to how epistemologists conceive of the relationship between words and things. And this tendency proper to the resemblance theory is all the more to be regretted since the proponents of this theory often begin most promisingly when pointing out the logical differences between description and depiction. The implication obviously is that the epistemological analysis of the relationship of true description and what it describes will be of little or no relevance to the problem of depiction and of aesthetic representation. But this auspicious start is then quickly spoiled when they ask how resemblance can account for the relationship between the represented and its representation. Resemblance then becomes the representational analogue of the criteria of truth that epistemologists always discuss. The problem of representation is thus reduced to that of epistemology, and we are required to see resemblance as the representationalist counterpart of the epistemological rules fixing the true statement to that about which it is true. But (aesthetic) representation should not be seen as a special case within a more general epistemological account of the relationship between a sign and what it signifies.

If we elaborate on this, an additional problem for the resemblance theory would be that it could be successful only if some identifiable content could be given to a more general epistemology of the sign, whatever this epistemology may actually look like. But that would require us to postulate an *x* (the subject of such a more general epistemological claim) that has depiction and description as its specific instances. However, what could this *x* possibly be? I am convinced that no plausible answer to this question can be given. Anyway, "representation" could not be the answer (in case one would feel tempted to try this one), since the view that description and depiction can both be considered as instances of representation is precisely the view that is *sub judice* here.

Since we happen to use the notion of sign in both the case of depiction and that of description, we are inclined to believe that the two *must* have some interesting philosophical properties in common that we may hope to discover by a painstakingly accurate philosophical analysis. But this is a perfect example of the kind of illusion that Wittgenstein attacked with his notion of the family resemblance. For the notion of "sign" is comparable to that of "utensil," rather than to that of, for example, "civil servant." There is little or nothing that ball-point pens, forks, and paperclips have in common apart from their all being classifiable as "utensils"; whereas police officers, judges, or deputy secretaries have a lot in common apart from the fact that they can all be classified as civil servants. Whereas, in the latter case, reflection on the notion of civil servant may substantially add to the list of properties shared by police officers and the others, reflection on the notion "utensil" will teach us nothing of interest that is true about ballpoints, forks, or paperclips. Similarly, it is one of the (many) sad and unfortunate facts about language that it happens to contain this notion of "sign" that suggests that there should be something "deep" and "fundamental" that description and depiction have in common, which a philosophical or epistemological analysis of that notion may be expected to bring to light. From this perspective one might say that semiotics, as a science or philosophy of the sign, has been the unwanted offspring of that otherwise so fruitful twentieth-century marriage of philosophy and language.

Furthermore, on the basis of the substitution theory it is easy to explain why depiction and description possess no interesting common denominator and why nothing is to be expected from an epistemological analysis of representation (i.e., of depiction). For, according to the substitution theory, both the represented and its representation belong to the (inventory of) the world—there is no ontological hierarchy between myself and the solicitor representing me in a lawsuit. Similarly, Marcus Aurelius and the statue at the Piazza del Campidoglio representing the emperor both belong to the inventory of the world, regardless of the fact that one of the two is (or, rather, was) of flesh and blood and the other of bronze. Consequently, the relationship between the represented and its representation—a world-to-world relationship—could never be modeled on the relationship between world and language (which is the exclusive domain of interest for the epistemologist). Speaking more generally, what makes representation such an interesting notion, especially now that we are beginning to lose our faith in the ideology of epistemology that so supremely ruled most of twentieth-century philosophy, is the impossibility of cramming it somehow in the traditional matrix of epistemological analysis. This, then, is the real problem with the resemblance theory: we will recognize its futility as soon as we realize that there is more between language and reality than epistemology has ever dreamed.

In our own time the substitution theory of representation has been defended by Ernst Gombrich in his famous meditations on a hobbyhorse; and a more recent and technically more detailed version of the theory can be found in the writings of Kendall Walton.[12] But the most elaborate and sophisticated defense of the theory occurs in Danto's aesthetics. As will become clear below, it is of the greatest importance to note that Danto distinguishes between two senses of representation. In the first sense we use the term "representation" for situations in which one and the same thing is "present" again, where it "re-presents" itself in the most literal sense of the word. For example, in the Dionysian rituals discussed by Nietzsche, the godhead himself may be present each time rituals are performed in his honor. Next, for the second sense of representation, think of an image that has been made of the godhead: here the image "represents" in the sense of making "present" to the believer the god who is "absent" himself. As Danto goes on to say: "This is the second sense of representation, then: a representation is something that stands in the place of something else, as our representatives in Congress stand proxy for ourselves."[13]

A few remarks are in order here. In the first place, Danto's view of representation demonstrates how big the differences between the substitution theory and the resemblance theory really are. For whereas the substitution theory has no difficulty in digesting the idea that Dionysius "re-presents" himself when he happens to be "present again" on several individual occasions, this use of the notion of representation puts the adherent of the resemblance theory in a bit of a quandary. At first sight this may reassuringly look like the very *ne plus ultra* of resemblance: here the re-presentation and its represented truly are *identical*.[14] Nothing resembles a thing more than it resembles itself. So it may seem that the adherent of the resemblance theory could not possibly desire more. But on closer inspection this situation must make the adherent of the resemblance theory feel uncomfortable: for we typically use the word "resemblance" to say something about two *different* things. The logic of the concept forbids us to use it in the case of identity: resemblance presupposes nonidentity. And we must conclude that Danto's first use of the concept of "representation" cannot properly be accounted for by the resemblance theory.

Certainly, the condition of nonidentity, with which the notion of resemblance is so much more at ease, is satisfied in the second sense of representation. But here resemblance is unable to account for representation for other reasons. In the first place, two cars of the same type will resemble each other more than any other object in the universe and yet they will not (normally) be considered to be "representations" of each other. So even next-to-perfect resemblance is insufficient to give us representation. But neither is resemblance a necessary condition of representation. For think of Gombrich's renowned hobbyhorse. The average table will more closely "resemble" a real horse than a hobbyhorse, and yet, as Gombrich so rightly insisted, the hobbyhorse more successfully represents a real horse than a table (for the simple reason that the hobbyhorse may *function* in the eyes of the child as a real horse, whereas the table will not).

So, the resemblance theory seems to be out of step with our actual uses of the notion of representation, whereas Danto's variant of the substitution theory respects these actual uses. And the explanation of the greater success of the latter in accounting for our uses of the notion of representation undoubtedly lies in the notion of identity. For the notion of identity shows much the same behavior as that of representation. On the one hand, we can well say that we have to do with one and the same identity when Dionysius or some person is present on several individual occasions. Next, we also know that identity may sometimes allow space for a dramatic amount of change. Think of the different phases of an individual from birth to death, or of the history of Poland's borders. Every conceivable criterion of resemblance has been flouted in such cases.

Against this background I suggest that the difference between the resemblance and the substitution theory has its origin in the fact that the resemblance theory tries to do in terms of resemblance what the substitution theory wants to do by means of identity. According to the resemblance theory, resemblance determines whether a representation represents a represented; however, for the substitution theory (as proposed by Danto) a representation re-presents, makes present again, the identity of the represented. But for a correct appraisal of this distinction between the two theories the following is absolutely essential. We should not conceive of (criteria of) resemblance and identity as each other's rivals, as if the substitution theory urges us to replace criteria of resemblance by criteria of identity. For the more interesting difference between the resemblance and the substitution theory is that the latter nowhere invokes or ever relies upon such criteria. And this is not because, when abandoning these criteria, the substitution theory wishes to emphasize that just anything can be seen as the representation of anything else. Though to a large extent this is true as well; for as Danto somewhere suggests, one might propose to see a fly as representing the New York World Trade Center (or even the reverse, if one would so prefer).

But this is not what is truly of interest here. What we should note is that the substitution theory differs from the resemblance theory by avoiding the suggestion of a conceptual hierarchy between the notions of representation and of identity. The resemblance theory inadvertently creates such a hierarchy by presenting resemblance as the link between identity and representation: if A sufficiently resembles B, what A represents is (or is identical with) B. Put differently, when A represents B it can be tailored by the criteria of resemblance in such a way that the result of all the tailoring will be (identical with) the represented B all over again. And this is different with the substitution theory: this theory does *not* posit such a conceptual hierarchy between identity and representation. Representation *is* the representation of identity because identity only comes into being by representation, and vice versa; there is not, first, an identity, which is or could, next, be represented—whether in agreement with certain criteria of resemblance or not—no, representation and identity both come into being *at one and the same time*. Recognizing this may also explain why both identities and representations can vary so enormously (as in the example of the fly and the World Trade Center given a moment ago) and successfully defy every conceivable proposal for criteria of resemblance that should be respected in the relationship between the represented and its representation.

For being dependent upon representation, identity is not something that is somehow present forever and always in the thing to be represented, in the way that a thing may have a certain color or weight. The identity of the represented only comes into being thanks to and at the same time as its representation. And with regard to representation, nothing is a priori impossible—as is amply shown by the history of art.

Lastly, it might be helpful, for an adequate appraisal of the merits of both theories, to consider an example where the two initially seem to apply equally well, but where then quickly we see which of the two is able meet the challenge and which is not. Such examples are not easy to find but are nevertheless provided by a series of well-known paintings by René Magritte, to which he gave the title *La Condition humaine*. Magritte gave the following clarification of what he had attempted to do in these paintings:

> I placed in front of a window, seen from inside a window, a painting representing exactly that part of the landscape that was hidden from view by the painting. Therefore, the tree represented in the painting hid from view the tree situated behind it, outside the room. It existed for the spectator, as it were, simultaneously in his mind, as both inside the room in the painting, and outside in the real landscape. Which is how we see the world: we see it as being outside ourselves even though it only is a mental representation of it that we experience in ourselves. In the same way, we sometimes situate in the past a thing which is happening in the present. Time and space thus lose the unrefined meaning which is the only one everyday experience takes into account.[15]

Leaving apart for the moment Magritte's (doubtful) speculations about how the painting represents our seeing of the world, we will observe that we have here an example of representation that at first sight seems to fit the two representation theories equally well. For, on the one hand, *ex hypothesi* the landscape on the painting completely satisfies the requirement that it resembles what it represents. There simply *could* be no difference: the landscape behind the painting and the one on the painting are the same down to the last molecule, since every molecule on Magritte's painting is intended to be part of both. But, next, it also satisfies both of Danto's uses of the word "representation" as defined in his substitution view. For in the first place, there also is identity, since the part of Magritte's painting in question is identical with itself—as each thing is identical with itself. But the painting in the room is also a *substitute* of what it represents—it even performs the substitution job ideally. For there *could* not possibly be any difference between the represented and its substitute in this case; the substitute and what it is a substitute of are completely identical here.

In order to correctly interpret this intriguing state of affairs, we should note that Magritte could only succeed in achieving this effect because it is achieved within a *representation*. It is only within the painting that he painted of the room, and of the painting placed before the window in that room, that this difference between the resemblance and the substitution theory lost its meaning. Nevertheless, even though there now seems to be no point anymore in having to choose between the two theories, a small but significant asymmetry should be observed. It is true that the relevant part of Magritte's painting is identical with itself (as part of the painting), but this part of the painting has *two* functions to fulfill: (1) to function as the landscape *itself* (in the way that paintings, according to the substitution theory are required to function as what is represented by them), and (2) to function as the *painting* of the landscape (i.e., as a *representation* of the landscape). Obviously, to make precisely this clear is what the Magritte painting is all about. Now, needless to say, the difference between these two functions is exactly analogous to that between (represented) reality and its representation. But this difference of functions disappears if we see the painting with the eyes of the adherent of the resemblance theory: for there is *no* difference in the resemblance relationship between (1) the landscape itself and that part of the painting for which the painting is the substitute, and (2) the landscape itself and its representation as presented by the painting in the room.

Therefore, the substitution theory is most successful in passing this pretty difficult test to which we subject the two theories: it is the theory that remains sensitive to the difference between the represented and its representation and is capable to account for it, whereas this distinction is lost if we interpret the Magritte painting in accordance with the resemblance theory. In sum, since the substitution theory succeeds in explaining and justifying our intuitions about representation, while the resemblance theory has to admit defeat, obviously we should prefer the former to the latter.

REPRESENTATION AND IDENTITY

We observed in the previous section that what is new in Danto's account of representation, where this account differs from all others from both past and present (and especially from all variants of the resemblance theory), is to be found in the close linkage of the notion of representation and that of identity. No account of representation deserves to be taken seriously that does not also account for identity; that is the all-important lesson that we should learn from Danto's analysis of representation.

But now two complications present themselves. In the first place this linkage obviously has an a priori plausibility insofar as we expect representation, such as painted portraits, to convey, or rather to define, something of the identity of the sitter. However, it would be absurd to maintain that the painting and the sitter are *identical*. So, in relationship to the notion of representation the substantive "identity" and the adjective "identical" seem to obey a different logic. The difference is also reflected in the fact that we say that something *has* an "identity," whereas things may (or not) *be* "identical." Since we will not say that we *are* what we possess (apart from the property of *being* in possession of what we possess), "being identical" seems to be bound up more intimately with a thing's nature than its identity. There is apparently an indeterminacy in "identity" that does not have its counterpart in "being identical." This tendency of the notion of identity to deviate from its cognate adjective will require us to be a little more precise about the linkage of representation and identity than we were in the previous section.

The second problem concerns the tension between Danto's substitution theory of representation and his method of indiscernibles. This method requires us to look for relevant differences between things that at first sight seem to be completely identical—such as a Brillo box at the grocer's and the Brillo boxes that Andy Warhol "transfigured" into a work of art by exhibiting them in a museum in the early sixties. This problem is much similar to the former: for whereas the substitution theory does not require the represented and its representation to be identical, the method of indiscernibles sets a premium on two things being identical in as many respects as possible. So both problems concern the notion of identity and the relationship between identity and being identical. These issues will occupy us for the remainder of this chapter. In this section the topic of representation and identity will be discussed; in the next we shall deal with the tension between the substitution theory of representation and Danto's method of indiscernibles.

To begin with, there is a thread in Danto's argument that relates the notion of identity exclusively to things in (represented) reality—hence, not to representation. Here his argument would be at odds with the thesis de-

Danto on Representation, Identity, and Indiscernibles   231

fended in the previous section, according to which identity is not something like color or weight, but, rather, something that only comes into being by and thanks to representation. Statements sinning against this view will be found in passages where Danto seems to have momentarily forgotten about the distinction between description and depiction—a distinction that is elsewhere so crucial in his argument, as we have seen. A good example of such a statement where (1) identity is detached from representation and pulled back to (things) in reality, and (2) representation is discussed in terms of the epistemological model of the relationship between language and reality, is the following:

> In the one case the relation was that of identity—in seeing the appearance one *was* seeing the thing—and in the other the relation was that of designation, a gap having opened up, so to speak, between the reality and its representations, comparable to, if not indeed the same as the gap that is perceived to separate language from reality when the former is understood in its representational, or descriptive capacity."[16]

Obviously, a statement like this undermines most of what Danto had previously said about (the substitution theory of) representation and about the shortcomings of epistemology if we wish to come to terms with the phenomenon of representation. Later on, in a similar context, Danto appeals to Gottlob Frege's distinction between *Sinn* and *Bedeutung* to clarify the notion of representation.[17] Now, since Frege's distinction was intended to explain linguistic meaning, clearly the suggestion is, once again, that representation (or depiction) and description are essentially the same. Even more explicit is Danto's following statement:

> Taken as having representational properties—as being about something, or of something—and hence subject to semantic identification—there exists an essential contrast between words and things, between representations and reality, as the latter in each instance is logically immune to such assessment since devoid of representationality.[18]

In statements like these, where identity is relegated to the represented only and is withheld from the notion of representation, most of the virtues of Danto's account of representation that we expounded above have been lost again.[19]

My hunch would be that in less guarded statements like these Danto has been misled by the unfortunate fact (identified a moment ago) that the notions of "identity" and of "being identical" obey different logics. How this affects Danto's position could be elucidated as follows. Think of Dionysius being "present again" each time rituals were performed in his honor. Surely each time we have to do with the same unique identity; hence the linkage between identity and this specific variant of representation. Obviously, it is no different with human beings. However, equally obviously, we will not always be exactly the *same* person at the different occasions that we "re-present" ourselves. We may be in a different mood, have gained or lost weight if compared to our previous presentations, or have become sadder and wiser, and so on. But the notion of representation is indifferent to these kinds of changes, and so is the notion of identity: think of philosophers such as David Wiggins or Derek Parfit, who so eagerly investigated the notion of "identity through time" and, by doing so, tried to account for the compatibility of unchanged identity and of not-being-identical. So, there is a use of the word "identity" that is compatible with being different on different occasions, and this is the notion of identity that we also must have in mind when we relate representation to identity. Within this use of the notion of identity there is nothing odd or absurd in saying, for example, that a good portrait (i.e., a representation) represents the identity of the sitter. Let us call this variant of representationalist identity "identity$_r$."

Let us now consider Leibniz's law of the identity of indiscernibles. According to this law two things A and B are identical if and only if what can truly be said about A can also be said about B, *salva veritate*, or, put differently, if and only if each true description of A is also true of B. Frege's distinction between sense and reference further contributed to this conception of identity. For by emphasizing that questions of sameness or identity should be phrased in terms of sense or meaning—as in his famous example of the identicalness of the morning star and the evening star—extra philosophical credit was given to Leibniz's view that truth determines identity. Let us call this variant of Leibnizian identity "identity$_l$." And we might add, in parentheses, that it is no coincidence that Danto's relapse from identity$_r$ into identity$_l$ took place (as we observed in the previous section) in the context of a discussion of the Fregean account of meaning. Now, obviously, Leibnizian identity clashes with "identity$_r$" and presents us with the kind of identity that is used when we say that one thing is "identical" with another thing. The easiest solution would be, of course, to acquiesce in this unhappy fact about language and conclude that there are apparently two different conceptions of identity, and that we should always pay attention to which of the two uses is at stake. Yet, by doing so we would miss a welcome opportunity to deepen our insight into the notion of identity.

If, then, we aim for an outright confrontation between identity$_r$ and identity$_I$, we should first make sure where a potential conflict between the two is to be expected and where differences are unproblematic or easy to reconcile. With regard to the latter possibility, it should be observed that the notion of identity$_r$ is ordinarily used in the context where we wonder *what* something is: for example, who exactly is this man?—a question that may concern something as simple as his nationality and something as complicated as his role in history, and anything in between. Identity$_I$, on the other hand, has to do with the similarities between *two* (or perhaps even more) things: for example, is this car the same, that is, identical to, that other one over there? Obviously, different uses and meanings of identity are at stake here, but these do not conflict and can unproblematically coexist together.

Real trouble arises only when the two notions of identity (and of being identical) happen to be applied to one and the same thing. This is the kind of trouble that gave rise to, for example, the problem of identity through change. When philosophers tried to deal with this problem, all difficulties stemmed from the fact that one and the same thing might differ at different phases of its history more dramatically from itself than from some other thing. For example, when you were a baby you resembled other babies more closely than the adult person that you presently are—or so one would hope. And then there *is* trouble: for you are the same person as the baby of so many years ago, while at the time you were *not* the same person as any of these other babies, although they cried just as hard as you did, had the same indignant look, and so on—all things that will rarely be true of you now. Identity$_I$ in this case contradicts identity$_r$. But, next, why would there necessarily be trouble even in such cases? For could one not say that in such cases identity$_I$ functions as a criterion for establishing identity$_r$? For example, the genetic codes of the baby are identical to those of the adult and differ from those of other babies, and thus the baby that you were so many years ago and the adult that you are now can safely be said to be one and the same person. This, obviously, is the intuition behind the search for the criteria of identity through change. Philosophers investigating this problem always try to identify some set of criteria (continuity through space and time, for example) that will allow us to establish identity$_r$.

But whatever one might like to invent in this connection will inevitably fall short of the desired reconciliation of identity$_l$ and identity$_r$. And problems will then invariably be caused, not by identity$_r$ (one of the most complaisant and accommodating of philosophical notions), but by identity$_l$. For it may well be that you have now the same genetic codes that you had when you were a baby. But in spite of that (or in spite of whatever else you may share with the baby that you were) it would be ridiculous to hold that you are identical$_l$ with the baby of so many years ago. Yet the baby is identical$_r$ with the adult: think of the many stories that could be told about you, beginning with the baby that you once were and ending with the adult that you presently are. And we must conclude that even these criteria of identity through change will not achieve a reconciliation between identity$_r$ and identity$_l$, because no set of such criteria will ever satisfy the impossibly high demands of identity$_l$.

As may have become clear from the foregoing, it was identity$_l$ that proved to be the real troublemaker in our (vain) efforts to create peace between identity$_r$ and identity$_l$. For in our last attempt to reconcile the two notions we appealed to criteria of identity through change. Now, from a logical point of view such criteria have much more affinity with identity$_l$ than with identity$_r$. With regard to identity$_r$ we need only recall the hobbyhorse: identity$_r$ apparently has not much use for such criteria (though it is not really opposed to the idea, nice, friendly, and easygoing as identity$_r$ always is). Identity$_r$ is satisfied already with each of the infinite number of possible stories that could be told about you and, as every historian will be able to tell you, no a priori criteria can be given of what may or may not count as such a story.[20] On the other hand, these lists of shared properties that might define identity through change obviously are subsets of the list of shared properties in the case that we may legitimately use the notion of identity$_l$. Yet even this concession has not made identity$_l$ more accommodating: it snubbed here, so to speak, its own ally.

So now we will begin to wonder what makes identity$_l$ into so intransigent a notion, a notion that is so extremely difficult to please. When asking ourselves this question in despair, the first thing to be observed is that identity$_r$ is an identity of *things*, whereas identity$_l$ *also* involves an identity of (sets of) *statements* about things (i.e., sets of true descriptions of things).

Whereas identity$_1$ inevitably requires us to move from the level of things to that of language (and backwards), identity$_r$ is content to keep within the domain of things. Even more so, adherents of identity$_r$ will point out that the advantage of their conception of identity, if compared to its rival, lies precisely in its successful avoidance of the thorny questions of the relationship between language and reality. So we could say that identity$_r$ presents us with an ontological account of identity, whereas identity$_1$ gives an epistemological-*cum*-ontological meaning to the concept. Identity$_r$ never leaves the realm of things, whereas the dimension *language* is also at stake in the case of identity$_1$ and, in this way, when defining the identity of *things*, does so by also involving the problem of the relationship between language and things that is so much the traditional domain of epistemological research. Identity$_1$ shares with epistemological concerns the pretension to define in terms of language (i.e., Leibniz's law) a truth about things (i.e., that two things are [not] identical). This may also help explain why identity$_1$ is so empty and useless a notion that it can only be used to express the fact that a thing is identical with itself—Leibniz himself admitted already that numerical difference is already sufficient to rule out identity$_1$. For what is at stake in identity is, so to speak, the intersecting line of ontology and epistemology. And insofar as identity permits us to move with absolute certainty from one thing to another (a kind of "tautology of things," as it were), the distinction between ontology and epistemology is momentarily suspended only in identity$_1$. It need not surprise us that only in the case of a most exceptional and unusual situation (i.e., a "tautology of things") can this most improbable suspension be achieved.

Several conclusions can be drawn from this. In the first place, we must conclude that identity$_1$ is an impractical notion that cannot really help us to explain our uses of the notion of identity: it is a typical philosopher's delusion that only creates new problems instead of solving old ones. Secondly, a meaningful notion of identity, a conception of identity that may help us explain our actual use of the notion, should carefully avoid implicating language in it in some way or other. Certainly, identity itself is a word, is part of our language, but what the notion stands for is not. Whoever is tempted to define identity in terms of language, since the word *itself* is part of language, will be a victim of the rationalist fallacy that truths of fact should always have their counterpart in truths about language. Thirdly, and most importantly in the context of the present discussion, the "gap" which according to

Danto is created by representation is not, as Danto argues himself, a gap between language and reality, but between things (between the represented thing and the thing representing it).

Having arrived at this stage, the following objection is to be expected. If identity should be restricted exclusively to the level of things, if it could not be contaminated by language in any way, if this representational "gap" is a gap between things and not between things and language, then what about, for example, historical representation? For surely the historian uses *language* in order to represent the past and in order to discern in it the identities that are the topic of his account of the past? What would be left of historical representation if the level of language were to be eliminated from it? So is it not an utter absurdity to claim (as we have been doing) that historical representation gives us this gap between things instead of between things (in the past) and (the historian's) language? Though I very much fear to make things even more complicated than they are already, I now unfortunately have to add the following critical remark about how we customarily and intuitively (but mistakenly) tend to define the levels of language and that of things. When we say that the representational gap is always a gap between *things* and not between *things* and *language*, we ordinarily suppose the words "thing" and "language" to fit within the traditional epistemological framework of the relationship of things (or reality) and language. Within this framework there is, on the one hand, reality and the things contained by it, and on the other hand, there is the language that we use for formulating true descriptions of reality. And epistemological debate presupposes that this is a completely unambiguous distinction in the sense that everything is either thing or language. This is the (familiar) framework that was presupposed in the foregoing discussion.

But precisely in the context of the representation of reality things are more complicated. For when language happens to be used to offer representations of reality (instead of paint or marble), language assumes, as I have demonstrated on several occasions, the properties of *things* (such as spots of paint or blocks of marble). Hence, there is not just (1) reality itself, the things that make up the inventory of reality, and (2) the language we use for speaking about reality; we should also discern (3) a category of "linguistic things" sharing the properties of both thing and language.[21] And one could say that these linguistic things are separated from reality by a double gap: (1) insofar as they contain true statements about reality, there is this epistemological gap that Danto had in mind, but (2) insofar as they are also things (representing other things), they are also separated by a representational gap with the things, phenomena, events, or whatever they represent. And about this latter gap, though *not* about the former, one can assert, with Danto, that the represented comes into being in a certain sense only thanks to the representation. As Danto put it himself: "something is 'real' when it satisfies a representation of itself, just as something is a 'bearer [of a name]' when it is named by a name."[22]

Indeed, names may function as representations in the way that individual true statements do not, though there are categories of *sets* of true statements—to which I gave the name of "narrative substances"—that may become representational.[23] This may also demonstrate what is true and false in the post-Fregean common wisdom that names have a meaning and that this meaning is equivalent to some identifying description of what is named by the name. For as soon as a name stands for a narrative substance it refers to a *representation* of (part of) the past and no longer to (something in) the past itself. For example, the name Napoleon in the statement "Napoleon contributed to the rise of nationalism" refers, when the sentence is interpreted descriptively, to the person of flesh and blood who lived from 1769 to 1821, but may also refer to a *representation* of Napoleon's historical role (presenting us with Napoleon's identity$_r$). This will become clear when we write before the name Napoleon in the sentence mentioned just now, for example, "this book's," or "historian X's." Even more obvious is this ambiguity of (historical) names in statements about things like the Renaissance or the Enlightenment. More often than not it will be impossible in practice to find out whether the proper name "the Renaissance" in a statement like "the Renaissance is x" refers to the past or to a specific representation of the past that a historian wishes to present to the readers of his book.

So our conclusion must be as follows. Representations are always *things* representing other things and should never be modeled on the relationship between *language* and reality that has been so much a challenge to the acuity of epistemologists. Nevertheless, language can be used representationally, and thus language will have become a *thing* from an ontological point of view. So, in a way, Danto was right with his claim about this representational "gap" between a representation and what it represents. But this is an *ontological* (or *aesthetic*) gap, a gap between *things*, and not an *epistemological* gap.

DANTO'S PHILOSOPHICAL METHODOLOGY

Let us now consider the philosophical methododology that Danto expounded on several occasions, and ask whether it agrees with his views on representation and, if not, which of the two we had best sacrifice in favor of the other. According to him, "philosophical problems arise in connection with indiscriminable pairs, the difference between which is not a scientific one."[24] The deep insight behind this idea is that philosophical knowledge should, as Wittgenstein already proclaimed, leave the world unchanged. A philosophical proposition that would "make a difference" in the sense of altering our conceptions of the world would be either bad philosophy or a scientific truth (or falsehood, as commonly will be the case, insofar as philosophers generally are poor amateur scientists). Philosophical truths should be compatible both with the world and with all the true statements that scientists can make about the world. Put differently, philosophical problems arise when we have two completely identical bits of the world (or of our knowledge of the world) that are yet to be perceived as different in some relevant sense. An obvious example would be the debate between idealists and realists: both the idealist and the realist can present their case in such a way that the world and all that we know about it are respected and yet there is somehow room for a meaningful philosophical debate. We have two worlds—the idealist's and the realist's—that are indiscriminable to all practical purposes and yet there seems to be an unbridgeable gap between the idealist and the realist account of these indiscriminable worlds. Or, to mention the example made famous by Danto's discussion of it, suppose that we have two Brillo boxes that are in all respects exactly identical. But one of the two Brillo boxes is in the grocery store and the other has been "transfigured" by Andy Warhol into a work of art. This gives rise to the philosophical problem of why one of this indiscernible pair of two Brillo boxes succeeded in acquiring the elevated status of a work of art while the other will probably end its short and unpresuming life in the dustbin. As Danto's argument so brilliantly makes clear, the method of indiscernible pairs is ideally suited for dealing with the problem of what art is. For, by comparing two objects that are materially completely indiscernible, while one belongs to the art world and the other does not, the question of the nature of art has taken on manageable proportions. All of the static caused by material differences—and that might mislead us when attempting to answer the question where art and reality differ—has been eliminated.

Now, it will be obvious that this method can only be used when we really have to do with indiscernible pairs. Perhaps the pairs need not be really identical in all respects—there were, after all, some easily discernible differences between Warhol's and real Brillo boxes or between Jasper Johns's *Painted Bronze* and two real Ballantine beer cans. But these differences should be considered irrelevant from the philosopher's point of view. Hence, let us suppose for the remainder of this argument that Danto's method will always present us with pairs that completely resemble each other.

But this presupposition presents a problem, since this method obviously has more affinities with identity$_1$ and with the resemblance theory than with identity$_r$ and the substitution theory of representation, defended by Danto elsewhere. For if we are justified in seeing Warhol's Brillo box as a representation of an ordinary Brillo box, the represented and its representation are completely similar here. In order to get rid of this nasty problem, two ways are open to Danto, as far as I can see. In the first place he could insist that when dealing with the Brillo box, the nature of art and not that of representation is the topic of his investigation. So no conflicts need necessarily arise if we see the substitution theory as our best candidate to account for the nature of representation and we use the method of the indiscernibles in order to account for the nature of art. Perhaps. But I suppose that most people would rather avoid making use of a philosophical method that presupposes as given what is explicitly rejected elsewhere as an inconsistent notion. The only possible way out would seem to be the argument that there is no overlap between art and representation. But it will not be easy to defend this counterintuitive view, and if the attempt were to be crowned with success at all, undoubtedly some very incisive adaptations would be needed elsewhere in Danto's aesthetics.

Another strategy for dealing with the problem—and one that Danto would presumably much prefer himself—would be to simply deny that Warhol's Brillo box should be seen as a representation of an ordinary Brillo box.[25] Surely, this would effectively solve the problem. But I'm not sure whether this strategy would really be convincing. For imagine Warhol in his studio devising this work of art. We don't know what precisely went on in his head at the time. But presumably it must have been something like this. He knew that he could have painted a still life of the Brillo box as exactly, realistically, and naturalistically as possible, maybe even aiming at the trompe l'oeil effect. But this would have caused no scandal and neither would it have given rise to problems about the nature of art. For since the days of Apelles' painting of grapes, which the birds themselves are said to have mistaken for real grapes, these things have often been tried; and the effort has been most respectable in the history of art. So Warhol realized that if he wanted to cause a scandal, he really had to take the Brillo box *as it is*. Only this might shock the public—and so it did.

If something like this makes sense, the following two remarks are relevant. First, we should see Warhol's experiment with the Brillo box within the context of a history of representation.[26] Things have been represented in many different ways in the course of that history, but nobody ever had the courage to do the kind of thing that Warhol did (of course, there had been Duchamp, but let's not go into that). And it is exclusively in *this* context that Warhol's Brillo box created the scandal at which Warhol had aimed. For if placed outside that context the Brillo box in the museum and the one outside it would be just as unrelated to each other as Rembrandt's portrait of Jan Six and, for example, the eleventh-century church of Anloo I always see from my writing desk. The Brillo box in the museum would be completely pointless outside the context of the history of representation; in that case the Brillo box would have the same status as a Brillo box that, presumably, one of the cleaning women of the museum had left lying around. In summary, if the Warhol Brillo box is not a representation of an ordinary Brillo box, it could never be the statement about the nature of art that Danto wants it to be.

Second, if the original Brillo box and Warhol's Brillo box are completely indiscernible, this is no mere coincidence. The work of art Warhol needed *really* had to have a counterpart in reality that it represents, and to be exactly similar to and present us with an exact resemblance of its counterpart. If these two conditions were not satisfied, the whole thing would not have worked. But this seems to lead us back to the resemblance theory of representation and to identity$_1$ as the kind of identity that we should associate with representation. So Danto's substitution theory of representation and his method of the indiscernibles are truly incompatible: acceptance of one of the two automatically implies the rejection of the other.

HISTORY

So this confronts us with the question whether we should opt for the substitution view of representation or for the method of indiscernibles. As it happens, Danto's own writings are our very best guide in this dilemma. This will become clear if we consider Danto's views on history as expounded in his *Analytical Philosophy of History*. The book belongs to the half a dozen or so of the most influential studies in the philosophy of history that have been written in English since R. G. Collingwood, and it has lost nothing of its freshness and originality. Of special importance in the present context is that this early work anticipates many of the themes that would dominate Danto's later philosophical writings.

Though the term is not used in this book, it can be read (from our present perspective) as an analysis of the nature of historical representation. Now, each account of historical representation has to deal, minimally, with two tasks. It should demonstrate, first, that there is such a thing as a historical reality that can be represented at all, and, second, what is the nature of the historian's representation of the past and its relationship to the represented past. Several theorists have doubted the existence of such a past reality that exists independently from the historian's representations of it;[27] and each theory of historical representation will have to deal with this challenge sooner or later. For what could (historical) representation be without there being something that is represented?

Fortunately, it will not be necessary to investigate all the arguments that have been given to justify these doubts, by either relativist historians themselves or by historical theorists with a bent for constructivism. In the present context it will be sufficient if we succeed in dealing with the strongest formulation of these skeptical arguments as presented by what is known as Russell's paradox: if we succeed in dealing with this paradox, we need no longer worry about weaker variants of skepticism. According to the Russell paradox, then, there is nothing that might refute the hypothesis that God created this world five minutes ago, with all of us and with all our memories of a remoter past and all the historical evidence for events in a past preceding these five minutes. So it might therefore well be that all that historians tell us about the past refers to a past that never existed;[28] historical writing would then be much like the fictive history of Europe since Charlemagne that was invented by Jean d'Ormesson and that provoked so much the ire of Georges Duby.²⁹ Needless to say, this is the kind of argument that fits nicely with Danto's method of the indiscernibles: *ex hypothesi* the real past and the fictive past suggested by Russell's paradox are indiscernible. And Danto even improves upon the paradox by pointing out that if it were true, the writing of history would be no less useful than it is in the case of a real past. The explanation is that for our present and future behavior, insofar as these are based on what we believe that the past has been like (think, for example, of promises made last week), it makes no practical difference whether the past really existed or not.³⁰

Nevertheless, if historical accounts are representations of the past, there must have been a real, represented past compared to which a fictive or imaginary past would leave us unsatisfied. In order to prove the reality of the past, Danto begins with the observation that Russell's five minutes are completely arbitrary. For why not reduce the five minutes to five seconds, or expand it to five centuries? So a really consistent skepticism à la Russell would conceive of a past that is fictive right up to *this* very moment.³¹ But if the skeptic is prepared to accept this criticism (and he could not do otherwise) he can be checkmated.³² For then we should ask him what he will answer tomorrow to our question at what moment the world came into being. If his answer (now) is that he will then say again that the world was created just now (i.e., today), he must recognize that he will accept tomorrow a past of one day—and in that case he is reduced again to the same kind of arbitrary option of accepting part of the past (i.e., one day) and not all of it. But if his answer is (and this is his only realistic alternative) that he will say tomorrow that the world was created tomorrow, there is an inconsistency between his position now and that of tomorrow. We would then have two creations of the world at two different times. Besides, it is not easy to see what we should make of the statement that the world will be created tomorrow (for what strange temporal limbo would we then be living in today?). So we cannot reasonably doubt the reality of the past and the existence of a past that is represented by the historian's representations of it, and we need no longer worry about whether there is a represented past corresponding to our representations of it.

So far, so good. But what, then, about the historian's representations of the past; and how do these representations relate to the represented past? It has often been argued—and Charles Beard is Danto's major source here—that since the past is inexorably past and therefore unobservable, all historical representation of the past and all historical writing is inevitably unreliable; reliable knowledge is only possible about what is given to us here and now, so the argument continues. But, as Danto most perceptively comments,

> this is an odd kind of lamentation. Our incapacity, which is granted, to observe the past, is not a defect in history itself, but a deficiency which it is the precise purpose of history to overcome. . . . That cities lie at a spatial distance from one another is not to be regarded as a defect in our systems of transportation: it is a deficiency, if one may style it such, which systems of transportation are precisely designed to overcome.[33]

What is so interesting about Danto's comment in the present context is that it does not dish up the customary kind of epistemological argument attempting to show what rational foundations can be given, after all, for our belief in what historians say about the past (as if the epistemologist would be of any help to us when we wonder whether we should or should not believe what historians say about the past). Danto's comment shows, rather, what is so "odd" about these epistemological worries and about our tendency to share them. It does so by emphasizing that we have a history, historical research, historical representations, discussions, and so on, precisely in order to overcome these epistemological anxieties. Hence, Danto's rejoinder to the skeptic is not so much an answer to an epistemological question as an exhortation that we should refrain from *asking* that kind of useless question. It is a useless question because the epistemological question fails to recognize that we have historical writing—and that it is even the very *purpose* of historical writing to bridge the kind of gap that the epistemologist (naively) hopes to bridge by means of vacuous epistemological argument. And no amount of historical epistemology could ever be an acceptable substitute for actual historical analysis. Too bad for the epistemologist, but this is what it is like.

We should note, next, that Danto explicitly appeals to pictorial representation in order to elucidate his refutation of historical skepticism:

> Imagine an artist who subscribed to the Imitation Theory of art, and who became so obsessed with the imitation of reality, which falls always short of reproducing the subject, that he decided that only the thing itself will do as an imitation of itself. He tries, accordingly, to go *all the way*, duplicating the landscape, using real trees, real water, real birds [and real Brillo boxes, we might add, with the Danto

of the *Transfiguration*]. Perfect success would, of course, be utter failure.... And we may say as much of histories of things. What Beard fails to understand is that even if we could witness the whole past, any account that we would give of it would involve selection, emphasis, elimination, and would presuppose some criteria of relevance, so that our account could not, unless it wishes to fail through succeeding, include everything.[34]

But, what is more important, even if we were to succeed in avoiding "selection, emphasis, elimination" and the application of criteria of relevance in the attempt to achieve "historical objectivity" and to protect the real past against each distortion, even then the attempt to achieve an account of the past *wie es eigentlich gewesen*, is doomed to failure. Or, preferably, it can be shown to be an inconsistent aspiration.

Danto's argument to that effect proceeds in two steps. In the first place, a Collingwoodian "reenactment" of the past, in the sense of a complete repetition of events as they took place in the actual past itself, is for obvious reasons out of the question. It would be idiotic to demand of historians that they should present us with, for example, another World War II in case we happen to be historically interested in that part of the past. Suppose this to be possible; we would become mortally afraid of asking historians any questions about the past because of the most redoubtable way in which they might satisfy our curiosity. But the idea is too silly to be seriously entertained even for less dramatic parts of the past—and not only for practical reasons.

This will become clear from Danto's account, if we consider his notion of the so-called Ideal Chronicle and the "narrative sentence." The fundamental insight behind these two notions is that we ask the historian for an *account* of the past, not merely because this is second best after we have abandoned (with a sigh of deep relief) the Collingwoodian view of historical representation that I mentioned just now, but for the far more compelling and convincing reason that such an account can only give us what even such a Collingwoodian "reenactment" of the past *wie es eigentlich gewesen* could *never* give us. When asking a historical question we want an *account*, a *comment* on the past, and not a *simulacrum* of the past itself. And these are not even *ideally* identical things. The Ideal Chronicle is defined by Danto as follows:

I now want to insert an Ideal Chronicler into my picture. He knows whatever happens the moment it happens, even in other minds. He is also to have the gift of instantaneous transcription: everything that happens across the whole forward rim of the Past is set down by him, as it happens, the *way* it happens. The resultant running account I shall term the *Ideal Chronicle* (hereafter referred to as I.C.).[35]

Now, two things should be observed about this I.C. In the first place, if we were to think of the linguistic counterpart of the past *wie es eigentlich gewesen*, surely this I.C. is what immediately comes to mind. The I.C. is a kind of linguistic facsimile of what the past itself has been like, and is intended by Danto to be seen as such. So, at first sight, the I.C. seems to be the (albeit unattainable) ideal of each historian and of all historical writing. But, second, as Danto goes on to demonstrate, on closer investigation the I.C. will turn out both in theory and in practice to be a useless notion at odds with what the writing of history and historical representation really are all about. This becomes clear as soon as we ask ourselves what could *not* be part of the I.C. In discussing this question Danto introduces the notion of the "narrative sentence." Narrative sentences are sentences like "The Thirty Years' War began in 1618" and in which one event (here, the outbreak of the war in 1618) is (implicitly) related to another, later event (here, the end of the war in 1648). Observe that the sentence presupposes knowledge of the fact that the war would end in 1648 and therefore could not possibly have been uttered in 1618.

Two further remarks should be made now. In the first place, it cannot reasonably be doubted that these narrative sentences are paradigmatic of all historical writing: facts are stated by historians for no other purpose than to relate them to *other* facts. Take away from historical writing these narrative sentences and what is effected by them, and you have transformed historical writing into a corpse without a heart. In the second place, it will be obvious that these narrative sentences present a problem for the I.C. Surely, the sentence could not be written down in the I.C. in 1618 when the war broke out, since nobody—not even the Ideal Chronicler—could know that it would last for thirty long and bitter years. But now the Ideal Chronicler might protest that *after* 1648 the sentence might be included in his account, so that it would need a mere extra effort on his part (and to which he is gladly disposed in order to satisfy us) to meet Danto's wishes. And since historians ordinarily discuss those parts of the past that are described in terms of the *perfectum* or even the *plusquam perfectum*, this would solve all problems, with the likely exception of contemporary history, which somehow lingers on in the present.

We certainly would be profoundly grateful to the Ideal Chronicler for his obligingness and yet remain dissatisfied. For we would now point out to him that historians often describe the past in terms of conceptual systems that were not yet available in the past itself—think of, for example, the vocabulary of economic history. Inclusion of all *these* descriptions in the I.C. require that the Ideal Chronicler would be acquainted with all these vocabularies. And that would also demand knowledge of vocabularies that will be developed only in the future. And, as we know since Popper, this is a logical impossibility, since if we knew now already the (scientific) vocabularies that will be used in the future, these would no longer be *future* vocabularies. There is a logical contradiction in the view that we, or even the Ideal Chronicler, might *now* know *future* knowledge.[36]

In sum, the I.C. may, in a certain sense, be more complete than any account that historians will ever give of the past, but in a far more important and relevant sense, in the sense that really belongs to the heart of the whole enterprise of the writing of history, the I.C. will be more incomplete, and more sadly so, than even the papers written by our undergraduate students. And we may agree with Danto when he writes: "it begins to dawn on one that a 'full description' does not adequately meet the needs of historians, and so fails to stand as the ideal which we hope our own accounts will approach."[37]

The nature of representation has been the main theme in this chapter. As we found when considering Danto's account of historical representation, a representation will necessarily differ from what it represents. Not merely because in the case of historical representation we somehow have to move from reality to language (with the possible exception of fields like intellectual history, where represented reality belongs to the realm of language as well), but for the more compelling reason that a representation that is identical to what it represents is simply not what we hope for when we are in need of representations. Such representations are not, as we might at first sight believe, unattainable ideals: they are not even ideals, but useless chimeras, and probably even worse since they tend to obstruct our access to what we really need.

This is, obviously, a *philosophical* insight into the nature of representation—an insight that has been achieved thanks to philosophical argument. It is from this perspective that we may have some hesitations with regard to the method of indiscernibles that was proposed by Danto for philosophical investigation. Certainly, there will be philosophical issues that can best be investigated when adopting this methodology: the realism-versus-idealism debate would be a case in point, and every reader of Danto's work of the last fifteen years will readily and immediately acknowledge the value of this methodology when dealing with the nature of art.

Nevertheless, as I suggested above, the method is not without its disadvantages when we have to deal with the problem of the representation of reality in either historical writing or art. Here the method of the indiscernibles clashes with the aesthetic gap inevitably existing between the represented and its representation(s). Here we will necessarily find, so to speak, a void or an absence in the place of one of the two indiscernibles.

Certainly, there seems to be no such absence or void in the case of the Brillo boxes. But does it really follow from this that the Brillo box is a covert statement about the nature of art? Maybe it is—for, once again, we don't know what went on in Warhol's mind when he came up with the Brillo box. The only thing we can say with certainty is that if this had indeed been Warhol's intention, he must have believed in some naive variant of the imitation theory of art and of (aesthetic) representation. For only on the basis of an acceptance of such a variant can the presentation of an identical copy of a real thing be considered of philosophical interest. Whoever believes in the substitution theory of art will not care much about the degree of likeness or difference between a thing and its representation, nor will he have good reasons for doing so. Adherents of this theory will tend to be interested, rather, in how and why one thing can function as a substitute for or representation of another—and within this approach to (aesthetic) representation the issue of material likenesses or differences between the represented and its representation is only of subsidiary importance. But it may well be that Warhol believed in the imitation theory—artists are not necessarily good theorists of art—and then the Brillo box would certainly have made sense to him.

Once again, we don't know what went on in Warhol's mind when he made the Brillo box. It may well be that he made the Brillo box because he was an adherent of the imitation theory of art and wanted to provide us with a material illustration of that theory, so that we could *see* for ourselves what the theory is like. But it might just as well be that he was aiming at a playful parody of the imitation theory: the fun would then be that with the

Brillo box the history of art paradoxically comes to an end at exactly the same place where it began three thousand years ago. For the presence of one and the same Dionysius on several individual occasions would then be the obvious theological anticipation of the presence of one and the same Brillo box at the grocery and in the museum. He might even have wished to improve on Danto's Hegelianism and to put into motion a new Vichian *corso e ricorso* of the history of art with the Brillo box.

Anyway, the only thing that we *can* be fairly sure about is that the evolution of art, at least since impressionism, is hard to reconcile with any variant of the imitation theory.

9

HAYDEN WHITE'S APPEAL
TO THE HISTORIANS

The relationship between philosophers of history and historians has never been an easy and relaxed one. Ranke's historism, with which modern historical writing came into being, was at least partly a reaction against Fichte's and Hegel's philosophies of history.[1] Hegel, in his turn, accused Ranke of being utterly unable to discern some kind of unity or general trend in the chaos of details that the past has left us.[2] And though there are a few shining exceptions, such as Droysen, Meinecke, or, to take a quite different example, the cliometricians of a generation ago, historians have generally remained suspicious of philosophers of history down to the present day.

In fact, this is strange. In fields such as intellectual history or the history of ideas there is considerable overlap between the domains of history and those of philosophy, so philosophy is really part of history proper there. One would have expected that this fact alone would have mollified historians' resistance to philosophical reflection about the nature of their own discipline. Moreover, historians' animosity toward the historical theorist does not seem to have its analogue elsewhere. In the social sciences, such as sociology and econometry, there has always been a fruitful interaction between the discipline in question and philosophy; linguistics and philosophy of language can even be said to be the two sides of one and the same medal; and this is no different for logic, mathematics, and philosophy. It is true that scientists tend to be indifferent with regard to the arguments of philosophers of science; insofar as scientists took any notice at all of debates such as those between Karl Popper and Thomas Kuhn, they rarely if ever discovered in them anything of relevance to their own occupations. But even the physicist's sovereign disinterest in philosophy of science never provoked the kind of skittish behavior that historians tend to display when confronted with historical theory and its practitioners.

One wonders why this is so. Part of the explanation undoubtedly is that historians feel more insecure about the scientific status of their discipline than the practitioners of any other field of scholarly research. They are painfully aware that historical debate rarely leads to conclusive results and that such regrettable things as intellectual fashions or political preference may strongly color their opinions about the past. In short, deep in their hearts historians know that, in spite of all their emphasis on the duties of accurate investigation of sources and of prudent and responsible interpretation, history ranks lowest of all the disciplines that are taught at a university. Since one of the main effects of the historical theorist's effort unfortunately is to confront the historian with these sad and disappointing facts about the discipline, it is only natural that the historian tends to project frustration about the uncertainties of the discipline onto the theorist. In short, the historical theorist is the historian's obvious target for working off an all too understandable professional inferiority complex.

But this is not all. Another illustrious hater of philosophy of history was Jakob Burckhardt—though Gombrich demonstrated some time ago that Burckhardt's own conception of history owed a lot more to Hegel than Burckhardt seems to have realized.[3] Right at the beginning of his *Weltgeschichtliche Betrachtungen* (Force and freedom: Reflections on history), Burckhardt accused philosophy of history of being "a Centaur" and he went on to explain why, in his opinion, philosophy of history is like this hybrid monster. Burckhardt says that history "coordinates," whereas philosophy "subordinates." That is to say, the historian tries to discover some unity in a chaos of (historical) facts, whereas the philosopher proceeds by logical deduction. Though this presentation of the nature of history and philosophy may be a bit too flattering with regard to the latter, this still seems to be much the essential difference between history and philosophy.

And this brings us to the heart of the matter. What irritates historians so much in philosophers of history is not that they also practice history, but that they practice it in a different manner. As Burckhardt's argument makes clear, historians above all resent it when philosophers of history make claims about the past on the basis of philosophical argument only, without feeling challenged to find support for their bold and unwarranted assertions in hard historical fact. And if this were not bad enough already, since the lay public for whom historians write their work is not ordinarily very interested in methodological subtleties, the lay public will often be more deeply impressed by and more interested in the *obiter dicta* of the Hegels, the Marxes, or the Toynbees than in historians' source editions and esoteric debates about, for example, the economics of seventeenth-century rural England. So what is at the basis of historians' hatred of philosophers of history is, in the end, that the latter are disloyal rivals, reducing with their intellectual brilliance all the unwearying industry of the historian to mere irrelevant pedantry that produces, at best, the material out of which the philosophers of history may construct their breathtaking panoramas. Burckhardt's argument therefore certainly goes a long way to explain historians' distrust of philosophy (of history). And his argument will also make clear, by the way, why sociologists and econometricians behave in a so much more relaxed way toward their philosophically minded colleagues than historians customarily do: for sociology and econometry share with philosophy this preference of "subordination" to "coordination," to use Burckhardt's terminology.

It might be objected now that contemporary philosophers of history abandoned speculative philosophy of history long ago and are now all doing critical philosophy of history, from which the interference with the results of historians' research is no longer to be feared. Self-evidently, there is much truth in this objection. Historians' professional sensitivities were hurt far less easily and frequently by analytical philosophy of history than by its speculative predecessor. It should be added, though, that most historians remained completely unaware of the existence of this new variant of historical theory, and insofar as they took any notice of it at all, they rightly dismissed it as irrelevant because of its propensity to ethereal talk about historical laws and because of its antediluvian conceptions of what historical writing is all about.

But this peaceful coexistence ended with the so-called linguistic turn in historical theory. The explanation is that the linguistic turn bored some small but treacherous holes in the hitherto safe barrier between language and reality, enabling historical theorists to regain access to historical reality. As soon as this happened, the historical discipline reacted as if stung by a wasp and all the old animosities against historical theory were revived.

ARTHUR MARWICK VERSUS HAYDEN WHITE

Now, no historical theorist has been more influential in introducing the linguistic turn in historical theory than Hayden White, and it need not surprise us therefore that White became a favorite object of historians' ire. Since the publication of White's *Metahistory* historians—from Gertrude Himmelfarb at one end of the spectrum of historical writing to Carlo Ginzburg at the opposite end—have fulminated against White and condemned his views as a dangerous and irresponsible caricature of what historical writing actually is.

Several years ago a new and sometimes hilarious chapter was added to this book of historians' guerrilla war against the historical theorist as personified by Hayden White. In 1995, Arthur Marwick, professor of history at the British Open University, wrote an essay in the *Journal of Contemporary History* that certainly marked an absolute low in the perennial battle of the historical discipline against the scourge of theory. It may surprise us that a reasonably sensible person, such as Arthur Marwick undoubtedly is, could write such a perfectly inane and silly tirade, which, as such things ordinarily go, must have injured its author more seriously than its target. So much is already clear; in the discussion that followed on the pages of that journal, several historians, even British historians, came to White's defense. And in a worthy and dignified manner, White himself also responded to Marwick's heated accusations.[4]

It would not be worthwhile to give a detailed exposition here of Marwick's invariably misinformed criticisms: however, for all its primitivity, there is something that demands our attention in the gut feeling from which his criticisms presumably originated. What *is* of interest in Marwick's *cri du coeur* is already suggested by its peculiar title: "Two Approaches to Historical Study: The Metaphysical (Including 'Postmodernism') and the Historical." What becomes clear from this title is that Marwick considers White, whom he mistakenly believes to be a postmodernist instead of the unrepenting structuralist that White still is, to be the true heir to speculative philosophers of history, who believed they had discovered the metaphysical essence of the past. And, as Ranke did a century and a half ago, Marwick severely castigates this metaphysical (and allegedly postmodernist) excess of certainty about the nature of the past: for all that we can know about the past results from the historian's painstaking and laborious work on the documentary evidence that the past has left us. It is to the *historian*, as Marwick assures us, and not to the idle speculations of White and of his noisy and obscurantist postmodernist gang, that one should turn if one wishes to know about the past.[5]

Now, even if one is only superficially acquainted with White's ability to hurt historians' sensitivities over the last two and half decades, one will be deeply surprised by Marwick's criticism. For ordinarily White is accused of precisely the reverse: White is attacked for his tropological relativism, for his rejection of the notion of historical truth, and for his claim that historians cherish naive and untenable views about historical truth and about how truth can be validated. It is not difficult to explain this more usual type of criticism. First, the tropological model of historical writing as proposed in *Metahistory*—too well known to be expounded here again—claims that the four tropes will determine historians' views of whatever part of the past they are investigating.[6] And the implication seems to be that the truth about "pretropological" historical reality, the Rankean past *wie es eigentlich gewesen*, is forever unattainable to historians. Second, because of this, historical debate is not, as historians like to believe, a debate about what the past was actually like, but an essentially linguistic debate about the pros and cons of the four tropes when applied to particular cases. Obviously, from this perspective Hayden White's historical theory is a harsh denial of all that historians have always striven for and thought to be both the nature and the only legitimate goal of their enterprise. And I would not wish to deny that there is at least some truth in *this* kind of criticism of White's views, nor that especially the introduction and the conclusion to *Metahistory* may rightly invite this kind of reading of White's work.

So, taking together Marwick's and the more traditional reaction to White's work, we may conclude that it is *historical reality* and the way historians encounter, describe, and explain historical reality that seem to be worrying practicing historians most. Next, this is a criticism that we *should* take seriously, since it concerns a crucial aspect of all practice of history. And if White's writings did indeed present us with the caricature of historians' relationship to historical reality that historians wish to discern in it, we could only agree with them. However, as I want to make clear in this chapter, if historians accuse White of having produced a caricature of historians' respect for historical reality, *this* accusation is no less a caricature of *Metahistory* and of all that White has written since *Metahistory*.

HAYDEN WHITE ON HISTORICAL REALITY

The best way to demonstrate this is by focusing not so much on White's books and essays separately, but on the general trend connecting them. Put differently, of course we should start by reading White's writings individually—where else could one possibly begin?—but then we must ask ourselves how his conceptions have developed over the years since *Metahistory*. And, more specifically, we must consider what we must see as the permanent challenge to which most of his writings have been a response.

Let us start then with *Metahistory*. The book can be read and interpreted in two ways that are fundamentally opposed. Indeed, we can read it as the unmasking of the historian's effort to get hold of historical reality and historical truth that I described a moment ago. But the book can also be interpreted as follows. Precisely by focusing on and by problematizing the historian's language, White demonstrates *not* that it is impossible to get hold of past reality, but the naivete of the kind of positivist intuition customarily cherished in the discipline for how to achieve this goal. More specifically, what these positivist intuitions proudly present as historical reality itself is a mere spectral illusion that is created by the historical discipline itself. Surely, there is a historical reality that is, in principle, accessible to the historian. But historians have forgotten about this historical reality and mistaken the product of their tropological encodation of the past for the past itself. Within this reading, not the practicing historian criticizing White but White himself is the realist who reminds us of the difference between reality and mere intellectual construction.

I shall now give two arguments in favor of this second reading of White's work. First, *Metahistory* was devoted to the great historians of the end of the eighteenth and nineteenth centuries. To these historians—Gibbon, Tocqueville, Macaulay, Michelet, Burckhardt, and even Ranke—the past was a sublime and quasi-divine spectacle that required the whole of their powerful personalities in order to become expressible in their writings. To them the past was not yet that tamed and domesticated reality that is the product and counterpart of the methods and canons of contemporary disciplinary historical writing. To them the past was a past that can only be rendered if it resonates in the depth of the historian's own soul and evokes there the essentially poetic response testifying to their actual encounter with past reality.

The author of *Metahistory* was clearly fascinated by how these historians and philosophers of history related to historical reality itself; and it would surely require a most perverse interpretation of *Metahistory* to read it primarily as the sad account of how the poetics of historical writing inevitably blinded them to that past's reality. For their poetic grasp of the past did not remove them from the past, did not create an insurmountable distance between the past and themselves—on the contrary, it was only thanks to their poetic genius that they caught a glimpse of it and could inform their readers about their experience of the past.

This brings me to my second argument. White makes clear that the greatness of these historians originated in the easy freedom with which they moved through the tropological grid, while defying those "elective affinities" to which mediocre historians ordinarily submit their encodation of the past. We are reminded here of how for Erich Auerbach, an author deeply admired by White, the realist representation of reality results from a mixture of the styles.[7] Both Auerbach and White propose their stylistic or linguistic protocols only to demonstrate how historical reality can be made visible not by a docile submission, but by a subtle and poetic evasion of these protocols. White's tropes will indeed often function as a screen between us and historical reality, as will be the case when the mediocre historian obediently submits to the dictates of one trope only.

The crucial point is that White's tropology shows us how these great eighteenth- and nineteenth-century historians succeeded in finding and exploiting the cracks and fissures in the tropological screen, and how precisely through these cracks and fissures they managed to get a glimpse of past reality that remained inaccessible to their less gifted colleagues. This also explains why irony is so prominent in White's tropology. Irony is the trope that confronts us with the limitations and shortcomings of the other tropes; it is, so to speak, the trope that is the natural ally of historical reality itself and that enables it to reassert its rights against the pressure of the other tropes. Irony naturally situates itself in these cracks and fissures between the other tropes, and is therefore the trope of historical reality itself.

On the basis of this second reading of *Metahistory* we have the best perspective for a correct understanding of the evolution of White's historical thought since *Metahistory*. Though this evolution follows a wide ellipse through the universe of theoretical questions, one could say that the historian's relationship to historical reality has been its permanent center of gravity. This becomes clear if we consider White's much discussed essay "The Politics of Historical Interpretation" (1982), which is, in my opinion, crucial for a correct assessment of the later development of White's thought.[8] The subtitle of this essay—"Discipline and De-Sublimation"—suggests what is of interest in the present context. For White discusses here an essay by Schiller of 1801 in which Schiller said that we should conceive of world history as "a sublime object"[9] forever transcending historians' attempt to fit it within their neat and orderly categories—or their tropes, as the White of *Metahistory* would have put it. Next, White contrasts Schiller's exhortation with how the disciplinization of history succeeded in changing the face of the past: "Historical facts are politically domesticated precisely insofar as they are effectively removed from displaying the aspect of the sublime that Schiller attributed to them in his essay of 1801."[10]

The idea here is the following. Undoubtedly the disciplinization of historical writing since the days of Ranke is a very good thing indeed; it has invaluably and immeasurably enriched our knowledge and our understanding of the past. But White wants to remind us that this also entailed an often unnoticed loss—a loss in our openness to historical reality. Those great eighteenth- and nineteenth-century historians discussed in *Metahistory* still possessed this openness: they felt a quasi-existential relationship to the past and they did not try or even wish to exclude any part of their highly complex intellectual individualities from their immersion in the past. Scientific history, however, gave us a neat, "domesticated" variant of the past, from which we tend to eliminate all that fits badly within the categories of a scientifically canonized past. The past now became like a seventeenth-century garden where nature was ruthlessly adapted to our conceptions of order, symmetry, and rationality. Historical discourse now presented us with mere intellectual constructions instead of with the account of the historian's experience of historical reality itself.

Obviously, there is a similarity here with the well-known argument in Nietzsche's *Use and Abuse of History*; in both cases the argument is that so-called scientific disciplinary historical writing does not function as a window enabling us to perceive historical reality itself, but rather as a screen obstructing our view of it. But the difference between Nietzsche and White is no less instructive. Nietzsche criticized "scientific," disciplinary history because it may both weaken our capacity for action *and* effect this "domestication" of the past. In short, Nietzsche first postulates a historical subject (the historian) and a historical object (the past) and then proceeds to show how the two always get in the way of each other. But White sidesteps this Nietzschean approach by asking the more helpful and constructive question of what kind of language, or use of language, might enable the historian to evade these subject/object dichotomies that give rise to Nietzschean worries. And this, then, is the question that we should turn to.

MODERNISM AS THE DISCOURSE OF HISTORICAL REALITY

A first clue to what kind of language will most respect historical reality is discovered by White in the Greek middle voice.[11] As you may recall from the Greek grammar taught at secondary school, classical Greek had not only the active and the passive voices but also the so-called middle voice, as in *elousamèn,* meaning "I washed myself," which is therefore indeed somewhere midway between the active "I wash" and the passive "I am washed." Hence the term "middle voice."

At first sight this may seem a most abstruse way of trying to deal with the issue of the representation of historical reality. But we will understand White's fascination with the middle voice when we recognize that the subject here is *also* the object of the action—and hence the middle voice indeed achieves a transcendence of the subject/object dichotomy where Nietzsche so unsatisfactorily left the problem of how to respect the sublimity of past reality.

The way we can profit from this insight into the peculiar workings of the middle voice is suggested in an example given by the French literary theorist Roland Barthes. Barthes considers the possibility of using the verb "writing" in the middle voice, as in "I write myself." According to Barthes, using the verb in this novel way would enable us to express the fact that we may sometimes truly become ourselves in and by the act of writing. For writing may show us what we really think and whom we really are: in that case we effectively "realize ourselves" in and by writing. In this way we enter into a contact with ourselves that transcends the subject/object dichotomy.

All this is most intriguing and thought-provoking, but the problem remains, obviously, how we should operationalize these insights for history and historical writing. Two steps can be discerned here in White's argument. First, he demonstrates the affinities between the middle voice and the kind of prose that is characteristic of the modernist novel as exemplified by Joyce, Virginia Woolf, or Proust.[12] The *monologue intérieur,* as we saw in Chapter 7, is the literary device, so characteristic of the modernist novel, that destroyed all clear boundaries between subject and object, between the self and what is outside the self. The interior monologue creates a world where the subject/object dichotomy has lost all relevance, inside and outside have become indiscernible—and it therefore effectively is a "thinking, speaking, or writing in the middle voice." A splendid example is the long introduction of Thomas Mann's *Lotte in Weimar* (called, in the U.S., *The Beloved Returns*), in which Goethe muses about his personal past and, in doing so, inextricably mixes his own love affair of half a century earlier with the fate of Germany before and after the Napoleonic wars.[13]

But though this may give us an idea of the kind of prose corresponding to the middle voice, it remains to be seen what it could mean for historians and their relationship to past reality. That brings us to a second step in White's argument: his discussion of what he refers to as "the modernist event."[14] After the foregoing it will not be hard to comprehend that by "the modernist event" White means the kind of event that, in being narrativized, loses what would *also* be lost if the modernist interior monologue were translated into a neat, orderly, and chronological narrative. Only the event's "outside" that presents itself to the historian could survive this act of translation, whereas its "inside," so carefully preserved in the modernist prose, would be lost forever. Put differently, ordinary disciplinary historical narrative effects this dichotomy of subject and object; and this is not, as we all believe, the kind of discourse that enables a historical subject, that is, the historian, to give the floor to historical reality itself. On the contrary, this is the kind of discourse in which the historian destroys historical reality in an effort to domesticate it and to adapt it to the constraints of conventional historicist language and of the tropes operative in it.

White does not imply that this loss would be inadmissible in all cases: on the contrary. However, when historians are required to "probe the limits of representation," to use Saul Friedlander's terminology, as in the case of the Holocaust or other "sublime" (in the technical sense of that word) historical tragedies, the modernist style will bring them closest to these "limits." As White put it: "What I am suggesting is that the stylistic innovation of modernism . . . may provide better instruments for representing 'modernist' events . . . than the storytelling techniques traditionally utilized by historians for representation."[15]

Though White does not mention this himself, Simon Schama's recent publications may give us an inkling of what all this might imply for historical writing. Experiments with the style of the modernist novel are found in his *Dead Certainties* of 1992.[16] The two parts of this book each begin with a lengthy interior monologue in which, as in Mann's *Lotte in Weimar*, personal recollection and the facts of history are inextricably linked together, and where reality has not yet been split up into a historical subject on the one hand and a past as seen by this subject on the other. But an even more daring experiment was made by Schama in his *Landscape and Memory*, where the past is presented as a frame story within the larger whole of Schama's own personal biography.[17] The past related by him—the way people have experienced the landscapes within which their lives unfolded—is part of this own personal past as well. And the reverse is also true, insofar as, for example, Schama's childhood experience of the Essex marshes, with which the book begins, is projected against the much larger whole of the relationship between landscape and memory in the West. And both renderings of Schama's book can be true since there is not yet a subject/object dichotomy favoring either.

Now, I suppose that most historians will have their doubts about Schama's most recent experiments, if not worse, and they will certainly consider them to be an unsuitable model for future historical writing. This is reasonable enough. Certainly these books are not models that should now be followed by all historians—and Schama himself never suggests that the books were written with this pedagogical intention. This kind of obtrusive meddlesomeness is completely alien to Schama. These books are daring and fascinating experiments and no dictates for future historical writing.

But this should not be our last word about them. For what we have been saying just now about Schama's experiments individually holds for the whole of the historical discipline as well. For is not the historical discipline, when considered as a whole, the interior monologue of contemporary Western civilization about a past from which it originated? Is our civilization not "writing itself," by means of historical writing, in the way meant by Barthes? Is historical culture not how our civilization, so to speak, "writes itself" in the style of the middle voice? Are history and historical writing not the place where our civilization becomes conscious of itself and of its own nature and, as Jörn Rüsen has emphasized, where our civilization achieves and becomes aware of its identity?[18] Is the historical discipline, taken as a whole, not the modernist text in terms of which we express our relationship to our past? From that perspective we have no reason to feel outraged by Schama's experiments: for what Schama attempted to do within the scope of a single volume is, in fact, what lies at the heart of the historical discipline as a whole. And that is what makes Schama's experiments so profoundly interesting.

When Arthur Marwick recently attacked White's alleged lack of interest in what past reality actually has been, no criticism could be more silly, more narrow-minded, and more wrong-headed. For it is precisely the reverse. Not White, but Marwick, is insensitive to the challenges of how to get hold of past reality. Not White, but Marwick, violates historical reality by claiming that it could never be more than what we may read about it in historical writing. Not White, but Marwick, preaches a complacent and lazy acceptance of the existing codes for representing the past—whether we identify these codes with White's tropes or with the methodological rules adopted in the discipline. Not White, but Marwick, encourages us to exchange the sublimity and authenticity of past reality for the intellectual constructions of disciplinary historical writing. Not White, but Marwick, thus compromises the discipline and its cultural assignment. For White's position is neither a critique nor a rejection of history as a discipline—on the contrary. We could and should not do without it. But what he tells us, again and again, is how we should *relate* to the discipline. And his exhortation is that we must not cowardly shun its boundaries, but always courageously probe and explore the area where the discipline begins to lose its grasp. For this is where we encounter past reality and all that is truly new and interesting (as is also the case in the sciences). It is here, too, that those great nineteenth-century historians that White discussed in his *Metahistory* acquire a renewed significance for us. For if we realize, with White, that disciplinary historical writing should be considered our servant rather than our dictatorial master, our guide rather than our goal, these historians antedating the disciplinization of historical writing may show us what to do with our newly regained intellectual freedom with regard to disciplinization.

These historians were the Schamas of their time. In their histories of the great Revolution and of the Napoleonic Wars, events that shook the very basis of Western civilization and sent their traumatic shock waves all through the nineteenth century, they succeeded in defining their own time in terms of its relationship to this deeply traumatic past. There was not, first, a nineteenth-century cultural identity that, next, sought to define its relationship to its past—no, it was only by defining this relationship that the identity of this culture could come into being. Historical reality is not something that we stumble upon in the way that we may find out about the chairs and tables in a room that we have just entered—that is the misguided pseudo-positivist model that has inspired Marwick's conception of historical reality and his attack on White. Historical reality, however, is only encountered in our attempts to define our relationship to our past, in our attempt to "write ourselves" by writing history. Here history functions as the mirror of the radically alien in which we can begin to recognize our own cultural identity.

This historical reality, which is not a positivist given but a permanent challenge to the historical discipline as a whole, is the historical reality lying at the end of the odyssey of Hayden White's historical thought since *Metahistory*.

10

RÜSEN ON HISTORY AND POLITICS

Every historical theory has a natural affinity with a certain variant of historical writing. Hermeneutics deals with the interpretation of texts and is therefore the historical theory that immediately comes to mind when we think of intellectual history. Collingwood's "reenactment theory" urges the historian to always ask for what purpose a historical actor did, thought, or made something. And by so strongly insisting on precisely this question, Collingwood's historical theory clearly demonstrates how much it owes to archeology, of which Collingwood himself was a most successful practitioner.[1] The "covering law model," in its turn, had such pronounced affinities with the notion of "history as a social science" that it can not surprise us that the cliometricians of a generation ago proposed covering law model theories as the methodological justification of their approach to the past.[2] I therefore would not hesitate to claim that no historical theory has ever been formulated that is completely neutral to the variants of historical practice.

RÜSEN AND POLITICAL HISTORY

If this claim makes sense, we may well ask ourselves what kind of writing of history is privileged by Jörn Rüsen's historical theory as developed in his *Grundzüge einer Historik* (Foundations for a historics), the trilogy that undoubtedly should be considered his major contribution to historical theory. When trying to answer this question, we must take two aspects of his historical theory into account. In the first place, Rüsen strongly emphasizes in his historical theory the interaction between historical writing and social reality, *Fachwissenschaft* and *Lebenspraxis*.

His relevant views here are best clarified by conceiving them to be a radicalization of the hermeneutic circle. The hermeneutic circle compels the historian to move continuously between the (documentary relics of the) past and the life experiences of the historian. None of the two is, in itself, sufficient for a correct understanding of the past. A continuous movement between the object and subject of understanding, where subjectivity is continuously corrected by objectivity and vice versa, enables the historian to achieve a continuous refinement of his understanding of the past. It is in this way that the meaning of the past can be approximated asymptotically, as it were.

And so it is in Rüsen's "disciplinary matrix," which describes both historical practice itself and the wider social and cultural context within which we account for our relationship to our past. The point of departure is the need of both the human individual and human society to situate themselves in the flow of time in order to be capable of meaningful action at all (*Orientierungsbedürfnisse*); this orientation to the past as the background for meaningful action is guided by criteria of meaning (*leitende Hinsichten auf die Vergangenheit*). It is only then that the rules codified within historical methodology (*Regeln der empirischen Forschung*) make their entrance: these rules determine how the evidence the past has left us can be transformed into knowledge of the past. Next, Rüsen emphasizes that historical knowledge must always be organized in the historian's text in agreement with certain forms for how to present the past (*Formen der Darstellung*)—here he obviously subscribes to the narrativist thesis. If historical knowledge has been organized accordingly, it will have acquired the form enabling it to function as a compass for our orientation to reality (*Funktionen der Daseinsorientierung*). But, lastly, this historical compass needs continuous refinement by historical research, which makes us move again to the *Orientierungsbedürfnisse*—and in this way the whole circle will repeat itself again and again.[3]

Secondly, we should take into account what Rüsen primarily considers to be the domain of individual and collective human existence where these *Orientierungsbedürfnisse* should be situated, and where *Fachwissenschaft* and *Lebenspraxis* both require and complement each other. At the end of his trilogy Rüsen comes closest to answering this question, arguing that utopian thought customarily is what informs our ideals for a better and more just world. Furthermore, he considers utopian thought to be an indispensable ingredient of our orientation to the future, but he goes on to emphasize that its defect has too often been to make us forget about the practical limits we should respect in our attempt to realize our political ideals, however lofty and well intentioned these ideals may be. And this is where history comes in: "Historical consciousness introduces into the set of parameters decisive for all orientation in human practice the dimension of experience, which transcends and supersedes utopian thought on behalf of the principle of hope. Historical consciousness thus dims exaggerated expectations insofar as these may guide collective action."[4]

But the reverse is true as well; the fixation of historical meaning presupposes a utopian background: "The production of sense and meaning by historical consciousness is itself in need of utopian orientation: for the giving of sense and meaning to the experience of the past is in need of an impulse moving the intentions of human action beyond the limits of the horizon of experience."[5] Consequently, the continual oscillation between *Fachwissenschaft* and *Lebenspraxis* demanded by Rüsen's disciplinary matrix for historical writing will result in a mediation between utopian ideals on the one hand and the practical constraints on responsible political action as presented by historical reality on the other.

It will now be clear that Rüsen's historical reality must, above all, be a *political* reality. For this mediation between utopian ideals and historical reality will necessarily make use of the language and the idiom of politics in order to articulate itself. Utopian thought primarily, if not exclusively, is a formulation of political ideals most often informed and sanctioned by a certain interpretation of the past. And it is therefore the political dimension of the past, or at least those dimensions of it that permit of politicization, where history can enter the kind of dialogue with utopian thought that Rüsen has in mind. Hence, if the question with which this chapter began was what variant of historical writing is favored by Rüsen's historical theory, it is *political* history that we should primarily think of.

POLITICS AS THE ORIGIN OF MODERN HISTORICAL CONSCIOUSNESS

As we all know, much of twentieth-century historical writing can be considered one long and sustained attack on political history, often mocked as the obsolete, arid, and elitist legacy of Rankean historism. So the affinities of Rüsen's historical writing and political history may raise some eyebrows. But instead of agreeing with these contemporary critics of political history, I would rather see here one of the outstanding merits of Rüsen's historical theory.

For in the first place we should realize, in agreement with Rüsen's own suggestions, that politics has been the domain where modern historical writing and historical consciousness originated, and furthermore that it is politics to which we must turn in order to understand the major evolutions that historical writing has undergone in the course of its history. Like so many other defining characteristics of the modern Western world, modern historical writing came into being in the Italian Renaissance. Sixteenth-century authors like Niccolo Machiavelli and Francesco Guicciardini were most painfully aware of Italy's political misfortunes following the French invasion of 1494, and they desperately tried to find an explanation for the seemingly unending chain of catastrophes striking the Italian peninsula and its helpless population since that fateful year. It was this desperate search for the causes of political disaster that for the first time in human history endowed the discipline of historical writing with a subject matter successfully differentiating it from all other disciplines. For it compelled Machiavelli, Guicciardini, and others to explain how a dismal political reality could have come into being that no Italian ruler could possibly have intended or wished for but that apparently was the logical and inevitable result of their ill-advised actions. In other words, their desperation about the disasters of contemporary Italian history put them on the hitherto unknown path of an investigation of the unintended consequences of intentional human action.

In this way, they defined a domain of human inquiry that was completely new. Before them, this sphere of potential historical meaning lying beyond human intentionality did not yet exist, let alone that human rationality was granted the quasi-godlike capacity to be to penetrate its secrets.

Before them there was a universe of human actions that could merely be labeled as either pleasing or displeasing in the eyes of God; and from the then all-important point of view of human salvation, this was all that could ever meaningfully be said about human action. There was no historical reality lying beyond this decisive dichotomy. The exclusive fixation on the individual human being's relationship to God left no room for this domain of the unintended consequences of intentional human action. It was in the hands of God (or Fate) whether human action and the results of human action would have a cause-and-effect relationship or not. Consequently, the Renaissance's urge to try to find an explanation for Italy's historical fate after 1494 meant a hitherto unheard-of secularization of what used to be a divine secret; and next, this secularization had to take the form of an investigation of the unintended results of intentional human action.

This going beyond the limits of a moral assessment of human action gave us history. This is what we owe to Machiavelli's daring attack on ethics as presented in his *Il principe* and elsewhere. And where the social sciences, with their origins in natural law philosophy, feel much at ease with ethics, history has remained, down to the present day, our only academic discipline requiring us to transcend the narrow limitations of ethics in order to get access to the most appropriate background for dealing with the question of what we should do.[6]

In sum, if disciplines owe their identity to their subject matter, we can assert that the writing of history only came into being thanks to a secularization of God's intervention in our world—a secularization that assigned to the historian the domain of the unintended results of intentional human action. And since it was the political realities after 1494 that were of paramount interest to sixteenth-century Italian historians, historical reality was for these historians primarily formed and molded by political action. History essentially is the history of politics or, as Hegel famously put it three centuries later: "Only the state presents us with a content that is not only appropriate for the prose of history but also contributes to it." And, as he had argued elsewhere, the state and politics is where we must discern the heart of all historical evolution, not only of politics itself, but of law, art, morality, and economy:

The true essence—and this is the unity of subjective will and the universal—is the state. The state is the reality in which the individual possesses and enjoys his freedom, since it is the knowledge, belief, and will of the universal. In this way, the state is the center of other concrete forms, such as law, the arts, of morality or of the conveniences of life.[7]

HISTORY AND POLITICS SINCE 1494

Hegel is of interest in this context for several reasons. In Rüsen's book on Droysen, his first major study, he emphasizes that "Droysen and Hegel have a shared interest, namely, the problem of history in the context of an emancipatory bourgeois society."[8] Hence, both Hegel and Droysen are striking illustrations of Rüsen's claim of the continuous dialogue between utopian thought (here, the emancipation of bourgeois social order) and history —and, therefore, of the transcendence of ethics by history. We could even argue that the different ways in which Hegel and Droysen tend to deal with "the problem of history" is in complete agreement with Rüsen's disciplinary matrix. For whereas Hegel's philosophy of history presented us with a dialectical dynamic in historical reality itself, Droysen set out to define in his *Historik* the *Regeln der historischen Forschung* ("rules for historical investigation") and in the book's famous chapter on *Topik* ("topics"), the *Formen der Darstellung* ("forms of representation") of all historical writing, to adopt the terminology of Rüsen's disciplinary matrix. Obviously this repeats Rüsen's thesis of how *Fachwissenschaft* and *Lebenspraxis* depend on and presuppose each other. Finally, in spite of the philosophical abstraction of Hegelian dialectics and of Droysen's fascination for culture (for example, his introduction of the concept of Hellenism), both emphatically agreed in seeing in politics the natural and real subject matter of history.

Machiavelli's and Guicciardini's discovery of the dimension of the unintended consequences of intentional human actions has its nineteenth-century counterpart in the historical thought of Hegel, Droysen, and most of their contemporaries. For the French Revolution, which had started with the loftiest ideals but ended in an unparalleled series of political catastrophes, was even more suggestive of the tremendous power of these unintended consequences than Italian history since 1494 had been. It need not surprise us therefore that nineteenth-century historical writing, being for the greater part an attempt to learn how to live with the traumatic realities of the French Revolution, triggered much the same reactions as 1494 had done. And the result was both an intensification of historical consciousness—an intensification resulting in the birth of German historism, which is still the matrix within which the historical discipline operates—and a renewed emphasis on the privileged position of political history, which had lost some of its natural preponderance because of the Enlightenment's experiments with the history of culture and civilization. And we should not have expected otherwise. Speaking generally, for a proper understanding of each new phase in the history of historical writing, this new phase can best be explained by relating it to the political realities of the day, or of a recent past.

But what about this almost unanimous attack on political history of our own time, to which I referred a moment ago? Now, what must strike the unprejudiced observer is that all this now so fashionable criticism of political history is invariably inspired by *political* idea(l)s. Are we not all acquainted with the traditional argument against political history, repeated ad nauseam, that we now live in a democratic age and *therefore* should no longer be interested in political history, that is, in the doings of kings, diplomats, generals, and so on? Historical writing has to be *democratized* in the sense of focusing on the masses, on the humblest individuals, on how they lived, what they thought and feared, desired and experienced. This is the kind of argument that is customarily proposed in order to justify socioeconomic history, the history of mentalities, micro-storie, and *Alltagsgeschichte*, against the alleged historical myopia of political history.

But, once again, this essentially is a *political* argument; and so the paradox is that political considerations were that in whose name the attack on political history was launched. Hence, contemporary, apparently nonpolitical variants of historical writing are, in the end, no less a variant of political history than political history proper. The only relevant change that we may observe is that these new forms of historical writing have been inspired by different, more "democratic" political ideals. So, after all, Machiavelli, Guicciardini, Hegel, Droysen—and Rüsen—were right when arguing that all history is, in the end, *political* history.

POLITICAL REPRESENTATION

But why is this so, we should now ask ourselves? Why are history and politics tied together so inextricably that the attempt to separate them will inevitably involve us in the kind of paradoxes mentioned just now? To try to answer this question, we are well advised to turn, first, to Hobbes's *Leviathan*, which is commonly seen as the first manifesto of modern political theory. In one of the most fascinating chapters of this book, Hobbes presents his readers with a definition of the person: "a PERSON, is he, *whose words or actions are considered, either as his own, or as representing the words and actions of another man, or of any other thing to whom they are attributed, whether Truly or by Fiction.*"[9] And Hobbes goes on to say that when the person owns his own actions, he will be called a *"Naturall Person,"* whereas when his actions represent those of others, he will be a *"Feigned"* or *"Artificiall person."* Using Hobbes's terminology as proposed here, one might say that *Leviathan* essentially is a book on how the transition is made from natural persons to artificial persons. For in the state of nature we have only natural persons, whereas civil society also presents us, in the person of the sovereign, with an artificial person.[10] But this transition is necessary in order to create a political society and the state; even more so, it is exclusively thanks to this transition that both can come into being. Or, as Hobbes writes: "A Multitude of men, are made *One* person, when they are by one man, or one Person, Represented; so that it be done with the consent of everyone of that Multitude in particular. For it is the *Unity* of the Representer, not the *Unity* of the Represented, that makes the Person *One*."[11]

So the state comes into being only when the *multitude* of isolated individuals is reduced to a *unity*, and it is the concept of *representation* that Hobbes explicitly employs in order to characterize the nature of this momentous transition. We may add to this the following from the perspective of our own contemporary democracies: surely, this reduction of a multitude into a unity can be observed for any form of government, whether it be a monarchy, aristocracy, democracy, or anything in between. Nevertheless, the kind of representative democracies that we presently have clearly remain closest to the scenario sketched by Hobbes. For whereas a monarchy or aristocracy would require some additional measures in order to be the result of Hobbes's scenario, representative democracy fits the bill without further specifications of the constitutional form of sovereign authority.[12] Representational democracy has less institutional overhead than we may expect from variants of aristocracy or of monarchy. Hence, representative democracy, or representation as institutionalized in our modern democracies, is the form of government that remains closest to how Hobbes accounts for the emergence of the domain of politics. The two notions of politics and of representation are thus inextricably linked together; for though politics may move beyond representation, it will always have to prove its legitimacy by showing where it is allegedly better than representative democracy. Representative democracy truly is the measure of things in the discussion of forms of government.

HISTORICAL REPRESENTATION

It is no different when we look at historical writing. Two arguments can be given for this structural similarity of politics and historical writing. In the first place, as has been argued by many historical theorists since Hegel proposed his notion of *das konkrete Universelle*, the historical representation of the past essentially is an attempt to discern a unity in manifold historical facts. Historians start with an investigation of the sources that the past has left us; these provide them with the evidence for the individual statements that they makes about past reality. But out of all the statements that they could possibly make about the past, historians select precisely those that will best enable them to reduce the manifold past to a coherent unity. Illustrative here is what William Walsh described as "colligatory concepts," that is, concepts like "the Renaissance" or "the Industrial Revolution," which may give a sometimes unexpected degree of coherence to a large number of at first sight completely *un*related historical phenomena.[13] In the same way that, as was suggested by Hobbes's argument, a political order can only come into being thanks to political representation, so what is historically represented owes its existence to historical representation.[14] Representation is the logical operation that we need *in both cases* in order to give more or less clear contours to either political or historical reality. Representation is the heart of both history and politics.

A second and more interesting argument to the same effect would run as follows. We observed above that modern historical writing came into being because authors like Machiavelli and Guicciardini became aware of the dimension of the unintended consequences of intentional action. Two remarks are relevant here. In the first place, this awareness should not be interpreted as if it were the discovery of a new domain of historical reality, in the way that, for example, *Alltagsgeschichte* could be said to be such a discovery. *Alltagsgeschichte*, to continue this example, may give us an account of what it was like to live in a certain age; and in order to give us such an account, the historian will have to focus on an aspect of the past that had always been part of it—even before it captured the historian's interest. The object of *Alltagsgeschichte* simply belongs, so to speak, to the past's inventory. But this is not the case with these unintended consequences. The awareness of unintended consequences arose from a shift in the *perspective* from which the historian considers the past. That is, historians like Machiavelli and Guicciardini saw the past from a perspective that was explicitly different from that of the agents themselves: they had a more or less adequate notion of what the intentions were of the primary political agents in fifteenth- and sixteenth-century Italy, and they observed, next, that the actions of these agents as inspired by these intentions often differed widely or were even diametrically opposed to what these agents had originally wished to achieve, to what their apparent intentions had been.

So Machiavelli and Guicciardini did not discover a new set of objects in the past that had never been noticed before them, in the way that one may suddenly become of a stone in one's backyard that had been lying there all along. Surely they made a discovery, but it was the discovery of a new way of looking at the past (and at human action) and not of a hitherto overlooked item of the past's inventory. For what they did was to link the intentions and actions of statesmen and politicians to results that had not been intended by them. And this would have seemed to their medieval predecessors a most absurd and perverse way of proceeding. For medieval thinkers, there were statesmen and politicians and their intentions and actions—and that was the end of it. Historical fate would decide whether these agents would succeed in achieving their goals—or not, as the case might be. But to relate intentions to what had *not* been intended would have been to the medieval mind just as absurd as it would be to us if someone argued that if S knows p, he may also know not-p. Our present paradigm of knowledge still inspired medieval man's paradigm of human action, so to speak. But now that Machiavelli and Guicciardini had, as historians, freed their perspective from that of the historical agent, these "absurdities" not only became thinkable but even, as we observed above, the very basis and heart of all historical writing. In sum, it was something on the side of the subject, something on the side of the historian—that is, the possibility of this shift of perspective—and *not* something on the side of the object from which modern historical consciousness and modern historical writing was born.

In the second place, these unintended consequences were most often unpleasant surprises, things that had been better avoided. Now, this datum can again be interpreted in two ways. One may argue that unintended consequences are *sui generis* unforeseeable and that, therefore, the discovery of this dimension of the unintended consequences could never have any practical implication for the politician and the statesman. But—and this is the other possibility—this was not the lesson that Renaissance authors like Machiavelli and (to a lesser extent) Guicciardini were inclined to learn from their discovery of (the subject matter of) modern historical writing. They were prepared to admit that no politician or statesman could ever succeed in completely avoiding *all* unintended consequences, but they were very much convinced that the recognition of the presence of this dimension of the unintended consequences is where all meaningful and responsible political action should begin. Not being aware of this dimension of political action would make the politician helplessly and fatally stumble over even the smallest obstacle lying in the way of his aims and purposes. Or, to put it in the terminology so dear to the sixteenth century itself, only after we have been willing to recognize the immense powers of that so whimsical goddess Fortuna can we hope that our *virtù* will enable us to restrain her harmful dominion within certain more or less acceptable limits.

In sum, as this second argument makes clear, modern historical consciousness and our notion of responsible political action (i.e., action taking into account the possibility of unintended consequences) inextricably belong together. They have their shared basis in the logic of historical representation, in the recognition that social and political reality can not be reduced to the intended consequences of human (and political) action. Only historical representation will give us the kind of language required for relating in a meaningful way action and its unintended consequences. Responsible political action always requires of politicians that at the very least they ask themselves the question of how future historians, from a perspective different from their own, might assess their courses of action. The link between history and politics is therefore truly indissoluble—and we have every reason to agree with Rüsen when his historical theory demands that we see it this way. Historical writing is either directly or indirectly the history of politics or it is nothing. And all those historians and historical theorists who wish to deny this simply do not know what they are talking about.

THE NATURE OF REPRESENTATION

I am well aware, of course, that this is a strong and provocative thesis, and that many people will vigorously contest it. Obviously, the linkage of politics and history as proposed here will have to be safeguarded against the arguments of these critics. When trying to do so below, I shall not deal with the well-known but uninteresting and ineffective argument that much if not most of contemporary historical writing does not present us with the history of past politics. As I pointed out above, the turn away from the history of politics merely reflects our success in politicizing domains and aspects of human existence that previous generations of historians considered to be outside the sphere of politics proper. Socioeconomic history, for example, reflects the extent to which we have succeeded in politicizing the details of the household; and we need only recall Marx's political philosophy in order to be aware of the *political* presuppositions and of the *political* impact of this variant of historical writing.

A far more interesting and alarming objection would begin with the observation that the notion of representation is the coping-stone in my argument, and go on to demonstrate that many theorists nowadays agree that a representation of reality is not possible. Especially authors that one may associate with postmodernism tend to sever in this way the ties between language (representation) and the world (the represented) and to conclude from this that the notion of representation suggests an unattainable and logically inconsistent ideal of a correspondence between language and the world. Hence, my whole argument could be shown to be built on philosophical quicksand.

Before proceeding further, I will have to make clear what is meant by this assertion that a representation of reality is not possible. Of course, nobody would deny that we have parliaments representing the people, works of art representing human beings or landscapes, and historical texts representing parts of the past. It would be quixotic to deny this. Hence, if the notion of representation is attacked, the attack cannot be directed against *attempts* to represent reality (in politics, art, and history); it therefore must rather have as its target the *chances of success* of all such attempts. Now, it is not easy to see what the reasons are for the common contemporary wisdom that all representation must fail. It seems to be an article of faith in circles of, predominantly, literary theorists rather than the result of a sustained and careful philosophical analysis. And insofar as the attack on representation is considered to be at all in need of elucidation, one is customarily reminded of the supposedly decisive arguments against it by authors such as Rorty (most often) or Hilary Putnam (sometimes). Thus, in his introduction to the collection *Realism and Representation*, George Levine states: "Representation—a category disbarred from Rorty's world where 'correspondence' between word and thing is a chimerical idea—figures importantly throughout the volume and not simply as object of critique."[15] And certainly Rorty's so-called antirepresentationalism will be our best guide if we wish to get a grasp of what is involved in the nowadays so popular attack on representationalism. So let us now concentrate on that.

As is suggested in the quote from Levine's introduction, the central role in Rorty's argument is the notion of correspondence. We often say that a statement is true (or, to use the vocabulary of this chapter, that it gives a correct representation of the world), if and only if it *corresponds* to a state of affairs in reality. The statement "The cat lies on the mat" is true if and only if that statement corresponds to the state of affairs that the cat lies on the mat. But as Rorty, following pragmatists such as James and Dewey, correctly points out, there simply is no such *third* thing like correspondence, apart from language and reality. There is no such *tertium quid*, no such frame behind and apart from language and the world, enabling us to establish that the right words are tied to the right part of the world. Language and reality are simply all we have. Hence, if the notion of representation is logically dependent on the notion of correspondence, we shall have to abandon the former together with the latter.[16]

As the foregoing suggests, when Rorty attacks representationalism it is the true statement that he has in mind. I shall not pronounce on the merits of this attack on correspondence explaining the truth of the individual singular statement (though I should add that Rorty's rejection of the notion of correspondence as a neutral background enabling us to compare language and the world has convinced me). But the crucial datum is this. When using the notion of representation, we rarely, if ever, think of (true) statements, but, instead of works of art, political assemblies, or historical texts (when taken as a whole and not as a long series of isolated true statements). And we may well doubt whether the way the true statement relates to reality is identical to how the work of art relates to a landscape, or a parliament to the electorate.

In fact, it will be worthwhile to investigate the differences between how the true statement and the representation relate to reality. However, when doing so within the context of the present argument, we must bear in mind that our point of departure here has been Rorty's discussion of the issue: it was *his* antirepresentationalism, it was *his* argument against the possibility of a reliable representation that was at stake here. Self-evidently, when arguing against antirepresentationalism, we must be sure about the exact nature of the argument that we are attacking. If not, our argument will have no proper target. The implication is, of course, that what follows need not necessarily be valid against antirepresentationalist arguments that differ fundamentally from the one put forward by Rorty. But we shall have to live with this restriction on the scope or our argument against antirepresentationalism.

Now, as we saw a moment ago, the notions of correspondence, and of the *tertium quid* functioning as a background for establishing correspondence, were the object of Rorty's attack on representationalism. These *tertia* (whatever their nature) supposedly enable us to move backward and forward between language (representation) and reality (the represented) in order to establish whether what we find on one level possesses its correct counterpart on the other. It was believed that this will explain truth. Now, it may well be that Rorty is right in rejecting this notion of the *tertia* for the true statement. But I wish to emphasize now that this whole idea of the *tertia*, whether defensible or not for the true statement, would make no sense at all with regard to representation, so that whatever one might conclude with regard to the plausibility of this notion could not possibly have any implication for the (plausibility of the) notion of representation.

This will become clear if we ask ourselves what cognitive ideal is suggested by the *tertia*. Obviously, this ideal must be that nothing at one level does *not* also possess its counterpart at the other. Equally obviously, the ideal will forever be unattainable because of the categorical difference between language and reality. As long as we remain convinced that such a categorical difference exists—and I would not know under what circumstances we might be prepared to abandon this conviction—we can be sure that this ideal can never be realized. For the ideal *could* only be realized if this categorical difference between language and reality had been eliminated in one way or other. If, then, this is the ideal behind the notion of truth (and of representation), we can only agree with Rorty that we had best abandon these conceptions of truth and representation.

However—and this brings us to the essence of the matter—whatever may be the case with truth, this emphatically is not the cognitive ideal that is suggested in or by the notion of representation. In order to see this, we should first realize that this cognitive ideal will require that the represented and its representation are the same for each description that we might give of them. For this is what correspondence demands: in case any description of the represented were false for its representation (or vice versa), there would be no correspondence between the represented and its representation. Hence, correspondence and the cognitive ideal suggested by it would require the kind of relationship between the represented and its representation demanded by Leibniz's law of identity (i.e., the law that two things are identical if and only if they are identical under each description of the two). But this is at odds with our notion of representation. As Nelson Goodman already pointed out long ago: "An object resembles itself to the maximum degree, but rarely represents itself."[17] And think of the representation of reality in the arts: it would be a most naive view of aesthetic representation to require the work of art to satisfy Leibniz's law. Or, as Virginia Woolf reportedly said somewhere: "Art is not a copy of the world; one of the damn things is enough." What makes art interesting, what made the evolution of art possible, is precisely this indeterminacy in the relationship between art and reality. And if this is true about aesthetic representation, it is no less true of political and historical representation.

REPRESENTATION IN POLITICS AND IN HISTORICAL WRITING

Let us start with political representation. Nothing could be more instructive here than how Rousseau in his discussion of political representation succeeds in paradoxically demonstrating precisely the reverse of what he wanted to demonstrate with his argument (a perfect example, I would say, of an unintended consequence in the realm of thought). When writing against the theater, Rousseau already showed his Platonist distrust of art and aesthetic representation,[18] so it need not surprise us that Rousseau was a staunch critic of political representation. And, indeed, in his *Du contrat social* Rousseau writes the following about political representation: "Sovereignty cannot be represented since it can be distorted by representation; sovereignty is essentially the general will, and this will cannot be represented: it is what it is, or what it is not—and there is nothing in between."[19] If we carefully analyze this *obiter dictum*, we must conclude that Rousseau's argument does not so much indicate what requirements political representation has to satisfy, but rather argues against all representation. Within

Rousseau's conception of it, political representation simply is impossible: for either we have something that looks like it, but this will be, on closer inspection, the represented itself (i.e., the sovereign people) all over again; or it is different from the represented (people), but then we are confronted with a perverse lie. So representation is either superfluous or a fraud; and that means the end of the notion of (political) representation. Hence, we may observe here how Rorty and Rousseau, *bien etonnés de se trouver ensemble*, present us with precisely the same kind of argument against (the possibility of) representation (and a shared misunderstanding of the concept of representation may explain this so unlikely alliance).

But a mere twelve years after Rousseau's dismissal of political representation, Edmund Burke took a quite different view of the nature of political representation. After his election to Parliament in 1774, Burke wrote in the letter to his constituents in Bristol the following:

Certainly, Gentlemen, it ought to be the happiness and glory of a representative to live in the strictest union, the closest correspondence, and most unreserved communion with his constituents. Their wishes ought to have great weight with him; their opinions high respect; their business his unremitted attention. It is his duty to sacrifice his repose, his pleasure, his satisfactions, to theirs,—and above all, ever, and in all cases, to prefer their interest to his own. But his unbiased opinion, his mature judgment, he ought not to sacrifice to you, to any man, or to any set of living men. These he does not derive from your pleasure,—nor from the law and the Constitution. They are a trust from Providence, for the abuse of which he is deeply answerable. Your representative owes you, not his industry only, but his judgment; and he betrays, instead of serving you, if he sacrifices it to your opinion.[20]

It is made admirably clear in this eloquent statement that the identity of represented and representation, of the voter and his representative on which Rousseau (and Rorty) had insisted so much, according to Burke ought to be rejected. For Burke the representative, after his election, possesses a responsibility of his own that he may never delegate or surrender to his voters. It is *his* conception of the common good, and not that of his *voters*, that must guide him in his political decisions. So in a representative democracy the mere datum of a difference between the voter and the representative would be an insufficient argument against adequate political representation. Even more so, it can be argued that from the possibility of this difference the unparalleled political creativity of representative democracy originates.[21]

Having a common origin in the sociopolitical matrix of sixteenth-century Italy and postrevolutionary Europe, it need not surprise us that the representation of the past in modern historical writing presents us with much the same picture. For just as we do not expect political representation to be an exact copy of the electorate, we do not demand of historical writing that it present us with an exact copy, or mimesis, of the past. And here too we should avoid seeing this as an inevitable shortcoming of historical writing, but rather as an indication of that for which we have historical writing. Rüsen is quite emphatic about the weaknesses of the (Rousseauistic) copy theory of historical representation, as may become clear from the following quote:

> Historical knowledge is constituted by specific interests, and these interests can be explicated as interpreted needs for temporal orientation. And in order to interpret what these needs are, you require criteria or ideas. These interests lead to questions or views of the past in order to understand the present. It is done by—what I call—leading ideas. These perspectives have now to be "filled" with empirical evidence, which is guided by methods and the rules of empirical research.[22]

As this quotation makes clear, we must abandon the Rankean ideal of a knowledge of the past *wie es eigentlich gewesen* with regard to "historical knowledge" as understood by Rüsen, since all historical knowledge requires these specific interests in order to be possible at all. And the presence of the dimension of these specific interests necessarily entails a rejection of the Rankean ideal. Furthermore, it should be observed that Rüsen explicitly speaks here about these specific interests as constituting historical knowledge, and that he does *not* say that we first have historical knowledge and that only then is this knowledge processed in some way or other by these specific interests. Rüsen's formulation makes clear that we should not discern here *two* phases: for him, these specific interests are part and parcel of all historical knowledge, just as for Kant the categories of the understanding could never be isolated from the knowledge we have of the phenomenal world. It follows that a theoretical reflection on the nature of historical knowledge as such already requires us to abandon the Rankean ideal. So Rüsen's position should not be (mis)construed as if he intended to say that, first, we all know what ideally historical knowledge would have to be like, but, second, why this ideal will always remain unattainable. Rüsen sidesteps this subjectivist or relativist adaptation of the Rankean ideal by subsuming these specific interests in the very notion of historical knowledge itself. And, once again, if we were to replace the notion of knowledge by that of representation, we must conclude that the difference between the represented and its representation is not a sad shortcoming of representation that we unfortunately shall have to live with, but that this difference is essential to *all* representation as such and is precisely why we need such a thing as representation. Without this difference, we no longer could speak of representation at all (as Goodman already pointed out so perspicaciously).

There is one last element in the quote from Rüsen that deserves our attention. Perhaps the best-known view of the nature of aesthetic representation is the one presented by Gombrich in his "Meditations on a Hobby Horse." The following quote from Gombrich's argument is of interest here:

> In many cases these "images" represent in the sense of "substitution." The clay horse or servant buried in the tomb of the mighty takes the place of the living. The idol takes the place of the God. . . . Can our substitute take us further? Perhaps, if we consider how it could become a substitute. The "first" hobby horse (to use eighteenth-century language) was probably no image at all. Just a stick which qualified as a horse because one could ride on it. . . . The *tertium comparationis*, the common factor, was function rather than form.[23]

If we now recall that within Rüsen's disciplinary matrix for historical writing a crucial role was assigned to *Daseinsorientierung*, this obviously is the "function" Rüsen would like to give to historical knowledge—or to historical representation. Historical knowledge essentially is *practical* knowledge, in the sense that it may, or rather should, help us in our effort to find our way about in sociohistorical reality. So if in the writing of history the represented and its representation will necessarily differ, the explanation is that historical writing has the *function* of presenting us with a *practical* knowledge of sociohistorical reality. And, equally obviously, this is what makes all historical writing so intimately related to the domain of politics. Our modern conception of politics and our modern historical consciousness are the two sides of one and the same coin, and once again we must conclude that all history is the history of past politics, or it is nothing.

Our contemporary postmodernist age, as exemplified by Rorty's so immensely influential attack on representationalism, rejects the idea that an adequate representation of (historical) reality is possible. In a certain sense, we may agree with this antirepresentationalism. It is true that knowledge (or representation) and reality (or the represented) will always differ. It is true, furthermore, that there are no *tertia comparationis* that will ever permit us to establish or to observe a complete correspondence of knowledge and reality.

But it would be wrong to discern in this mere datum a sufficient argument against representationalism. For, as we have seen in this chapter, we sin against the very logic of representation when requiring this correspondence (however defined) of the represented and its representation. For that they differ, that no such correspondence can or will ever be achieved, is precisely what is an essential part of the notion of representation.

Next, the difference between the represented and its representation may take on many different forms. And no exhaustive list of the nature of these differences could ever be made. For if we would possess such a list, it would enable us to eliminate these differences. Similarly, if we knew where the meaning of words in one language may differ from those in another, precisely this knowledge would enable us to achieve both a complete identity of meaning and a perfect translation from one language into another. But as Gombrich taught us so many years ago, all we can say is that *function* is responsible for these not only inevitable, but also welcome and aesthetically creative, differences—differences that are not regrettable shortcomings of representations, but precisely what we have representation *for*. And it was from the perspective of this question of function that we have been able to discern the close relationship of history and politics. We have every reason to be grateful to Rüsen for reminding us once again of this relationship—for this is a truth that we have tended to forget somewhat these last few decades.

EPILOGUE

The central theme is this volume has been the notion of representation. In the first chapter, the notion was contrasted with the more familiar one of true description, and we saw that representation cannot be reduced to description. A true description identifies an object in reality by means of its subject-term to which a property is attributed by the predicate-term of the description. This well-known structure, which has painstakingly been analyzed by philosophers of language since Frege, is absent in the case of representation. Though historical representations are built up of true descriptions, a (historical) representation itself cannot be interpreted as one large (true or false) description. I would not hesitate to say that this—and nothing else—is the central problem in all philosophy of history. On the one hand, there are philosophers of history of a scientistic inspiration who try somehow to fit historical representation within the matrix of true description. And to the extent that historical writing can be made to fit the ideal of "history as a social science," these attempts will not be wholly unsuccessful. For the problem of truth in the sciences can undoubtedly be usefully approached in terms of the truth of description. Certainly many problems will remain, but there is no a priori reason to doubt that the philosopher of history will here be less successful than the philosopher of science.

On the other hand, there are those philosophers of history who correctly recognize that most of existing historical writing can not be reduced to the model of true description. One may think here of theorists following Hayden White, of narrativists, and of theorists with a postmodernist orientation. After having rejected the scientific description model of historical representation, their problem now was to find a suitable model for understanding and clarifying the nature of historical representation. Since philosophy of language and even the history of the philosophy of history did not provide them with such models, they decided to turn to literary theory, a perfectly understandable strategy. For literary theory had developed since Russian formalism, since structuralism, since the New Criticism and deconstructivism (to mention only a few of the most influential movements in literary theory) an impressive array of instruments for dealing with texts. Moreover, only a philistine would deny that great literature sometimes expresses some deep truths about the *condition humaine*. So it seemed to follow that literary theory would present the historical theorist with the means to come to an understanding of the narrative representation of the past. And one need only think of how historiography, the study of the history of historical writing, was revolutionized by Hayden White, Lionel Gossman, Hans Kellner, Ann Rigney, and many others, to recognize how much contemporary historical theory owes to literary theory.

But an important problem remained. If the great literary texts succeed in expressing these Truths about the *condition humaine*, literary theory rarely investigated how it could do so. Undoubtedly this has been a wise decision. For having to deal with this kind of truth would inevitably have involved literary theory in the difficult problems of philosophical anthropology and of philosophy of life. It would then have started upon a hapless journey from which in all likelihood it would never have returned. So literary theory wisely restricted itself to what happens at the level of the text and refrained from investigating the domain of the relationship between text and reality. Admittedly, some incursions have been made into that domain—one may think of the deconstructivist's notorious *il n'y a pas dehors texte* and of their infatuation with the helpless "always already" kind of argument—but the theoretical and practical value of such intuitions have rightly been doubted. And their contributions to a philosophy of language (rarely going beyond a sometimes absurd and self-defeating skepticism) have been negligible.

Moreover, even if literary theory had developed a theory of truth for these truths about the *condition humaine*, it is unlikely that this would have been of much help for the historical theorist. For one may well doubt that these truths (if truths they are) have much in common with the kind of truth in which the historian is interested. The kind of consideration that will convince us of the plausibility of a representation of the history of natural law philosophy in the seventeenth and eighteenth centuries will be of an entirely different order than those that make us admire Shakespeare's or Dostoyevsky's picture of the depths of the human soul. It is true that some realist novelists—think of Zola's *Rougon-Marquart* series—attempt to depict the social realities of a certain country at a certain time. But if we wish to pronounce on the veracity of such depictions we will first have to reformulate the content of the novel into a quasi-historical account of what social life was like, say, in France during the reign of Napoleon III. And if we had to decide about the truth of such a reformulation we would, after a detour along the novel, have to return again to considering what criteria historians apply for assessing the veracity of historical representations.

So little is to be expected from literary theory if we wish to explain why some historical representations are better (or worse) than others, or, as I have phrased it in this book, the rationality of the writing of history. On the one hand this obviously is a most disappointing setback, but on the other hand it is a challenge in which philosophers of history should rejoice. For precisely this will enable them to add a new and important chapter to contemporary philosophy of language. Philosophers of language have over the last century and a half closely scrutinized the notions of truth, of reference, and of meaning, in order to clarify the relationship between the true statement and that of which it is true. But they have never ventured upon the problem of the text, and surely this is an important aspect of our use of language. For much of what we say is text, rather than true description. This is not only the case for the writing of history, but also in daily life, in conversation, in business, or in jurisdiction. So what the philosopher of history might discover about the relationship between historical representation and past reality is of crucial importance not only for our understanding of historical writing, but no less for countless other contexts of the use of language in our social and professional lives. To put it in a provocative way, philosophy of history is an integral part of the philosophy of language. And philosophy of language will remain a mere theoretical torso unless it takes seriously the kind of problem that is addressed in philosophy of history.

The main claim of this book is that such a complement to existing philosophy of language will have to be a reflection on the notion of representation. The three central notions of philosophy of language—reference, meaning, and truth—have to be redefined in order to come to an adequate understanding of the nature of representation. Reference should be replaced by "aboutness": a representation does not refer to what it represents, but is about it. Meaning has to be replaced by "intertextuality": the meaning of the text of a historical representation can never be identified if one takes into account only the text itself. Its meaning only reveals itself in a comparison with other texts about (roughly) the same represented. And this necessarily has its consequences for the notion of truth. Representations are not true or false in the proper, technical sense of these words, but only more or less plausible. And their relative plausibility articulates itself in this comparison with these other texts. In Chapter 2 we found which are the two criteria for a representation's plausibility: (1) the best representation is the one that succeeds in achieving a maximum of unity in a set of maximally diverse historical phenomena, and (2) the best representation is the most original one. And the two requirements can be taken together in the claim that the best representation is the most metaphorical one.

Lastly, "representation" is a primarily aesthetic term. The work of art is the prototypical representation. So, in a sense, there is much truth in the claim that has been reiterated all through the centuries that historical writing is an art rather than a science. But this does not mean that the historian has the same freedom when representing the past as the artist has. The artist recognizes representational constraints only in order to transcend them. The whole of the history of art is nothing but the history of the continuous questioning and rejection of previous representational constraints. This is different in the writing of history, since the constraints mentioned in the previous paragraph will always be respected. This does not imply that there could be no change or development in how the past is represented by historians. But however revolutionary such changes may be, if they are to be successful and to have a lasting impact on the history of the writing of history, the rationale for such revolutions can always be explained and defended in terms of these constraints.

All this may prove what fruits may be expected from a philosophical analysis of the notion of representation. Not only will such an analysis contribute to a better understanding of aesthetic representation and of historical representation. Representation also is the heart of representative democracy—and it is therefore to be expected that a better understanding of the notion of representation will also contribute to a better understanding of politics and of democracy. This is the topic of my *Political Representation*, the present book's companion volume.

REFERENCE MATTER

NOTES

INTRODUCTION

1. See for this W. E. Krul, "Huizinga's definitie van de geschiedenis," in J. Huizinga, *De taak van de cultuurgeschiedenis: Samengesteld, verzorgd en van een nawoord voorzien door W. E. Krul* (Groningen, Neth., 1995), 284.

2. Huizinga would later replace *a* culture by *the* culture in his definition. As Krul makes clear, he did so in order to emphasize his antirelativism.

3. This was the title of Habermas's *Die neue Unübersichtlichkeit: Kleine politische Schriften* (Frankfurt am Main), 1985.

4. H. Kellner, "Disorderly Conduct: Braudel's Menippean Satire," in Kellner, *Language and Historical Representation* (Madison, Wisc., 1989), 162.

5. For this conjunction in contemporary theory of the contingent on the one hand and the sublime on the other, see H. V. White, "The Politics of Historical Interpretation: Discipline and De-Sublimation," in White, *The Content of the Form: Narrative Discourse and Historical Representation* (Baltimore, 1987), 50–83.

6. H. Fenichel-Pitkin, *Fortune Is a Woman: Gender and Politics in the Thought of Niccolo Machiavelli* (Berkeley, Calif., 1987).

7. Illustrative is the indignant remark that an English reader had written down in 1702 in the margin of one of the pages of Bayle's *Dictionnnaire*: "How strangely some words lose their primitive sense: by a Critick was originally understood a good judge; with us nowadays it signifies no more than a Fault finder." Quoted in R. F. Beerling, *Ideeën en Idolen* (Arnhem, Neth., 1968), 123–24.

8. "It will suffice here to have shown that in the last century mankind has become more enlightened from one end of Europe to the other than in any previous age." With these self-congratulatory words, Voltaire ends his book. (General note: all translations in this book are mine, unless otherwise stated.)

9. W. Welsch, *Unsere postmoderne Moderne* (Darmstadt, Ger., 1991), 295.

10. Ibid., 305–6.

11. For a further elaboration of the striking similarities of historism and postmodernism, see my *History and Tropology: The Rise and Fall of Metaphor* (Berkeley, Calif., 1994), chap. 7.

12. This is what I have attempted to do in my *Aesthetic Politics: Political Philosophy Beyond Fact and Value* (Stanford, Calif., 1997).

13. As I have argued already in chapter 3 of my *History and Tropology*; see esp. 88–94.

14. One may think here, for example, of White's otherwise unexceptionable assertion that "the governing metaphor of an historical account could be treated as a heuristic rule which self-consciously eliminates certain kinds of data from consideration as evidence." See H. V. White, "The Burden of History," in White, *Tropics of Discourse: Essays in Cultural Criticism* (Baltimore, 1978), 46.

15. It seems likely that this practical problem of all philosophy of history has always functioned as a standing invitation to the philosopher to focus on the details, or on parts of the historical text rather than on the text as a whole. This may explain why the secrets of the historical text have been investigated so rarely by philosophers of history and why this main vehicle of historical insight still is so much a *terra incognita*.

16. This is the literal translation of the original Dutch title of Huizinga's book.

17. The preface is not included in English versions of *The Autumn of the Middle Ages*.

18. A. Momigliano, "Gibbon's Contribution to Historical Method," in Momigliano, *Studies in Historiography* (London, 1966). Momigliano also mentions Gibbon's farewell to all theological interpretation of history: "Gibbon followed Voltaire in boldly sweeping away every barrier between sacred history and profane history" (52).

19. An extreme example of this tendency is R. Berkhofer, *Beyond the Great Story: History as Text and as Discourse* (Cambridge, Mass., 1995); for Berkhofer's program, see esp. 4–16.

20. See my *Narrative Logic: A Semantic Analysis of the Historian's Language* (The Hague and Boston, 1983), 120–34. See also Chapter 8 in the present book.

21. For a further elaboration of this dialectical logic of historism, see my *History and Tropology*, chaps. 5, 6, and 7.

22. One may think here of Pierre Nora's seven-volume *Les Lieux de mémoire* (Paris, 1984–92), or P. Hutton's *History as an Art of Memory* (Hannover, Ger., 1993).

CHAPTER 1: *The Linguistic Turn*

1. R. Rorty, ed., *The Linguistic Turn: Recent Essays in Philosophical Method* (Chicago, 1967), 3 and 33 ff.

2. In Hume's famous formulation:

> When we run over libraries, persuaded of these principles, what havoc must we make? If we take into our hand any volume; of divinity or school metaphysics, for instance; let us ask, *Does it contain any abstract reasoning con-*

cerning quantity or number? No. *Does it contain any experimental reasoning concerning matter of fact and existence?* No. Commit it then to the flames; for it can contain nothing but sophistry and illusion.

See D. Hume, *An Enquiry Concerning Human Understanding*, ed. L. A. Selby-Bigge (Oxford, 1972), 165.

3. W. V. O. Quine, *Word and Object* (Cambridge, Mass., 1975), 272.

4. W. V. O. Quine, "Two Dogmas of Empiricism," in Quine, *From a Logical Point of View* (Oxford, 1971), 20.

5. R. Rorty, *Philosophy and the Mirror of Nature* (Oxford, 1980), 169.

6. C. Brinton, *The Anatomy of Revolution* (New York, 1965), 7.

7. T. Skocpol, "A Critical Review of Barrington Moore's *Social Origins of Dictatorship and Democracy*," *Politics and Society* 4, no. 1 (1973–74): 14; see also 5–6.

8. C. Lorenz, *Konstruktion der Vergangenheit: Eine Einführung in die Geschichtstheorie* (Cologne, 1997), 273.

9. For a discussion of the nature of these criteria, see the section "Against the Empiricists," below.

10. A problem that we will certainly have to face in historical discussion insofar as historical discussion could be described as a conflict between different historical "languages" (or vocabularies). But dealing with this issue falls outside the scope of the present chapter.

11. For a more technical defense of this claim, see my *Narrative Logic: A Semantic Analysis of the Historian's Language* (The Hague and Boston, 1983), 140ff.

12. F. R. Ankersmit, "Texts and Pictures," in F. R. Ankersmit and H. Kellner, eds., *The New Philosophy of History* (London, 1995), and Ankersmit, "Representation as the Representation of Experience," *Metaphilosophy* 31, nos. 1–2 (January 2000): 148–69.

13. For a brilliant exposition of these differences, see H. Schulte Nordholt, *Het beeld der Renaissance* (Amsterdam, 1948).

14. It is here that we may discern a resemblance between how a historical representation relates to the past and Tarski's *T*-sentences. According to convention *T* a statement like "Snow is white" is true if snow is white. The idea is, roughly, that a *T*-sentence (such as "'Snow is white' if snow is white") is a sentence formulated in metalanguage stating about a sentence in object-language (such as "Snow is white") what is the case, if the sentence in object-language is true. The *T*-sentence thus is, in the first place, a statement formulated in metalanguage about what makes a sentence in object-language true of the world. And, in the second place, *T*-sentences always do this for individual sentences formulated in object-language (such as "Snow is white"). Now, these two things are true as well of representation. For representations always bring us to the level of "speaking about speaking," hence to the level of metalanguage fixing the relationship between

object-language and the world; and they do so in the same way as the *T*-sentence. Furthermore, representations are always related to one individual represented only.

This observation is not without its interest if we recall that representation belongs to the domain of ordinary language rather than to that of formalized languages. Now, Hintikka has recently claimed to be able to formulate a theory of truth for ordinary languages avoiding any (Tarskian) appeal to metalanguage. But if my analysis of representation in this chapter is correct, such an anti-Tarskian theory of truth is not likely to be successful. See J. Hintikka, "Post-Tarskian Truth," *Synthese: An International Journal for Epistemology, Methodology, and Philosophy of Science* 126 (2001).

15. This may serve as an answer to the objection made by Zammito that there is an asymmetry between pictorial and historical representation that is insufficiently appreciated in my proposal to use pictorial representation as a means to clarify the nature of historical representation. See J. Zammito, "Ankersmit's Postmodernist Historiography," *History and Theory* 37, no. 3 (1998): 341.

16. H. Fain, *Between History and Philosophy* (Princeton, N.J., 1973).

17. For an analysis of this account of historical ontology and "on what there is" in historical reality, see my *Narrative Logic*, 155–69. See also C. Lorenz, "Can Histories Be True?" *History and Theory* 37, no. 3 (1998): 311, no. 5, which gives a short summary of the idea.

18. In order to obviate the objection that my use here of the distinction between synthetic and analytical truth is at odds with Quine's attack on what he had labeled "the first dogma of empiricism," I remind the reader that Quine was not arguing against the meaning of the terms "analytical" and "synthetic truth," but against the empiricist's claim that each truth is (reducible to) either of these two.

19. R. Berkhofer, *Beyond the Great Story: History as Text and as Discourse* (Cambridge, Mass., 1995).

20. D. Munslow, *Deconstructing History* (New York, 1997), 18–19.

21. R. J. Evans, *In Defence of History* (London, 1997), 253.

22. Zammito, "Postmodernist Historiography," 343.

23. Ibid.

24. C. Lorenz, "Can Histories Be True?" 313.

25. Ibid., 316.

26. Ibid., 328–29.

27. Ibid., 313–14.

28. Ibid., 314.

29. Ibid., 325.

30. Ibid.

31. Ankersmit, *Narrative Logic*, 220–48.

32. Elsewhere Lorenz presents his readers with an adequate exposition of how I had argued the scope criterion. See C. Lorenz, *Konstruktion der Vergangenheit*, 139–47.

33. C. Behan McCullagh, *The Truth of History* (London, 1998), 64. I shall not comment on McCullagh's propensity to replace argument for invective and for a feigned or (probably) actual incapacity to understand my argument. Though I must confess that I found it a strange experience to discover such an aversion for

rational and dispassionate argument in the writings of someone who elsewhere praises "truth" and "fairness" in such high-pitched wordings.

34. Ibid., 65.

35. Strictly speaking, this is philosophical mumbo-jumbo: historians describe the past, not "patterns," though they may describe the past *by* discerning patterns in it. But what enables us to achieve something is not identical with what is achieved itself: a car may enable us to make a journey, but cars themselves are not journeys.

36. In order not to create new misunderstandings, I will clarify that I have nothing more in mind here than that, by common agreement, in a true statement (or description) only the subject-term, and not the predicate-term, is said to refer. Unless one holds the counterintuitive view that, apart from green or red objects, reality also contains such things as "greenness" or "redness." This is, of course, what the medieval scholasticists called "realism."

37. A. A. L. de Caulaincourt, *De Moscou à Paris avec l'Empéreur* (Paris, n.d.), 174.

38. For this all-important issue—and where the necessity of the linguistic turn for historical writing announces itself—see also Chapter 8 of the present volume.

39. McCullagh, *The Truth of History*, 68.

40. McCullagh mistakenly gives 1957 as its date of publication.

41. Ibid.

42. J. Huizinga, "Abaelard," in Huizinga, *Verzamelde Werken*, 9 vols. (Haarlem, 1949), 4: 120.

43. McCullagh, *The Truth of History*, 67–68.

44. "Further, I shall try to show that there are disputes, centered on the concepts which I have just mentioned, which are perfectly genuine: which, although not resolvable by argument of any kind, *are nevertheless sustained by perfectly respectable arguments and evidence.* This is what I mean by saying that there are concepts which are essentially contested, concepts the use of which inevitably involves endless disputes about their proper uses on the part of their users" (emphasis mine). See W. B. Gallie, "Essentially Contested Concepts," in Gallie, *Philosophy and the Historical Understanding* (New York, 1968), 158.

45. Since statements like these tend continuously to be misinterpreted by my readers, I hasten to add that this does *not in the least* imply a rejection of the rationality of historical writing and of historical discussion. On the contrary, I think that I am an even stauncher believer in the rationality of the discipline of history than my empiricist detractors, since they are, in the end, often compelled to make an almost ritual concession to relativism in order to explain away junctures at which the facts about historical writing are at odds with their proud empiricist claims (I remind the reader here of my comments on Evans's book, or of Lorenz's view that to a certain extent the historian is, either willingly or unwillingly, always at the mercy of ethical and political values). My position *nowhere* obliges me to make such defeatist concessions. My thesis is merely that we should not appeal to truth in order to explain and justify historical rationality.

46. See for this the next chapter of this book and the last chapter of my *Narrative Logic*. To avoid misunderstanding: truth is, of course, a nonnegotiable requirement and a *conditio sine qua non* at the level of description.

47. For an exposition of White's linguistic Kantianism, see the introduction of my *History and Tropology: The Rise and Fall of Metaphor* (Berkeley, Calif., 1994).

48. These are the categories in which Richter subdivided contemporary literary theory in his textbook *The Critical Tradition*, 2d ed. (Boston, 1998). Strangely enough, narrativist theorists of history have rarely paid much attention to narratology. An exception is K. Pihlainen, *Resisting History: The Ethics of Narrative Representation* (Turku, Fin., 1999).

49. For an excellent exposition of the problem to what extent language can be seen as just one more part of the world, see A. C. Danto, "Historical Language and Historical Reality," in Danto, *Narration and Knowledge* (New York, 1985), esp. 305–10. Danto reminds us that pragmatism and ordinary language philosophy also tend to "naturalize" language and, hence, come closest to how literary theory demands us to deal with language. It should be pointed out, lastly, that the naturalization of the historian's language that was advocated in this chapter took place within a semantics of historical language. For I have attempted to make clear how and why representation transcends the matrix of the semantics of description or of the true statement. And this could only been done by taking one's point of departure in semantics.

50. See the previous note for this and for a further elaboration. A. C. Danto, *The Transfiguration of the Commonplace* (Cambridge, Mass., 1981), chap. 7.

51. As I have attempted to demonstrate in my "The Use of Language in the Writing of History," in my *History and Tropology*, 75–97.

52. Exemplary is R. Rorty, *Contingency, Irony, and Solidarity* (Cambridge, Mass., 1989).

53. R. Barthes, *Michelet par lui même* (Paris, 1954); H. V. White, *Tropics of Discourse: Essays in Cultural Criticism* (Baltimore, 1978); H. Kellner, *Language and Historical Representation* (Madison, Wisc., 1989); L. Gossman, *Between Literature and History* (Cambridge, Mass., 1990); A. Rigney, *The Rhetoric of Historical Representation: Three Narrative Histories of the French Revolution* (Cambridge, Eng., 1990).

54. And do the ambiguities in his position thus not reflect Burckhardt's own highly ambiguous relationship to romanticism?

55. Unparalleled are Gossman's analyses of Thierry and Michelet in his *Between Literature and History*.

56. These historians have now found a powerful ally in the writings by Mark Bevir. See M. Bevir, *The Logic of the History of Ideas* (Cambridge, Eng., 1999). For a lengthy discussion of Bevir's untimely views, see *Rethinking History* 3 (December 2000).

57. I italicize this phrase in order to demarcate the linguistic imperialism dis-

cussed here from the relationship between the claims of language and of experience as expounded by the linguistic turn.

58. And this is where this "skin" differs from the "thicker skin" in the formalism of White's tropology, and where the "skin" does have a material content of its own.

CHAPTER 2: *In Praise of Subjectivity*

1. Quoted in F. Wagner, *Geschichtswissenschaft* (Munich, 1951), 34.
2. See W. H. Walsh, *An Introduction to Philosophy of History* (London, 1967), 93–117.
3. A. C. Danto, *Analytical Philosophy of History* (Cambridge, Eng., 1968), 98.
4. Its most serious rival is the resemblance theory of representation. For a discussion of the relative merits of these two theories, see Chapter 8.
5. See ibid.
6. A. C. Danto, *The Transfiguration of the Commonplace* (Cambridge, Mass., 1983), 81.
7. Within the weltanschauung of nineteenth-century historism (not to be confused with Popper's historism), the nature of a nation, a cultural or intellectual tradition, and so on, lies in its history. A thing is what its history is.
8. Of course, this is not idealism. Representation does not actually create what it represents, but merely defines it or, as we shall see in a moment, is a proposal for how it *should* or had best be defined. And this is crucial for any intellectual grasp of the world. For without such proposals reality would remain as inaccessible to us as a well-protected strong room to the potential bank robber.
9. For this relationship between politics and ethics, see F. R. Ankersmit, "Against Ethics," introduction to Ankersmit, *Aesthetic Politics: Political Philosophy Beyond Fact and Value* (Stanford, Calif., 1997).
10. The issue is intensively discussed in S. Friedlander, ed., *Probing the Limits of Representation: Nazism and the "Final Solution"* (Cambridge, Mass., 1992). See also Chapter 6 in this volume.
11. See also S. G. Crowell:

> My argument is that historical narrative (as opposed to fictional narrative) *necessarily* involves links between (at least) two "heterogeneous" language games or discourses, each with its own aim—viz., the cognitive and the normative—and in so doing poses the difficult philosophical problem of determining, first, the "stakes" of this sort of discourse, so that, second, we can see what a proper standard for evaluating it might be.

Crowell, "Mixed Messages: The Heterogeneity of Historical Discourse," *History and Theory* 37, no. 2 (1998): 222.

12. Though this account is complicated by the tradition of natural law philos-

ophy, which until the end of the eighteenth century succeeded in keeping together what was later recognized as the domain of the cognitive with that of the normative.

13. K. R. Popper, *The Logic of Scientific Discovery* (London, 1972), 41.

14. F. R. Ankersmit, *Narrative Logic: A Semantic Analysis of the Historian's Language* (The Hague and Boston, 1983), 239ff.

15. M. Howard, "Lords of Destruction," *Times Literary Supplement*, 12 November 1981, 1323.

16. This exchange of ethics for history as our primary guide for political action was recommended already by Machiavelli, according to whom political evil arises not only "from the weakness into which the present religion has led the world," but even more "from not having a true knowledge of histories, through not getting from reading them that sense nor tasting that flavor that they have in themselves." See N. Machiavelli, *Discourses on Livy*, trans. Harvey C. Mansfield and Nathan Tarcov (Chicago, 1996), 6.

CHAPTER 3: *History as Metamorphosis*

1. E. Gibbon, *Autobiography of Edward Gibbon*, ed. O. Smeaton (New York, 1923), 141.
2. L. Gossman, *The Empire Unposses'd* (Cambridge, Eng., 1980), chaps. 7 and 8.
3. Gibbon, *Autobiography*, 141.
4. P. Gay, *Style in History* (London, 1974), chap. 1.
5. H. V. White, *Metahistory: The Historical Imagination in Nineteenth-Century Europe* (Baltimore, 1973).
6. D. Womersley, *The Transformation of "The Decline and Fall of the Roman Empire"* (Cambridge, Eng., 1988), 89.
7. "The successor of Charles V may disdain their brethren of England [it was widely believed in Gibbon's days that Fielding was a descendant of Charles V]; but the romance of *Tom Jones*, that exquisite picture of human manners, will outlive the palace of the Escurial, and the imperial eagle of the house of Austria." See Gibbon, *Autobiography*, 4.
8. L. Braudy, *Narrative Form in History and Fiction* (Princeton, N.J., 1970), 214–15.
9. Ovid, *Metamorphoses*, trans. and intro. Mary M. Innes (London, 1955), 83.
10. Ibid., 86.
11. Ibid., 87.
12. E. Gibbon, *The History of the Decline and Fall of the Roman Empire*, 12 vols. (Basel, 1787–94), 2: 137.
13. Ibid., 1: 74.
14. Ibid., 1: 75.
15. Ibid., 4: 73–74.

16. K. H. Eller, *Ovid und der Mythos der Verwandlung: Zum mythologischen und poetischen Verständnis des Metamorphoses-Gedichts* (Frankfurt am Main, 1982), 23.

17. Gossman, *The Empire Unposses'd*, 58.

18. G. K. Galinsky, *Ovid's* Metamorphoses: *An Introduction to the Basic Aspects* (Berkeley, Calif., 1975), 45.

19. Ovid, *Metamorphoses*, 29.

20. Galinsky, *Ovid's* Metamorphoses, 61.

21. Obviously, metamorphosis typically involves identity. Even more so, the whole point of metamorphosis ordinarily is to preserve identity despite (often dramatic) change. An intriguing exception to this rule is Alison Lurie's "The Double Poet," a story about the fight of Karo McKay, a highly esteemed poetess, with a double trying to impersonate her. Finally, like a vampire, this double succeeds in taking over McKay's identity, and the original McKay is changed into Carrie Martin, an unemployed, anonymous elderly woman. The only property preserved through change is the poetess's being the mother of "a sensible and wonderful grown daughter" (A. Lurie, in *Women and Ghosts* [London, 1994], 182) and is therefore implicitly presented by the story as her only and true identity.

The most ingenious story is further complicated by its carefully upholding the possibility that McKay suffers from a delusion. And it is interesting that insofar as McKay would really be deluded, two possibilities present themselves: either there never was a double and the end of McKay's career was caused by her mere belief that there was such an impostor, or we are being told the story of this impostor who, initially imagining herself to be McKay, finally discovered that she was merely the anonymous Carrie Martin and had her peace with that.

McKay's *not* being deluded about what happened to her is, of course, compatible with this second possibility, but then the end of the story makes clear that we have all the time been reading it from the wrong perspective. That is to say, the story is not about McKay but about Carrie Martin, and written from the latter's perspective.

22. In the short proem of the *Metamorphoses* Ovid informs his readers that they may expect a "continuous poem running from the beginning of the world down to my own time." The juxtaposition of *perpetuum* and *deducite* is interpreted by Myers as a challenge of the generic codes given by Callimachos in his *Aetia*. See K. S. Myers, *Rerum Causae: Ovid's "Metamorphoses" and Aetiological Narrative* (Ann Arbor, Mich., 1990), 1ff.

23. P. B. Craddock, *Edward Gibbon: Luminous Historian, 1772–1794* (Baltimore, 1989), 152.

24. Historians have much discussed the question of whether the views Ovid attributed to Pythagoras are actually his own. Most often the question is answered in the affirmative. Thus Otis writes: "The Pythagorean discourse embraces the entirety of Ovid's *carmen perpetuum* and represents metamorphosis as the universal key to the secrets of both nature and history" (Myers, *Rerum Causae*, 150).

25. Ovid, *Metamorphoses*, 341.
26. Ibid., 29.
27. Ibid., 31. For these negative characteristics in Ovid's text, see B. Gatz, *Weltalter, goldene Zeit, und sinnverwante Vorstellungen, Sudasmata* 16 (Hildesheim, Ger., 1967), 74.
28. Ovid, *Metamorphoses*, 339.
29. Galinsky, *Ovid's Metamorphoses*, 47.
30. Gibbon, *Decline and Fall*, 1: 102.
31. Ibid., 1: 1.
32. J. G. A. Pocock, "Between Machiavelli and Hume: Gibbon as Civic Humanist and Philosophical Historian," in G. W. Bowersock, J. Clive, and S. R. Graubard, eds., *Edward Gibbon and the Decline of the Roman Empire* (Cambridge, Eng., 1977), *passim*. For a magisterial elaboration of Pocock's interpretation of Gibbon, see J. G. A. Pocock, *Barbarism and Religion* (Cambridge, Eng., 1999), vol. 2.
33. Gibbon, *Decline and Fall*, 1: 12–13.
34. Ibid., 1: 70–71.
35. Virgil, *Aeneid*, trans. W. F. Jackson Knight (Harmondsworth, Eng., 1956), 1: 278–79.
36. Gatz, *Weltalter, goldene Zeit*, 72.
37. Myers, *Rerum Causae*, 154.
38. Gibbon, *Decline and Fall*, 12: 186.
39. Ibid., 8: 323.

CHAPTER 4: *The Dialectics of Narrativist Historism*

1. K. Mannheim, "Historismus," in Mannheim, *Wissenssoziologie* (Neuwied am Rhein, Ger., 1970), 246–47.
2. Ibid., 246–309.
3. J. Rüsen, "Historisches Erzählen zwischen Kunst und Wissenschaft," in Rüsen, *Konfigurationen des Historismus* (Frankfurt am Main, 1993), 117.
4. J. Locke, *An Essay Concerning Human Understanding* (London, 1972), 245.
5. E. Gibbon, *The History of the Decline and Fall of the Roman Empire*, 12 vols. (Basel, 1787–94), 1: 102.
6. E. Gibbon, *Autobiography of Edward Gibbon*, ed. O. Smeaton (New York, 1923), 159.
7. Before he decided to write the history of the fall of the Roman empire, it had been Gibbon's plan to write a history of the city of Rome in the Middle Ages. See Gibbon's famous but perhaps not entirely reliable account of the inception of his work in his *Autobiography* (124).
8. For an exposition of the too neglected issue of the "indispensability of periodization," see J. Huizinga, *Verzamelde Werken*, 9 vols. (Haarlem, 1950), 7: 85–95.
9. Gibbon, *Decline and Fall*, 6: 186.

10. Ibid., 6: 190.

11. Ibid., 12: 186.

12. For Gibbon's own formulation of this analysis of the cause of Rome's fall, see Chapter 3.

13. I would therefore disagree with Womersley when he explains this evolution in Gibbon's analysis in the following way: "The question in his mind seems less to be 'What are the causes of this event?' than 'What sort of thing is cause?'" However, Womersley's comment that Gibbon is moving here from a "sociological interest" to "a more metaphysical interest" is closer to my view. See D. Womersley, *The Transformation of "The Decline and Fall of the Roman Empire"* (Cambridge, Eng., 1988), 188.

14. "Historians only inform us about the internal divisions that are said to have been fatal: but they do not show that they were necessary for Rome's fall. For they had always been there and would always be there. It was only its size that did all the evil and that transformed popular unrest into civil wars." See C. L. de Montesquieu, *Considérations sur les causes de la grandeur des Romains et de leur décadence* (Paris, 1834), 81.

15. Gibbon, *Decline and Fall*, 1: 74; Montesquieu, *Considérations*, 106.

16. Cited in Womersley, *The Transformation of "The Decline and Fall,"* 44.

17. J. Rüsen, "Historisches Erzählen zwischen Kunst und Wissenschaft," 118.

18. P. F. Strawson, *Individuals: An Essay in Descriptive Metaphysics* (London, 1959).

19. Quoted in F. Wagner, *Geschichtswissenschaft* (Munich, 1966), 198.

20. For this tendency of historism to evolve into two diametrically opposed directions, see F. R. Ankersmit, *Narrative Logic: A Semantic Analysis of the Historian's Language* (The Hague and Boston, 1983), 120 ff.

21. For Burckhardt's proto-postmodernism, see J. Rüsen, "Jacob Burckhardt and Historical Insight on the Border of Postmodernism," *History and Theory* 24, no. 3 (1985): 235–47; and, recently, L. Gossman, *Basel in the Age of Burckhardt: A Study in Unseasonable Ideas* (Chicago and London, 2000), esp. part 4.

22. See F. R. Ankersmit, "History and Postmodernism," in Ankersmit, *History and Tropology: The Rise and Fall of Metaphor* (Berkeley, Calif., 1994), chap. 7.

23. W. von Humboldt, "On the Historian's Task," in G. G. Iggers and K. von Moltke, *The Theory and Practice of History* (Indianapolis, 1973), 19.

24. For an exposition of these immensely fruitful insights proposed by historism, see F. R. Ankersmit, *Denken over geschiedenis* (Groningen, Neth., 1986), 178 ff.

25. Humboldt, "On the Historian's Task," 14, 23.

26. Obviously, I am thinking here of Droysen's *erster Fundamentalsatz*:

> This is the first important and fundamental law of our discipline, namely that what it wants to discover about the past is not to be looked for in the past itself, for this past is no longer available, but in what the past has left

us, in whatever form, and can be empirically investigated. Only what has survived the past and is present still now, in whatever changed form, and can empirically be grasped, will and can provide the historian with the data he is looking for.

See J. G. Droysen, *Historik* (Munich, 1971), 20.

27. See Ankersmit, *Narrative Logic*, chaps. 5 and 6, for the logical properties of these narrative substances.

28. See F. R. Ankersmit, "The Use of Language in the Writing of History," in H. Coleman, ed., *Working with Language* (Berlin and New York, 1989). For a further discussion of this claim of narrativist language being a *thing* from an ontological perspective, see also the Introduction and Chapter 1 of this book.

29. For a further elaboration, see the Introduction to this book and F. R. Ankersmit and J. J. A. Mooij, introduction to Ankersmit and Mooij, *Knowledge and Language: Metaphor and Knowledge* (Dordrecht, Neth., 1993).

30. It should be emphasized, once again, that this criterion, in spite of the fact that it enables us to decide *rationally* between alternative historical representations, can never be reduced to any theory of truth. For truth is a property of constative statements expressing knowledge of the past; whereas historical representations are *non*cognitive, in that they offer us not knowledge, but *organizations* of knowledge.

31. Rüsen, "Historisches Erzählen zwischen Kunst und Wissenschaft," 114.

32. J. Kocka, "Th. Nipperdey, Einführung," in Kocka, ed., *Theorie der Geschichte*, 3 vols.; vol. 3, *Theorie und Erzählung in der Geschichte* (Munich, 1979), 9.

33. See, for example, A. Janik and S. Touchin, *Wittgenstein's Vienna* (New York, 1973), and C. E. Schorske, *Fin-de-Siècle Vienna* (London, 1960).

34. H. von Hofmannsthal, "Ein Brief," in Hofmannsthal, *Sämtliche Werke*, 43 vols.; vol. 31, *Herausgegeben von Ellen Ritter* (Frankfurt am Main, 1991), 48.

35. Ibid.

36. Ibid., 50.

37. A striking parallel is to be found in Michel Tournier's *Vendredi ou les limbes du pacifique* (Paris, 1972). Completely condemned to himself by the solitude of the island on which he is living, Robinson Crusoe recognizes:

> I may well speak aloud incessantly, and never have an intuition or idea without addressing it immediately to the trees or the clouds [his substitute fellow language users], each day I see sink away whole corners of the verbal citadel in which our thought has found its shelter and where it moves around at its pleasure, like a mole in its system of tunnels. (68)

38. Hofmannsthal, "Ein Brief," 51.

39. Ibid.

40. Quoted in J. M. Krois, *Cassirer: Symbolic Forms and History* (New Haven, Conn., 1987), 107.

41. See H. White, "The Modernist Event," in White, *Figural Realism* (Baltimore, 1999); see also Chapter 9 of this book.

42. D. LaCapra, *Representing the Holocaust: History, Theory, Trauma* (Ithaca, N.Y., 1994); and LaCapra, *History and Memory After Auschwitz* (Ithaca, N.Y., 1998).

43. E. Runia, *Waterloo Verdun Auschwitz: De liquidatie van het verleden* (Amsterdam, 1999), 9.

44. It might now be asked how the French Revolution could have been such a powerful stimulus of historiographical innovation. Surely this was an event full of meaning and, in this respect, to be compared with the Holocaust rather than with the historiography of what had hitherto been meaningless? And surely few events have revolutionized historical writing more than the French Revolution. The answer to this query is as simple as it is obvious. The French Revolution has certainly given us a wholly new form of historical writing and of historical representation. But what it gave us is the *historist* model of historical writing aiming at synthesis and cohesion, which is the background of the present discussion and against which the new forms of historical writing discussed here articulate themselves.

45. See, for example, L. Hunt, ed., *The New Cultural History* (Berkeley, Calif., 1989).

46. A comprehensive and succinct summary of the relevant features of these newer forms of historical writing can be found in G. G. Iggers, *Geschichtswissenschaft im 20. Jahrhundert* (Göttingen, Ger., 1993), 73–84. Without denying the important innovations brought by these newer forms of historical writing, Iggers emphasizes their indebtedness to the tradition of *Geschichte als Sozialwissenschaft*.

47. Ibid., 84.

48. Ibid., 75.

CHAPTER 5: *The "Privatization" of the Past*

1. J. Habermas, "Die neue Unübersichtlichkeit," in Habermas, *Die neue Unübersichtlichkeit* (Frankfurt am Main, 1985), 143.

2. See L. Orr, "Postrevolutionary Syndrome: Stael, Michelet, Tocqueville," in F. R. Ankersmit and H. Kellner, eds., *A New Philosophy of History* (London, 1995), 89–108.

3. F. R. Ankersmit, *History and Tropology: The Rise and Fall of Metaphor* (Berkeley, Calif., 1994), 204.

4. P. Hutton, *History as an Art of Memory* (Hanover, N.H., 1993), xxiv.

5. Ibid., xiii.

6. Similarly, Nora observes that, until quite recently, the West defined its relationship to the past in terms of continuity; and this continuity (as embodied in the history of a dynasty, nation, social class, etc.) gave to the historian *le principe explicatif* for both understanding and telling the past. But, as Nora goes on to say,

"it is this relationship which has broken down"—and this has transformed the past from an object possessing a certain intrinsic order into a chaos of *faits divers*: "The loss of one unique explanatory principle has thrown us into an exploding universe, while it has, at the same time, endowed each object, however humble, however unlikely, however inaccessible, with the dignity of historical mystery." Instead of telling us the familiar story of the gradual unfolding of the nation, we now expect the historian to give us "the feel of the past," *l'authenticité du direct*, by intimating to readers the experience of "the soil on one's shoes, the heavy hand of the Devil in the year 1000, and the stench of eighteenth-century cities." See P. Nora, "Entre mémoire et histoire," in Nora, ed., *Les Lieux de mémoire*, 3 vols.; vol. 1, *La République* (Paris, 1984), xxxi, xxxii.

7. M. Halbwachs, *Les Cadres sociaux de la mémoire* (Paris, 1976), 7 ff.

8. Ibid., 108–9.

9. For this peculiar, and strangely Kantian argument, see H. Bergson, *Durée et simultanéité* (Paris, 1922).

10. For Halbwachs's comments on this argument, see M. Halbwachs, *Het collectief geheugen* (Leuven, Belgium, 1991), 36 ff.

11. Ibid., chap. 1.

12. Quoted in W. Lyons, *The Disappearance of Introspection* (Cambridge, Mass., 1986), 115.

13. Ibid., 152.

14. For an elaboration of this view, see my "Between Language and History: Rorty's Promised Land," *Common Knowledge* 6, no. 1 (1997): 44–79.

15. R. Rorty, "Nineteenth-Century Idealism and Twentieth-Century Textualism," in Rorty, *The Consequences of Pragmatism* (Brighton, Eng., 1982), 139–60.

16. H. Kellner, "'Never Again' Is Now," *History and Theory* 33, no. 4 (1994): 132.

17. B. Lang, *Act and Idea in the Nazi Genocide* (Chicago, 1990). For a critique of Lang's position see W. Kansteiner, "The New Approach to Nazism and the 'Final Solution,'" *History and Theory* 33, no. 2 (1994): 145–74.

18. I am referring here to C. R. Browning, *Ordinary Men: Reserve Batallion 101 and the Final Solution in Poland* (New York, 1992).

19. G. H. Hartman, "The Book of Destruction," in S. Friedlander, ed., *Probing the Limits of Representation: Nazism and the "Final Solution"* (Cambridge, Mass., 1992), 334.

20. H. G. Gadamer, *Wahrheit und Methode* (Tübingen, Ger., 1960), 429.

21. Ankersmit, *History and Tropology*, 209–10.

22. S. Felman and D. Laub, *Testimony: Crises of Witnessing in Literature, Psychoanalysis, and History* (New York, 1992), 204.

23. Ibid., 213.

24. For an example of how testimony may function as a correction of history, see the section titled "Testimony and Historical Truth" in chapter 2 of *Testimony*.

25. Ibid., 59.
26. Ibid., 62.
27. A. W. M. Mooij, "Het werkelijke als trauma," *Feit en Fictie* 1, no. 2 (1993): 12.
28. Felman and Laub, *Testimony*, 65.
29. D. Lowenthal, *The Past Is a Foreign Country* (Cambridge, Eng., 1985), 195.
30. J. Banville, *Ghosts* (London, 1993), 196–97.
31. P. Nora, "L'Ere de la commémoration," in Nora, ed., *Les Lieux de mémoire*, vol. 3, *Les Frances* (Paris, 1992), 977–1012. See also, J. R. Gillis, ed., *Commemorations: The Politics of National Identity* (Princeton, N.J., 1994).
32. Quoted in F. Yates, *The Art of Memory* (Aylesbury, Eng., 1966), 22.
33. C. Amalvi, "Le 14 Juillet," in P. Nora, ed., *Les Lieux de mémoire*, 1: 426.
34. Nora, "L'Ere de la commémoration," 983.
35. C. S. Maier, "A Surfeit of Memory," *History and Memory: Studies in the Representation of the Past* 5, no. 2 (1993): 150. Furthermore, according to Maier, the present emphasis on memory testifies to a lack of confidence in a collective project: "Why, to return to a question that motivated this discussion of public commemoration, does memory now seem to play a larger role in political and civic life? My own belief is that at the end of the twentieth century Western societies have come to an end of a massive collective project" (147).
36. According to Gillis, this shift is encouraged by entrusting memory to historical amateurs: "of course, taking memory out of the hand of specialists, diffusing its practice over time and space, runs the risk of merely privatizing it rather then democratizing it." See J. R. Gillis, introduction to Gillis, ed., *Commemorations*, 19.
37. Ibid., 17. See note 5 in the next chapter for a further comment on the counter-monument.
38. G. W. F. Hegel, *Vorlesungen über die Philosophie der Weltgeschichte*, vols. 2–4 (Hamburg, 1976), 640–41, 644.
39. Several studies have been devoted in the last two decades to the fascination with history in the sixteenth century that seemed to anticipate, in many ways, late-eighteenth-century historism. Cartesian rationalism quickly put an end in the seventeenth century to this fledgling sense of history.
40. Felman and Laub, *Testimony*, 206.
41. W. Johnston, *Postmodernisme et bimillénaire: Le Culte des anniversaires dans la culture contemporaine* (Paris, 1992), 14.
42. Nora, "L'Ere de la commémoration," 1011.

CHAPTER 6: *Remembering the Holocaust*

1. For an elaboration of this claim, see Chapter 4.
2. For an exposition of nostalgia as a dimension of contemporary historical consciousness, see my *History and Tropology: The Rise and Fall of Metaphor* (Berkeley, Calif., 1994), 197 ff.

3. J. Webber, *The Future of Auschwitz: Some Personal Reflections* (Oxford, 1992), 3.

4. E. van Alphen, "Armando's oorlog," *Feit en Fictie* 1, no. 1 (1993): 109–25.

5. James Young described the first of these counter-monuments as follows:

> Unveiled in 1986, this twelve meter high, one-meter-square pillar is made of hollow aluminum, plated with a thin layer of soft, dark lead. A temporary inscription near its base reads—and thereby creates constituencies in—German, French, English, Russian, Hebrew, Arabic, anbd Turkish: "We invite the citizens of Harburg, and visitors to the town, to add their names here to ours. In doing so, we commit ourselves to remain vigilant. As more and more names cover this 12-meter-tall lead column, it will gradually be lowered in the ground. One day it will have disappeared completely, and the site of the Harburg monument against fascism will be empty. In the end, it is only we ourselves who can rise up against injustice." A steal-pointed stylus, with which to score the soft lead, is attached at each corner by a length of cable. As one-and-a-half-meter sections are covered with memorial graffiti, the monument is lowered into the ground, into a chamber as deep as the column is high. The more actively visitors participate, the faster they cover each section with their names, the sooner the monument will disappear. After several lowerings over the course of four or five years, nothing will be left but the top surface of the monument, which will be covered with a burial stone inscribed to "Harburg's monument against fascism." In effect, the vanishing monument will have returned the burden of memory to visitors: one day, the only thing left standing here will be the memory-tourist, forced to rise and to remember himself.

See J. E. Young, *The Texture of Memory: Holocaust Memorials and Meaning* (New Haven, Conn., 1993), 30.

6. Quoted in ibid., 244. See also, for further information about Yad Vashem, *Yad Vashem*, published by the Holocaust Martyr's and Heroes' Remembrance Authority (Jerusalem, n.d.).

7. Young, *Texture of Memory*, 66.

8. Paul Celan, "Todesfuge," ll. 25–26, trans. Michael Hamburger, from the Paul Celan home page at www.polyglot.lss.wisc.edu/german/celan.

9. As was argued by Robert Musil in his *Het posthume werk van een levende* (Amsterdam, 1987), 63–68. This translation into Dutch of Musil's thoughts on monuments was taken from his *Nachlass zu Lebzeiten* (Reinbek, Ger., 1978).

10. Quoted in Young, *Texture of Memory*, 254.

11. A. Margalit, "The Kitsch of Israel," *New York Review of Books*, 24 November 1988, 23.

12. H. Broch, "Kitsch und Tendenzkunst," in G. Dorfles, ed., *Der Kitsch* (Tübingen, Ger., 1969), 70. This is also why Broch identifies kitsch with *das radikal Böse*: it follows from the statement quoted in the text that the *ne plus ultra* of aestheticism must necessarily also be the *ne plus ultra* of evil (see also p. 76).

13. Ibid., 58.
14. H. Broch, "Einige Bemerkungen zum Problem des Kitsches—ein Vortrag," in Broch, *Gesammelte Werke*, 4 vols.; vol. 1, *Dichten und Erkennen* (Zurich, 1955), 295–309.
15. S. Freud, *Totem und Tabu*, in Freud, *Studienausgabe*, 10 vols.; vol. 9, *Fragen der Gesellschaft, Ursprünge der Religion* (Frankfurt am Main, 1982), 363.
16. S. Freud, "Über eine Weltanschauung," in Freud *Studienausgabe*, vol. 1, *Vorlesungen zur Einführung in die Psychoanalyse* (Frankfurt am Main, 1982), 588.
17. I. Kant, *Kritik der Urteilskraft* (Hamburg, 1924), 66.
18. I am referring here to the lecture read by J. Rüsen for the history department at Groningen University, on April 24, 1995, entitled "Mourning."
19. S. Freud, "Trauer und Melancholie," in Freud, *Studienausgabe*, vol. 3, *Psychologie des Unbewussten* (Frankfurt am Main, 1982), 199.
20. For an excellent account of the history of melancholia, see R. Kuhn, *The Demon of Noontide: Ennui in Western Literature* (Princeton, N.J., 1976).
21. Freud, "Trauer und Melancholie," 203.
22. Ibid., 200–201.
23. Ibid., 201.

CHAPTER 7: *Why Realism?*

1. E. Auerbach, "Epilegomena zu *Mimesis*," *Romanische Forschungen* 65, no. 1 (1954): 1, 18.
2. In one of his essays Auerbach wrote: "The discipline I'm representing, Romance languages, is one of the more modest branches of the tree of romantic historism." See F. Schalck, "Einleitung," introduction to E. Auerbach, *Gesammelte Aufsätze zur romanischen Philologie* (Bern, 1967), 7. And the intellectual matrix of mimesis Auerbach defined as follows: "It has grown from the inspiration and methods of German philology and intellectual history, and would not have been possible in any other tradition than that of Hegel and German romanticism." See E. Auerbach, "Epilegomena zu *Mimesis*," 1.
3. E. Auerbach, "Vico's Contribution to Literary Criticism," in Auerbach, *Gesammelte Ausätze zur romanischen Philologie*, 261. In this essay, Auerbach both defines and expresses his agreement with the generally accepted meaning of the word "historism," according to which the nature of a thing is to be found in its history. Vico had already formulated this conception of historism in *La scienza nuova* (see p. 260).
4. T. M. De Pietro, "Literary Criticism as History," *CLIO* 8 (1979): 377; see also G. Green, *Literary Criticism and the Structures of History: E. Auerbach and L. Spitzer* (Lincoln, Nebr., 1982), 11.
5. E. Auerbach, *Vier Untersuchungen zur Geschichte der Französischen Bildung* (Bern, 1951), 7.

6. H. G. Gadamer, *Wahrheit und Methode* (Tübingen, Ger., 1960), 162–229.

7. F. Meinecke, *Die Entstehung des Historismus* (1936; reprint, Munich, 1965), 6. The whole of Auerbach's oeuvre, including *Mimesis*, has its "basis in the development of perspectivist historism, whose influence Auerbach underwent and that he tried to give a new foundation to with his interpretation of Western literature—an effort completing Meinecke's book on historicism" (see Schalck, "Einleitung," 17).

8. "Friedrich Meinecke's book on the origins of Historism is the finest and most mature treatment that I know." E. Auerbach, *Mimesis: The Representation of Reality in Western Literature* (Princeton, N.J., 1968), 444.

9. "Above all, it is wrong to believe that historical relativism or perspectivism makes us incapable of evaluating and judging the work of art, that it leads to arbitrary eclecticism, and that we need, for judgment, fixed and absolute categories. . . . Historical relativism has a twofold aspect: it concerns the understanding historian as well as the phenomenon to be understood. This is an extreme relativism, but we should not fear it." See E. Auerbach, "Vico's Contribution to Literary Criticism," 262. For Auerbach's relaxed attitude toward relativism, see furthermore Green, *Literary Criticism*, 53–54.

10. See my *Narrative Logic: A Semantic Analysis of the Historian's Language* (The Hague and Boston, 1983), esp. 140–50.

11. The same is true for Schiller, for whom Auerbach has a profound dislike. Auerbach is prepared to admit the realism of Schiller's rendering of speech and dialogue in his *Luise Millerin*. But here realism is used for the purposes of ideology: "*Luise Millerin* is much more a political and even demogagic play than a truly realistic one" (*Mimesis*, 440). Because of his own recent experiences of Hitler's Nazi propaganda, Auerbach was not willing to see even in Schiller's Enlightened humanist values an excuse for his political (ab)use of realism.

12. Auerbach, *Mimesis*, 355.

13. Ibid., 349.

14. Ibid., 385 ff.

15. A. de Tocqueville, *Democracy in America* (New York, 1945), 2: 84–89.

16. A classification that the French classicists had inherited from the notion of the "Rota Vergilii" and from classical rhetoric.

17. If we recall Roland Barthes's claim, as developed in his well-known "L'Effet de réel," that realism requires the amalgamation of "notation" (corresponding to Auerbach's low style) and "prediction" (corresponding to Auerbach's elevated style), the similarities between Barthes's and Auerbach's conceptions of literary realism will be obvious. For Barthes, see R. Barthes, "L'Effet de réel," in Barthes, *Le Bruissement de la langue*, vol. 4 (Paris, 1984).

18. The shortcoming of allegory is that it may formally come quite close to the notion of *figura*, which will be dealt with in the next section, but by moving only "vertically" from the historical event to its allegorical meaning, the movement essentially is a movement away from historical reality. It therefore misses the realist

dimension of *figura*, because *figura* always ties together two secular events, even though this happens via the "vertical" link that both have to their shared figurative meaning. Allegory sends us to the *civitas Dei*, but *figura* always sends us back again to the *civitas terrena*. See for this contrast between medieval allegory and *figura*, E. Auerbach, "Figura," in *Gesammelte Aufsätze zur romanischen Philologie*, 77.

19. Auerbach, *Mimesis*, chap. 8.

20. Or, to mention another aspect of Dante's style that is expounded by Auerbach himself, when Farinata interrupts the conversation between Dante and Virgil in order to speak to Dante, "We hear, not, 'Tuscan, stop!' but 'O Tuscan, who . . . may it please to linger in this place'"—surely not a very "realist" locution. See Auerbach, *Mimesis*, 179.

21. Thus Zola, in the preface to his *Thérèse Raquin*, about his realist aspirations.

22. Auerbach, *Mimesis*, 73. For Auerbach's most detailed analysis of *figura*, see Auerbach, "Figura," 55–93. Exactly the same definition that was mentioned just now can be found in this essay on p. 77.

23. L. O. Mink, *Historical Understanding*, ed. B. Fay, E. O. Golob, and R. T. Vann (Ithaca, N.Y., 1987), 56, 57.

24. For the realism of historical writing, see my *History and Tropology: The Rise and Fall of Metaphor* (Berkeley, Calif., 1994), chap. 4.

25. One important difference between *figura* and "configurational comprehension" should be borne in mind. Though *figura* has to do with historical reality itself and is in the end an ontological notion, Mink's "configurational comprehension" is an answer to the question of the nature of historical knowledge and has therefore an epistemological status.

26. Auerbach, *Gesammelte Aufsätze zur romanischen Philologie*, 56 ff.

27. Auerbach sees, as the main difference between *figura* and historical understanding, that the provisional character of all historical meaning has in *figura* its origins in the vertical link between the historical event and its transcendent meaning. In historical understanding, however, it is our imperfect knowledge of the horizontal dimension, where the event, together with other historical events, has to be situated, that renders all our interpretations of the past provisional and subject to later correction. See Auerbach, "Figura," 81.

28. On many occasions I have argued that historical "forms" or "ideas" can only articulate their contours when they have been contrasted to *other* forms or ideas. See, for example, my *History and Tropology*, chap. 3. To put it succinctly, if we have only *one* historical form, we have *no* historical form at all.

29. This is clearly the intention of the passage in which Auerbach comes closest to explaining the realism of *figura*: "both figure and fulfillment possess—as we have said—the character of actual historical events and phenomena. The fulfillment possesses it in a greater and more intense measure, for it is, compared with the figure, *forma perfectior*." Auerbach, *Mimesis*, 197; see also p. 72 (where St. Augustine is presented as the inventor of *figura*), 116, 119.

30. Auerbach himself uses these metaphors of "horizontality" and "verticality" (73ff). There is a striking similarity between Auerbach's notion of *figura* and the way in which John Pocock characterized the medieval historical consciousness as influenced by the writings of St. Augustine and Boethius's *De consolatione philosophiae*. See J. G. A. Pocock, *The Machiavellian Moment: Florentine Political Thought and the Atlantic Tradition* (Princeton, N.J., 1975), 31–49; see also my *Exploraties*, 3 vols.; vol. 1, *De spiegel van het verleden* (Kampen, Neth., 1996), chap. 1.

31. Auerbach, *Mimesis*, 259.

32. "Hier verschwindet alles Einzelne und Besondere menschlicher Interessen und Zwecke vor der absoluten Grösse des Endzweckes und Ziels aller Dinge; zugleich aber steht das sonst Vergänglichste und Flüchtigste der lebendigen Welt objektiv in seinem Innersten ergründet, in seinem Wert and Unwert durch den höchsten Begriff, durch Gott gerichtet, vollständig episch da." See G. W. F. Hegel, *Vorlesungen über die Ästhetik*, 3 vols. (Frankfurt am Main, 1986), 3: 406–7.

33. On several occasions in his writings, Auerbach emphasizes that his notion of *figura* owes much to the characterization of Dante given by Hegel in his *Ästhetik*. He even praises Hegel for having given us "one of the most beautiful passages ever written on Dante"; see *Mimesis*, 191.

34. Green, *Literary Criticism*, 66ff. We may observe here, incidentally, a difference between Hegel's conception as expounded just now and Aristotle's conception of poetry. "Poetry," writes Aristotle, "is a more philosophical and higher thing than history: for poetry tends to express the universal, history the particular" (see Aristotle, *Poetics*, 9.3–4). Thus, where Aristotle tends to oppose the universal and the particular (in order to distinguish poetry from history), Hegelian dialectics aims at the most perfect union and synthesis of the two.

35. Auerbach, *Mimesis*, 495.

36. See note 2 of the present chapter.

37. Auerbach, *Mimesis*, 490.

38. The *locus classicus* is I. Kant, "Analytik des Erhabenen," in *Kritik der Urteilskraft*.

39. See for this R. Kuhn, *The Demon of Noontide: Ennui in Western Literature* (Princeton, N.J., 1976); and for the relationship of the sublime to history and to historical experience, see my *De historische ervaring* (Groningen, Neth., 1993), and my *History and Tropology*, chap. 7.

40. "Das hoffnungslose Schrecken hat in der Literatur seinen überlieferten Platz; es ist eine Sonderform des Erhabenen; es findet sich bei manchen antiken Tragikern und Geschichtsschreibern, natürlich auch bei Dante; es besitzt höchste Würde." See Auerbach, *Vier Untersuchungen zur Geschichte der Französischen Bildung*, 108.

41. "Entscheidend ist die Eindringlichkeit der Evokation, und in diesem Sinne ist Baudelaires Gedicht aufs äusserste realistisch." See ibid., 111.

42. Auerbach, *Mimesis*, 503.

43. Though it must certainly be conceded that there is an intimate relationship

between the realist novel and the pessimism of the *fin de siècle*; for, as is shown in J. Pierrot, *L'Imaginaire décadent* (Paris, 1977), this pessimism had Schopenhauer as its intellectual guide. And one might well defend the view that Schopenhauer's system is essentially an exploration of what Kant, as "noumenal reality," had resolutely placed outside the philosopher's grasp (philosophers always succumbing to the temptation to "eff the ineffable," as Rorty once put it so nicely). And this noumenal reality has its obvious affinities with the sublime, in the sense of being its counterpart on the side of the object, while, furthermore, Schopenhauer used all his considerable philosophical and literary talents to present it as the source of all that is evil, painful, and melancholic about human existence. The way Schopenhauer transformed the Kantian system certainly goes a long way toward giving a philosophical justification of the literary preoccupations of the realist novelists. And from that perspective we need not be surprised by the fact that the realist novel and neo-Kantianism are each other's exact contemporaries.

44. Auerbach, *Mimesis*, 86 ff.

45. Ibid., 208–9.

46. Auerbach points out that the tragic dimension is almost absent from Rabelais. So, in fact, Rabelais is not the kind of author one would expect to see discussed in *Mimesis* (282).

47. Auerbach, *Vier Untersuchungen zur Geschichte der Französischen Bildung*, 8. And note the implicit references to sensory experience in Schalck's comment on Auerbach's analysis of Dante's early work: "His good ear, his artistic susceptibility, made him hear the soft and magic tone of the poem of the youthful Dante." (Schalck, "Einleitung," 13).

48. De Pietro, "Literary Criticism as History," 378.

49. Auerbach, *Mimesis*, 200.   50. Ibid., 60.

51. Ibid., 91.   52. Ibid., 552.

53. Quoted in ibid., 285.

54. "It is true that the representations of reality that are evoked in it are meant symbolically; nevertheless they make concrete in a most penetrating manner a horrible state of affairs, a terrible reality—even if the checks of reason enable us to see that we have to do with reality as we know it." Auerbach, *Vier Untersuchungen zur Geschichte der Französischen Bildung*, 111.

55. "The nakedness of the most general and concrete being of an epoch has been expressed here in a most perfect and new way by the poet, whose personality has been so very peculiar." Ibid., 126.

56. G. W. Leibniz, *The Monadology*, in Leibniz, *Philosophical Papers and Letters*, trans. and ed., Leroy E. Loemker (Dordrecht, Neth., 1969), 648.

57. I would like to thank Professor Bernhard Scholz for having called my attention to this interesting problem.

58. Auerbach, *Mimesis*, 535.

59. Ibid., 534.

60. For Kant's exposition of the a priori character of time (and of space), see I. Kant, *Kritik der reinen Vernunft*, B46–B73.

61. Auerbach, *Mimesis*, 536.

62. Ibid., 540–41.

63. Ibid., 547.

CHAPTER 8: *Danto on Representation, Identity, and Indiscernibles*

1. A. C. Danto, *The Transfiguration of the Commonplace* (Cambridge, Mass., 1983), 207.

2. A similar opposition of wide scope and simple, unpretentious language that evokes there the same kind of elegiac mood is found is found in Danto's short and fascinating characterization of the nature and history of philosophy. See A. C. Danto, *Connections to the World: The Basic Concepts of Philosophy* (New York, 1989), 3–5. When we read passages like these, Danto's *Wahlverwandschaft* with Hegel need no longer surprise us.

3. The issue of style in philosophical writing is most fruitfully dealt with in C. van Eck, J. McAllister, and R. van de Vall, eds., *The Question of Style in Philosophy and the Arts* (Cambridge, Eng., 1995).

4. I am using the term "naive" here in the sense meant by Schiller in his essay on naive and sentimental poetry: "Each true genius must be naive, or is not a genius. . . . Ignorant of the rules which are the supports of weakness and the disciplinarians of ineptitude, guided only by nature or instinct (its protective angel), the genius moves quietly and self-confidently through all the aberrations of bad taste." See F. von Schiller, "Ueber naive und sentimentalische Dichtung," in Schiller, *Schillers sämtliche Werke*, 12 vols. (Stuttgart, n.d.), 12: 118.

5. See p. 128 in Schiller's essay referred to in the previous note: "I have been saying that the poet either is nature, or he will aspire to it; the former is the naive and the latter the sentimental poet." A gap has come into being between nature and expression after the naïveté of the work of art has been recognized at a later stage in the history of art, and sentimental poetry will then (vainly) attempt to bridge the gap again.

6. M. Rollins, introduction to Rollins, ed., *Danto and His Critics* (Cambridge, Mass., 1993), 1.

7. E. Burke, *A Philosophical Inquiry into the Origins of Our Ideas of the Sublime and the Beautiful*, ed. and intro. A. Phillips (1757; reprint, Oxford, 1992), 157.

8. N. Goodman, *Languages of Art: An Approach to a Theory of Symbols* (Indianapolis, 1976), 3ff. Goodman points out, for example, that nothing more "resembles" itself than itself, yet we cannot say that a thing "represents" itself. Next, representations, such as paintings, will ordinarily "resemble" each other (in the sense of all being pieces of canvas with paint spots on them) more than what they "represent" (such as castles, human individuals, etc.).

9. One of the (many) oddities of Goodman's aesthetics is that, for all his uncompromising criticism of the resemblance theory of representation, he gives the adherents of this theory the best argument for sustaining their case. For according to Goodman's conventionalism, pictorial conventions explain the resemblances between the represented and its representation. But if we accept this conventionalism, words can also properly be said to "resemble" what they represent, because of our linguistic conventions for relating words to things.

10. For a conception of political representation that is in agreement with the substitution view of aesthetic representation, see F. R. Ankersmit, *Aesthetic Politics: Political Philosophy Beyond Fact and Value* (Stanford, Calif., 1997), and Ankersmit, *Exploraties*, 3 vols.; vol. 3, *Macht door representatie* (Kampen, Neth., 1997).

11. It is of interest, in this context, to observe that contemporary adherents of the resemblance theory exclusively have pictorial representation in mind when they deal with the issue of representation. See, for example, F. Schier, *Deeper into Pictures: An Essay on Pictorial Representation* (Cambridge, Eng., 1986), and R. van Gerwen, *Art and Experience* (Utrecht, Neth., 1996). The great merit of analyses like these is that they do not lose from sight (as is the case with semiotic theories of representation, such as that defended by Nelson Goodman) the logical distinctions between description and depiction. But the price to be paid for their welcome respect of this distinction is an undesirable restriction of the scope of the notion of representation.

12. See especially K. L. Walton, *Mimesis as Make-Believe: On the Foundations of the Representational Arts* (Cambridge, Mass., 1990).

13. Danto, *The Transfiguration of the Commonplace*, 19.

14. I disregard here the objection that no thing could be identical to itself at different phases of its existence.

15. Cited in S. Gablik, *Magritte* (London, 1970), 87.

16. Danto, *The Transfiguration of the Commonplace*, 21.

17. Ibid., 72.

18. Ibid., 79.

19. I should emphasize that Danto is quite explicit about the importance of this part of his argument; this is certainly not some mere accidental sideline in his thought. According to him the whole enterprise of philosophy is at stake here. For Danto, philosophy only comes into being when the "society within which it arises achieves a concept of reality." See Danto, *The Transfiguration of the Commonplace*, 78. In his opinion philosophy originates when man becomes aware of the gap existing between the world itself and the representations and descriptions he gives of the world. It is only then that he will start to ask himself (philosophical) questions about the relationship between notions like reality, the true statement, representation, illusion, art—in short, about the whole set of issues that are the core of all philosophy.

Elsewhere Danto praises Descartes for having been the first to draw up the philosopher's agenda in the "basic cognitive episode" of his *Meditations*:

> The basic cognitive episode, as I have called it, is composed of three elements and three relationships, and in as much as these are the fundamental concepts of philosophy, it might be worth dwelling on them before our image becomes clouded with detail. The components are the subject, the representations, and the world. The relations are between the world and the subject, between the subject and its representations, and between representations and the world.

For this definition of the matrix for all meaningful philosophy, see Danto, *Connections to the World*, xii, xiii.

20. It might be objected now that this is turning things upside down. For does not identity$_r$ presuppose identity$_1$ (or some of its variants) in the sense that we can only write the histories of things, or of human individuals, if we know how to reidentify$_1$ them through historical change? This is, indeed, where most if not all of contemporary misunderstanding of historical writing originates. As long as one allows oneself to be convinced by this objection, the writing of history will inevitably appear either as an unfathomable mystery or an irresponsible play of the human intellect.

But think of notions like "Gothicism," "the Renaissance," "the Industrial Revolution." There are no "things" that these names refer to and that are given to us in the way that tables or chairs are given to us. It is only thanks to *historical representation* that these "identities" can come into being at all; there is not, first, a thing that we happened to come across in the past and that we have called "the Renaissance" and that, next, we follow on its complex path through space and time. Here identity$_r$ comes into being without presupposing identity$_1$; here identity$_r$ precedes (re)identification (which is logically related to identity$_1$) and does not presuppose the latter.

And in historical writing it is no different with individuals like Napoleon, even though these individuals, unlike things such as "the Renaissance," *can* be reidentified in the sense of identity$_1$ as well. For observe that a historical discussion of Napoleon's identity$_r$ *never* is dependent on or reducible to issues of Napoleon's identity$_1$: such discussions are not discussions about whether *this* individual human being or *that other* human being was Napoleon, but about the historical role of *this* individual whom everybody knows as the bearer of the name Napoleon. Napoleon's identity$_1$ is just as irrelevant to this discussion as the fact that the historians involved in the discussion should know the meanings of the words they use or how to read and write. Certainly, in a way these things *are* presupposed in meaningful historical discussion—I grant that—but *not* in the sense of historical discussion being *logically dependent* on such presuppositions. So much may be clear already from the example of the Renaissance of a moment ago. Similarly, if I were dead I would be unable to prove the theorem of Pythagoras—but the truth of this theorem does not presuppose my, or anybody else's being alive (or dead).

For an exposition of this all decisive issue, which truly is the *conditio sine qua non* of all narrativist philosophy of history, see for example F. R. Ankersmit, *Narrative Logic: A Semantic Analysis of the Historian's Language* (The Hague and Boston, 1983), 179–97. For the last fifteen years, I have vainly tried again and again to get this message across in my writings on historical (and political) theory and I therefore recite it here merely *pour acquit de conscience*. See also the third and fourth sections of Chapter 1 for a further elaboration of this issue.

21. See F. R. Ankersmit, *History and Tropology: The Rise and Fall of Metaphor* (Berkeley, Calif., 1994), 90 ff.

22. Danto, *The Transfiguration of the Commonplace*, 81.

23. For an exposition of the logical nature of these narrative substances and of the indispensability of this notion for a proper understanding of the nature of historical representation, see my *Narrative Logic*, chaps. 5 and 6. For a short summary of the views expounded there, see F. R. Ankersmit, "Reply to Professor Zagorin," *History and Theory* 29, no. 3 (1990): esp. 278–84.

24. Danto, *Connections to the World*, 11.

25. As he suggested himself when discussing the problem during the conference that was devoted to his work in Bielefeld, Germany, in May 1997.

26. This would, of course, be wholly in agreement with the Hegelianist character of Danto's own argument.

27. From the perspective of the previous section it should be emphasized that I'm speaking here about past *reality* and not about the *identity$_r$* of the past, or aspects of it. For these identities$_r$ do indeed require representation.

28. I shall refrain here from discussing once again the good old problem of how to assess the truth claims of statements about fictive referents.

29. J. d'Ormesson, *La Gloire de l'Empire* (Paris, 1971).

30. A. C. Danto, *Analytical Philosophy of History* (Cambridge, Eng., 1968), 79.

31. Ibid., 83 ff.

32. What follows is not in Danto's argument itself.

33. Ibid., 95–96.

34. Ibid., 114.

35. Ibid., 149.

36. For a detailed, technical discussion of the pros and cons of Popper's argument, see Werner Habermehl, *Historizismus und kritischer Rationalismus* (Munich, 1980).

37. Danto, *Analytical Philosophy of History*, 152.

CHAPTER 9: *Hayden White's Appeal to the Historians*

1. "Often a certain conflict has been observed between an immature philosophy and history. By way of a priori thinking, conclusions were drawn about what must be. Without being aware, that such ideas are exposed to many doubts, men

went about trying to find these ideas in the history of the world. Out of the infinite number of facts those were chosen which seemed to confirm these ideas. This kind of writing has been called philosophy of history." See L. von Ranke, *The Theory and Practice of History*, ed. and intro. G. G. Iggers and K. von Moltke (Indianapolis, 1973), 29.

2. Having Ranke in mind, Hegel condemns his writings as "die bunte Menge von Detail, kleinlichen Interessen, Handlungen der Soldaten, Privatsachen, die auf die politische Interessen keinen Einfluss haben,—unfähig ein ganzes, einen allgemeinen Zweck zu erkennen." G. W. F. Hegel, *Vorlesungen über die Philosophie der Weltgeschichte*, 4 vols.; vol. 1, *Die Vernunft in der Geschichte* (Hamburg, 1955), 15.

3. E. H. Gombrich, *In Search of Cultural History* (Oxford, 1956).

4. For this "discussion," see A. Marwick, "Two Approaches to Historical Study: The Metaphysical (Including 'Postmodernism') and the Historical," *Journal of Contemporary History* 30, no. 1 (1995): 1–35; H. V. White, "Response to Arthur Marwick," *Journal of Contemporary History* 30, no. 3 (1995): 233–45. Further participants in the debate were Wulf Kansteiner, Geoffrey Roberts, Beverley Southgate, and Christopher Lloyd. The last probably further added to the confusion by linking White's case to that of his own sociologically oriented approach to historical writing. For these contributions, see the 1996 (no. 2) issue of the journal mentioned, pp. 191–228.

5. Marwick, "Two Approaches to Historical Study," 12.

6. H. V. White, *Metahistory: The Historical Imagination in Nineteenth-Century Europe* (Baltimore, 1973). For a succinct summary of the major theses defended in *Metahistory*, see H. V. White, "The Historical Text as a Literary Artifact," in White, *Tropics of Discourse: Essays in Cultural Criticism* (Baltimore, 1978), 81–101.

7. E. Auerbach, *Mimesis: The Representation of Reality in Western Literature* (Princeton, N.J., 1968). For White's present view of Auerbach, see H. V. White, "Auerbach's Literary History: Figural Causation and Modern Historicism," in S. Lerer, ed., *Literary History and the Challenge of Philology: The Legacy of Erich Auerbach* (Stanford, Calif., 1996). For an exposition of the link between Auerbach's notion of the mixture of the styles and the sublimity of the real, see Chapter 7.

8. H. V. White, "The Politics of Historical Interpretation: Discipline and De-Sublimation," in White, *The Content of the Form: Narrative Discourse and Historical Representation* (Baltimore, 1987), 58–83.

9. Ibid., 69.

10. Ibid., 72.

11. H. V. White, "Historical Emplotment and the Problem of Truth," in S. Friedlander, ed., *Probing the Limits of Representation: Nazism and the "Final Solution"* (Cambridge, Mass., 1992), 27–54. See also White, "Writing in the Middle Voice," *Stanford Literary Review* 9, no. 2 (1992): 132–80.

12. See the essay mentioned in note 8.

13. T. Mann, *Lotte in Weimar* (Frankfurt am Main, 1959).
14. H. V. White, "The Modernist Event," in V. Sobchack, ed., *The Persistence of History: Cinema, Television, and the Modern Event* (New York, 1996), 17–38.
15. Ibid., 32.
16. S. Schama, *Dead Certainties: Unwarranted Speculations* (New York, 1992).
17. S. Schama, *Landscape and Memory* (London, 1995).
18. This is one of the main insights developed in Rüsen's trilogy. See, for example, J. Rüsen, *Historische Vernunft* (Göttingen, Ger., 1983), where Rüsen writes: "Historical narrative is a medium for the formation of human identity" (57).

CHAPTER 10: *Rüsen on History and Politics*

1. R. G. Collingwood, *The Idea of History*, ed. and intro. J. van der Dussen (Oxford, 1994), 490–92.
2. An instructive example is P. D. McClelland, *Causal Explanation and Model Building in History, Economics, and the New Economic History* (Ithaca, N.Y., and London, 1975), chap. 1.
3. J. Rüsen, *Historische Vernunft: Grundzüge einer Historik*, 3 vols.; vol. 1, *Die Grundlagen der Geschichtswissenschaft* (Göttingen, Ger., 1983), 21ff.
4. J. Rüsen, *Lebendige Geschichte: Grundzüge einer Historik*, 3 vols.; vol. 3, *Formen und Funktionen des historischen Wissens* (Göttingen, Ger., 1989), 125.
5. Ibid., 127.
6. See F. R. Ankersmit, "Against Ethics," introduction to Ankersmit, *Aesthetic Politics: Political Philosophy Beyond Fact and Value* (Stanford, Calif., 1997).
7. G. W. F. Hegel, *Vorlesungen über die Philosophie der Weltgeschichte*, 4 vols.; vol. 1, *Die Vernunft in der Geschichte* (Hamburg, 1955), III, 164.
8. J. Rüsen, *Begriffene Geschichte: Genesis und Begründung der Geschichtstheorie J. G. Droysens* (Paderborn, Ger., 1969), 16.
9. T. Hobbes, *Leviathan* (London, 1970), 83.
10. To which it should be added that Hobbes is at pains to point out that the sovereign need not necessarily be a monarch. The function of the sovereign can also be performed by an assembly, as is the case with our modern parliaments.
11. Hobbes, *Leviathan*, 85.
12. See also note 10, above.
13. See W. H. Walsh, *An Introduction to Philosophy of History* (London, 1967). Similar views are defended in W. B. Gallie, *Philosophy and the Historical Understanding* (New York, 1968); P. Munz, *The Shapes of Time* (Middletown, Conn., 1977); and L. O. Mink, *Historical Understanding*, ed. B. Fay, E. O. Golob, and R. T. Vann (Ithaca, N.Y, 1987). In my *Narrative Logic: A Semantic Analysis of the Historian's Language* (The Hague and Boston, 1983), I tried to develop a formal justification of this conception of the nature of historical writing.
14. Which should not be taken to imply the absurdist thesis of the idealist that

historical representation effectively *creates* the past; we should rather think of how a country only comes into being after people started to use its name. In a sense there was no France before that name came into use—but that does not imply that the very use of that name itself created rivers, hills, trees, and so on. See for an elaboration of this anti-idealist interpretation of historical representation F. R. Ankersmit, *Exploraties*, 3 vols.; vol. 2, *De macht van representatie* (Kampen, Neth., 1996), 166.

15. G. Levine, *Realism and Representation: Essays on the Problem of Realism in Relation to Science, Literature, and Culture* (Madison, Wisc., 1993), 6.

16. R. Rorty, "Davidson, Pragmatism, and Truth," in Rorty, *Philosophical Papers*, 2 vols.; vol. 1, *Objectivity, Relativism, and Truth* (Cambridge, Eng., 1991).

17. N. Goodman, *Languages of Art: An Approach to a Theory of Symbols* (Indianapolis, 1976), 4.

18. For an exposition of Rousseau's relevant ideas and for why we should prefer Diderot's views of the theater, see Ankersmit, *De macht van representatie*, chap. 4.

19. J. J. Rousseau, *Du contrat social* (Paris, 1962), 301–2.

20. E. Burke, "Speech at the Conclusion of the Poll," in Burke, *The Works of Edmund Burke*, 12 vols. (Boston, 1866), 2: 95–96.

21. Ankersmit, *Macht door representatie*, chap. 6.

22. J. Rüsen, *Studies in Metahistory* (Pretoria, S. Africa, 1993), 53–54.

23. E. Gombrich, "Meditations on a Hobby Horse," in Morris Philips ed., *Aesthetics Today* (New York, 1980), 175. Gombrich's view of representation was anticipated by Burke: "Hence we may observe that poetry, taken in its most general sense, cannot with strict propriety be called an art of imitation. . . . But *descriptive* poetry operates chiefly by *substitution*; by the means of sounds, which by custom have the effect of realities." See E. Burke, *A Philosophical Enquiry into the Origins of our Ideas of the Sublime and the Beautiful*, ed. and intro. A. Phillips (1757; reprint, Oxford, 1992), 157.

INDEX

Adorno, Th. W., 6
Aesthetics, 11, 90, 95, 284; aesthetic criteria of representational success, 96–101; as having priority to value, 95, 96
Amalvi, C., 170
Anti-representationalism, 273, 274–76
Arendt, H., 193
Armando, 178
Auerbach, E., 25, 197–217, 219, 255, 305; on Cervantes 199, 200; on experience, 210, 211; on *figura*, 203–5; his Hegelianism, 205, 206; on historism 197–201; on modernism, 211–17; on realism, 197–217; his realism and Leibnizian monadology, 212–17; on the sublime, 206–8
Ayer, Sir A. J., 30

Bann, S., 123
Banville, J., 167
Barthes, R., 84, 85, 257, 259, 306
Baudelaire, C., 207, 208, 212
Bauman, Z., 6, 193
Bayle, P., 4
"being about," 13, 15, 16, 41, 46–48; continuity between reference and, 46
Bergson, H., 156, 157
Berkhofer, R., 48
Bevir, M., 294
Braudy, L., 108
Brinton, C., 33
Broch, H., 187–89

Burckhardt, J., 69, 120, 134, 250; and metaphor, 17–20
Burke, E., 222, 277, 316

Cassirer, E., 143
Causality, 125–28
Celan, P., 182
Change (historical), 22, 23
Children's Memorial, 185–88, 192
Coherence (narrative), 131, 135
Collingwood, R. G., 262
Commemoration, 165–75
Condorcet, M. J. A. N., marquis de, 5
Countermonument, 172, 179
Craddock, P. B., 115
Crowell, S., 295

Dante Alighieri, 202–5, 210
Danto, A. C., 25, 79, 82, 218–48; on history, 241–46; on the "Ideal Chronicler," 244–46; on identity of indiscernibles, 230–36; on narrative sentences, 245; on philosophical methodology, 238–40; on representation, 218–48; on style, 218–21
De-disciplinization of history, 153
Derrida, J., 2, 48, 67, 152, 160
Description (compared with representation), 12–15, 39–48, 73
Diderot, D., 167
Droysen, J. G., 135, 267, 299, 300

Ehrenzweig, P., 87

Empiricism, 30–32, 36, 37, 74; critique of, 45–47, 49–63; linguistic turn and, 45–47
End of history (Fukuyama), 5
Enlightenment, 4–7, 23
Enlightenment historical writing, 124, 147; and causality, 125–29; and change as metamorphosis, 125; and natural-law philosophy, 124; ontology of, 124, 125; and rhetoric, 23, 124, 126, 130–32, 136, 150; its substantialism, 124–26, 129, 134
Epistemology: representation not being reducible to, 11–13, 82–86, 223–25, 236, 243
Evans, R. J., 49, 50
Experience, 148; Auerbach on, 210, 211; Hofmannsthal on, 141–43; and the Holocaust, 162, 163

Fain, H., 44
Felman, S., 163, 164, 174
Fierens Gevaert, H., 20
Flaubert, G., 206, 208
Formalism and historical writing, 71–73, 203, 204
Foucault, M., 86, 200
Frege, G., 37, 231, 232
Freud, S., 155–58, 188–92
Friedlander, S., 144, 177, 258
Frye, N., 2, 3
Fukuyama, F., 5

Gadamer, H. G., 162
Galinsky, K., 113, 114
Gallie, W. B., 62
Gay, P., 108
Gerwen, R. van, 311
Geyl, P., 50
Gibbon, E., 23, 107–22, 124–31; absence of tragedy in, 113–16; and beginnings and endings, 127, 128; and change as metamorphosis, 110–13, 116–21; and metaphor, 17–20
Gillis, J. R., 172

Ginzburg, C., 50, 51
Gombrich, Sir E., 80, 225, 226, 279, 280
Goodman, N., 55, 222, 276
Gossman, L., 21, 113, 120, 122, 123
Grammatical delusion, 45–47, 58
Guicciardini, F., 265–67, 270, 271

Habermas, J., 2
Halbwachs, M., 155–60, 171
Hall of Remembrance, 183–88, 191, 192
Hartman, G., 162
Hegel, G. W. F., 86, 172, 173, 308; Auerbach on, 205, 206; and the historians, 249, 250; on politics as the essence of history, 266, 267, 270
Hilberg, R., 163
Historism, 10, 22, 23, 83, 123, 138; as the matrix of *all* historical thought, 148; its antimetaphysical slant, 136; Auerbach on, 197–201, 305; perverse dialectics of, 133, 139, 140, 146, 147; and "historical ideas," 134; as the historicization of substance, 130–36; as anticipating postmodernism, 11; versus speculative philosophy of history, 10; and rhetoric, 131, 132
History: as academic discipline, 150–52; privatization of, 153–55, 171–75
History of mentalities, 24, 154, 155; and the memory issue, 158
Hobbes, Th., 268, 269
Hofmannsthal, H. von, 140–45
Holocaust, 144, 145, 160–63, 176–93
Horkheimer, M., 6
Huizinga, J., 1, 4, 17–20, 59, 60
Humboldt, W. von, 134, 135
Hume, D., 30, 290, 291
Hutton, P., 154

Identity, 146, 226–37, 313; of indiscernibles, 232, 233
Iggers, G. G., 147, 148
Indeterminacy of (historical) representation, 15, 16, 42, 43, 87–89; and the linguistic turn, 37, 48

Indexicality, 178, 179
Indiscernibles, 221, 230, 238–40
"Inverted positivism," 50–53

Johnston, W., 174
Julian the Apostate, 111, 112

Kafka, F., 114, 115
Kant, I., 9, 11, 95, 189, 190, 207
Kellner, H., 5, 161
Kitsch, 186–88
Kocka, J., 139
Krul, W. E., 1

LaCapra, D., 144, 301
Lang, B., 6, 7, 161, 176, 193
Language: semanticization/naturalization of, 64–66
Lanzmann, C., 184
Laub, D., 163, 164
Leibniz, G.W. Freiherr von, 212–17, 232, 235, 276
Levine, G., 274
Lieux de mémoire, 168, 180
Linguistic turn, 21–23, 29–32; as a corrective on the grammatical delusion, 45–48; and the Holocaust, 160, 164; and literary theory, 64–74; and representation, 41, 42; and semantic ascent, 31, 41, 42; as shading off into linguistic idealism, 160, 161; and truth, 33–39, 44, 46, 47, 62, 63; and Hayden White, 30, 63, 64, 251, 252
Literary theory, 21, 29, 283; difference between philosophy and, 64–74
Locke, J., 125
Lorenz, C. L., 35, 52–56
Lowenthal, D., 167
Lucian, 75
Lurie, A., 297
Lyons, W., 159, 160
Lyotard, F., 6, 10

Machiavelli, 4, 95, 96; and the emergence of historical consciousness, 265–67, 270, 271; on why politics is prior to ethics, 91
Magritte, R., 228, 229
Maier, C. S., 171, 303
Mann, Th., 258, 259
Mannheim, K., 123
Margalit, A., 186, 188
Marwick, A., 252, 253, 260, 261
McCullagh, C. B., 56–62
Megill, A., 123
Meinecke, F., 123, 198
Memory, 25; collective, 154–57; and commemoration, 166–70; and the Holocaust, 177–79
Menippean satire, 2, 3
Metamorphosis, 22, 23; as a model for the history of "the return of the repressed," 120; as a model of historical change, 109–22; its untragic character, 113–16
Metaphor, 13–19, 23, 24; as embracing both reality and text, 14; on how to decide between competing metaphors, 14–20, 22; Lorenz on, 52; as the trope of historism, 138, 139, 177
Metonymy, 178, 179
Michelet, J., 20, 98
Mink, L. O., 203
Modernist novel, 211; and monadology, 214–16
Momigliano, A., 20
Montaigne, M. Eyquem de, 211
Montesquieu, C. L. de Secondat, baron de, 299
Moore, Barrington, 34, 35
Munslow, A., 49

Narcissus, 109–11
Narrative, 13, 135–38
Narrative substances, 57, 135–38
Narrativism, 52–56, 135, 136; as a corrective on the Enlightenment's substantialism, 137
neue Unübersichtlichkeit, 2, 3
Nietzsche, F., 225, 256, 257

Nora, P., 167, 168, 175, 301, 302

Objectivity, 75–78
Orr, L. 152
Ory, P., 170
Ovid, 22, 23, 122; and metamorphosis, 108–17; and Stoicism, 117

Pocock, J. G. A., 118
Popper, Sir K. R., 6, 7, 246; and the plausibility of representations, 63, 97, 138, 139
Postmodernism, 6, 7, 20, 21, 120; affinities with historism, 11; and fragmentation, 134, 171; Ginzburg's attack on, 51; its Marwick's attack on, 252, 253; relationship to the past, 153–55
Precision, 16, 17, 42, 43, 87–89
Privatization of the past, 24, 25, 153, 160; by commemoration, 168–75; in the Holocaust, 164
"propositional attitude," 47
Psychoanalysis, 1

Quine, W. V. O.: on "semantic ascent," 31, 32, 41, 42

Ranke, L. von, 75, 133, 134, 152
Rationality of historical writing, 14, 17, 20, 22, 96, 97, 139, 293
Realism: Auerbach on, 197–217; and Leibnizian monadology, 212–17
Reason, 5–10; and "historical Reason," 10, 14, 15; as "transversal Reason," 7–10
Reference, 13, 39, 40, 41, 46–48, 237; continuity between, and "being about," 46
Representation: is aesthetic, 11–13, 284; and analytical and synthetic truth, 46, 47; and "being about," 41, 46–48; as being irreducible to epistemology, 11–13, 82–86, 223–25, 236, 243; Danto on, 221–29; as different from description, 12, 13, 39–48; and evidence, 51; and experience, 141–43, 148, 162, 163; and formalism, 72, 73; Hofmannsthal on the experiential limits of, 141–43; its apparent "idealism," 45; and identity, 81, 226–37, 313; the indeterminacy of, 15, 16, 17, 42, 43, 48, 87–89 (*see also* precision of); as "instant epistemology," 74; the limits of, 144, 162, 164, 177; and the linguistic turn, 11, 19–75; and metaphor, 13, 14, 17–20; and narrative, 88, 89; and the objectivity issue, 80–88; and ontology, 11–13, 81, 82, 236, 237; the opacity, of, 13, 44; the plausibility of, 14–16, 22, 96–101, 284; as different from photography, 84, 85; and pictorial representation, 42, 43, 83, 84; political, 268, 270, 276–79; and precision, 16, 17, 42, 43, 87–89 (*see also* indeterminacy of); as proposals (or definitions), 32, 33, 86, 89–94; and reality, 14, 15; and reference, 13, 40, 41, 46, 48; rejection of, 273, 274–79; and its relationship to the represented, 13, 44, 45, 72, 73, 82, 83; resemblance theory of, 222–29, 240; and "semantic ascent," 31, 32, 41, 42; as speaking about speaking, 36, 37, 47, 56, 74, 137 (*see also* and "semantic ascent"); substitition theory of, 80, 81, 222–31, 240; and Tarski's semantic theory of truth, 291, 292; *tertia comparationis*, exclusion of, 274–76; and truth, 33–39, 44, 46, 47, 55–63; and truth *de dicto* and *de re*, 36–39; and unintended consequences, 270–72; values, sources of, 98, 99
Resemblance theory of representation, 222–29, 240
Rhetoric: of Enlightenment and historist historical writing, 123, 124, 126–32, 136–38
Rorty, R., 30, 32, 67, 160, 161; and anti-representationalism, 274–79
Rousseau, J. J., 276, 277

Runia, E., 145
Rüsen, J., 25, 130, 139, 262–80; on the "disciplinary matrix" of history, 263, 264; and political history, 264; and representation, 278, 279
Russell, B. Lord, 46, 241, 242
Ryle, G., 159, 160

Schama, S., 259, 260
Schier, F., 311
Schiller, F. von, 220, 310
Schopenhauer, A., 3, 309
Semantic ascent, 31, 32, 41, 42
Semiotics, 224
Skocpol, T., 34, 35
Socrates, 172, 173
"Speaking and speaking about," 36, 37, 47, 56, 74, 137; and semantic ascent, 31, 32, 41, 42
Stoicism, 121
Strawson, Sir P. F., 130
Style, 68, 107; Danto on, 218–21
Subjectivity, 75–78, 99–103; sweet fruits of, 99–103
Sublime, 142, 206–8, 256, 258
Substitution theory of representation, 80, 81, 222–31, 240

Talmon, J. L., 6
Tarski, A., 291, 292
Tertia comparationis, 274–76
Testimony, 163, 164, 178
Tournier, M., 300
Transversal Reason, 7–10; as "historical Reason," 14, 15
Trauma, 164, 192

Truth: *de dicto* and *de re*, 36–39, 63; limited significance of, 55–63; linguistic turn and, 33–39, 44, 46, 47, 62, 63; Lorenz on, 55, 56; McCullagh on, 56–62

Unintended consequences, 271, 272

Values: historical representation as the source of our, 98–101; and truth 77, 93, 94;
Voltaire (François-Marie Arouet), 5

Walsh, W., 77, 78, 79, 270
Walton, K., 225
Warhol, A.: Danto on, 230, 238–40, 247, 248
Webber, J., 178
Welsch, W., 7–11
White, H. V., 20, 21, 29, 249–61, 282; on Gibbon, 108, 123; on the historian's assignment, 252, 253, 260; and historical reality, 254–57; and the linguistic turn, 25, 29, 30, 63, 64, 70; Lorenz on, 52, 53; and modernism, 144, 257–60; on tropology, 14, 21, 68, 71–74, 255, 256
Wilde, O., 187
Windschuttle, K., 62, 70
Wittgenstein, L., 30, 60, 61, 72
Womersley, D., 108
Woolf, V., 211

Yad Vashem, 25, 180–93
Young, J., 184, 304

Zammito, J., 50, 52

Cultural Memory | *in the Present*

F. R. Ankersmit, *Historical Representation*

F. R. Ankersmit, *Political Representation*

Elissa Marder, *Dead Time: Temporal Disorders in the Wake of Modernity (Baudelaire and Flaubert)*

Reinhart Koselleck, *Timing History, Spacing Concepts: The Practice of Conceptual History*

Niklas Luhmann, *The Reality of the Mass Media*

Hubert Damisch, *A Childhood Memory by Piero della Francesca*

Hubert Damisch, *A Theory of /Cloud/: Toward a History of Painting*

Jean-Luc Nancy, *The Speculative Remark: (One of Hegel's Bons Mots)*

Jean-François Lyotard, *Soundproof Room: Malraux's Anti-Aesthetics*

Jan Patočka, *Plato and Europe*

Hubert Damisch, *Skyline: The Narcissistic City*

Isabel Hoving, *In Praise of New Travelers: Reading Caribbean Migrant Women Writers*

Richard Rand, *Futures: Of Derrida*

William Rasch, *Niklas Luhmann's Modernity: The Paradoxes of Differentiation*

Jacques Derrida and Anne Dufourmantelle, *Of Hospitality*

Jean-François Lyotard, *The Confession of Augustine*

Kaja Silverman, *World Spectators*

Samuel Weber, *Institution and Interpretation,* second edition

Jeffrey S. Librett, *The Rhetoric of Cultural Dialogue: Jews and Germans in the Epoch of Emancipation*

Ulrich Baer, *Remnants of Song: Trauma and the Experience of Modernity in Charles Baudelaire and Paul Celan*

Samuel C. Wheeler III, *Deconstruction as Analytic Philosophy*

David S. Ferris, *Silent Urns: Romanticism, Hellenism, Modernity*

Rodolphe Gasché, *Of Minimal Things: Studies on the Notion of Relation*

Sarah Winter, *Freud and the Institution of Psychoanalytic Knowledge*

Samuel Weber, *The Legend of Freud,* expanded edition

Aris Fioretos, ed., *The Solid Letter: Readings of Friedrich Hölderlin*

J. Hillis Miller / Manuel Asensi, *Black Holes / J. Hillis Miller; or, Boustrophedonic Reading*

Miryam Sas, *Fault Lines: Cultural Memory and Japanese Surrealism*

Peter Schwenger, *Fantasm and Fiction: On Textual Envisioning*

Didier Maleuvre, *Museum Memories: History, Technology, Art*

Jacques Derrida, *Monolingualism of the Other; or, The Prosthesis of Origin*

Andrew Baruch Wachtel, *Making a Nation, Breaking a Nation: Literature and Cultural Politics in Yugoslavia*

Niklas Luhmann, *Love as Passion: The Codification of Intimacy*

Mieke Bal, ed., *The Practice of Cultural Analysis: Exposing Interdisciplinary Interpretation*

Jacques Derrida and Gianni Vattimo, eds., *Religion*